The *Länder*
and German fed

MANCHESTER
UNIVERSITY PRESS

ISSUES IN GERMAN POLITICS
Edited by
Professor Charlie Jeffery, Institute for German Studies
Dr Charles Lees, University of Sussex

Issues in German Politics is a major new series on contemporary Germany. Focusing on the post-unity era, it presents concise, scholarly analyses of the forces driving change in domestic politics and foreign policy. Key themes will be the continuing legacies of German unification and controversies surrounding Germany's role and power in Europe. The series includes contributions from political science, international relations and political economy.

Already published:

The *Länder*
and German federalism

Arthur B. Gunlicks

Manchester University Press
Manchester and New York
Distributed exclusively in the USA by Palgrave

Published by Manchester University Press
Oxford Road, Manchester M13 9NR, UK
and Room 400, 175 Fifth Avenue, New York, NY 10010, USA
www.manchesteruniversitypress.co.uk

Distributed exclusively in the USA by
Palgrave, 175 Fifth Avenue, New York,
NY 10010, USA

Distributed exclusively in Canada by
UBC Press, University of British Columbia, 2029 West Mall,
Vancouver, BC, Canada V6T 1Z2

British Library Cataloguing-in-Publication Data
A catalogue record for this book is available from the British Library

Library of Congress Cataloging-in-Publication Data applied for

ISBN 0 7190 6532 1 *hardback*
0 7190 6533 X *paperback*

First published 2003

11 10 09 08 07 06 05 04 03   10 9 8 7 6 5 4 3 2 1

Typeset in Minion
by Northern Phototypesetting Co. Ltd, Bolton
Printed in Great Britain
by Bell & Bain Ltd, Glasgow

Contents

Maps, figures, and tables

Maps

Figures

Tables

Preface

In doing research on local government reforms in Germany in the 1970s, it soon became apparent that there was very little information in English in the scholarly literature on local government in Germany. I attempted to fill this gap by writing a book on the subject (*Local Government in the German Federal System*) that was published by Duke University Press in 1986. While writing that book, I became aware of the lack of information in English on the German *Länder* and German federalism in general. There are some edited books on German federalism that have appeared in English, but they generally deal with selected current issues or with the functioning of German federalism overall. There was little or nothing that provided an overview of the origins of the current German *Länder*, their constitutional or administrative framework, financing, or parliaments. Much has been written in English on German parties and elections, but there has been very little focus on the *Länder* in these areas.

Given the importance of Germany, the role federalism has played in the democratic experience of that country since 1949, and the influence German federalism has had in Europe and elsewhere, it seems obvious that a relatively detailed overview in English of the *Länder* and the federal system within which they operate is long overdue. The purpose of this book, then, is to provide that overview and close another gap in the literature on German politics and institutions.

I have many people to thank in helping me to achieve this goal. For reading and commenting on one or more chapters, I am indebted to Professors Willi Blümel and Gisela Färber, both at the German Postgraduate School of Administrative Sciences in Speyer; Professor Arthur Benz, Fern-Universität Hagen; Gert Hilmann, Leitender Ministerialrat, Hanover and Honorarprofessor, Göttingen; Klaus-Eckart Gebauer, Director of the Cabinet Staff in Rhineland-Palatinate; Uwe Leonardy, Ministerialrat a.D,

Bonn; and Peter Lindemann, President of the *Land* Social Court in Lower Saxony, a.D. For institutional support, I thank the University of Richmond for various and sundry grants and other support; the German Institute for Federalism Studies in Hanover and its director, Professor Hans-Peter Schneider; the library staff at the Parliament of Lower Saxony and the Chief Administrator of the Lower Saxon Parliament, Professor Albert Janssen; and I am especially grateful to the Research Institute at the German Postgraduate School of Administrative Sciences in Speyer and its director, Professor Karl-Peter Sommermann. I also thank my wife, Regine, for her patience and understanding for the time spent away from her.

A note on terminology

American and European usage of certain political concepts and terms is not always identical, and I have tried in this book to make the reader aware of potential misunderstandings that might arise from these differences. A common problem of semantics and a potential source of confusion is the term "government." In Europe, "government" usually means "cabinet" or "executive leaders," or "administration," while for Americans it often means what Europeans would call "the state." Therefore, what Americans call the "federal" or "national" government (or especially in the past, "the Union") may be called the "state" in German; however, Germans are more likely to use the more precise term of *Bund* or "federation." The *Bundesregierung*, or, literally, "federal government," is the cabinet, or what Americans call "the Administration." Thus it's the "Kohl or Schröder government" in Germany, but the "Clinton or Bush Administration" in the United States. In this book "government" will usually mean "cabinet" unless the context is clear that the more general American sense of the term, i.e., the European "state," applies.

To complicate matters further, both Americans and Germans use the term "state" to describe their respective subnational regional units. While the German "states" have been called *Länder* (plural form) since 1919, "state" can still refer either to the subnational *Land* (singular form) or national political system. Indeed, "state" administration in the German context usually means administration by the *Land*.

Another term that is used commonly in Britain and on the Continent is "competences" for what Americans call "powers." In this book I will follow American practice and hope for the tolerance of European readers and others who might be unfamiliar with American terminology.

In Germany the ceremonial head of the national state is the president. The head of government is the chancellor. As in the United States, there is only a head of government at the *Land* level: the minister-president. Since this term is so foreign to American readers, I will use instead the common term for the head of government in a parliamentary system, the prime minister. The American term, governor, is inappropriate because it suggests direct election by the people, not selection by the majority party or coalition of parties of a parliament.

The term "liberal" can also be easily misunderstood by European and American readers. In Europe "Liberal" usually refers to classical liberalism, i.e., the European philosophical tradition of individualism that supports policies of *laissez faire* in both civil liberties and economics. In the United States "liberal" generally refers to someone who supports both civil liberties and a significant role for government in the economic and social arenas. Thus a European "Liberal" is generally in the center or even right of center on the ideological spectrum between "left" socialists or social democrats and "right" conservatives, while the American "liberal" is "left" of center.

Germans and Americans also use the term "dual federalism" in different ways. In the United States the term emphasizes separate spheres of activity for the executive and legislative branches of the federal and state government. Thus, the federal government is responsible for old-age security, the states for education and highways. This kind of dualism still exists to some extent, but since the New Deal and the Great Society, the federal and state governments have been sharing more and more responsibilities, including the financing of a wide variety of public policies. Thus American federalism today is not as much a dual federalism as it is a cooperative federalism based on intergovernmental relations. In Germany the concept of dual federalism usually refers to the focus at the national level on legislation and the focus at the *Land* level on administration. But cooperation and sharing in a variety of forms have also led Germans to talk more of cooperative federalism or *Politikverflechtung*, a form of interlocking intergovernmental relations. As a result of these different conceptions of dual federalism, the use of terms such as "functional federalism" or "horizontal" and "vertical" relationships can have different meanings in the two countries. On the other hand, some Germans also use these terms in the American sense, which can be confusing to the reader who thinks he or she has made the appropriate adjustment to general usage in each country.

Some disagreement exists in the United States about the use of the concept of "levels" when describing national, state, and local governments. Daniel Elazar insisted that speaking of different arenas or, better yet, "planes," would be better, because "levels" suggests hierarchy, higher and lower, more important and less important. He preferred thinking of federal systems in terms of a matrix, in which "there are no higher or lower power centers, only larger or smaller arenas of political decision making and action."1 For a number of reasons, I will use the more conventional concept of "levels." First, because "level" is the term used in both countries by most people when they identify the different units of government and distinguish among them. Second, because it (*Ebene*) is the term used virtually without exception by German legal scholars as well as the general public. And third, because while it is true that one level may not in fact be "higher" than another in some hierarchical order, a distinction is frequently made today between "high" and "low" politics, terms which generally refer to policies with international or major domestic consequences as opposed to those that have only a more limited even if important domestic impact. National governments of federations are responsible for "high" politics, not subnational units.

Notes

1 Daniel Elazar, *Exploring Federalism* (Tuscaloosa: University of Alabama Press, 1987), pp. 37, 200–201.

Introduction

Germany, like most European states, has a well-established parliamentary system with the typical array of rights and liberties associated with all recognized, functioning democracies. It is also clear to anyone who travels to Germany that the country is a federation. Even the most unobservant foreigner knows that Bavaria is somehow separate and distinct from other regions of Germany, and he or she may even be aware of the existence of the fifteen other states (*Länder*) that constitute the country. A beginning student of Germany soon learns something about the names and locations of sixteen capital cities other than the national capital, Berlin, including the anomaly of two capitals that are across the Rhine River from each other (Mainz and Wiesbaden). Later the student may learn that, unlike Washington, DC, Berlin is not the home of a number of very important federal institutions, such as the Federal Constitutional Court and other federal courts, the Federal Employment Office in Nuremberg, the Federal Statistics Office in Wiesbaden, and some ministries left in Bonn after the general move to Berlin at the turn of this century. The student also learns that in this respect Germany is very different from the typically more centralized, unitary European states such as Great Britain, France, or Sweden.

Making comparisons among democratic states

When comparisons are made between and among democratic political systems, one of the first steps is to distinguish between presidential, semi-presidential, and parliamentary institutions. The United States is the model for most of the few functioning presidential systems, which are characterized by the direct and separate election of the president – who is both head of state and head of government – and the legislature. The American model is also characterized by a strong system of separation of powers between the executive, judicial, and legislative branches, the latter of which is further divided into two independent and co-equal legislative chambers. The French semi-presidential model provides for a directly elected president as head of state, who then appoints the prime minister as head of government. This head of government is responsible both to the president, who can dismiss him or her virtually at will when he has majority support in parliament, and to the popularly elected parliament, which can remove him or her in a vote of no-confidence under certain conditions. This provides a certain control of the otherwise rather weak legislature over the premier as head of government but not over the president as head of state. As suggested above, the president has more power over the premier when he has majority support in the parliament, but his options are rather limited if he is faced with a parliamentary majority in opposition. The president is not limited to ceremonial duties as head of state; indeed, there can be considerable overlap between the duties of head of state and head of government, especially in defense policy, foreign affairs, and other "high politics" areas. The degree of overlap depends to a considerable extent on the support or opposition the president has in parliament and whether the president can appoint a premier of his choice or is forced to "cohabit" with a premier who comes from the opposition. The semi-presidential system became popular in Eastern Europe after the collapse of communism, for example, in Russia, where the president has become even more dominating than in France.

Most democracies are parliamentary systems, of which there are many different models. The British "Westminster" model is characterized by a single-party government that is led by a strong prime minister as head of government who is supported by a disciplined party that has majority control of parliament. The role of the opposition party or parties is to offer alternatives, criticize the government, and draw public attention to the perceived flaws in the government's policies. Given the nature of the "Westminster" model, however, there is little or nothing the other parties can do to change or delay government policy. The continental European models are more consensus-oriented, because with very few exceptions the governments (cabinets) are composed of coalitions of two or more parties (which is largely the result of the electoral system), with the head of government (prime minister, chancellor) usually drawn from the ranks of the largest party. Though the degree of party discipline varies to some extent among different parties and countries, the parties are typically rather strongly disciplined. The reason, of course, is that the stability of the cabinet depends largely on the disciplined support it receives in the parliament, which has the right to call for a vote of no-confidence in the government under certain conditions. In all democracies, including parliamentary systems, there is a separation of powers between the judicial branch and the other branches; however, in contrast to the presidential systems, and especially to the American model, there is no clear separation of powers between the executive and legislative branches, because the executive emerges out of the legislature, i.e., the prime minister and all or most of the cabinet ministers are also members of parliament, the majority of which has the responsibility of supporting the cabinet. The separation of powers that does exist between the executive and the legislature is between the government and its majority on the one hand and the opposition party or parties on the other.

Democratic federal states

In addition to the institutional comparisons above, comparisons are made based on distinctions in territorial organization – that is, unitary, federal, and confederal organization of territory for governing and administrative purposes. Most states, including democracies, are unitary, while there are twenty-three federations, most but not all of which are also democracies. There are no states organized as confederations today, but Ronald Watts suggests that the European Union (EU), Commonwealth of Independent States (CIS), Benelux, and the Caribbean Community are examples of contemporary confederations. The twenty-three federations contain about 2 billion people or 40 percent of the world population.[1] India alone has almost a billion people, and most of the other billion come from the United States, Russia, Brazil, Mexico, Nigeria, and Germany. Many of these federations also cover very large territories, for example, Australia, Canada, Brazil, Russia and the United States. There are five federations in Europe: Germany, Switzerland, Austria, Spain and Belgium.

Some of the twenty-three mostly democratic federations have parliamentary systems, others have some form of presidential system. The differences between the federal parliamentary and federal presidential systems have consequences for the nature of the political system. For example, as noted above the separation of powers between the executive and legislative branches is weaker in parliamentary systems, and the direct popular election of a president as opposed to the selection or confirmation of a prime minister by a parliament can affect not only the party system but also the relationships between the head of government at the national level with the heads of governments of the individual regional territorial units such as states or provinces.

The size of the overall state is one factor which may lead to federation. The large states listed above, for example, Canada and the United States, would be difficult to govern from a central government in a unitary system. Another factor that may lead to federalism is racial, ethnic, religious, language, and cultural differences among the people who may live in distinct parts of the federation that encompasses them, for example, India and Russia, or even Canada with its French-speaking minority in Quebec province, where it is the majority. Federation is a practical alternative to fragmentation into small independent states if there is sufficient recognition among these people of the common economic, security, or other advantages of union that they might enjoy while also retaining some degree of autonomy. A third reason for federation is history. It is difficult to imagine the federations in Germany or Switzerland without considering the impact of the Holy Roman Empire, and, in Germany, the German Confederation after 1815, the Bismarck Reich after 1871, the Weimar Republic from 1919 to 1933, and the Third Reich from 1933 to 1945. Some would argue that the role of the Allies in the postwar years was an even more important factor in the re-emergence of federalism in Germany after 1949.[2] It is also difficult to imagine federalism in the United States without the experience of the colonial era, the Revolutionary War, and the Articles of Confederation. A fourth reason is the promise of more grassroots democracy and popular participation in public affairs offered by a federal system. Switzerland is a good example of this, but so is Germany since 1945. If one looks at the number of elected public offices in Germany, for example, in comparison with France or Great Britain, there is a very significant difference. Thus, there are almost 2,000 deputies elected to the parliaments of the German *Länder* who have no counterparts in France, Great Britain, or in the other unitary political systems of Europe. A fifth and more abstract reason that has been important in American political theory and to some extent in Germany is the division of power that federalism promotes. In other words, American theory suggests that a tyrannical state can be prevented or countered not only by the institutional separation of powers mentioned above but also by the division of government into different territorial spheres of influence and activity.[3] This was one of the reasons why the Americans, in particular, pushed for the federal organization of Germany after 1945. The division of power is related also to popular participation in that political parties may not be so successful at the national level but may have a strong regional base which may reduce potential centrifugal pressures from frustrated supporters. An example for Germany would be the Greens in the 1980s and the PDS (Party of Democratic Socialism) and some right-wing parties in the 1990s. That these considerations may be completely irrelevant for another federation is one indication of the variety of federations.

While perhaps not consciously proposed reasons for forming a federation, there may be some positive consequences of a federal system that can be important at times. For example, the regional governments in a federation may engage in certain policy or administrative experiments that are of interest to other regions and to the national government. This "laboratory function" is especially important in federations in which the regional units enjoy a high degree of autonomy. Sometimes federalism is also seen as a means of relieving the central government of responsibility for certain problems that are region-specific. Regional elections might also be seen as providing voters with the opportunity to demonstrate support or opposition to national policies.

The basic notion behind a federal system is that there is a combination of shared rule for some purposes and regional self-rule for other purposes within a single political system so that neither is subordinate to the other. But federations differ, not only in the ways mentioned above, but also in the character and significance of the underlying economic and social diversities; in the number of constituent units and the degree of symmetry or asymmetry in their size, resources and constitutional status; in the scope of the allocation of legislative, executive, and expenditure responsibilities; in the allocation of taxing power and resources; in the character of federal government institutions and the degree of regional input to federal policy making; in procedures for resolving conflicts and facilitating collaboration between interdependent governments; and in procedures for formal and informal adaptation and change.[4]

The variety of federal structures, procedures, and conditions is reflected in the large number of adjectives used to describe different federal systems. We speak, for example, of dual federalism, cooperative federalism, picket-fence federalism, coercive federalism, fiscal federalism, "fend-for-yourself" federalism, and many other "kinds" of federalism in the United States. Germans also speak of dual federalism, cooperative federalism, administrative federalism, executive federalism, participatory federalism, and, more recently, competitive federalism. One author found as many as 500 such terms in the scholarly and popular literature in 1984,[5] and many more have been added since then.

If the twenty-three federal states that Ronald Watts has identified differ in a variety of both minor and important ways, what kind of federal state is Germany? Is it more like the former British colonial states of the United States, Canada, and Australia, each of which has a history and a territorial expanse very different from Germany's? More like the multiethnic and religiously fragmented India or Russia? More like Switzerland, which contains ethnic divisions quite different from India's or Russia's? Or is federalism in the relatively homogeneous German state *sui generis*? A systematic comparison of German federalism with other federal states is not the purpose of this book, but the many unique features of this system will become apparent to any reader with some knowledge of or background in comparative politics and institutions of government. The purpose of this book is to present in some depth the major features of German federalism, including its origins and development, especially since the founding of the Federal Republic of Germany in 1949. We will be taking a close look at the German model of federalism which has been the subject of much admiration as well as criticism, depending on one's understanding of federalism and the expectations one has from that understanding.

Notes

1 Ronald Watts, *Comparing Federal Systems in the 1990s* (Kingston: Queen's University Instutute of Intergovernmental Relations, 1996), pp. 4, 10–11.
2 Roland Sturm, "Das Selbstverständnis des deutschen Föderalismus im Wandel," in *Krise und Reform des Föderalismus*, edited by Reinhard C. Meier-Walser and Gerhard Hirscher (München: Olzog Verlag, 1999), p. 111.
3 Arthur B. Gunlicks, "Can Comparative Federalism Really Be Comparative?," in *The American Federal System*, edited by Franz Gress *et al.* (Frankfurt and New York: Peter Lang, 1994), pp. 217–226.
4 Watts, *Comparing Federal Systems*, pp. 1–2.
5 Ellis Katz, "Cooperative – Dual – Competitive Federalism: The Pros and Cons of Model Building," in Gress et al., The American Federal System, p. 91.

1

The origins of
the *Länder*

Introduction

Where is Germany? What are its constituent parts? Who is a German? These questions may not be entirely unique to Germans; they are sometimes asked in many nation-states in Europe and elsewhere. But questions about identity have been asked for centuries in Germany and to some extent are still asked today. For hundreds of years "Germany" was a group of tribes located in north-central Europe, most but not all of which became a part of the empire of Charlemagne and, after the death of Charlemagne, a part of what would become the Holy Roman Empire. This empire consisted of hundreds of political units of widely varying sizes and shapes, including noncontiguous territories, speaking different dialects and developing different cultures, headed by kings, princes, dukes, counts, bishops, and various and assorted minor nobility generally referred to as knights. Those who lived within the borders of the empire were not all Germans by today's standards, but most were even if they did not know it. For in the middle ages, people did not think in terms of nationality. They were the parochial subjects, not citizens, of a prince or lord, and nationality was not a meaningful concept for them.

Later, in the sixteenth century, they became divided also by religion. This and other divisions led to a devastating Thirty Years' War (1618–48) between Protestants and Catholics, both German and foreign, on German territory. For many decades this had far reaching negative effects on the economic, cultural, and political development of Germany. The Holy Roman Empire, not a "state" but a historically unique league of princes with some confederate features, was naturally weakened by the Thirty Years' War and other conflicts between and among the princes, but it continued to exist in some form until Napoleon forced its dissolution in

1806. One important change between the Thirty Years' War and 1806, however, was the Treaty of Westphalia in 1648 which, among other things, is generally credited with having introduced the modern concept of the state. Subjects were now more likely to identify themselves as Bavarians, Württemberger, Hanoveranians, Saxons, and so forth.

Following the French Revolution, the concept of the state was modified to include a particular kind of state: the nation-state. This meant that it was now the goal of people who identified with one another – whether because of geography, language, religion, history, or culture – to form a state which included this distinct group of people. This led to the rise of nationalism, which generally replaced religion as the major focus of common identity. Napoleon had manipulated national feelings to great personal advantage, and the monarchical heads of state in the German and Austrian territories had good reason to fear the consequences of nationalism in their own highly divided and fragmented states.[1]

In 1815, with the final defeat of Napoleon at Waterloo, the German Confederation of thirty-nine states, including Austria, was formed. It was a very loose confederation, the main purpose of which was to provide internal and external security. This confederation, supplemented by a Customs Union of 1834, which excluded Austria, continued to limp along until 1866, when the two major German states, Prussia and Austria, fought a brief war that led to their final separation within even as loose an arrangement as the German Confederation. In 1867 more than twenty German states joined in the formation of the North German Federation, led and dominated by Prussia. Following a brief war in 1870 between France and Prussia, the states in the North German Federation and the four separate and independent South German states joined to form a united German state for the first time in history.

But the questions of where Germany is and who is German were not resolved. The German population in Austria and the majority German population in Switzerland did not become a part of the new German state. Then, following defeat in the First World War, many Germans who had been a part of the Kaiserreich were now in France or Poland, and even more Germans who had been a part of the Austro-Hungarian Empire were now in various, mostly newly created, separate countries, such as Czechoslovakia, Italy, and Romania. These developments fed nationalistic fervor among many Germans, with the result that the most radical nationalistic elements under the leadership of Adolf Hitler and his National Socialist Party were able to capture the German state and launch a war to unite all Germans and expand German territory in the East at the expense of the peoples living there. They also, of course, led to the Holocaust and other crimes against any and all opponents of Nazi rule.

Following the Second World War, the questions arose again. Where is a Germany that has lost one-fourth of its pre-war territory and many former citizens to Poland and the Soviet Union, has had to absorb as many as 12 million refugees and expellees, is divided first among the four Allies into four zones and then into two hostile camps facing each other throughout the Cold War, and then is presented suddenly and unexpectedly with the opportunity to unite in peace? This latest unification seems to have answered once and for all the question of where Germany is if not in every case who is German. But now Germany is faced with two other questions that are new to the post-war era: where and how does Germany, and, for that matter, where do the other European states, fit into an increasingly integrated Europe? And, less dramatically but still of considerable importance, where and how do the current German states (*Länder*) fit into a united Germany? Are there too many of these *Länder*? Should they be joined in ways that would reduce their number from sixteen to perhaps eight or ten? Would the predicted economic and administrative benefits outweigh the potential costs in loss of traditions and regional identity? Is there a strong German identity that is shared between former East and West Germany in spite of forty years of experiences with profoundly different regimes?

This chapter and this book cannot answer all of these questions satisfactorily, but they can help to provide some background and a framework for understanding how Germany and the Germans literally have come to where they are today. The focus, then, will be less on the larger issues of German identity over the past decades and more on the sources of identity of the people within Germany for the regions in which they live today.

The Holy Roman Empire

Following Charlemagne's death, the Treaty of Verdun in 843 divided his "Roman Empire" into three parts: the West Frankish Kingdom, the Middle Kingdom, and the East Frankish Kingdom. The West Kingdom would become the core of France, the East Kingdom the core of Germany. The Middle Kingdom would become the Netherlands, Belgium, Luxembourg, and areas later contested by France and Germany, such as Alsace-Lorraine and the west bank of the Rhine. There were five "stem duchies"

(*Stammesherzogtümer*) in the East and Middle Kingdoms, based originally on Germanic tribes (Saxony, Franconia, Swabia, Bavaria, and
Lorraine – which included the Netherlands, Belgium, and Luxembourg
on today's map). They did not, however, prove to be durable territories.
Election of kings by the nobility in the Carolingian Empire was a
Germanic influence that complemented the Roman administrative institutions adapted to the local conditions. This meant that the king was
more *primus unter pares*, and that the kingdom represented a central
authority versus particularistic tendencies.[2] The empire followed this tradition of election in the selection of emperors by the stem dukes before
the tenth century and again after the beginning of the thirteenth century.

By "the middle of the eleventh century the realm was firmly united
under its ruling dynasty and all traces of particularism seemed on the
point of disappearance."[3] The emperors gained power at the expense
of the duchies by dividing territories, for example, the emergence of
an important part of Austria from eastern Bavaria in 1156, and by
using their authority to appoint the high clergy whose administration
competed with that of the dukes. Nevertheless, the tendency was for the
Reich to divide into smaller units of rule, so that while the stem duchies
disappeared, smaller territorial duchies and territories led by the
"princes" emerged in their place. These smaller territories provided
the actual government over their subjects, but the rulers were not sovereign and enjoyed their power only as a part of the Reich and in alliance
with the emperor.[4]

The emperor ruled through the princes, who in turn ruled through the
lesser nobility, such as the knights. In the imperial free cities small groups
of oligarchs, usually from the guilds, were in charge. There was no capital city of the Reich, and the emperor traveled from place to place with his
entourage to demonstrate his authority. His territorial base consisted of
his own lands.[5] Only in these territories did the emperor rule directly.
While the princes of the realm were not sovereign, they did enjoy considerable autonomy (*Landeshoheit*). The empire served to protect the
smaller territories from annexation by their more powerful neighbors,
and it provided some protection from outside threats to their territorial
integrity. The nobility was based on heredity, but that, of course, did not
apply to the ecclesiastical princes. In the early centuries the emperor
appointed them and used them for purposes of administration. He also
received the moveable inheritance of the bishops and other revenues. In
return, the Church received various lands, customs duties, and other
benefits. In the twelfth century the emperor relinquished his right to

appoint archbishops, but his presence at their election still gave him considerable potential influence (map 1.1).[6]

At this time the controversies over the appointment of the Pope, whose power and actions had weakened the empire, led to a strengthening of the territorial princes at the expense of the emperor.[7] The princes were also strengthened by the reestablishment in 1198 of the traditions of electing

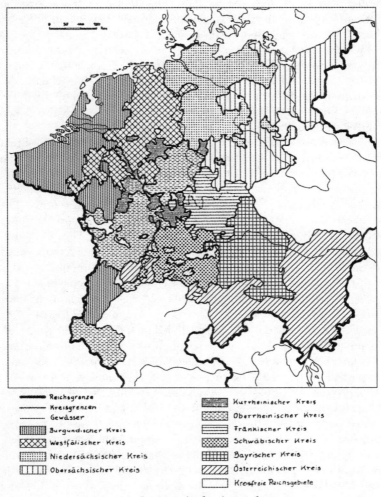

▬▬▬ Reichsgrenze	▦ Kurrheinischer Kreis
─── Kreisgrenzen	▨ Oberrheinischer Kreis
─── Gewässer	▤ Fränkischer Kreis
▥ Burgundischer Kreis	▦ Schwäbischer Kreis
▧ Westfälischer Kreis	▦ Bayrischer Kreis
▨ Niedersächsischer Kreis	▧ Österreichischer Kreis
▥ Obersächsischer Kreis	□ Kreisfreie Reichsgebiete

Map 1.1 **Germany in the sixteenth century**

the emperor. Election of the emperor was confirmed by the Golden Bull of 1356, which gave the right of selection to three ecclesiastical and four secular princes (*Kurfürsten*) and broke the bonds of papal subjugation.[8] But the rejection of an hereditary emperor also weakened the empire, because some of the newly elected emperors had to start anew (emperors from Luxembourg were chosen from the middle of the fourteenth to the middle of the fifteenth century).[9] Indeed, Barraclough renders the harsh verdict that "[t]he monarchy was [after the Golden Bull] a nullity and German unity a mere façade."[10] Such a negative view is not, however, shared by many contemporary historians.[11]

Even the territorial princes had to contend with a division of their authority owing to the rights of the aristocracy, e.g., the knights, and of the free cities, with which they were also in conflict.[12] But feudal independence from the princes was doomed in the fifteenth century with the vulnerability of castles to destruction by cannon. The princes also gained control over the Church.[13]

By the end of the fifteenth century the lack of imperial territory that could be used as a basis for support for the emperor meant that only an emperor with extensive territories outside as well as inside the empire could even afford to accept the crown. Thus the Austrian Habsburg line became the dynastic rulers of the empire in the fifteenth century. The result was that imperial policy became Habsburg policy, and Habsburg policy was only partially in the interests of Germany.[14] This, of course, continued to be the case even after Emperor Maximilian of Austria added "of the German Nation" to the old title, "Holy Roman Empire."[15]

By the end of the fifteenth century the emperor had been weakened to an alarming degree. The territorial units were fighting each other, feuds were common, and the princes were using force to extend their territories. Finally, an imperial reform concluded in 1500 by the *Reichstag*, an assembly of princes, about an "eternal public peace" which intoduced the principle that the state, not individuals, must secure peace in the land; established the Imperial Chamber Court (*Reichskammergericht*) consisting of princes who would decide cases dealing with matters that fell under the jurisdiction of the empire but not within the individual territories; created an Imperial Authority (*Reichsregiment*) which did not last long after two failed attempts; and divided the empire into "imperial circles" (*Reichskreise*) which enforced imperial chamber court decisions with troops assembled in the circles. The circles established their own circle assembly (*Kreistag*) that mirrored the *Reichstag*. There were ten circles by 1512.[16] These circles, according to Hermann Wellenreuther, became the key "federal" elements in holding the empire together as intermediate-level organizations until the end in 1806.[17] From settling local and regional disturbances of public peace to taxation, coinage, and various administrative tasks and making public proclamations of imperial law to providing "circle" troops to serve the empire in a number of causes, including the struggle against Turkish forces in the east, Neuhaus argues that the circles were crucial factors in explaining the continued existence of the empire, including the period after 1648.[18] Hartmut Lehmann, on the other hand, argues that Neuhaus exaggerates the role of the circles and ignores other important factors. He points instead to the influence of at most a dozen of the larger territories that were not identical with but often dominated the imperial circles in promoting some kind of federal principle in the empire.[19]

By 1500 the "Holy Roman Empire of the German Nation" was "a patchwork of dynastic and ecclesiastical territories dotted with imperial free cities and castles of independent imperial knights."[20] The rulers of the seven electoral principalities elected the emperor and therefore enjoyed a higher status, but there were also another twenty-five major secular principalities, around ninety ecclesiastical principalities, over 100 territories led by counts, a large number of lesser noble holdings, and many free cities. These territories were organized in the *Reichstag* which was equal to the emperor and consisted of three chambers: one for the seven electoral princes (the bishops of Mainz, Cologne, and Trier, and the secular princes of Saxony, the Palatinate, Brandenburg, and Bohemia); one for the other princely rulers (four archbishops, forty-six bishops, eighty-three other spiritual rulers, twenty-four secular princes, and 145 counts and lords); and one for the eighty-three imperial free cities.[21] These 392 territories did not generally include the knights and their small estates.[22]

The Reformation, which began officially in 1517 with Martin Luther's nailing of his ninety-five theses on the door of the castle church in Wittenberg, served to strengthen the territorial princes even further, as did their victories in the Peasants' War in 1524. Charles V was the last emperor to be crowned by the Pope in 1529. A religious split occurred with the Catholic princes siding with the emperor and the Lutheran princes determined to protect their beliefs and autonomy. The emperor defeated them in battle in 1547, but it was a Pyrrhic victory in that it aroused the concern of all princes about the emperor's power. At the Augsburg *Reichstag* in 1555 the princes came to decide which religion their subjects would embrace,[23] which reflected the decline in power of the Catholic Church as well as the emperor. However, spiritual princes who changed religion were to lose their principalities.[24] Charles V resigned in 1556.

During the Thirty Years' War from 1618 to 1648, the emperor at first gained power *vis-à-vis* the princes, but by the end the princes had reestablished their autonomy. Barraclough again comes to a harsh conclusion with his assertion that "after 1648 the subordination of the principalities within the empire was a form of words without political significance, the empire a shadow without substance, beyond all hope of resurrection or reform."[25] And Daniel Elazar suggests that "[t]he Thirty Years' War . . . effectively ended the traditional confederation of German states known as the Holy Roman Empire. Although its shell survived until 1806, the rise of Prussia and Austria as modern states destroyed that basis of its existence."[26] But others have noted that the empire had possessed a "grandiose historical mystique" as a "living and legitimate successor of ancient western and Christian Roman Empire as renewed by Charlemagne and his successors."[27] Gagliardo also suggests that recent scholarship has shown "the consciousness of being part of an imperial structure was still a very important factor in the policies of German territories large and small right up to the dissolution of the Empire in 1806."[28]

The Thirty Years' War and the Treaty of Westphalia in 1648 did not bring about major territorial changes, except for Brandenburg, which gained the eastern half of Pomerania and the bishoprics of Magdeburg, Halberstadt, Minden, and Kammin. The Cleves duchies had been added by inheritance in 1614, and in 1721 Western Pomerania was added from Sweden. Silesia was wrested from Austria in 1741 by Frederick the Great and West Prussia was gained from Poland in 1772. In the west the empire had lost Alsace and Lorraine to the French in 1681 and 1766.[29]

There were also some changes in the "constitution" of the Empire. The Treaty of Westphalia functioned as a basic law until the empire's demise in 1803–6. It gave the princes certain rights and privileges, including the right to conclude treaties among themselves and with foreign powers as long as they were not directed against the emperor and empire.[30] Technically, this did not give the princes legal sovereignty, but the autonomy (*Landeshoheit*) they enjoyed was close to it and amounted practically to internal sovereignty.[31]

With the addition of Bavaria after 1648, there were eight, rather than seven, electors. In 1692 the number was increased to nine with the addition of Hanover.[32] After 1663 the *Reichstag* met permanently in Regensburg, whereas before then the emperor had called the meetings in different cities. The *Reichstage* (diets) were not representative in the modern sense;

membership was not legitimated by elections but by property. However, they can be seen as a part of the evolutionary development of representative systems, in part because the emperor's powers were tied to the consent of the estates meeting in the *Reichstag*.[33]

The period after 1648 was the beginning of the age of monarchical absolutism, especially in Austria and Prussia. The princes became the undisputed rulers in their territories, eclipsing the powers of the ecclesiastical authorities and incorporating them into territorial churches. Whether in terms of the selection of the Church hierarchy, the administration of Church property, the taxation of the Church, or the submission of the Church to the judiciary of the territory, the prince became the dominant power. This included the knightly estates and the (mostly small) free cities as well. The goal of the princes became increasingly to achieve a tight coordination and rule over their territory which for the first time was becoming a modern state administered by offices and civil servants rather than vassals.[34] According to Vierhaus, however, the goal was never achieved fully, because at least the lesser princes lacked the tools and personnel to assume the various administrative and judicial functions performed by the lower nobility.[35]

In spite of their inclusion in the empire, some princes were oriented toward Sweden (Brandenburg), some toward France (Bavaria), and some remained loyal to the emperor. Austria grew in strength, not because the emperor was Austrian, but because of his own territorial base, which included lands outside the empire (e.g., territories in what are today Hungary, southern Poland, Slovenia, Croatia, northern Italy and parts of Romania). Some other princes also had territories outside the empire. Thus the electoral princes of Saxony were also the King of Poland from 1697 to 1763, and the electoral princes of Hanover were also the Kings of England, which made it more difficult for the Austrian Emperor to maintain authority over them.[36] There were also German speaking territories outside the empire in East Prussia (where the Duke of Brandenburg was King), Switzerland, and Alsace as well as non-Germans within the empire, e.g., Flemings, Walloons, Italians, Czechs, and some other Slavs.[37]

In the eighteenth century, as before, there were four categories of territories. First, there were the ecclesiastical states, ruled as distinct principalities by prince-prelates of the Catholic Church. They ruled their territories essentially like secular princes and at the same time had ecclesiastical oversight of districts which did not necessarily coincide with the political boundaries of their states. Most of these states were small, and they saw the empire as their guarantor.[38] The second and most powerful group was the secular principalities, governed by the hereditary high nobility with titles of king (Bohemia), duke, count, landgrave, margrave, etc., and simply "prince." The size of territories varied dramatically, but in most the landed nobility, towns, and Catholic clergy had formal rights of representation in the territorial diets (*Landtage*).[39] The number of territories formally listed as independent for certain military and financial obligations declined from 405 in 1521 to 314 in 1780.[40] Third were the imperial cities or towns, which accounted for only about 2 percent of the total population. The fifty-one cities were governed by "exclusive and often self-perpetuating patrician oligarchies,"[41] and most were in the west and southwest. Some cities like Bremen, Hamburg, and Lübeck prospered owing to trade, while others declined to mere villages. They were especially loyal to the empire as a protection against the territorial princes.[42] The fourth group consisted of the imperial counts and knights, found mostly in the west and southwest. Most of their territories, especially those of the knights, were very small, numbering between 1,600 and 1,700, but they also enjoyed autonomy. This often gave them a personal authority over their few subjects which was more complete than that of the more powerful princes. Given the rule of primogeniture, positions outside the estate had to be found for the other heirs. In Catholic families, these were often with the imperial Court or with ecclesiastical princes, while in Protestant families they were generally with a secular prince.[43]

The attack on Austria by Frederick the Great in 1740 by which Prussia gained Silesia was a serious blow to the cohesion of the empire, and the Seven Years' War from 1756 to 1763 which again involved Prussia against Austria served to weaken further the empire and emperor. The institutions of the empire were used increasingly to air differences between Prussia and Austria, and the smaller states began to consider alliances to ally themselves against both of the larger states. Prussia took up the idea on its own and formed an Alliance of German Princes which in 1785 consisted of Prussia, Hanover, Saxony, and later others, with the goal of protecting and preserving the constitutional order of the empire. Soon, however, the Alliance failed and the empire was in a desultory condition when the French Revolution broke out in 1789.[44]

The French Revolution and its aftermath

In the year of the French Revolution, 1789, the empire, including Austria, included 314 secular and Church territories and imperial cities and 1,475 knightly estates, or 1789 political units of widely varying size and power.[45] Soon after the Revolution the empire was at war with France, which quickly occupied the left bank of the Rhine. The armies of the empire were weak and easily defeated, and even Prussia agreed to a separate peace, even though this was an egregious violation of imperial law.[46] Following a second Austrian defeat in 1800, the Peace of Lunéville was concluded in 1801 according to which the emperor accepted the French Republic on behalf of the empire and of Austria as well as the loss of the west bank of the Rhine. The secular princes who lost territory on the left bank were to be compensated by the secularization of ecclesiastical territories on the right bank.

The *Reichstag* created an Imperial Deputation, consisting of plenipotentiaries of five electors and three other princes, with the purpose of drawing up a specific plan of indemnification. But between July 1801 and May 1802 several states of the empire made a separate peace with France, which in turn guaranteed them substantial shares in the indemnification and removed many decisions from the Imperial Deputation which had not yet convened. After a few minor changes, the French-induced plan was accepted by the Deputation in 1803, approved by the *Reichstag*, and ratified by the emperor. This is the famous *Reichsdeputationshauptschluss* or "Final Recess" that dissolved around 112 political units: all ecclesiastical principalities (about twenty archbishoprics and prince-bishoprics and forty abbeys and convents) and all but six free imperial cities (Bremen, Hamburg, Lübeck, Frankfurt, Nuremberg, and Augsburg). Thus the spiritual principalities were secularized, which meant the elimination of spiritual rule and the annexation of church property into the state. Bishops were no longer the equal of the prince, and the churches fell under the regulation of the individual states. To compensate for losses on the left bank of the Rhine, Prussia gained even more territory on the right bank, as did Baden:[47]

> With these compensations, Bonaparte realized one of the great goals of his German policy: the creation of a group of enlarged German client states on or near the French border, of sufficient size and internal cohesion as to diminish their sense of dependence on Austria, yet not so large as to be able to forget that their recent good fortune as well as their possible future expansion was due to the good will of France.[48]

The growing influence of Napoleon on the south and central German princes and other factors led Austria to enter into an offensive alliance with Russia and Britain against France. But France, in alliance with Baden and

Württemberg, again defeated Austrian forces at Austerlitz, and Austria had to accept the Peace of Pressburg in December 1805. Prussia was forced to give up territories on the east bank of the Rhine, while Baden, Württemburg, and Bavaria were recognized by France as sovereign states.[49]

In July 1806 several German princes declared their withdrawal from the empire and formed the *Rheinbund* (Confederation of the Rhine). Napoleon demanded that the emperor lay down the imperial crown, thus ending the empire for good. Prussia presented France with an ultimatum to withdraw from all of Germany, but in the ensuing war France defeated Prussian forces at Jena in October 1806. France now controlled all of Germany, and Prussia was saddled with reparations to France. The *Rheinbund* started with sixteen states, but after the Prussian defeat and the Treaty of Tilsit in 1807, it grew to thirty-nine. Only Austria, Prussia, Danish Holstein, the Hanseatic cities, and Swedish Pomerania remained outside. Through consolidation of imperial cities and further secularization, Napoleon increased the size of Baden, Württemburg, Bavaria, and Hesse-Darmstadt. The Grand Duchies of Berg (a new territory created on the east bank of the Rhine) and Würzburg were expanded and the Grand Duchies of Frankfurt and the Kingdom of Westphalia were formed. At the same time, the *Rheinbund* states had to relinquish some territory to France, and though formally sovereign were now under the dominance of Napoleon.[50]

A *Bundestag* (federal assembly) was established in Frankfurt as the common organ of the *Rheinbund*. Not unlike the imperial *Reichstag*, its purpose was to deal with common interests and resolve disputes between member states. Each member was obliged to come to the aid of any other member that was involved in a continental conflict. Intervention, of course, was determined by Napoleon, which meant that the sovereignty of the members was in fact circumscribed politically if not legally. In any case the *Bundestag* never met. Officially the *Rheinbund* was a confederation of German states, but in practice it was more a French protectorate.[51]

The assessment of the *Rheinbund* varies among historians, but it certainly had important consequences. Numerous reforms and territorial changes were introduced,[52] and a growing homogeneity of living conditions in different states created the basis for the development of a middle class. Absolute monarchism was promoted by the sovereignty the territories now enjoyed – even if limited by Napoleon – and a national sentiment began to grow. Indeed, the idea of a German nation grew with the writings of nationalist poets and philosophers and the rise of a middle class that replaced the estates weakened by secularization and the consolidation of cities.[53] Thus "the tendency of the empire to create autonomous territories from dependent states changed in the direction of autonomous territories combining to form a federation and therefore coming closer together."[54]

With the French defeat in Russia in 1812, Russia, Austria, and Prussia formed an alliance in 1813. Prussia declared war on France and was joined by a large coalition of European states whose forces defeated Napoleon at Leipzig in 1813. Napoleon retreated to Paris, he was exiled to Elba, and his domination of Germany for two decades was ended. It was now left to the Congress of Vienna, interrupted by Napoleon's return and the Battle of Waterloo in 1815, to establish a new order for Europe and Germany. Prussia ended up with a small part of Poland, part of Westphalia, territories on the left bank of the Rhine and on the Saar that had been taken by France (but not Alsace). Bavaria was given Landau in the Palatinate (map 1.2)

In the meantime the *Rheinbund* had ceased to exist, and the German Confederation (*Deutscher Bund*) was established in 1815. It consisted of thirty-nine states, excluding the eastern parts of the territories of Prussia and Austria. Some historians suggest that it continued the old Reich in a new form.[55] It was established for the limited purposes of securing the states against both internal and external dangers and for the promotion of trade. Though a clear expression of federal powers was not contained in the founding document, the Federal Treaty, there was a general clause which authorized the confederation to carry out its purposes. As time went on, the confederation became the means of internal restoration or reaction rather than an instrument of external protection which in practice was left up to the individual states. In other words, the states retained their sovereignty, but the confederation served to protect the status quo.[56]

The confederal organ responsible for common matters was a permanent federal assembly or diet (*Bundestag*) in Frankfurt. Otherwise there was no head of state, no government, no administration, and no courts. The *Bundestag*, chaired by Austria, consisted of representatives who served their states with an imperative mandate, i.e., as delegates rather than trustees. When the assembly met in full session for the purpose of voting, a two-thirds majority or even unanimity was required. The seven largest states had 4 votes each, the other thirty-two states 1 vote. An executive committee consisted of the largest eleven states with 1 vote each. Another 6 votes were distributed among the smaller states. Decisions of the committee were made by majority vote in general, but in some cases unanimity was required.[57]

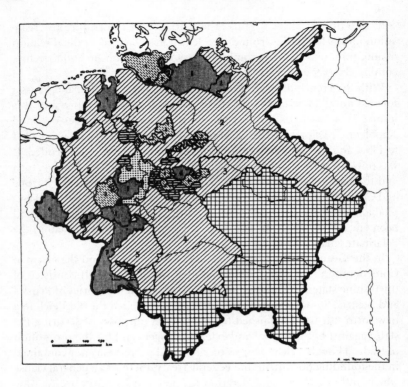

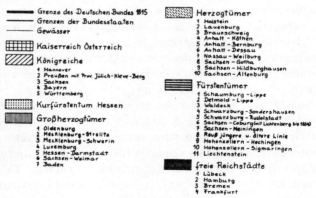

Map 1.2   **The German Confederation, 1815**

There were some important reforms in Prussia and in other German states – especially in the south – at this time, but in Prussia reforms ended in 1819, and in general the German Confederation was noted until 1848 for the Austrian Prince Metternich's promotion of policies of restoration and hostility to democracy, liberalism, and nationalism because of the threat each posed for multi-national Austria. South German states continued to make some modest reforms, but these were not allowed to challenge the monarchical principle. Restoration was more the norm in northern Germany. Yet while the constitutional order of the German Confederation stagnated, economic and social modernization were taking place. One result was the Hambach Festival in 1832 which demanded German unification and popular sovereignty; but this brought about even more reactionary measures pushed by Metternich. On the other hand economic changes also led to the establishment of a Prussian–German customs union in 1834 in which Austria did not participate.[58]

After the defeat of Napoleon and the Congress of Vienna in 1815, Prussia was located in the East as well as the West of Germany, with a hole in the middle. Though Prussia was an absolutist state, it was not really a unitary state. Historical regions retained their characteristics, e.g., Brandenburg, East and West Prussia, and Silesia, while the new territories in the West, Westphalia and the Rhine Province, were not historical. The country was divided into ten, then eight, provinces, which were subdivided into administrative districts (*Regierungsbezirke*). The period before 1848 was "pre-constitutional," in that the king resisted any efforts to promulgate a constitution; however, government was not arbitrary, for it was bound to abide by the rule of law.[59]

The Customs Union (*Zollverein*) of 1834, which was formed under Prussian leadership, was the result of a reluctant but steady increase in support for free trade. It is ironic that Prussia therefore succeeded in achieving considerable economic unity while together with Austria and the *Bundestag* it continued to suppress the national and liberal movements. Unlike the German Confederation established in 1815, the Customs Union did not include Austria, Bremen, or Hamburg, but it did include Luxembourg. It had no assembly of delegates, but it did have a general conference of governments with one vote each. Again, it was another form of confederation that overlay the German Confederation of 1815.[60]

The Revolution of 1848 to the Second (Bismarck) Reich of 1871

The Revolution in March 1848, which followed revolutionary uprisings in France, was a key event in German constitutional and political history, an event comparable in some ways to the disturbances in East Germany in 1989.[61] It was the culmination of a national movement, which derived the idea of a German nation-state from the French Revolution, the writings of nationalist philosophers, and from increasing democratic pressures. But the idea of a liberal nation-state did not find favor in the governments of the individual states,[62] in spite of the fact that by 1848 all but four German states had constitutions; however, the two key states, Prussia and Austria, did not.[63] One of the many ramifications of the Revolution was the efforts of the Frankfurt Assembly in the Paulskirche, elected in May by relatively democratic procedures throughout the German Confederation, to devise a constitution for a united, federal Germany that would meet basic democratic requirements, satisfy the many monarchical ruling houses in the German states, and somehow accommodate the conflicting interests of the two major German powers, Prussia and Austria, whose reemergence after Napoleon's defeat had "left no room for a nationalistic agenda."[64] By this time the idea of a federal state, as opposed to the more traditional German idea of a loose confederation, had taken root with the United States often perceived as a kind of model.[65] But the conditions in Germany were different from those faced by the American Founding Fathers. In the first place the territorial developments in Germany were very different: from hundreds of states at the end of the eighteenth century, there were still thirty-nine states ranging in size from thousands to many millions of inhabitants and in territory from city states to large monarchies; there was no unitary legal system; economic unity was inadequate in spite of the Customs Union; and reformers faced states with an authoritarian, feudal–absolutistic tradition. Second, economic prosperity was generally lacking, a proletariat had formed, and as a result there was resistance by many to universal male suffrage. Third, the German Confederation had been hostile to democratic and progressive change. There was no political center, but rather two restorative powers competing for hegemony. Thus, in the United States the issue was separation from a distant political center in London and the gradual formation of a nation, while in Germany "the aim was to unite different sovereign states with rather distinctive peculiarities and to create a powerful central government in opposition to internal particularistic forces but also in opposition to the great powers in Europe, which were not interested in the formation of a new powerful state."[66]

By the fall of 1848, it became clear to the ruling houses of Prussia and Austria that they still enjoyed the loyalty of the military and could resist the pressures of the Frankfurt Assembly. The initial hopes of a majority of the Assemblymen that they could forge a united Germany including Austria were dashed in November by the Austrian government's rejection of any such plan. Efforts to form a "small" Germany without Austria continued with the writing of a constitution for the other states of the German Confederation. The Constitution of March 1849 provided for a federal state with enumerated powers for the federation and reserve powers for the states. The federation was made responsible not only for foreign affairs; war and peace; internal law and order; trade, currency, weights and measures; immigration and citizenship; postal affairs, etc., but also railways and health. Provisions for achieving unitary economic conditions were included, and there was an implied powers clause not very different from the American "necessary and proper clause." The result was a constitutional draft somewhat more centralist than the American model. On the other hand, only the navy was under national control, while ground forces were to be provided by the states. Only in wartime would they come under national command. The federal parliament was to pass the laws, but the states were to execute them in order to preserve the monarchical character of the states and their bureaucracies. The federation was to have only supervisory powers over the execution of the laws. These provisions reflected "the ambivalence of the unitarian–particularistic German approach very clearly."[67]

The Frankfurt Constitution of 1849,[68] accepted by twenty-nine states of the German Confederation, was doomed to failure, however, when the Prussian King, Frederick William IV, rejected the offer to become the crowned head of state of a new, united Germany, on the grounds that it "does not bear the stamp 'by the grace of God' on its head."[69] The Prussian and Austrian delegates to the Frankfurt Assembly were recalled, and in May the central authority that had been established dissolved the Assembly. Left- wing elements decided to fight, but they were easily defeated by Prussian troops by the end of July.[70]

In 1850 the king of Prussia reluctantly accepted a constitution which provided for an upper house composed of the nobility and a plutocratic parliamentary assembly, one-third of which was elected by those very few Prussians who paid the top one-third of the taxes, one-third by a modest proportion of citizens who paid the next one-third in taxes, and one-third by the remainder of the citizens who paid taxes. Austria did not follow with a constitution until 1861. In the meantime most of the other

German states became more authoritarian, even though the principle of representative government was not abandoned.[71]

Following the dissolution of the Frankfurt Parliament in 1849, Prussia proposed a plan for German unification which would provide for Prussian executive dominance in a league of princes with a plutocratically elected parliament. Austrian objections, supported by Russia, led to abandonment of the effort by several German states, and an assembly elected in early 1850 as a first step toward establishing the new league was dissolved by the end of the year. By the spring of the following year Prussia and Austria had reestablished the German Confederation. In 1851 the Customs Union was also reestablished, again under Prussian leadership.[72]

In 1859 representatives of several German states gathered together to discuss the adoption of common civil and criminal laws for the Confederation and a German supreme court. Committees were formed to begin the process of codifying civil and commercial laws in 1862, and in 1861 the Saxon head of government proposed a plan of German unification in which executive power would be shared by Prussia, Austria, and a third German state. Austria expressed interest and proposed a revised alternative plan. Prussia was wary of having to share power in such a federal arrangement and proposed its own plan which was another version of its 1850 plan for unification. A commercial code which Prussia had worked out for the Confederation and a free-trade arrangement between Prussia and France which Austria could not accept led to tensions between the two large states, and Prussia refused to attend a conference in Frankfurt in 1863 at which Austria presented its ideas for German unification. This led to failure of efforts to unite Germany with Austria as a member state.[73]

In 1864 Prussia and Austria joined forces to defeat Denmark in a brief war over Denmark's intention to annex Schleswig and perhaps Holstein as well. Rather than create a new German state for the Confederation, Prussia and Austria divided the new territory so that Prussia secured Schleswig and Austria occupied Holstein. In 1866 the two quarreled over the spoils, and Austria took its case to the Assembly of the Confederation. Prussia seized Holstein in retaliation, and Austria responded by seeking approval from the Frankfurt Assembly to mobilize against Prussia. It won the support of most of the kingdoms, including Saxony and Hanover, while Prussia was supported mostly by smaller states in the North. In the brief war that followed, Prussia quickly defeated the forces of Hannover, Hesse-Kassel, and Bavaria before they could join with the Austrians, and then went on to defeat the Saxon and Austrian armies at Königgrätz. The Confederation was dissolved, and Austria withdrew from Germany.

Schleswig and Holstein were annexed by Prussia, as was Hannover, Hesse-Kassel, Nassau, and Frankfurt. Prussia stopped at the Main River, however, to avoid provoking France. Prussia formed the North German Confederation in 1867, which left three Germanies: one in the North, including Saxony; one in the South; and Austria. South Germany was in the French zone of influence, but the South German states of Hesse-Darmstadt, Baden, Württemberg, and Bavaria agreed secretly to give Prussia high command in case of war. No territory was taken from Austria, nor was any given to the bitterly disappointed Napoleon III.[74]

After the war Prussian proposals for a new constitutional order were accepted by twenty-three states. A *Reichstag* was elected and, after several changes, approved the constitution on 16 April 1867. It had rejected the demands of the progressive Left for a unitary state, which Bismarck had opposed in favor of a federation that would be legally less problematic, would grant the states considerable autonomy, and would serve as a barrier against parliamentary-democratic tendencies. It had also rejected particularistic demands from the traditional aristocratic feudal Right and the newer parliamentary particularism found especially in newly annexed states.[75] The new "Constitution of the North German Federation" then went into effect on 1 July 1867. Prussia, with a large majority of the population and territory, was, of course, the dominant state in the Federation. The executive head of the Federation was the "Federal Praesidium" which consisted of the King of Prussia. He was authorized to appoint the chancellor as head of government, who had to countersign all acts of the Federal Praesidium, and he had the overall command of the armed forces. The states and their princes were represented in the *Bundesrat*, which was the "carrier" of sovereignty in the Federation rather than the individual states; however, law enforcement, religion, and education were retained by the states. Prussia had 17 of 43 votes in the *Bundesrat*, enough to prevent amendments without its consent. The *Reichstag* was the chamber that represented the people and was elected by what was then in Europe a remarkably democratic system of universal male suffrage (in contrast to the plutocratic class system of voting for the Prussian legislature which continued without change). Indeed, the Frankfurt Parliament had passed a law in February 1849 that called for universal male suffrage by secret ballot, in spite of serious opposition from many middle-class delegates.[76] Though its powers were limited, the *Reichstag* had to approve all domestic legislation passed by the *Bundesrat* and signed by the King of Prussia. Of course the North German Federation was formed essentially as the result of a revolution "from above" by governments, in contrast to the efforts of the Frankfurt Parliament of 1848; on the other hand the revolutionary changes introduced by the Federation were supported by the people "from below" through the political parties. The new Federation signed a customs treaty with the four South German states in July 1867, which created a unified economic area for all of Germany except Austria.[77]

In 1870 Chancellor Bismarck maneuvered Napoleon III into declaring war on the Federation, which was joined by the South German states in defeating French forces at Sedan and Metz. The South German states expressed an interest in unification, and they joined with the North German Federation to form the Second German Reich (also Kaiserreich, Hohenzollern Reich or Bismarck Reich) in January 1871. Thus was created for the first time a German "center" in the capital of Berlin (map 1.3):

> The ubiquity of territorial politics in the history of Germany before unification necessarily had the consequence that there was no centre. As a result of this fact the picture which most Germans have of their past differs profoundly from the historical images familiar in Britain, France or Spain where there is a long experience of government from a dominant capital city. There has been no single all-pervasive centre in the German political evolution.[78]

From the Second Reich to the Third Reich

The constitution of the German Reich was modeled closely after the constitution of the North German Federation. The highest organ of the German Reich was the emperor (Kaiser), who was also the King of Prussia. He appointed the Chancellor who was also the Minister-President (prime minister) of Prussia and was responsible to the Kaiser as head of government. The Chancellor chaired the *Bundesrat* meetings and had to answer to the *Reichstag*, but he was not dependent on the confidence of that body as was the case in the British parliamentary model. The legislative bodies consisted of the *Bundesrat* and *Reichstag*. Both chambers had to approve all legislation. The dominance of Prussia in this constitution is reflected by Koppel Pinson: "The men of '48 had wanted Prussia 'to merge itself' into a greater Germany. Bismarck annexed the non-Prussian Germany to Prussia in order to create an enlarged Prussia."[79]

The *Reichstag* was elected in single-member districts by universal male suffrage for those who were over twenty-five years of age, and its members were "representatives of all the people." However, its powers were limited in several ways. First, it had no influence on the appointment or

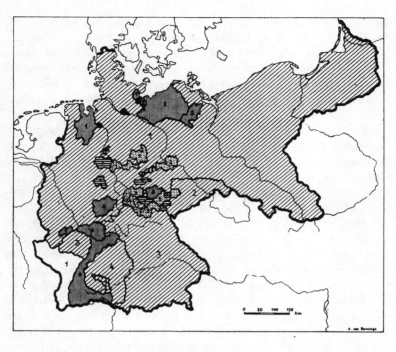

Map 1.3   **The Bismark Reich, 1871**

removal of the Chancellor. Second, it had to share legislative powers with the *Bundesrat*. The list of legislative powers in Article 4 of the Constitution was modest, but it expanded in practice, e.g., in the area of courts, judicial procedures, and a nation-wide code of civil law still in operation today. By the end of the century it had become the major factor in legislation in spite of the *Bundesrat*, promoted strongly by the national political parties.[80]

The *Bundesrat* consisted of delegates from the twenty-five states listed in Article 1 of the Constitution[81] that made up the new Reich (twenty-two monarchies and three city states; Alsace-Lorraine became a special *Reichsland* with representation in the *Reichstag*), and they voted by instruction from their state governments, led mostly by the traditional princes (actually four kings, six grand dukes, five dukes, and seven princes). The *Bundesrat* was the first organ mentioned in the Constitution, and it "carried" the sovereignty of the Reich. This meant that the individual states were no longer sovereign, even though they retained considerable autonomy in a number of areas. It was the organs and activities of the Reich, however, that represented sovereignty, including the Kaiser, the Chancellor, the Reich administration, the *Reichstag* and *Bundesrat*, foreign policy, and army and navy that had never existed before for Germany as a whole. Prussia had 17 of the 58 votes in the *Bundesrat*, in spite of the fact that it had about three-fifths of the population and two-thirds of the territory of the Reich. On the other hand, amendments to the Reich Constitution required 14 votes. The three kingdoms of Bavaria, Württemberg, and Saxony had 14 votes together (6, 4 and 4, respectively). The seventeen small states had 1 vote each.[82]

Since the Kaiser was the supreme commander of the armed forces, over which there was no civilian control and therefore no parliamentary control, "the Kaiser virtually remained an absolutist monarch in the military field."[83] Indeed, Pinson suggests that the Prussian army was the core of the Prussian state and therefore of the Kaiserreich. Therefore, it "was the most obvious instrument of power and influence in the new Reich."[84] The constitutional order of the Reich remained stable, in spite of numerous challenges, for example, from Protestant–Catholic tensions and the growing working class and their leaders.[85] The challenge which it did not survive, however, was the First World War. Facing certain defeat, the High Command pressed for an armistice that would be signed by a new parliamentary-democratic government led by the former opposition, the Social Democrats, Left liberals, and Catholics. While deemed necessary at the time owing to the fear that the Allies would not conclude an armistice or conclude peace with a government lacking democratic legitimacy, the result was that it was the democratic opposition, not the Kaiser and his government, that ended up facing charges of treason by the extreme nationalists. In October 1918 the necessary changes were made in the constitution to bring it more into conformity with a democratic parliamentary system. The *Reichstag* approved the necessary changes, but the November Revolution and the overthrow of the Kaiser and the old order required the writing of a new constitution.

Elections in January 1919 for the constitutional assembly (National Assembly) in the small city of Weimar yielded a majority for the Social Democrats, German Democratic Party (progressive liberals), and the Catholic Center Party, which together formed the center-left democratic coalition responsible for writing the Weimar Constitution (map 1.4). The far left and far right were not well represented. In the meantime the states also elected constitutional assemblies for their own new constitutions, in spite of the fact that the Social Democrats in Weimar (but not state leaders!) favored a unitary state together with the leadership of the German Democratic Party.

In his proposals of early January 1919, the constitutional scholar, Hugo Preuss, did not call for a federation but rather for sixteen territories of approximately equal size, including Austria, that would become administrative units in a decentralized unitary state. His goal was to break up Prussia, but the identity of the people with their traditional states was too strong. Even the national leaders of the Social Democratic Party, who supported Preuss, had to deal with the party's leaders in Prussia, who, with the elimination of the old Prussian three-class voting system for the state parliament, were now confident that they would be (and indeed did become) the dominant force in Prussia.[86] As a result of these kinds of pressures, Preuss' draft, along with four others, was rejected. A committee of states was formed at the end of January with the agreement that it had to approve proposals brought before the Weimar National Assembly, which had the effect of guaranteeing the continuation of a federal system. Nevertheless, Preuss insisted that "'[t]he foundation of the entire Weimar Constitution is that this republic is not an association, a league of German states, but that the German state is and shall be the political organisation of the unified German people living within this state.'"[87] A new constitution was drafted and accepted, and it went into effect in August 1919.[88]

The Weimar Constitution[89] provided for a parliamentary democracy in which the government, with a chancellor as head of government, was made dependent on the *Reichstag*. The head of state was a popularly

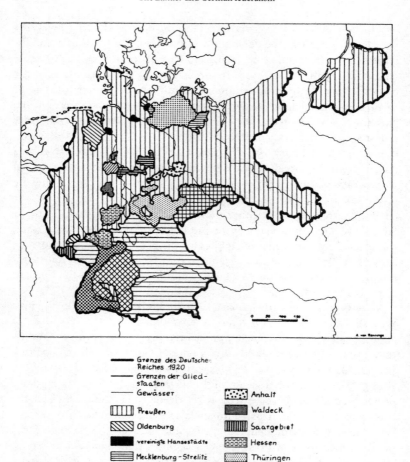

Map 1.4   **The Weimar Republic, 1920**

elected president. The new republic was a federation, with the *Reichsrat* replacing the *Bundesrat*; however, the *Reichsrat*, which had 66 votes, was not made a regular participant in the legislative process and could be overridden by the *Reichstag*. Prussia received two-fifths of the votes, but half of the Prussian delegation of twenty-six came from the Prussian government, the other half from the Prussian provincial administrations represented by political parties. The states were now called *Länder* and over the years were reduced in number from twenty-five to seventeen by 1932. Territorial changes remained minor, however, in comparison with Napoleon and even Bismarck.[90]

The seventeen *Länder* were: Prussia, Bavaria, Saxony, Württemberg, Baden, Thuringia (created in 1920), Hesse, Mecklenburg-Schwerin, Oldenburg, Brunswick (Braunschweig), Anhalt, Lippe, Mecklenburg-Strelitz, Schaumburg-Lippe, and the three city states of Bremen, Hamburg, and Lübeck. Austria, which wanted to join the new federation, was prevented from doing so by the Allies. Unlike the Constitution of the Kaiserreich, the *Länder* were not listed in the Weimar Constitution on the grounds that the Reich territory, including Prussia, would be reorganized so that the *Länder* would be of roughly equal size. As it turned out, however, territorial reorganization of the kind envisaged by Preuss receded into the background in light of many more urgent problems.[91]

Under the Weimar Constitution the relationship between Prussia and the Reich was changed dramatically. Prussia lost its hegemony through the elimination of the *Personalunion* between the prime minister of Prussia and the chancellor of the Reich. The powers of the Reich were also expanded. A Reich administration of financial matters was created alongside the finance administrations of the *Länder*, and by 1930 a reform commission consisting of delegates from the Reich and the *Länder* were calling for the dissolution of Prussia; creation of new *Länder* from Prussian territory that would have less autonomy than the larger, older, *Länder*; and the consolidation of small *Länder*. These proposals never reached the *Reichstag* owing to more pressing matters.[92]

In contrast to the Constitution of the Kaiserreich, the *Reichstag*, rather than the *Bundesrat* (now called the *Reichsrat*) was the first organ to be mentioned in the Weimar Constitution. The *Reichstag* was elected by men *and* women by proportional representation, with only 60,000 votes making up one parliamentary seat. This system led to fair representation, but it also led to a greater role for the political parties and promoted a fragmented multi-party system. The *Reichsrat* represented the *Länder*, which received one vote for each million inhabitants; however, the largest

Land (Prussia) could not have more than two-fifths of the total membership in spite of its population which was more than three-fifths of the total. In addition, half of the Prussian votes were from the various provinces rather than from the central government of Prussia. [93]

The Chancellor was appointed and dismissed by the popularly elected Reich President; however, the Chancellor and his ministers were also dependent on the support of a majority of the *Reichstag*. These provisions of the Weimar Constitution which are very similar to those of the French Fifth Republic today broke down by the end of the 1920s because of the inability of the polarized multi-party system to form stable majority coalition governments. This, in turn, led to an increasing dependency on the emergency rule of the President under Article 48. In the end, exasperation with these conditions led to the invitation to Adolf Hitler to form a government.

When the National Socialists came to power in January 1933, they began the process of *Gleichschaltung*, the "coordination" of the *Länder*, first by replacing non-Nazi governments in ten *Länder* by Reich commissioners, then by giving the *Land* governments (cabinets) legislative powers. By April a kind of governor (*Reichsstatthalter*) was placed over the *Land* governments, and in January 1934 the autonomy of the *Länder* was transferred to the Reich. The *Länder* became administrative districts of the Reich, acting only on behalf of the central administration. As a result the *Reichsrat* became superfluous, and it was dissolved in February 1934. The *Land* parliaments were also dissolved, and the *Land* governments were appointed by the Reich. In the meantime the two Mecklenburg *Länder* were consolidated, Lübeck was absorbed by Prussia, and the Saarland was placed under the *Gauleiter* (regional party leader) of the Palatinate, which was part of Bavaria. Over time the *Gauleiter* assumed greater importance than the *Länder*.[94] Both the Nazi Party and the state which it governed under the highly centralized dictatorship of Adolf Hitler made no pretense of the contempt with which any semblance of regional or local autonomy and democratic rule were held.[95]

The *Länder* in the Federal Republic of Germany

There was a dramatic shake-up of German states with the dissolution of the old Reich in 1806, a dramatic growth in size by Prussia in 1815, a struggle over hegemony between Prussia and Austria and the incorporation of several states into Prussia in 1866, and the collapse of the Kaiserreich in

1918 followed by a reduction in the number of states from twenty-five to seventeen during the fourteen years of the Weimar Republic. But none of these changes could compare to the events following the defeat of the Third Reich in 1945.

Germany was divided into four zones of occupation, with the supreme commander in each zone, a general from the United States, Great Britain, France, and the Soviet Union, respectively, acting as the highest authority. Berlin, like Vienna and the rest of Austria, was also occupied by the four Allies. In each case a council was established to provide for coordination and cooperation in the whole of Germany or Berlin, but from the beginning tensions among the Allies prevented almost all common actions. Territories east of the Oder/Neisse Rivers were placed under Polish and Soviet "administration," and several millions of their German inhabitants became the victims of "ethnic cleansing." The Soviet Zone consisted of the five pre-war *Länder* of Mecklenburg-Strelitz and Mecklenburg-Schwerin, Anhalt, Thuringia, Saxony, and the two Prussian provinces of Brandenburg and Saxony. In the zones of the three Western Allies, old *Länder* with administrative continuity included only Bavaria, Württemberg, Baden, Hesse-Darmstadt in the south, and tiny Schaumburg-Lippe, and the city states of Bremen and Hamburg in the north. Most of the territory in the north consisted of former Prussian provinces. The military governments decided whether to use the administrative structures in the old *Länder* or to create new ones.[96]

The American zone

The Americans, who wanted a federal structure from the beginning, created three *Länder* in the South in September 1945.[97] They re-created the old *Land* of Bavaria without the Bavarian enclave of Landau in the Palatinate; other than that minor territorial loss, Bavaria was the only *Land* in the three Western zones other than Bremen and Hamburg that emerged unchanged. A new constitution for Bavaria was drafted during the first half of 1946 and approved by an elected constitutional assembly and a popular referendum on the day of the first election to the Bavarian parliament in late autumn of 1946.[98]

The Americans also created the new *Land* of Württemberg-Baden, consisting of the northern halves of the former *Länder* with these names. The Americans had given the southern half of Baden, rather than all of it, to France for its occupation zone in order to prevent the French from separating territories along the Rhine from the rest of Germany. Dissatisfaction with the creation of this *Land* and the one created by the French in their zone led to further changes which are discussed below.[99]

Finally, the new *Land* of Hesse was created. "Large Hesse" (*Grosshessen*), as it was called initially, consisted of the older *Land* of Hesse, without Rheinhessen, which went to the French zone; the former Prussian province of Nassau, without four counties that went to the French zone; and the former Prussian province of *Kurhessen*.[100] Each of these three *Länder* drew up a constitution in 1946 which was approved by an elected constitutional assembly. The northern city-state of Bremen, which the Americans secured as a port of entry, was re-created in January 1947.[101] Local elections in the south were held in early 1946, county elections and elections in the larger cities in the spring, and constitutional assemblies approved draft constitutions in late autumn. At the same time *Land* parliaments were elected and *Land* governments formed.[102]

The French zone

The French zone was carved out of the original British and American zones, because the Soviets insisted at Yalta on retaining their zone that had been drawn by the British, Americans, and Soviets without the French in mind.[103] It consisted of several Prussian territories: the southern part of the Rhine province of Prussia, parts of the former province of Nassau, the Saar, the Palatinate, and Hohenzollern. It also got parts of four older *Länder*: Rheinhessen from Hesse, the southern halves of Baden and Württemberg, and the Bavarian territory in the Palatinate around Landau. In 1947 the southern half of Baden was created as a new *Land*, (South) Baden, and the southern half of Württemberg and the Prussian enclave of Hohenzollern became the *Land* of Württemberg-Hohenzollern. The new *Land* of Rhineland-Palatinate was formed from the Prussian administrative districts (*Regierungsbezirke*) of Koblenz and Trier, four counties of the former Prussian administrative district of Wiesbaden, the former Hessian administrative district of Rheinhessen, and the former Bavarian enclave of Landau mentioned above.[104]

The Saarland was a special case. It had been occupied by Napoleon from 1801 to 1815, and Napoleon III had expected to receive it in compensation for standing by when Prussia went to war against Austria in 1866. After the First World War it was occupied by France but returned to Germany as a result of a referendum in 1935. In 1946 the French separated it from Germany again and turned it into a legally autonomous but in fact dependent territory of France. The French went so far in 1948 as to change the nationality of the inhabitants from German to a "Saarland nationality." With efforts by the French and German leaders to move in the direction of European integration, and after German complaints to the Council of Europe about violations of basic rights, the French began to modify their position and to be more conciliatory. After numerous ups and downs and the apparent success of efforts to "Europeanize" the Saarland, the French allowed the voters to decide whether to accept this solution in 1955. They rejected it, and a new *Land* parliament was elected for the first time with pro-German parties. The French finally accepted majority sentiment and agreed to return the Saarland to Germany on 1 January 1957; however, the Saarland remained in economic union with France until the end of December 1959.[105]

The British zone

The British waited somewhat longer with the territorial reorganization of their zone, which was more heterogeneous than the others. It consisted of the four previous Prussian provinces of Hannover, Schleswig-Holstein, Westphalia, and the northern part of the Rhine province; the four small *Länder* of Braunschweig (Brunswick), Oldenburg, Lippe-Detmold, and Schaumburg-Lippe; and the city-state of Hamburg. The other city-state in the north, composed of Bremen and Bremerhaven, was occupied by the Americans, who wanted to have control over the port of entry for American troops and supplies.

North-Rhine Westphalia was formed from the province of Westphalia, the northern part of the Rhine province, and, somewhat later, the small *Land* of Lippe-Detmold. These territories incorporated the heavily industrialized and densely populated *Ruhrgebiet* which made this new *Land* then and still today the most densely populated in all of Germany. It was first created in August 1946, with Lippe being added in January 1947. The first *Land* parliament was appointed in October 1946. Work on the first constitution was begun in the spring of 1947 but, owing to much controversy, not completed until the spring of 1950.[106]

Lower Saxony was formed in 1946 from Hanover, Oldenburg, Braunschweig, and Schaumburg-Lippe, the smallest traditional *Land* in Germany. In September 1946 the British appointed a *Land* parliament, which approved a temporary constitution in February 1947. A few months later, the members of the first elected *Land* parliament entered office. A second "temporary constitution" was passed by the *Land* parliament in 1951 and went into effect in May of that year. Some efforts were made to separate

Oldenburg and Schaumburg-Lippe from Lower Saxony, but they were unsuccessful.[107]

Schleswig-Holstein, including the former city-state of Lübeck which lost its autonomy in 1937, was elevated to the status of a *Land* in 1946. It is the only former Prussian province that became a *Land* with no change of boundaries.[108] The first *Land* elections took place in April 1947. The Social Democrats wanted to combine Schleswig-Holstein, Hamburg, and Lower Saxony into one large "Northwest State," but Hamburg was vehemently opposed.[109] The constitution, which did not go into effect until December 1949, reflected an agreement with Denmark which guaranteed minority rights for the Danes in Schleswig-Holstein and for the Germans in Denmark.[110]

The traditional city-state of Hamburg was re-established as a *Land* in 1946, and the first election for its parliament was held in November 1946. The first constitution, however, was not completed until June 1952. As noted above, Bremen and Bremerhaven, at first occupied by the British, were turned over to the Americans who proclaimed them to constitute a *Land* in January 1947. It was and remains today the smallest *Land* in population and territory.[111]

The Soviet zone

In 1945 American and British troops occupied Thuringia, parts of Saxony, Halle-Merseburg, Magdeburg, and Mecklenburg. In accordance with the Yalta Agreement, these troops were withdrawn from these territories in July 1945, and they were replaced by Soviet troops. The territories east of the Oder/Neisse River – Pomerania, Silesia, and the lower half of East Prussia – were given to Poland for "administration," while the northern half of East Prussia was annexed by the Soviet Union. In the Soviet Zone west of the Oder/Neisse River there were five older *Länder*: Mecklenburg-Strelitz, Mecklenburg-Schwerin, Anhalt, Thuringia, and Saxony; and two Prussian provinces: Brandenburg and Saxony. These were used for administrative purposes and given constitutions in 1947, when Prussia was formally dissolved.

In June 1946 the Americans formed a provincial government in Thuringia which was replaced by the Soviets in July with a government completely dominated by communists. A new constitution for the *Land* of Thuringia went into effect in 1947, and in 1948 the capital was moved from Weimar, where the Americans had placed the seat of government, to Erfurt.[112]

The old Kingdom of Saxony, which had been turned into a republican *Land* in the Weimar Republic, was occupied in 1945 by American troops in the west and Soviet troops in the east. This led to the appointment by the Americans in their half of mostly social democratic and middle-class politicians and of communists and left-wing social democrats in the Soviet half. The Soviets occupied the entire territory in July 1945, and local elections and parliamentary elections were held in September and October 1946, respectively. In spite of Soviet support, the communists (Socialist Unity Party, SED, see below) received a little less than half of the seats in the parliamentary elections. A constitution was passed by the *Land* parliament in February 1947.[113]

In 1945 Soviet forces entered Mecklenburg from the east, while British and American troops entered from the west and south. The Soviets occupied all of the two Mecklenburg territories and the western portion of Pomerania in July 1945. Not only was the territory east of the Oder given to Poland; Polish gains also included the area around Stettin just west of the Oder. In spite of considerable Soviet harassment, the non-communist parties received half the seats in parliamentary elections in October 1946. The new government that was formed was, however, controlled by the communist-dominated SED. A constitution for the new *Land* consisting of the two Mecklenburgs and western Pomerania was passed by the parliament in January 1947.[114]

Like Mecklenburg, the former *Land* of Anhalt and the Prussian province of Saxony which contained Halle-Merseburg and Magdeburg were occupied by British, American, and Soviet troops, but they became part of the Soviet zone in July 1945. The Soviet military government organized an administration for Halle-Merseburg and Magdeburg and the *Land* of Anhalt with the seat of government in Halle. Deputies of a provisional consultative assembly were appointed in July 1946, and county and parliamentary elections were held in October. Again, the SED failed to gain an absolute majority of seats, but it did dominate the coalition government that was formed. A new constitution for the region went into effect in January 1947. After the dissolution of Prussia, Saxony-Anhalt was declared a *Land*.[115]

The Prussian province of Brandenburg was occupied by Soviet forces in 1945, which began immediately with the construction of a communist administration. Potsdam was made the seat of government. In June 1946 a consultative assembly was organized. Local elections were held in September, parliamentary elections in October. Even though the SED did not receive an absolute majority in spite of Soviet support, it became the dominant partner in a coalition government. A constitution was passed and went into effect early in 1947, and with the dissolution of Prussia on 25 February 1947 Brandenburg became a *Land*. In the elections of 1950, a "unitary" list of parties was presented to the voters in all of the *Länder* in the Soviet Zone, which meant for all practical purposes that any meaningful opposition in the parliament was eliminated.[116]

At the Yalta Conference in September 1944, the Allies agreed to divide Berlin into three occupation sectors just as Germany was divided into three zones of occupation. A common administration was to be exercised by the three sector commanders (*Kommandatura*). The city was captured by Soviet forces in April and May 1945, and a city administration was formed that was one-half communist. Western Allied troops, including French forces, which received part of the British sector, entered the city in July. Soon controversy emerged over the transit corridors for the Western Allies. Rail traffic and air routes were regulated in the autumn of 1945, and agreement was reached in May 1946 on road and canal traffic. The Soviets began to take a separate path early in 1946, when they tried to force a merger of the old Communist Party of Germany (KPD) and the Social Democratic Party of Germany (SPD) to form the SED. Outside the Soviet sector the SPD members voted against the merger by 80 percent; however, the merger took place in the Soviet sector and in the rest of the Soviet Zone of occupation. The Allied *Komandatura* issued a provisional constitution in August 1946, and it went into effect in October. In the first and only free election that followed, the Social Democrats received 49 percent of the vote, the Christian Democrats 22 percent, the Liberals 9 percent, and the communist-dominated SED only 20 percent. Increasing Soviet–Western differences made the work of the city government increasingly difficult, and in the spring and summer of 1948 the Soviets left the Allied Control Council and *Kommandatura*, respectively. The Western currency reform took place on 20 June 1948, and in response the Soviets introduced the East German Mark. In an attempt to force the Western Allies out of West Berlin, the Soviets began the Berlin Blockade on 24 June 1948; the Blockade failed and was lifted on 5 May 1949. In the meantime the SED in the eastern half of the city stopped their cooperation with their Western colleagues, and the city administration was effectively divided by the end of 1948. The SED refused to participate in the elections of December 1948, which then led to two city administrations, one in the East and one in the West.[117]

Largely in response to the West German Basic Law, an East German constitution, like the previous *Land* constitutions in the Soviet Zone modeled after the Weimar Constitution but largely ignored by the communist-dominated SED, went into effect in October 1949. The *Volkskammer* (Peoples' Chamber) was the popularly elected body dominated completely by the SED. The deputies of the five *Länder* parliaments elected representatives to a second body, the *Länderkammer* (*Länder* chamber), but it was given little authority and attention. As Georg Sante noted, in East Germany

> [t]he *Länder* are the atavistic and contrary element of the constitution. They point to the example of the Weimar Constitution, to past history, which is to be superseded in its old form. They contradict the socialist, communist principle of "democratic socialism," which amounts to a unitary state.[118]

In effect the *Länder* became administrative districts, and they were dissolved *de facto* in July 1952 when they were subdivided into the three administrative districts created from each *Land* that reported directly to East Berlin, which was one of the fifteen districts. The three districts within each *Land* (except Saxony-Anhalt, which had two) continued to elect delegates to the *Länderkammer* until 1958, when it was finally dissolved officially.[119]

Developments after the creation of the new *Länder* in the West

Political developments

In the West it became apparent that the *Länder* or administrative regions that had been created were too small for economic purposes, so the Americans formed a *Länder* council in November 1945, and the British formed a similar council for consultative purposes in February 1946. In January 1947 the two were joined economically to form the British–American Bizonia. The French, in the meantime, tried to administer their zone with as little contact with the other Allies as possible. They had the most centralized, rigorous and strict administration of the three Western zones. In May 1947 an economic council – in effect a parliament – was added to the Bizonal administration. This council, located in Frankfurt, consisted of delegates from the *Länder* parliaments. The French did not create a zonal consultative body, but they did join the Bizonia early in 1948. The administration of this combined economic zone introduced the famous currency reform of Ludwig Erhard on 20 June 1948. Together with the Marshall Plan of June 1947, this reform was an important element in the so-called German "economic miracle" that began soon after. The growing tensions between the Western Allies and the Soviets led to the Berlin Blockade from June 1948 to May 1949.[120]

In July 1948 the Western Allies gave the eleven prime ministers of the *Länder* in their three zones the "Frankfurt Documents" which called for a constitutional convention to draft a democratic, federal constitution for the territory of the three Western zones. The prime ministers were also asked to propose changes for *Land* boundaries in order to avoid both too small and too large *Länder*. The first reaction was generally negative, on the grounds that a constitution for the Western zones would effect a permanent division of Germany. However, the prime ministers finally agreed, after the military governors accepted a compromise according to which the new state would be provisional, not with a constitution but a "basic law."[121]

On 10 August 1948 the first meeting of the constitutional convention was called by the prime ministers in Herrenchiemsee, a palace located on an island of a large lake in Bavaria. Each *Land* had one legal expert as a representative. Together they prepared a draft constitution for the Parliamentary Council, consisting of representatives elected by the eleven *Land* parliaments. The Basic Law was approved by the Parliamentary Council on 23 May 1949 and passed by ten of the eleven *Land* parliaments. Bavaria refused to pass it, but it had agreed to abide by the decision of the majority.[122]

Additions and subtractions, 1949–60

At the time the Federal Republic was created, the *Länder* were Hamburg, Schleswig-Holstein, Lower Saxony, and North-Rhine Westphalia in the British zone; Bremen, Hesse, Bavaria, and Württemberg-Baden in the American zone; and the Rhineland-Patatinate, Württemberg-Hohenzollern, and Baden in the French zone. The Saarland, as noted above, was incorporated economically and to some extent even politically into France after 1945, but it was returned to Germany as a *Land* in January 1957.

More complicated – though without the international implications associated with the Saarland – was the question of the three *Länder* in the southwest, Baden, Württemberg-Hohenzollern, and Württemberg-Baden, which had been created from four parts: northern and southern Baden and northern and southern Württemberg (including the Prussian administrative district of Hohenzollern). Considerable dissatisfaction with the fragmentation represented by these three *Länder* was expressed even before the Federal Republic was created in 1949, and discussions had taken place among representatives of the four parts of the two former *Länder* in 1948 regarding the creation of a new *Südweststaat* (southwest state). But so much disagreement ensued concerning proposals for a referendum that the issue was put on hold until the Federal Republic had been established. A non-binding referendum was held in September 1950, and the results in the four parts as a whole favored a *Südweststaat*. South Baden voted against a combined state, and together with the northern part of the former *Land* a very slight majority of voters favored retention of their former state. Article 118 of the Basic Law permitted the *Bundestag* to pass legislation regulating the disposition of the territories in the southwest, and it did so in May 1951. The law allowed the creation of a new combined state if approved by a majority of voters in three of the four territories and if that majority constituted a majority for the combined area. South Baden vehemently opposed the bill and took it before the Federal Constitutional Court. The Court delayed the referendum from September until December 1951, but it rejected South Baden's suit. The referendum that was held had results very similar to the non-binding referendum in 1950. In the area as a whole almost 70 percent voted for the new state; however, in South Baden the vote was 62 percent for the old *Land* of Baden, while in the North and South together the vote was 52 percent for the old *Land*. Since, however, the three territories other than South Baden voted in favor and the total majority vote in the four territories was decisive, a new provisional government was formed in April 1952 for the new *Land* of Baden-Württemberg.[123]

In the meantime Schleswig-Holstein, which was a poor *Land* with a population that had doubled since the war because of refugees from the East, expressed a strong interest in gaining Hamburg and a strip of land from northern Lower Saxony. Lower Saxony did not want a poor *Land* to its north and suggested that Bremen be included in the annexation. Since both Hamburg and Bremen were vehemently opposed to the idea of joining Schleswig-Holstein, no action was taken.[124]

Changes and proposals for change after unification

In December 1989 the government of East Germany formed a commission to consider the possibility of restoring the five *Länder* that had been dissolved in 1952. Newly created "Roundtables" in the various administrative districts were also looking at the *Länder* and found that many East Germans no longer wanted to be identified as citizens of the German

Democratic Republic (GDR) but rather as Saxons, Mecklenburger, and so forth. It became clear that the restoration of the *Länder* could help re-establish a sense of legitimacy for the emerging political system.[125]

Soon, however, disputes began to arise over a variety of issues. One of these concerned the lack of congruence that could be found in many cases between the boundaries of the former *Länder* and the administrative districts that replaced them. Another was the desire of the inhabitants in some areas, such as Rostock and West Pomerania, to form new, separate *Länder*. A third issue was the location of the capital of Saxony-Anhalt. The Soviets had made Halle the capital from 1947 to 1952, but Magdeburg, which had been the seat of government of the Prussian province of Saxony, laid claim to the title and did, indeed, become the capital after the first *Land* elections in October 1990. There was also some question about certain territories and the *Länder* to which they belonged.[126]

During the spring and summer months of 1990, numerous proposals concerning the boundaries of the five new *Länder* were discussed in and out of government circles.[127] The simplest options saw the fourteen districts without Berlin combined into five *Länder*, either within the boundaries of the districts or of the *Länder* as of 1952. The third option called for a division of East Germany into four *Länder* by merging Saxony-Anhalt into Brandenburg and Saxony. A fourth option was to divide the GDR into three *Länder*, which would combine Saxony and Thuringia on the model of Baden-Württemberg. This would have made this *Land* the third largest in the united Germany, thus giving the East a large *Land* that could compete with the four large *Länder* in the West. A final option would have been to create one very large *Land* out of the GDR which would have been roughly comparable in population size to North-Rhine Westphalia.

In the end, of course, five *Länder* were re-created along with a united Berlin (map 1.5). The borders of the new *Länder* ran along the lines of the administrative districts; however, the questions of which border territories (in this case, counties) should go to which *Land* were settled in non-binding referenda at the end of July 1990.[128]

At this time there were also some proposals for combining parts of West and East Germany, for both sentimental and economic reasons. One serious proposal was to combine Schleswig-Holstein and Hamburg with Mecklenburg, perhaps with either Hamburg or Lübeck as the capital. Another was to combine Hesse and Thuringia, and there was also some talk of combining Lower Saxony and Saxony-Anhalt. Finally, some counties in the East sought to join their western neighbors. Heiligenstadt, the major city in the Eichsfeld in the East, for example, suggested that it

Map 1.5   **The Federal Republic of Germany, 1990**
Source: *Das Parlament*, 38 (14 September 1990), p. 32.

should join its sister city, Duderstadt, in Lower Saxony, and leave Thuringia. None of these proposals was implemented.[129]

The dramatic changes in the GDR and the creation of the new *Länder*, in addition to the debate about whether Bonn or Berlin should be the capital of a united Germany, initiated an intense debate about a *Neugliederung* or reordering of *Länder* boundaries in West Germany. In principle this debate was nothing new. In the late 1960s there was much discussion of territorial reform in Germany, including boundary reforms for the villages, towns, cities, and counties. As a result major territorial reforms were enacted at the local level in the eight territorial states (as opposed to the three city-states of Bremen, Hamburg, and West Berlin).[130] While these reforms were being enacted by *Land* legislatures, a special commission, called the *Ernst-Kommission*, recommended major boundary changes for the *Länder*.[131] It proposed that the Federal Republic have either five or six *Länder*: North-Rhine Westphalia, Baden-Württemberg, Bavaria; a combination of the Saarland, Rhineland-Palatinate, and Hesse; and either a combination of Schleswig-Holstein, Hamburg, and part of Lower Saxony on the one hand and Bremen and Lower Saxony on the other hand, or a joining of all these *Länder* – Schleswig-Holstein, Lower Saxony, Hamburg, and Bremen – into one very large *Nordstaat*. While no action was ever taken, the discussion of boundary reform continued unabated over the years.

The debate in the western *Länder* that was rekindled by the restoration of the *Länder* in the East did not resolve the differences between the protagonists and opponents.[132] One of the arguments made for boundary reform was that "now," i.e., during the first half of the 1990s, is the time to act, because the new *Länder* in the East have not yet established a strong identity among East Germans, and there was much more interest in boundary reform even in western Germany since unification. In spite of this and many other arguments in favor of boundary reform, no action was taken except for the effort to join the city-state of Berlin with its surrounding territory, Brandenburg. The political elites in both *Länder* favored consolidation, but in the referendum held in 1996 the majority of East German votes in East Berlin and Brandenburg that were in opposition exceeded the majority of votes in West Berlin that favored consolidation. The failure of the efforts to consolidate Berlin and Brandenburg has had a discouraging effect on plans to initiate consolidations elsewhere in Germany. Nevertheless, by the end of the decade there was again an intense debate about boundary reform that was brought about largely because of dissatisfaction concerning the financing of the *Länder*, and in particular the system of fiscal equalization involving the transfer of funds from richer to poorer *Länder*.[133] These issues will be considered again later in this book.

Conclusion

German history has not been kind to the concept of a German nation-state. The Holy Roman Empire was a league of secular and religious princes which became more of a league of semi-independent states after the Treaty of Westphalia in 1648. Like the EU today, it was a unique political entity, difficult to define and compare. In a legal work published in 1667, Samuel von Pufendorf suggested that the "Holy Roman Empire of the German Nation" could only be called by the rules of classification "an irregular and monster-like state body."[134] It consisted of more than 300 states when Napoleon entered the scene but, following the dissolution of the Holy Roman Empire (the First Reich) in 1806 and the many consolidations brought about by the pressure of Napoleon and his German allies, only thirty-nine remained. The Confederation which they formed in 1815 could be said to constitute "Germany" culturally, but it was no "nation-state" like France or even a "state."

Not until 1867, with the formation of the twenty-two-member North German Federation, did a German federation with a credible central authority emerge. This Federation, in turn, served as the foundation for the united twenty-five-member Germany of 1871 that did not include German Austria (nor, of course, German Switzerland). During the fifteen years of the Weimar Republic, the number of states, now called *Länder*, was reduced to seventeen. The *Länder* were weakened during the fourteen years of the still "federal" Weimar Republic and practically ceased to exist during Hitler's Third Reich.

After the Second World War, Germany was divided into four zones and then into two antagonistic states, each within opposing camps of states with dramatically different political and economic systems. For West Germany, the Allied occupation led to the creation of several new *Länder*, including the former Prussian province of Schleswig-Holstein, Lower Saxony, North-Rhine Westphalia, Hesse, and Rhineland-Palatinate. Only three older *Länder* survived the occupation: Bavaria and the city-states of Bremen and Hamburg. In 1952 Baden-Württemberg was formed, and in 1957 France returned the Saarland to Germany. These ten *Länder* made up the Federal Republic of Germany, while West Berlin remained legally under Allied occupation throughout the Cold War. In spite of their origins, the *Länder* that constituted the Federal Republic formed a political system under the Basic Law of 1949 that provided not only for democratic government, which had existed also in the Weimar Republic, but also a federal system identified clearly with democracy. Weimar had been a federation, but the *Länder* were so weak that they were practically administrative units in an otherwise centralized democratic system.

In the Soviet Occupation Zone, the older *Länder*, Saxony and Thuringia, were recreated, while the two older Mecklenburg *Länder* were combined with western Pomerania to form Mecklenburg. The former Prussian province of Brandenburg west of the Oder River became the *Land* of Brandenburg, and an older *Land* was combined with a Prussian province to form Saxony-Anhalt. These *Länder* were dissolved in 1952, but they were revived in 1990 with the second unification of Germany.

Today, of the sixteen *Länder* in united Germany, only five existed as *Länder* in 1933, and two of these are small city-states. Only Baden-Württemberg was created by the Germans themselves. The other ten *Länder* were created under the pressure of the Allied occupation authorities. Today there is considerable discussion of boundary reforms that might lead to a reduction in the number of *Länder*, but it is not a little ironic that in the past major boundary reforms brought about by annexations and consolidations of various kinds have taken place only as the result of war. With the possible exception of the creation of Baden-Württemberg in 1952, only minor adjustments have been made in peacetime circumstances. Perhaps the strains of fiscal federalism will force some changes on reluctant parties, or perhaps developments in the process of European integration will provide an inducement to change. But in the meantime popular identities with the existing *Länder* have developed some deep roots, and meaningful boundary reforms will not come easily.

United Germany today consists of four large *Länder* in the West and none in the East. There are five relatively poor to very poor "new" *Länder* in the East and a currently poor united Berlin and ten relatively rich-to-very-rich *Länder* in the West. A north–south economic and political gap in the West now faces a new and deeper East–West economic and political gap. A largely Protestant North, a largely Catholic South, and a largely formerly Protestant East – now a secular East – contribute further to internal tensions. Taken together, these differences present the new, united Germany with a set of major challenges. These challenges may not include the old question of where is Germany, but they do include the issue of regional identity. (Immigration in Germany – and elsewhere in Europe – has, of course, also again raised the question of who is or can become German.) Germans will have plenty to occupy them in the future when it comes to answering the questions which all of these issues and others pose regarding the *Länder* and their place in German federalism.

Notes

1 For the historical development of nationalism, see E. J. Hobsbawn, *Nations and Nationalism Since 1870*, 2nd edn (Cambridge: Cambridge University Press, 1990).

2 Georg Wilhelm Sante and A. G. Ploetz-Verlag (eds), *Geschichte der deutschen Länder "Territorien-Ploetz,"* vol. 1: *Die Territorien bis zum Ende des alten Reiches* (Würzburg: A. G. Ploetz Verlag, 1964), pp. 2–4.

3 Geoffrey Barraclough, *The Origins of Modern Germany* (Oxford: Basil Blackwell, 1947), p. 76.

4 Sante, *Geschichte*, vol. 1, pp. 9–10.

5 Ibid., pp. 17–18.

6 Ibid., pp. 13–16.

7 Ibid., pp. 15–16.

8 Ibid., pp. 34–35 and Barraclough, *The Origins*, pp. 316–317.

9 Sante, *Geschichte*, vol. 1, pp. 17 and 32; Barraclough, *The Origins*, p. 317.

10 Barraclough, *The Origins*, p. 319.

11 Hartmut Lehman, "Another Look at Federalism in the Holy Roman Empire," in *German and American Constitutional Thought*, edited by Hermann Wellenreuther (New York: Berg, 1990), p. 80.

12 Barraclough, *The Origins*, pp. 330–332.

13 Ibid., p 343.

14 Ibid., pp. 355–362.

15 Ibid., p. 368.

16 Sante, *Geschichte*, vol. 1, pp. 40–41.

17 Helmut Neuhaus, "The Federal Principle and the Holy Roman Empire," in Wellenreuther, *German and American Political Thought*, pp. 38 and 48.

18 Ibid., pp. 42–44.

19 Lehmann, "Another Lok," p. 84.

20 Mary Fulbrook, *A Concise History of Germany* (Cambridge: Cambridge University Press, 1990), p. 27.

21 Ibid., pp. 27, 34.

22 Sante, *Geschichte*, vol. 1, p. 37.

23 Bruno Gebhardt, *Handbuch der deutschen Geschichte*, vol. 2 (Stuttgart: Union Verlag, 1955), p. 103.

24 Sante, *Geschichte*, vol. 1, pp. 42–44.

25 Barraclough, *The Origins*, p. 373.

26 Daniel Elazar, *Exploring Federalism* (Tuscaloosa: University of Alabama Press, 1987), p. 132.

27 John G. Gagliardo, *Reich and Nation: The Holy Roman Empire as Idea and Reality, 1763–1806* (Bloomington: Indiana University Press, 1980), p. vii.

28 Ibid., p. x; see also Joachin Whaley, "Federal Habits: The Holy Roman Empire and the Continuity of German Federalism," in *German Federalism:*

Past, Present, Future, edited by Maiken Umbach (New York: Palgrave, 2002), pp. 15–41.

29 Ilja Mieck, "Deutschlands Westgrenze," in *Deutschlands Grenzen in der Geschichte,* edited by Alexander Demandt (München: Verlag C. H. Beck, 1990), pp. 210–212.

30 Rudolf Vierhaus, *Germany in the Age of Absolutism,* trans. by J. B. Knudsen (New York: Cambridge University Press, 1988), pp. 9 and 90.

31 Sante, *Geschichte,* vol. 1, p. 51; Gagliardo, *Reich and Nation,* pp. 4–5; Vierhaus, *Germany,* p. 90.

32 Gagliardo, *Reich and Nation,* p. 18. The Palatinate lost its electorate title again in 1778.

33 Vierhaus, *Germany,* p. 88 and 90.

34 Sante, *Geschichte,* vol. 1, pp. 50–52.

35 Vierhaus, *Germany,* p. 89.

36 Gagliardo, *Reich and Nation,* p. 10.

37 Ibid., p. vii.

38 Ibid., pp. 5–7.

39 Ibid., p. 8.

40 Karl Otmar von Aretin, *Heiliges Römisches Reich, 1776-1806,* vol. 1 (Wiesbaden, 1967), p. 69, cited in ibid., n. 3, p. 308.

41 Gagliardo, *Reich and Nation,* p. 11.

42 Ibid.

43 Ibid., pp. 13–15.

44 Bernd Grzeszick, *Vom Reich zur Bundesstaatsidee* (Berlin: Duncker & Humblot, 1996), pp. 70–71.

45 Franz-Ludwig Knemeyer, *Regierungs- und Verwaltungsreformen in Deutschland zu Beginn des 19. Jahrhunderts* (Köln: Grote'sche Buchhandlung, 1970), p. 21; In contrast to the figures given by Knemeyer, Eric Dorn Brose, *German History 1789–1871: From the Holy Roman Empire to the Bismarckian Reich* (Providence and Oxford: Berghahn, 1997), p. 4, says there were 350 secular states, fifty-one imperial city-states, and a total of "462 largely sovereign political entities of the Holy Roman Empire" in 1789.

46 Grzeszick, *Vom Reich,* p. 97.

47 Gagliardo, *Reich and Nation,* pp. 192–195; Georg Sante, "Reich und Länder – Verfassung und Wirklichkeit," in *Geschichte der deutschen Länder,* vol. 2: *Die deutschenLänder vom Wiener Kongress bis zur Gegenwart* (Würzburg: A. G. Ploetz, 1971), pp. 839–840.

48 Ibid., p. 195.

49 Grzeszick, *Vom Reich,* p. 105.

50 Ibid., pp. 140–143, 150.

51 Ibid., pp. 152–155.

52 Brose, *German History,* pp. 52–58.

53 Grzeszick, *Vom Reich,* pp. 180–181.

54 Ibid., p. 188.

55 Sante, "Reich und Länder," in *Geschichte*, vol. 2, p. 836.

56 Grzeszick, *Vom Reich*, pp. 228–231.

57 Ibid., pp. 232–233 and Brose, *German History*, p. 82.

58 Ibid., pp. 241–246, 272–273, 298.

59 Sante, "Reich und Länder," in *Geschichte*, vol. 2, p. 871.

60 Ibid., p. 872.

61 Brose, *German History*, p. 248.

62 Sante, "Reich und Länder," in *Geschichte*, vol. 2, pp. 836 and 846.

63 Ibid., p. 874.

64 Brose, *German History*, p. 76.

65 Hans Boldt, "Federalism as an Issue in the German Constitutions of 1849 and 1871," in Wellenreuther, *German and American Constitutional Thought*, pp. 260–261.

66 Ibid., pp. 263–264.

67 Ibid., pp. 266–269.

68 For the English text of the 1849 Constitution, see Elmar M. Hucko, *The Democratic Tradition: Four German Constitutions* (New York and Hamburg: Berg, 1987), pp. 79–117.

69 Cited in Brose, *German History*, p. 261.

70 Ibid., pp. 244 and 262.

71 Ibid., pp. 266–268.

72 Ibid., pp. 274–275.

73 Ibid., pp. 283–284, 334–335; Sante, "Reich und Länder," in *Geschichte*, vol. 2, p. 896.

74 Brose, *German History*, pp. 336–343; Sante, "Reich und Länder," in *Geschichte*, vol. 2, p. 902.

75 Ernst Rudolf Huber, *Deutsche Verfassungsgeschichte seit 1789*, vol. III, *Bismarck und das Reich*, 3rd edn (Stuttgart: W. Kohlhammer Verlag, 1988), pp. 655–657.

76 Hucko, *The Democratic Tradition*, pp. 16–17.

77 Huber, *Deutsche Verfassungsgeschichte*, p. 671; Borse, *German History*, pp. 352–353; Sante, *Geschichte*, vol. 2, pp. 905–907.

78 Nevil Johnson, "Territory and Power: Some Historical Determinants of the Constitutional Structure of the Federal Republic of Germany," in *German Federalism Today*, edited by Charlie Jeffery and Peter Savigear (New York: St. Martin's Press, 1991), p. 11.

79 Koppel S. Pinson, *Modern Germany: Its History and Civilization*, 2nd edn (New York and London: Macmillan, 1966), p. 161.

80 Sante, "Reich und Länder," in *Geschichte*, vol. 2, p. 910; Hucko, *The Democratic Traditon*, p. 35.

81 For the English text of the Constitution of 1871, see Hucko, *The Democratic Tradition*, pp. 121–145.

82 Sante, "Reich und Länder," in *Geschichte*, vol. 2, pp. 910–915; Huber, *Deutsche Verfassungsgeschichte*, vol. III, p. 787, 791, 799–800.

83 Hucko, *The Democratic Tradition*, p. 31.

84 Pinson, *Modern Germany*, p. 162.

85 Brose, *German History*, pp. 355–358.

86 Bruno Gebhart, *Handbuch der deutschen Geschichte*, vol. 4 (Stuttgart: Union Verlag, 1959), p. 113.

87 Quotation from Hucko, *The Democratic Tradition*, p. 50.

88 Sante, "Reich und Länder," in *Geschichte*, vol. 2, pp. 919–921.

89 For the English text of the Weimar Constitution, see Hucko, *The Democratic Tradition*, pp. 149–190.

90 Sante, "Reich und Länder," in *Geschichte*, vol. 2, p. 922.

91 Hucko, *The Democratic Tradition*, p. 51.

92 Sante, "Reich und Länder," in *Geschichte*, vol. 2, pp. 922–923.

93 Hucko, *The Democratic Tradition*, pp. 53, 57–58.

94 Sante, "Reich und Länder," in *Geschichte*, vol. 2, pp. 924–926.

95 For an excellent review of the *Länder* during the Third Reich, see Jeremy Noakes, "Federalism in the Nazi State," in Jeffery and Savigear, *German Federalism*, pp. 113–145.

96 Volker Wagner, "Bildung der Länder in den westlichen Besatzungszonen und Entstehung der Bundesrepubik Deutschland," in Sante, *Geschichte*, vol. 2, pp. 658–659.

97 Theodor Eschenburg, *Geschichte der Bundesrepublik Deutschland*, vol. 1: *Jahre der Besatzung 1945–1949* (Stuttgart: Deutsche Verlagsanstalt, 1983), pp. 77–83.

98 Ernst Deuerlein, "Bayern," in Sante, *Geschichte*, vol. 2, pp. 756–757; see also Manfred Vasold, "Bayern," in *Die Länder und der Bund: Beiträge zur Entstehung der Bundesrepublik Deutschland*, edited by Walter Först (Essen: Reimar Hobbing Verlag, 1989), pp. 7–32.

99 Günter Haselier, "(Nord-) Württemberg-Baden 1945–1952," in Sante, *Geschichte*, vol. 2, pp. 714–715.

100 For details, see Walter Mühlhausen, "Hessen," in Först, *Die Länder und der Bund*, pp. 75–107.

101 Dirk Bavendamm, "Hamburg und Bremen," in Först, *Die Länder und der Bund*, p. 64.

102 Karl E. Demandt, "Land Hessen seit 1945," in Sante, *Geschichte*, vol. 2, pp. 771–772.

103 W. R. Smyser, *From Yalta to Berlin: The Cold War Struggle Over Germany* (New York: St. Martin's Press, 1999), p. 14.

104 Wagner, "Bildung der Länder," p. 660; Heinrich Küppers, "Rheinland-Pfalz," in Först, *Die Länder und der Bund*, pp. 165–188.

105 Hans-Walter Herrmann, "Das Saarland," in Sante, *Geschichte*, vol. 2, pp. 701–712; Eschenburg, *Geschichte*, vol. 1, pp. 100–102.

106 Peter Hüttenberger, "Nordrhein-Westfalen seit 1945," in Sante, *Geschichte*, vol. 2, pp. 670–685; Walter Först, "Nordrhein-Westfalen," in Först, *Die Länder und der Bund*, pp. 135–164.

107 Waldemar R. Röhrbein, "Niedersachsen 1945–1970," in Sante, *Geschichte*, vol. 2, pp. 779–784; Dieter Brosius, "Niedersachsen," in Först, *Die Länder und der Bund*, pp. 109–134.

108 Kurt Jürgensen, "Schleswig-Holstein," in Först, *Die Länder und der Bund*, p. 190.

109 Wagner, "Bildung der Länder," p. 659; Eschenburg, *Geschichte*, vol. 1, pp. 86–89.

110 Alexander Scharff, "Schleswig-Holstein als Bundesland," in Sante, *Geschichte*, vol. 2, pp. 794, 798; Jürgensen, "Schleswig-Holstein," pp. 189–219.

111 Hermann Kellenbenz, "Die Hansestädte nach 1945," in Sante, *Geschichte*, vol. 2, pp. 791–793.

112 Werner John, "Thüringen 1945–1952," in Sante, *Geschichte*, Band 2, pp. 828–830.

113 Werner John, "Das Land Sachsen 1945–1952," in ibid., pp. 831–835.

114 Werner John, "Mecklenburg 1945–1952," in ibid., pp. 822–824.

115 Werner John, "Sachsen-Anhalt 1945–1952," in ibid., pp. 825–827.

116 Werner John, "Brandenburg 1945–1952," in ibid., pp. 819–821.

117 Werner John, "Berlin 1945–1970," in ibid., pp. 807–813.

118 Sante, "Reich und Länder," in *Geschichte*, vol. 2, p. 938.

119 Werner John, "Die Länder in der SBZ und in der DDR," in ibid., pp. 814–818. For a good overview in English, see Mary Fulbrook, "Democratic Centralism and Regionalism in the GDR," in Jeffery and Savigear, *German Federalism*, pp. 146–171.

120 Wagner, "Bildung der Länder," in Sante, *Geschichte*, vol. 2, , p. 663; Eschenburg, *Geschichte*, vol. 1, p. 95; Henry Ashby Turner, Jr., *Germany from Partition to Reunification* (New Haven: Yale University Press, 1992), pp. 20–21, 25–27.

121 Wagner, "Bildung der Länder," in Sante, *Geschichte*, vol. 2, p. 667; Sante, "Reich und Länder," in *Geschichte*, vol. 2, p. 929.

122 Turner, *Germany*, pp. 33–36.

123 Theodor Eschenburg, "Die Entstehung des Landes Baden-Württemberg," in *Baden-Württemberg: Eine politische Landeskunde*, edited by Landeszentrale für politische Bildung Baden-Württemberg, 3rd edn (Stuttgart: Verlag W. Kohlhammer, 1985), pp. 44–59; Eschenburg, *Geschichte*, 474–475; Eberhard Gönner, "Die Entstehung des Südweststaates," in Sante, *Geschichte*, vol. 2, pp. 738–739; Klaus-Jürgen Matz, "Baden und Württemberg," in Först, *Die Länder und der Bund*, pp. 33–60.

124 Eschenburg, *Geschichte*, vol. 1, pp. 471–472.

125 Arthur B. Gunlicks, "Federalism and German Unification," *Politics and Society in Germany, Austria and Switzerland*, vol. 4, no. 2 (1992), p. 54.

126 Ibid., pp. 54–55.

127 See especially Karlheinz Blaschke, "Alte Länder – Neue Länder: zur territori-alen Neugliederung der DDR," *Aus Politik und Zeitgeschichte*, B 27/90, 29 June 1990, pp. 39–54, cited in Gunlicks, "Federalism and German Unifica-tion", p. 63.

128 Gunlicks, "Federalism and German Unification," p. 55.

129 Ibid., pp. 56–57.

130 See Arthur B. Gunlicks, *Local Government in the German Federal System* (Durham: Duke University Press, 1986), Ch. 4 and *Local Government Reform and Reorganization: An International Perspective* (Port Washington: Ken-nikat Press, 1981), Ch. 10.

131 Bundesministerium des Innern, *Bericht der Sachverständigenkommission für die Neugliederung des Bundesgebiets (Ernst-Kommission)* (Bonn, 1973).

132 For the different arguments made then and now, see Gunlicks, "Federalism and German Unification," pp. 58–59 and Arthur B. Gunlicks, "The Future of Federalism in the Unified Germany," in *The Domestic Politics of German Uni-fication*, edited by Christopher Allen *et al.* (Boulder: Lynne Rienner, 1993), pp. 156–159.

133 For a strong argument in favor of boundary reform as a part of fiscal reform, see Uwe Leonardy, "Deutscher Föderalismus jenseits 2000: Reformiert oder deformiert," *Zeitschrift für Parlamentsfragen* 30, no. 1 (February 1999), pp. 135–162.

134 Quoted in Rudolf Vierhaus, "Historische Grundlagen des Bundesrates: Poli-tische Einheit und Staatenvielfalt in der deutschen Verfassungsgeschichte," in *Vierzig Jahre Bundesrat*, edited by the Bundesrat (Baden-Baden: Nomos Verlagsgesellschaft, 1989), p. 24.

2

Theory and constitutional framework of German federalism

Introduction

As in the case of the American states, the German *Länder* existed before the federation. But unlike the United States, there is no legal controversy in Germany over the role of the states as opposed to the "people" in creating the federation.[1] Representatives from the *Länder* met at Herrenchiemsee in 1948 to draft the new constitution and formed the Parliamentary Council which negotiated with the Allies over the final text in 1949. The German Constitution, or Basic Law, was then *approved* by the parliaments of the *Länder* (except Bavaria) rather than by popular referendum. This does not make the Federal Republic the creature of the German *Länder*, however; the Preamble states specifically that the Basic Law is the result of an act by the German people.

In accordance with the tradition of civil law countries on the European continent, the Basic Law is long and detailed in comparison to the very brief US Constitution.[2] The Basic Law has 146 articles, in comparison to seven original articles and twenty-seven amendments in the American Constitution. It has been amended fifty times since 1949 in comparison to seventeen times for the American Constitution since the first ten amendments were added in 1791. Some of the German amending laws have contained multiple changes of old articles or additions of new articles, so that the total number of changes is actually much larger than fifty. As these numbers suggest, it is easier to change the Basic Law by a two-thirds majority vote in the *Bundestag* (the popularly elected national parliament) and *Bundesrat* (a second legislative chamber in which the governments [cabinets] of the *Länder* are represented) than in the United States, which requires not only a two-thirds vote in the House and Senate but also majority approval by the legislatures in three-fourths of the

states. It can be argued, of course, that the Supreme Court is an instrument of continuing constitutional change in the United States, since its
decisions serve in some ways as a substitute for formal constitutional
amendment. But this is true also, if perhaps to a lesser extent, of the Federal Constitutional Court in Germany.

About one-half of the articles of the Basic Law are related in a direct or
indirect manner to federalism, and most amendments have concerned
some aspect of the subject. In the first paragraph of Article 20, the Federal Republic is described as "a democratic and socially conscious
[*sozialer*] federal state." Federalism, though not defined by the Basic Law,
is even protected by a "perpetuity clause" (Article 79, para. 3) which for-
bids changes in "the division of the federation into *Länder*" or which
affects their fundamental participation in the legislative process. The first
clause does not protect individual *Länder* from boundary changes or consolidation as prescribed elsewhere in the Basic Law (Article 29); however,
it does exclude any fundamental change from a federal to a unitary state.[3]
The second clause concerning participation in the legislative process
means participation in the *Bundesrat*.

Two or three tiers?

Controversy over the nature of federalism in the United States has always
focused on the federal government, i.e., the Union, the federation, federal
level, federal tier, or federal plane vs the states. The Civil War decided the
issue of the right of American states to secede, and the Supreme Court
declared in 1868 that the United States was an indestructible union
composed of indestructible states.[4] The issue of contention has usually
been disagreement over the location of sovereignty between two tiers of
government or, at the very least, over the proper distribution of powers
between them.[5] When Ronald Reagan claimed in his inaugural presidential address in 1981 that the states created the Union, thus implying state
sovereignty, few legal scholars agreed. But just where sovereignty does
lie is still an unresolved question. Daniel Elazar, for example, insists that
in a democratic federal system sovereignty is shared; each arena or
"plane" (he rejects the term "level") of government derives its sovereignty
from "the people," and no one arena is superior to the other.[6] Paul Peterson, on the other hand, speaks of "levels" and argues that since the Civil
War sovereignty has been "concentrated in the hands of the national
government."[7]

While German scholars since 1949 have not argued about the location of sovereignty, there have been some differences among them over the conception of the German federal state as having two or three tiers or levels. Those who see a two-tier or two-systems model "see the *Länder* as subsystems of the federation." The *Bund* is the federation and is endowed with the powers of a federal government. Advocates of the three-tier or three-systems model "distinguish among the *Länder*, the central state, and the federation." The *Bund* is the central state with the powers of a federal government, while the "federation is seen as a rather powerless system embracing both the *Länder* and the central state. The central state is a mere subsystem of the federation, as are the *Länder*." *Bund* and *Länder* are almost equal partners, "both subject to the all-embracing though somewhat nebulous federation."[8] In this case the federal president and the Federal Constitutional Court would be organs of the federation, while the federal government (*Bundesregierung*) and the *Bundestag* would be organs of the central state and the federation. In the two-tier model, on the other hand, all federal organs are organs of the federation.[9]

An early decision of the Federal Constitutional Court seemed to suggest that the Court accepted the three-tier model, but later it made clear its preference for two tiers. Some scholars believe that "a resurrection of the "three systems model" cannot be excluded,"[10] while others argue vehemently that "the Federal Republic is *no* three-tier federation."[11] The two-tier model seems to be the consensus among scholars today.[12]

The division of legislative, executive, and judicial powers

As we shall see below, a general principle guides the division of powers or functions in the Basic Law. That principle is contained in Article 30, which says that "state [Americans would say "governmental"] powers and the implementation of state [governmental] tasks are the responsibility of the *Länder*," unless the Basic Law provides otherwise. This creates a presumption that governmental powers – legislative, executive, and judicial – lie with the *Länder* in cases of doubt.[13] But as with the Tenth Amendment[14] to the American Constitution, the provisions of Article 30 are somewhat misleading.[15] Indeed, Fritz Scharpf has suggested that such provisions are a "living lie [*Lebenslüge*] of federalism."[16]

Division of legislative powers between the federal and Land governments[17]

The general provisions of Article 70

An entire section (Section VII) of fifteen articles in the Basic Law deals with legislation. The first of these, Article 70, is closely related to Article 30 above. It states simply that "the *Länder* have the right of passing legislation insofar as this Basic Law does not grant legislative authority to the federation." This means that in contrast to the United States there is little room or necessity for implied powers. There is a somewhat similar doctrine in German law of granting powers based on the "nature of the material" (*aus der Natur der Sache*) and "subject interrelationship" (*Sachzusammenhang*), but these are used only rarely and under certain conditions and are not considered really comparable to American implied powers.[18]

Article 70, para. 2, says that legislative authority is granted in the form of exclusive and concurrent legislative powers. A third important source of legislative authority for the federation, not mentioned in Article 70, is found in framework legislation, which is taken up in Article 75. As indicated above, one can also add unwritten powers based on "the nature of the material" or "subject interrelationship," but these are highly restricted by the requirement of Article 70 that powers of the federation are derived from provisions of the Basic Law. Finally, one should add European law as an increasingly important source of law in Germany which affects both federal and *Land* lawmaking powers.

The constitutional reality today is that there are relatively few legislative powers that have not been granted to the federal level by various means.[19] Areas generally left to the *Länder* are local governments; culture, including schools as well as the visual or performing arts and electronic media; public safety, e.g., police; and some aspects of civil service and health care.[20]

Exclusive federal powers

In spite of the provisions of Articles 30 and 70, the legislative powers of the federation are much greater than those of the *Länder*. This is made clear in Articles 71–75. Article 71 denies the *Länder* any powers in the areas of exclusive federal jurisdiction unless they have been granted specifically by federal law. Thus a law passed by a *Land* legislature or a popular referendum in a *Land* or unit of local government that demanded some action or inaction by the federal government in an area of its exclusive jurisdiction, e.g., national defense, would be unconstitutional.[21]

The exclusive legislative powers of the federation are listed in Article 73. There are twelve "paragraphs," most of which contain rather obvious responsibilities for the federal government, for example, foreign affairs and defense; national citizenship; currency, weights and measures; customs and foreign trade; air and rail transport owned by the federation; postal and telecommunications services; and several other matters. The list is not complete, because many other federal responsibilities can be found in other provisions of the Basic Law.[22] The power to regulate asylum seekers, for example, is found in Article 16, while the regulation of political parties and political finance is authorized in Article 21. There are also certain executive powers, such as planning, that are found in other articles.[23] There is no comparable catalogue of powers for the *Länder*, because they retain under Articles 30 and 70 all legislative powers not granted to the federation. In the case of foreign affairs, Article 73, para. 1, does not mention specifically foreign aid, which has led the *Länder* to establish their own separate foreign aid programs while recognizing the primacy of the federation in this area (Article 32).[24]

Concurrent powers

Articles 72 and 74 are concerned with concurrent powers. Both articles became subjects of discussion as a result of Article 5 of the Unification Treaty of 1990 which "recommends" that the *Bundestag* and *Bundesrat* consider constitutional changes "with respect to the relationship between the federation and the *Länder* . . ."[25] In 1992 these two legislative bodies formed a Joint Constitutional Commission which recommended a number of modest changes to the Basic Law, including some changes to Articles 72, 74, and 75 which deal with the distribution of legislative powers between the federation and the *Länder*.[26] The changes recommended by the Joint Constitutional Commission were generally accepted by the *Bundestag* and *Bundesrat*, but some revisions were made.[27] The final result of these efforts was a 42nd amendment law that changed eleven Articles of the Basic Law and added three new ones.[28]

The revised Article 72 contains three paragraphs. The first of these states simply that the *Länder* have the power to act in the area of concurrent legislation so long and so far as the federation has not "used" its power to pass legislation in the area of concern ("has used" was inserted in 1994 to mean having gone through the entire legislative process[29]). According to the Basic Law, any action the federal government takes in the area of concurrent legislation preempts any *Land* legislation covering the same subject, not just provisions that may be in conflict, as in the United States.[30] That is, there is no "dual authority."[31] Therefore, some legal scholars suggest that "precedence" legislation might be a better term than "concurrent" legislation.[32]

The changes made to Article 72 in the 1994 amendments are rather subtle and esoteric but nevertheless important. In para. 2 the federation can now claim a concurrent power for itself only if it is "essential" or "required" (*erforderlich*) and not just because it perceives a "need" (*Bedürfnis*) to act. In the past the federation could claim a "need" to act because a matter could not be regulated effectively by individual *Länder*, because regulation by a *Land* could affect the interests of other *Länder* or the whole (in both cases rare occurrences[33]), or because the legal and economic unity of the country required the "uniformity [*Einheitlichkeit*] of living conditions." These were, of course, such general provisions that they allowed the federation very broad authority. As of October 1994, however, the federal government can claim a federal preemption to be "essential" only in the general interest of preserving "equivalent [*gleichwertige*] living conditions" or the legal and economic unity of the country. The standard of *equivalency* is less strict than *uniformity*, about which there was considerable misunderstanding in Germany among politicians and even some jurists.

Some legal experts insisted that "uniform living conditions" never did mean equality in any literal or leveling sense; rather, it meant providing equal opportunities in education; necessary infrastructure for a modern economy, including transportation; certain environmental standards, including green spaces and recreation facilities, etc.,[34] in addition to an adequate standard of living to be achieved, if necessary, through the welfare state. Whatever the original intent might have been, some scholars have concluded that the uniformity clause was an "empty formula" that could be filled to suit a variety of purposes.[35]

There can be little doubt that demands to eliminate differences in living standards – emerging not only from constitutional interpretation but also from the public – have had a strong "unitary" or centralizing effect on the federal system in Germany.[36] This is why there was pressure even before German unification, but especially afterwards, to make Article 72 less sweeping in its language. Thus, it was thought that it is more feasible for the *Länder* to provide for "equivalency" in their territory than to achieve "uniformity" of living conditions, because equivalency can vary from *Land* to *Land*. Furthermore, under a new provision added to Article 93 by the changes introduced in 1994, the *Land* governments, *Land* parliaments, and the *Bundesrat* can take any disagreements over what is "essential" to the Federal Constitutional Court, which they could not do before the 1994 changes.[37]

Finally, a third paragraph for Article 72 was introduced in 1994 in order to return power to the *Länder*[38] if and when a "requirement" for federal action no longer exists.[39] Whether this and the changes noted above will in fact have much of an impact on the legislative power relations between the federation and the *Länder* remains to be seen. The federation already has virtually exhausted its possibilities in the area of concurrent powers, and it seems doubtful that it will agree to transfer many – or any – of the subjects it now regulates back to the *Länder*.

Article 74 provides a list of the concurrent powers that in theory at least could have remained with or been assumed by the *Länder*. The list now contains twenty-eight subject areas, including numerous areas that have always been and remain responsibilities of the American states, such as civil and criminal law. The American concept of concurrent legislation also permits the states to pass or retain legislation in areas in which the federal government has acted except in cases where specific provisions are in conflict. In general the German federation has assumed most of the powers in the general areas of economics, employment conditions, welfare, and justice affairs. As we saw above, the *Länder* have retained responsibility for other areas, especially "culture," which includes schools as well as the arts and electronic media; local government; police; and a few other matters.

While these are important functions, they pale in significance to the concurrent legislative powers of the federation. These are even more extensive than Articles 72 and 74 suggest. For example, in order to eliminate financially damaging competition among themselves, the *Länder* agreed via the *Bundesrat* to grant to the federation in Article 74a the concurrent power of regulating the salary and benefits of the civil service (*Beamte*), including the *Land* civil service, insofar as this power is not already included in the federation' s exclusive powers. This was a rather significant voluntary abdication of the right of the *Länder* to regulate their own personnel.[40] The tax provisions of Article 105, para. 2, are another example of concurrent power that will be discussed in a later chapter.[41] Finally, in case of war Article 115c gives the federal government certain concurrent powers normally in the hands of the *Länder*.[42] In each of the above cases, however, the federal government needs the approval of a majority of the *Bundesrat*.

Framework legislation

In addition to exclusive and concurrent powers, framework legislation as provided by Article 75 of the Basic Law is an important source of power for the federation. Framework laws are different from the laws passed under the federation' s exclusive and concurrent powers, however, in that they are directed at the *Land* legislators for further legislative action by them. It is assumed that the legislative details to be completed by the *Land* legislators are of some significance and are arrived at freely; indeed, in order in part to prevent the repetition of some past federal intrusiveness, a new paragraph inserted in Article 75 in 1994 states specifically that framework legislation may go into detail only in exceptional cases.[43] Some restrictions have been placed on the federation by the changes of 1994 in that the provisions of Article 72 apply, according to which the federation must now demonstrate not merely a "need" but rather a "requirement" for framework legislation. An additional item, the protection of cultural artifacts against foreign acquisition, was added in 1994 to the list of six general subjects that can be regulated by framework legislation, while film (movies) was removed and given to the *Länder*. One subject, the regulation of public service personnel, must be seen in conjunction with Article 74a, discussed above, which regulates the salary and benefits of civil servants (*Beamte*) as a special category of public service personnel. The general regulation of universities in framework legislation must also be viewed together with Article 91a and 91b, which established a number of "joint tasks" (*Gemeinschaftsaufgaben*) in the constitutional reforms (Finance Reform) of 1969.

Administration in the German federal system

Article 83 and "dual federalism"

Just as one section of the Basic Law deals with the distribution of legislative powers between the federation and the *Länder*, another (Section VIII) deals with the implementation of federal legislation. The first article (Article 83) of this section states simply that "[t]he *Länder* implement federal legislation on their own responsibility so long as this Basic Law does not provide otherwise." The language of this Article shows its relationship to Articles 30 and 70 above in granting sweeping authority to the *Länder* unless the Basic Law provides otherwise.

Article 83 is a reflection of the concept of "dual federalism" in Germany. As we have seen above, the federation in fact carries most of the responsibility for legislation, while the *Länder* are primarily responsible for administration. For this reason, German federalism is sometimes referred to as "administrative federalism." The division of responsibilities in German federalism is not one of strict separation, however; rather, it is a system of cooperation, interconnections, and interrelationships. The federation carries the greatest responsibility for legislation, but the *Länder* participate in legislation via the *Bundesrat*. The *Länder* are generally responsible for administration, but in carrying out federal laws they may be subject to many federal instructions and restrictions which they can usually influence via the *Bundesrat*.[44] The exception to the general rule is found at the local level, where certain core functions are protected by Article 28, para. 2, from any direction from above.[45]

This is very different from the American concept of "dual federalism" or "dual sovereignty," according to which a duality exists between the federal government and its executive *and* legislative powers on the one hand and the states and their executive *and* legislative powers on the other hand.[46] While these two concepts of dual federalism are not as distinguishable in practice as one might assume, they do represent a clear difference in the German and American federal traditions. They also contribute to some confusion in the sense that some German scholars speak of a "functional" division between federal legislative and *Land* administrative responsibilities, while American scholars (as well as some Germans[47]) usually focus on the distinction between public "tasks" or "functions" performed by federal authorities and those performed by state or local governments when referring to "functional" divisions.

We saw above that once the federation has acted in the area of concurrent legislative power, any legislation already passed by the *Länder* on the same subject is preempted by the federal law, i.e., there is no dual legislative responsibility in Germany except in the limited cases that fall under framework laws and "joint tasks." In principle either one level or the other has legislative responsibility, not both. The same principle applies in administration; however, here there are numerous exceptions to the rule.[48] Indeed, the many exceptions, whether by design or by practice, have contributed to the concept of "cooperative federalism" which is now commonly used in describing German federalism. It is a concept borrowed from the United States, where "cooperative federalism" was used to describe the reality of shared financing and administrative responsibilities that emerged during and after the New Deal in contrast to the theory of "dual federalism" that prevailed before the 1930s.[49] As noted above, the Finance Reform of 1969 in Germany led to a number of constitutional changes that included the introduction of two new articles providing for the carrying out of "joint tasks" (*Gemeinschaftsaufgaben*) by the federation and the *Länder*. Article 91a and 91b.

The administration of Federal and Land laws

The German "state"at the federal level is a lawmaking state, while at the *Land* level it is an administrative state. The federation is more dominant in legislation than the *Länder* are in administration, but administration is still the key element of *Land* autonomy.[50] Article 83 of the Basic Law, translated above, makes this clear. However, as in the cases of Article 30 and Article 70, which reserve legislative powers to the *Länder* unless the Basic Law provides otherwise, there are many opportunities for federal involvement in administration based on provisions of the Basic Law. Indeed, Section VIII provides three methods of administering federal law.

Bundeseigene Verwaltung   An obvious, but not common, method is administration solely by federal officials (*Bundeseigene Verwaltung*) as either required or authorized by the Basic Law.[51] This takes place directly in state agencies, e.g., finance administration, or indirectly, e.g., social insurance agencies, where unity throughout the Federal Republic is required. The Basic Law lists the areas that fall under exclusive federal administration in Articles 87, 87a and 87b, 87d–87f, and 88–89. Article 87, para. 1, provides for federal administration of the foreign service, federal finances, federal waterways and shipping; it also authorizes the federal government to establish administrative agencies for border patrol, certain federal police services, and constitutional protection. Paragraph 2 calls for direct federal administration in cases of social insurance programs when the territory covered goes beyond a single *Land*. The other articles mentioned above deal with federal administration of military forces; air transportation; railroads, post office and telecommunications (railroads, many post office functions and telecommunications were privatized in whole or in part in the mid-1990s); the *Bundesbank* (federal reserve bank); and federal waterways.[52]

Bundesauftragsverwaltung   A second method is administration by the *Länder* of federal laws delegated to them (*Bundesauftragsverwaltung*), that is, administration by the *Länder* according to federal instructions (Article 85).[53] It represents a "middle way" between administration by federal agencies and by *Land* agencies on their own responsibility; however, it is still *Land* administration.[54] The federal government pays the functional costs, but the *Länder* pay the administrative costs. Federally delegated administration occurs only if provided by the Basic Law or because of a constitutionally authorized federal law.[55] *Land* administration of the federal autobahns and other federal long-distance highways and the administration of major taxes are provided directly by Article 90 and Article 108, para. 1, respectively. Other subjects, such as nuclear energy and some aspects of air transportation, *can* be given to the *Länder* with the approval of the *Bundesrat* (Article 87c and 87d), and, upon application, federal waterways can be administered by a *Land*.

The delegation of federal laws to the *Länder* for administration increased with the passage of the Finance Reform package of 1969. Article 104a, for example, provides that when the federation pays 50 percent or more of the costs of a program, that program is to be delegated to the *Länder* for administration. An example is educational assistance legislation (*Bundesausbildungsförderungsgesetz*), under which about one-third of higher-level pupils (*Schüler*) and more than 40 percent of university students receive varying degrees of financial aid for expenses other than tuition, which is free (by the end of the 1990s, there was growing pressure to introduce modest tuition charges). The complex relationships between federal and *Land* agencies involved in the administration of this legislation is eased to some extent by vertical contacts between the administrators involved and the effort by the federal authorities to coordinate the federal directives with the *Land* authorities. But such examples of delegated administration remain somewhat problematic, because the federal ministries end up heavily involved in administration.[56]

Under Article 85 the federation provides for uniform rules of training for higher and middle-level civil servants who will be involved in implementing federal laws; blue-collar public employees (*Arbeiter*) are not included in this training. In rare cases the federal government also approves the heads of specialized "middle agencies" that execute delegated federal law, e.g., the head of the high finance offices. These provisions and the right of the federal ministries to issue instructions to the *Land* ministries under which the federal laws are administered demonstrate the extent of federal influence in *Land* administrative agencies. This influence was curtailed somewhat in 1999, when the Federal Constitutional Court ruled that the federal cabinet, with the approval of the *Bundesrat*, could issue administrative regulations for the implementation of federal laws.[57] Before this decision federal ministers alone sometimes issued instructions to the *Land* authorities. On the other hand, federal guidelines and recommendations usually emerge as a result of committee and commission meetings composed of federal and *Land* officials.[58] Thus federal instructions do not mean a federal takeover of *Land* administration; rather, the *Land* agencies are required to follow the "federal will."[59] It should also be noted that federal agencies must not ignore federal comity, which in this case means providing the *Land* agencies with opportunities to respond and react to the federal instructions before taking the extreme actions authorized in Article 85 of demanding documents and sending officials to the *Land* agencies to ensure compliance with the "federal will."[60]

Landeseigene Verwaltung   A third type of administration, which is the most common of all, is that carried out by the *Länder* themselves. That is, the *Länder* and local governments, to which the *Länder* send as many as 75 percent of "state" (federal and *Land*) laws for execution,[61] have the right to administer higher-level laws on their own responsibility. According to Article 84, if the *Länder* execute federal legislation, they establish the agencies and regulatory procedures under their organizational powers as matters of their own responsibility (*als landeseigene Angelegenheit*), which is generally referred to as autonomous Land administration (*Landeseigenverwaltung*);[62] however, a federal law, to which the *Bundesrat* has consented, may provide for federal involvement in the establishment of agencies or in administrative procedures. Where the *Länder* administer federal laws on their own responsibility, they pay both the administrative and functional costs; however, in cases where the *Länder* pay more than 25 percent of the functional costs, consent of the Bundesrat is required. (According to Article 104a, as noted above, if the federation pays for more than 50 percent of the costs, the law must be delegated to the *Länder* for administration by federal instructions.) Since there is nothing in Article 84 to suggest that the federation has to demonstrate a "need" to intervene but rather can do so to ensure an effective administration, there is a broad opportunity for federal involvement.[63] Nevertheless, federal involvement occurs only with the approval of the *Bundesrat*, which means that in the final analysis the *Länder* – actually, the *Land* governments, i.e., cabinets – control the extent to which the federation becomes involved in *Land* administration.

Examples of this category of administration include federal traffic laws, federal emission control laws, waste disposal laws, and federal construction law. Federal laws administered by the *Länder* on their own responsibility can be based on exclusive or concurrent federal powers, and, to some extent, framework powers. Increasingly, the *Länder* are also implementing EU legislation on their own administrative responsibility.[64]

In implementing federal laws, the *Länder* are supervised by federal authorities to ensure compliance and uniformity; however, whereas supervision in the case of delegated laws is both legal and functional, in the case of implementing federal laws on their own responsibility the *Länder* are under legal supervision only. If there is a conflict and no satisfactory resolution occurs, either side may take the case to the *Bundesrat* for a decision. If dissatisfied with this decision, either side can appeal to the Federal Constitutional Court.[65]

Since there are so many federal laws administered by the *Länder*, the consent of the *Bundesrat* is now required for more than half of the legislation passed by the *Bundestag*. It was originally thought by the founding fathers in 1949 that about 10 percent of federal laws would be consent laws.[66] In part the increased role of the *Bundesrat* is due also to the interpretation by the Federal Constitutional Court that any federal law that contains a single provision concerning how the statute is to be administered by the *Länder* requires, as a whole, the consent of the *Bundesrat*.[67] This makes it more difficult, but not impossible, for the government and *Bundestag* to separate one legislative bill's section from the others in order to avoid opposition and even a veto by the *Bundesrat*.

Administration of Land laws   The Basic Law is silent concerning the fourth type of *Land* administration, i.e., the right of the *Länder* to administer their own laws and organize their own administrative structures. *Land* authority for these functions is presumed by Article 30. Thus *Land* constitutions and legislatures are decisive in the area of "own-law" administration.[68]

Federal–Land cooperation

As a general rule, German law does not permit a combination or mixture of federal and *Land* administration in a hierarchical relationship[69] (*Mischverwaltung*) any more than it accepts dual legislative powers over the same subject. As indicated above, however, there are certain exceptions that are commonly referred to as "administrative cooperation" or, since the late 1970s, as "political–administrative interconnections"(*Politikverflechtung*[70]), a term similar to, but not quite the same as, "intergovernmental relations" in the United States.[71] Cooperation between the federation and the *Länder* is sometimes referred to also as *vertikale Verwaltungsverflechtung* (vertical administrative interconnection).[72] This occurs formally, of course, when the *Länder* participate in federal policy making via the *Bundesrat*, and, one might add, when they participate in EU policy making via the *Bundesrat* and their missions in Brussels.

A well-known form of cooperation which is even cited as an example of *Mischverwaltung* takes place under the category of "joint tasks"

(*Gemeinschaftsaufgaben*) that are specified in the Basic Law in Article 91a and 91b. Article 91a, discussed briefly above, gives the federation the right of codecision (*mitwirken*) with the *Länder* in university building construction, in improving regional economic structures, and in improving conditions in agricultural and coastal areas. This requires joint planning between the federal and *Land* governments, described in the chapter on *Land* administration.

The "joint tasks" have been the subject of considerable discussion among German jurists, administrators, and politicians.[73] Some point out that Article 91a and 91b recognized or even made constitutional a number of contractual agreements between the federation and the *Länder* that already existed before the Finance Reform of 1969.[74] The lack of a clear constitutional authorization for these cooperative agreements led to the creation of the Troeger Commission which issued a report in 1966[75] that served as the basis for the Finance Reform of 1969 and the addition of Articles 91a, 91b, and 104a to the Basic Law.[76] (Article 104a provides the federation with the authority to make financial grants to the *Länder* and is sometimes discussed along with Article 91a and 91b as an "ungenuine" joint task.[77]) In spite of this background, these new provisions soon became very controversial and a subject of investigation in a federal commission on constitutional reform (*Enquete-Kommission Verfassungsreform*) in 1976; however, no serious efforts were made to revise the joint task provisions.

The joint tasks are defended not only on historical grounds but also on the grounds that otherwise the federal government would have no constitutional authorization to act in important areas. However, federal authorities cannot require action. The federal government participates only in framework planning; every *Land* government has the right to reject its application in its territory. The federal government does not become involved in detailed planning, and each *Land* implements the framework as it wishes. The projects are financed jointly.[78]

The basic criticism of these provisions, however, is that they have added significantly to the legislative and administrative powers of the federation at the cost of the *Länder*. These may have been compensated to some extent through their participation via the *Bundesrat*, but joint administration and joint financing in particular have been responsible for a general trend toward a reduction in the importance of the *Länder*.[79] The federation has used extensively the instruments of cooperation granted it in Article 91a and 91b, with the result that the *Länder* see a continued narrowing of their freedom of decision making and of their financial room for maneuver.[80] The agreements among bureaucrats in participating ministries at the federal and *Land* levels serve to narrow the room left for decision making by those drawing up budgets at both levels and for the *Land* parliaments that can do little to change the executive decisions already reached.[81]

A form of cooperation takes place also when the federal government provides the *Länder* with grants-in-aid under Article 104a, para. 4. As in the United States, complaints are sometimes heard that these grants interfere with *Land* or local autonomy, but empirical evidence does not support these claims. In any case, as with the joint tasks, the federation is responding more to the needs expressed by the *Länder* than to any goals of its own.[82]

The weakest form of federal participation in *Land* administration is federal supervision and control. If the *Land* is administering a federal law delegated to it, the responsible federal minister has the power of subject matter and legal supervision; he or she exercises legal supervision only if the law is being administered as a matter of *Land* responsibility. In practice supervision usually consists of an exchange of information and consultation.[83]

Cooperation among the Länder
There are numerous examples of cooperation between the *Länder* and the federal government and among the *Länder* themselves. Indeed, the *Land* parliament of North-Rhine Westphalia conducted a study in 1989 according to which there were 330 federal–*Land* commissions and 120–140 commissions involving North-Rhine Westphalia and other *Länder* without federal participation.[84] These are examples of vertical and horizontal coordination, respectively. The purpose of such coordination efforts is to resolve practical problems, usually requiring cross-boundary cooperation, that can be either temporary or permanent in nature.[85]

Horizontal cooperation between and among the *Länder* is said to take place at a kind of extra-constitutional "third level" between the federation and the *Länder*. The conferences of *Land* prime ministers take place about every three months to consider common demands on the federation, and subject ministers in the *Länder* meet regularly to consider a wide variety of themes, including draft legislation.[86]

The most common and best-known legal instrument of cooperation among the *Länder* is the interstate compact. It is based neither on federal law nor on *Land* law but rather on "cooperative customary law" (*Kooperationsgewohnheitsrecht*) that exists between the federation and the *Länder* at the "third level."[87] There are two forms of compact: the "administrative agreement" and the "state contract." The difference is that the first form is restricted to the executive authorities of the *Länder*, e.g., the administrative agreement in 1952 among the *Länder* and, in this case, the federation, regarding the German Postgraduate School of Administrative Sciences (*Deutsche Hochschule für Verwaltungswissenschaften*) in Speyer,[88] whereas the second form, the "state contract," binds the *Länder* as such and must be approved by the *Land* parliaments, e.g., compacts establishing certain public radio and television networks and their listening and viewing fees or the compact regulating the distribution of students among the various universities.[89] Compacts may involve all or only some of the *Länder*; for example, common planning institutions have been established for Hamburg and Lower Saxony and for Hamburg and Schleswig-Holstein, although the success of these institutions has been limited.[90]

In addition to formal, legally binding compacts, there is the "political understanding" (*politische Absprache*), which is usually the result of a recommendation of a conference of *Land* ministers, whose goal, for example, might be to reach agreement on model legislation. These "understandings" are not legally binding, but they are considered to be politically and morally binding.[91]

The interstate compacts described here do not include certain well-known activities such as the conference of *Land* prime ministers (*Ministerpräsidentenkonferenz*), the conferences of *Land* subject ministers, or the permanent conference of ministers of education and culture (*Kultusminsterkonferenz (KMK)*) or their various committees. These are executive cooperative bodies that do not possess any autonomous administrative authority.[92] They are, however, important elements in the federal political process. The conference of *Land* prime ministers, for example, serves a variety of functions, including guarantor of continuity for *Land* government actions in spite of changing majorities in the *Bundesrat*; control instrument *vis-à-vis* the federation and watchdog over EU developments; clearing house for various compacts among the *Länder*; and umpire for *Land* ministerial meetings. The rule of unanimity and rotating leadership of the prime ministers' conferences discourage a strong partisan approach.[93]

A *"unitary federal state"* through interlocking, intergovernmental relations?

Taking examples from both federal–*Land* cooperation, e.g., joint tasks, and cooperation among the *Länder*, critics point, among other things, to the inequality in the arrangements between the federation on the one hand and the *Länder* on the other; to the invasion of *Land* autonomy that results; and to the strengthening of *Land* executive powers at the cost of the *Land* parliaments.[94] This is symbolized in part by the "traveling federalism" of high-level federal and *Land* ministerial bureaucrats who establish a "coordination bureaucracy" sometimes referred to as "vertical brotherhoods of experts" (*Fachbrüderschaften*).[95] Some scholars argue that while cooperation is necessary and desirable, given the demands of a modern society and welfare state, practice in the Federal Republic may have exceeded the limits required for maintaining the autonomy of the *Länder* within the federal system.[96]

The numerous cases of federal–*Land* administrative cooperation and the "self-coordination" among the *Länder,* together with federal dominance in the legislative arena and the resulting federal supervision of the *Länder* in the administration of numerous federal laws, have led many scholars to speak of a "*unitary* federalism" in Germany.[97] "Unitary federalism" does not quite conform to Daniel Elazar's description of a "decentralized" unitary state, because the former is the result more of voluntary cooperation and coordination by the federal units than of central direction.[98]

With the 1969 Finance Reform, "*unitary*" federalism was complemented and to some extent replaced by the term "cooperative federalism." This term was borrowed from the United States and was introduced to describe the growing practices of intergovernmental relations. As noted in several places above, Article 91a and 91b are examples frequently cited, as are the joint taxes and selected legislation. A later, somewhat narrower, concept that reflects the centralizing trends described above and the complex interrelationships among various levels and institutions of government is "political–administrative interconnections" (*Politikverflechtung*),[99] a term mentioned above that is similar to but not exactly the same as the American term "intergovernmental relations."[100] *Politikverflechtung* has become identified with numerous criticisms of German federalism, e.g., that the responsibility for policy making for and financing of various projects involving the federal and *Land* levels is unclear; that the budgets of the *Länder* both in respect to the initial project funding and follow-up costs are too restricted; that the sectoral planning between the federal and *Land* levels takes place at the cost of coordinated general planning at federal and *Land* levels, respectively; that the freedom of decision making in the parliaments at the federal and *Land* levels is narrowed; that the federal balance is endangered, the *Länder* weakened, the federation given too much planning power, and a systematic fiscal equalization in the federal system made more difficult; and that *Politikverflechtung* is characterized by a bureaucratized and expensive administrative procedure.[101]

Gerhard Lehmbruch, while acknowledging the contributions of Fritz Scharpf and his colleagues, suggests that "policy networks" would be a more descriptive term than *Politikverflechtung*. He sees this term as focusing too narrowly on interbureaucratic relations linking autonomous administrations and neglecting their links with societal actors, especially the political parties.[102]

Fritz Scharpf is known not only as the originator of the term *Politikverflechtung*; he is also widely cited for his thesis that the German federal system – and, for that matter, the EU – is characterized in much of its decision making by a "joint-decision trap." This "trap" is found especially in the decision-making process regarding the "joint tasks" but also in other areas, such as the *Bundesrat*, and it refers to the necessity of reaching compromises on all important issues since none of the parties in the decision-making group can dominate the others and unanimity is required for action.[103] This thesis has become a very influential and widely cited explanation for the – for many Germans frustrating – "gridlock" or difficulty in achieving reforms in a variety of important political areas. Of the many current examples, one could name fiscal equalization (Chapter 5) and the related issue of territorial boundary reform of the *Länder*, health insurance, and tax policy (especially under Chancellor Kohl).

Organization of the judiciary[104]

The division of judicial powers, court organization, and certain procedures are found in Section IX of the Basic Law. As we saw above, Article 30 establishes the presumption that "state functions" are the responsibility of the *Länder*, and Article 92, though less clearly than Articles 70 and 83, presumes that judicial authority rests with the *Länder*.

Nevertheless, the Federal Constitutional Court is mentioned even in the first article of Section IX, i.e., Article 92. It is a constitutional organ to which *Land* courts must turn for interpretations of the Basic Law, therefore making unnecessary a case like *Marbury* v. *Madison*[105] which established the right of judicial review in the United States. A ruling of a *Land* constitutional court can also be challenged via an individual "constitutional complaint" brought before the Federal Constitutional Court. Of course decisions of this court are binding on the *Land* constitutional courts. Thus there is some hierarchy in the relationship between the federal and *Land* constitutional courts, but not in a formal, structural sense. As in the United States, the constitutional courts of the two levels are basically separate in their fields of operation. An interesting difference to the United States, however, is that a *Land*, for example, Schleswig-Holstein, may decide to turn over to the Federal Constitutional Court all constitutional questions rather than to establish a separate *Land* constitutional court of its own.

The federal court system

The Basic Law (Article 95) requires the establishment of five federal courts. These are the Federal Court of Justice in Karlsruhe (not to be confused with the Federal Constitutional Court in Karlsruhe), which is the highest appeals court for civil and criminal law; the Federal Administrative Court in Berlin (moved to Leipzig after 2002); the Federal Finance Court in Munich; the Federal Labor Court in Kassel (which will be transferred to Erfurt); and the Federal Social Court in Kassel. Unlike the Federal Constitutional Court, these are not constitutional organs. Their authority is not set by the Basic Law but by federal statutory law. These courts are the highest authorities within their subject area. The boundaries between them and their respective *Land* courts are set by federal law, and uniformity in their decisions is maintained by a "common senate" in Karlsruhe. Judges for these courts are selected by the federal ministers responsible for the subject area together with their counterpart ministers in the *Länder* and an equal number of *Bundestag* members.

Other federal courts may also be established by federal law. These are courts of first instance that answer to the Federal Court of Justice in Karlsruhe. Since the Basic Law went into effect in 1949, federal law has established a Federal Patents Court, disciplinary courts for public servants, military courts, and a disciplinary court for judges. With the consent of the *Bundesrat*, *Land* courts can rule on federal law in certain criminal cases involving agitation against other peoples or for aggressive war.

Land *courts*

All of the *Länder* except Schleswig-Holstein have established *Land* constitutional courts. These are autonomous courts whose organization, authority, and procedure are set by *Land* constitutions and laws. In contrast to the other courts, the *Länder* determine the salaries and compensation of their own constitutional court judges.

In accordance with Article 92, the bulk of judicial activity in Germany is at the *Land* level. The courts are organized at the lower and middle instances, i.e., at local and regional levels, and they follow the specialization of the federal courts as outlined above. Thus in normal civil and criminal cases, the levels are local (*Amtsgericht*), regional (*Landgericht*), and *Land* (*Oberlandesgericht*); for cases involving administrative law, there are the administrative courts and higher administrative courts; for labor cases, the labor courts and the *Land* labor court; and for social welfare cases, the social courts and the *Land* social court; and one finance court for each *Land*. The federation has used its powers of concurrent legislation to regulate the organization, authority, and procedures of these courts. The *Land* Minister of Justice and a judicial selection committee decide on the selection of judges, but the pay and benefits of the judges are set by federal law.

While the *Länder* have an important role in performing judicial functions, the German legal system is characterized by the dominance of federal law. Court organization, boundaries, and procedures are generally regulated by federal law. Except for the *Land* constitutional courts, pay and benefits are set by federal law. The interpretation of constitutional law and of ordinary federal law are basically left to the Federal Constitutional Court and the federal superior courts. All of this leads, of course, to the uniformity of judicial decision making in the German federal system.

Conclusion

The German federal system is based far more on relatively detailed written constitutional principles than is the federal system in the United States, which has evolved in reaction to political and economic developments in a long, often difficult and discontinuous historical process in which the Supreme Court has played the key role. While Federal Constitutional Court decisions have been more important in the German political system since 1949[106] than court rulings in other European countries and have clarified many provisions of the Basic Law, the brevity and vagueness of the American Constitution have offered the Supreme Court even greater opportunities to shape and control the federal system in the United States.

Although the detailed written constitutional principles of the German Basic Law stand in contrast to the very general and frequently ambiguous provisions of the American Constitution, the Basic Law is still misleading in its provisions regarding the federal system. Article 30 suggests that the *Länder* are the repository of most governmental powers unless exceptions have been made by other provisions of the Basic Law. Article 70 gives the impression that the *Länder* have significant legislative powers, and Article 83 appears to give the *Länder* the right to implement federal laws on their own authority. Constitutional reality, as German legal scholars like to say, presents a quite different picture. The conditional clause, "unless the Basic Law provides otherwise," has in fact provided for federal dominance in legislation and a complex interrelationship in administration.

In terms of legislative powers, the Basic Law granted the federation a number of key exclusive powers, and from the rather long list of concurrent powers the federation has taken virtually every item for itself. Even under framework legislation, the federation has expanded its range of activities in areas normally thought to lie within the competence of the *Länder*. It is true that most federal laws now require the approval of the *Bundesrat*, but this guarantees the participation only of the *Land* governments (cabinets), not of the *Land* parliaments. It also means that *Länder* in the minority in *Bundesrat* decisions find themselves relinquishing some degree of autonomy without their consent. In spite of some minor improvements in the position of the *Länder* as a result of recent constitutional changes, relatively little has been left to them over the years for autonomous decision making.

While the *Länder* are dominant in the administrative arena, as Article 83 suggests they are, the federal government can and does become involved in administration in a number of ways. It administers on its own the laws passed under its exclusive powers, and it delegates many other laws to the *Länder* for administration with federal instructions. The remaining federal laws are administered by the *Länder* on their own responsibility, but the federal government retains some right of legal supervision. The federal government also participates with the *Länder* in planning and financing numerous "joint tasks."

The *Länder* are an important part of the judicial system, and most courts are *Land* courts.

But in the final analysis the federation is the dominant partner in judicial matters, especially since all courts of final appeal are federal courts and federal law regulates the organization and activities of the *Land* courts. As a result, there is little problem in establishing a country-wide uniformity in judicial decision making.

The result of the many centralizing tendencies in constitutional reality has led to a federal system that has been commonly described as a "*unitary* federation," while the complex administrative and financial interrelationships between federal and *Land* authorities and among the latter have promoted a system of "cooperative federalism." Some scholars, in turn, see cooperation as having led to *Politikverflechtung* or a kind of joint decision making that ends up hindering transparency and accountability. It is apparent, then, that the German federal system, like the American federal system, is a complicated array of practices and procedures and a source of continuing debate and controversy.

Notes

1 Most scholars argue that the American Constitution was created by a contract of the people rather than by a compact among the states, especially but not only because ratification took place in ratifying conventions elected by the people and not by the already existing state legislatures. See, for example, Melvin I. Urofsky, *A March of Liberty: A Constitutional History of the United States* (New York: Alfred A. Knopf, 1988), pp. 173, 274; Robert McClosky, *The American Supreme Court* (Chicago: University of Chicago Press, 1960), pp. 62–64; Daniel J. Elazar, *Exploring Federalism* (Tuscaloosa: University of Alabama Press, 1987), pp. 93–95; Alfred H. Kelly and Winfried A. Harbison, *The American Constitution: Its Origins and Development* (3rd edn; New York: Norton, 1963), p. 310.

2 In Daniel Elazar's terms, the US Constitution is the classic example of "the constitution as frame of government and protector of rights," while most Western European countries have "the constitution as code." *Exploring Federalism*, pp. 158–159.

3 Theodor Maunz in Theodor Maunz *et al.*, *Kommentar zum Grundgesetz* (München: C. H. Beck'sche Verlagsbuchhandlung, 1989), Article 79 III, Rdnr 28-36 and Hans Ulrich Evers in *Bonner Kommentar zum Grundgesetz* (Heidelberg: C. F. Müller Juristischer Verlag), Article 79 Abs.3, Rdnr 212 Zweitbearbeitung.

4 *Texas* v. *White*, 7 Wall. 700 (1869).

5 Urofsky, *A March of Liberty*, pp. 173, 274; Kelly and Harbison, *The American Constitution*, pp. 306–311.

6 Elazar, *Exploring Federalism*, pp. 35, 199.

7 Paul E. Peterson, *The Price of Federalism* (Washington, DC: The Brookings Institution, 1995), p. 9.

8 Gunter Kisker, "The West German Federal Constitutional Court as Guardian of the Federal System," *Publius: The Journal of Federalism* 19, no. 4 (Autumn 1989), pp. 47–49.

9 Klaus Stern, *Das Staatsrecht der Bundesrepublik Deutschland*, vol. I (2nd edn;

München: C. H. Beck'sche Verlagsbuchhandlung, 1984), pp. 650–651.

10 Kisker, "The West German Federal Constitutional Court," p. 49.

11 Bruno Schmidt-Bleibtreu and Franz Klein, *Kommentar zum Grundgesetz* (8th edn; Neuwied: Luchterhand Verlag, 1995), pp. 490–491 and 1091.

12 Stern, *Das Staatsrecht*, vol. I, p. 651; Konrad Reuter, *Föderalismus: Grundlagen und Wirkungen in der Bundesrepublik Deutschland* (5th edn; Heidelberg: Hüthig, 1996) p. 22.

13 Maunz in Maunz et al., *Grundgesetz Kommentar*, Article 30, Rdnr 2; Heinz Laufer, *Das Föderative System der Bundesrepublik Deutschland* (Bonn: Bundeszentrale für politische Bildung, 1991), pp. 86–87; Reuter, *Föderalismus*, p. 49.

14 The Tenth Amendment reads: "The powers not delegated to the United States by the Constitution, nor prohibited by it to the States, are reserved to the States respectively, or to the people."

15 Bodo Dennewitz in Evers, *Bonner Kommentar*, Article 30, Rdnr 2; Laufer, *Das Föderative System*, p. 86; Reuter, *Föderalismus*, p. 49.

16 Fritz Scharpf, "Kann es in Europa eine stabile föderale Balance geben?," in Scharpf, *Optionen des Föderalismus in Deutschland und Europa* (Frankfurt: Campus Verlag, 1994), p. 125.

17 There are several excellent commentaries on the Basic Law, some more detailed than others. See, for example, the detailed discussion of Articles 70–82 in Maunz and Dürig., cited above. For briefer references, see Schmidt-Bleibtreu and Klein, also cited above, and *Grundgesetz Kommentar*, edited by Michael Sachs (München: C. H. Beck'sche Verlagsbuchhandlung, 1966). More general discussions are offered in Heinz Laufer and Ursula Münch, *Das föderative System der Bundesrepublik Deutschland* (Bonn: Bundeszentrale für Politische Bildung, 1997); Heiderose Kilper and Roland Lhotta, *Föderalismus in der Bundesrepublik Deutschland* (Opladen: Leske & Budrich, 1996), pp. 100–104; Laufer, *Das Föderative System*, pp. 87–94; and Reuter, *Föderalismus*, pp. 39–53.

18 Maunz in Maunz and Dürig, *Grundgesetz Kommentar*, Article 30, Rdnr 21-26.

19 Ibid., Rdnr 11.

20 Ibid., Rdnr 17; Reuter, *Föderalismus*, pp. 51–53.

21 Ibid., Article 71, Rdnr 30-31.

22 Ibid., Article 30, Rdnr 10; for a list of such authorizations outside of Article 73, see Schmidt-Bleibtreu and Klein, *Kommentar*, p. 932.

23 Maunz in Maunz and Dürig, *Grundgesetz Kommentar*, Article 73, Rdnr 6.

24 Ibid., Rdnr 34 and 43.

25 For the text of theUnification Treaty, see *Europa Archiv* 45 (25 October 1990), pp. D515–536.

26 For useful articles summarizing the work of the Joint Constitutional Commission, see the entire issue *of Das Parlament*, vol. 44 (14 January 1994). The

official government publication that deals in considerable detail with the Joint Constitutional Commission is the "Bericht der Gemeinsamen Verfassungskommission," Deutscher Bundestag, 12. Wahlperiode, *Drucksache* 12/6000, (5 November 1993).

27　An excellent discussion of the background to and results of the work of the Joint Constitutional Commission can be found in Karl Peter Sommermann, "Die Stärkung der Gesetzgebungskompetenzen der Länder durch die Grundgesetzreform von 1994," *Jura*, no. 8 (1995), pp. 393–399. For a brief overview in English, see Arthur B. Gunlicks, "German Federalism After Unification: The Legal/Constitutional Response," *Publius: The Journal of Federalism* 24 (Spring 1994), pp. 88–91.

28　Grundgesetznovelle vom 27.10. 94, BGBl I, p. 3146.

29　Schmidt-Bleibtreu and Klein, *Kommentar*, p. 943.

30　Daniel Halberstam and Roderick M. Hills, Jr., "State Autonomy in Germany and the United States," *The Annals of the American Academy of Political and Social Science* 574 (March 2001), pp. 177–178.

31　Ibid., p. 921 and 932; Maunz in Maunz and Dürig, *Grundgesetz Kommentar*, Article 72, Rdnr 2, 4, and 6 and Article 74, Rdnr 32. See also Sommermann, "Die Stärkung," p. 395.

32　Schmidt-Bleibtreu and Klein, *Kommentar*, p. 936 and Maunz in Maunz and Dürig, *Grundgesetz Kommentar*, Article 72, Rdnr 6.

33　Maunz in Maunz and Dürig, , Article 72, Rdnr 21-22.

34　For an excellent discussion of this issue in English, with a specific *Grundgesetz Kommentar* reference to land-use planning, see Clifford Larsen, "What Should be the Leading Principles of Land Use Planning? A German Perspective," *Vanderbilt Journal of Transnational Law* 29, no. 5 (November 1996), pp. 991–996.

35　Ursula Münch, *Sozialpolitik und Föderalismus: ZurDynamik der Aufgabenverteilung im sozialen Bundesstaat* (Opladen: Leske & Budrich, 1997), pp. 143–154, especially p. 152.

36　Ibid., p. 90, 143–145.

37　See Sommermann, "Die Stärkung," p. 395.

38　Maunz in Maunz and Dürig, *Grundgesetz Kommentar*, Article 74, Rdnr 1.

39　Schmidt-Bleibtreu and Klein, *Kommentar*, p. 941.

40　Paul Feuchte, "Die rechtliche Ordnung der Verwaltung im Bundesstaat und ihre Entwicklung," in *Deutsche Verwaltungsgeschichte*, vol. 5, edited by Kurt G.A. Jeserich, Hans Pohl und Georg-Christian von Unruh (Stuttgart: Deutsche Verlags-Anstalt, 1987), p. 131.

41　Schmid-Bleibtreu und Klein, *Kommentar*, p. 939.

42　Maunz in Maunz and Dürig, *Grundgesetz Kommentar*, Article 74, Rdnr 3.

43　Ibid., Article 75, Rdnr 32; Schmidt-Bleibtreu and Klein, *Kommentar*, p. 1011; also Sommermann, "Die Stärkung," p. 397.

44　Lerche in Maunz and Dürig, *Grundgesetz Kommentar*, Article 83, Rdnr 8.

45 For a discussion in English of the constitutional protection of German local governments, see Arthur B. Gunlicks, *Local Government in the German Federal System* (Chapel Hill: Duke University Press, 1986), pp. 103–104 and "Constitutional Law and the Protection of Subnational Governments in the United States and West Germany," *Publius: The Journal of Federalism* 18, no. 1 (Winter 1988), pp. 141–158.

46 Arthur B. Gunlicks, "Principles of American Federalism," in *Germany and Its Basic Law: Past, Present and Future – A German–American Symposium*, edited by Paul Kirchhof and Donald P. Kommers (Baden-Baden: Nomos Verlagsgesellschaft, 1993), pp. 91–108.

47 Frido Wagener always distinguished between "functional administration" (administration by tasks or functions) and "territorial administration" (*Gebietsverwaltung*), by which he meant unity of command, i.e., all administrative tasks carried out in one administrative territory. See, for example, his "Äußerer Aufbau von Staat und Verwaltung," in *Öffentliche Verwaltung in der Bundesrepublik Deutschland*, edited by Klaus König, Hans-Joachim von Oertzen, and Frido Wagener (Baden-Baden: Nomos Verlagsgesellschaft, 1981), pp. 76–80. This book was also published in English: *Public Administration in the Federal Republic of Germany* (Boston: Kluwer–Deventer, 1983).

48 Lerche in Maunz and Dürig, *Grundgesetz Kommentar*, Article 83, Rdnr 85 and 92.

49 Peterson, *The Price of Federalism*, pp. 55–56.

50 Rainer Wahl, "Die Organisation und Entwicklung der Verwaltung in den Ländern und in Berlin", *Deutsche Verwaltungsgeschichte*, vol. 5, p. 209. See also Lerche in Maunz and Dürig, *Grundgesetz Kommentar*, Article 83, Rdnr 4.

51 Willi Blümel, "Verwaltungszuständigkeit," in *Handbuch des Staatsrechts der Bundesrepublik Deutschland*, edited by Josef Isensee and Paul Kirchhof, vol. IV, p. 904.

52 See also Stern, *Das Staatsrecht*, vol. II, p. 780.

53 Lerche in Maunz and Dürig, *Grundgesetz Kommentar*, Article 83, Rdnr 21-25.

54 Dittmann in Michael Sachs (ed.), *Grundgesetz Kommentar* (München: C. H. Beck'sche Verlagsbuchhandlung, 1996), Article 85, Rdnr 1-5; Blümel, "Verwaltungszuständigkeit," p. 887.

55 Stern, *Das Staatsrecht*, vol. II, pp. 808–809.

56 Feuchte, "Die rechtliche Ordnung," pp. 128–129.

57 BverfGE of 2 March 1999, in *Deutsches Verwaltungsblatt* (15 July 1999), pp. 976–978.

58 Blümel, "Verwaltungszuständigkeit," pp. 890–891.

59 Dittmann in Sachs, *Grundgesetz Kommentar*, Article 85, Rdnr 19.

60 Ibid., Rdnr 22, 23 and 34.

61 Daniel Thürer, *Bund und Gemeinden* (Berlin: Springer Verlag, 1986), p. 34.

62 Lerche in Maunz and Dürig, *Grundgesetz Kommentar*, Article 83, Rdnr 21.
63 Ibid., Article 84, Rdnr 16.
64 Blümel, "Verwaltungszuständigkeit," pp. 870–871.
65 Dittmann in Sachs, *Grundgesetz Kommentar*, Article 84, Rdnr 28-30.
66 Feuchte, "Die rechtliche Ordnung," p. 126.
67 Kisker, "The West German Fedral Constitutional Court," pp. 50–51.
68 Blümel, "Verwaltungszuständigkeit," pp. 860, 863–864.
69 Ibid., p. 935, and Dittmann in Sachs (ed.), *Grundgesetz Kommentar*, Article 83, Rdnr 4.
70 Fritz W. Scharpf, Bernd Reissert and Fritz Schnabel, *Politikverflechtung: Theorie und Empirie des kooperativen Föderalismus in der Bundesrepublik* (Kronberg: Scriptor Verlag, 1976).
71 See Deil Wright, *Understanding Intergovernmental Relations* (3rd edn; Pacific Groves: Brooks/Cole, 1988).
72 Arthur Benz, "Verflechtungen der Verwaltungsebenen," in *Öffentliche Verwaltung in Deutschland*, edited by Klaus König and Heinrich Siedentopf (Baden-Baden: Nomos, 1996), pp. 169–172.
73 See, for example, Arthur Benz, "Intergovernmental Relations in the 1980s," *Publius: The Journal of Federalism* 19, no. 4 (Autumn 1989), pp. 206–209.
74 Kilper and Lhotta, *Föderalismus*, pp. 196–197.
75 Kommission für die Finanzreform, Gutachten über die Finanzreform in der Bundesrepublik Deutschland (Stuttgart: Verlag W. Kohlhammer, 1966); for a discussion of this report, see Kilper and Lhotta, *Föderalismus*, pp. 183–186; for a brief review in English, see Karl H. Cerny, "Federalism in the West German Republic," in *Federalism: Infinite Variety in Theory and Practice*, edited by Valerie Earle (Itasca, IL: F. E. Peacock Publishers, 1968), pp. 175–177.
76 Stern, *Das Staatsrecht*, vol. II, pp. 833–834; Feuchte, "Die rechtliche Ordnung," p. 140.
77 Blümel, "Verwaltungszuständigkeit," p. 945.
78 Stern, *Das Staatsrecht*, vol. II, pp. 834–838.
79 For a view of general decline of Land powers over the past decades, see Herbert Schnoor, "Zur Lage der Länderverwaltung nach 30 Jahren Grundgesetz," *Die öffentliche Verwaltung* 23, no. 10 (May 1979), pp. 355–362. For administrative cooperation in particular, see p. 357; with particular emphasis on social policy, see Münch, *Sozialpolitik und Föderalismus*, pp. 22–33.
80 Maunz in Maunz and Dürig, *Grundgesetz Kommentar*, Article 91a, Rdnr 3.
81 Kilper and Lhotta, *Föderalismus*, p. 198.
82 Benz, "Verflechtung der Verwaltungsebenen," p. 171.
83 Ibid., pp. 171–172.
84 Ibid., pp. 131–132; Rolf Grawert listed 224 administrative agreements in the mid-1960s covering twenty-two general topics in his book, *Verwaltungsabkommen zwischen Bund und Ländern in der Bundessrepublik Deutschland* (Berlin: Duncker & Humblot, 1967), pp. 299–341.

85 Lerche in Maunz and Dürig, *Grundgesetz Kommentar*, Article 83, Rdnr 92.
86 Benz, "Verflechtung der Verwaltungsebenen," p. 172.
87 Gunter Kisker, *Kooperation im Bundesstaat* (Tübingen: J. C. B. Mohr (Paul Siebeck), 1971), pp. 75 and 79.
88 Blümel, Verwaltungszuständigkeit," p. 961.
89 Stern, *Das Staatsrecht*, vol. II, pp. 786–787.
90 Benz, "Verflechtung der Verwaltungsebenen," p. 173.
91 Stern, *Das Staatsrecht*, p. 787.
92 Blümel, "Verwaltungszuständigkeit," pp. 960–961.
93 Lorenz Menz, "Die Ministerpräsidentenkonferenz – ein unverzichtbares Element politischen Handelns in der Bundesrepublik Deutschland," in *Der Landtag – Standort und Entwicklungen*, edited by Erich Schneider (Baden-Baden: Nomos Verlagsgesellschaft, 1989), pp. 86, 88–90.
94 Kisker, *Kooperation*, pp. 143 and 161.
95 Frido Wagener, "Gemeinsame Rahmenplanung und Investitionsfinanzierung," in *Die öffentliche Verwaltung*, no. 16 (August 1977), p. 588; Lerche in Maunz and Dürig, *Grundgesetz Kommentar*, Article 83, Rdnr 98.
96 Kisker, *Kooperation*, pp. 166–167, 303–304.
97 The scholar most frequently cited for this concept is Konrad Hesse, *Der unitarische Bundesstaat* (Karlsruhe: C. F. Müller, 192). See also Lerche in Maunz and Dürig, *Grundgesetz Kommentar*, Article 83, Rdnr 4.
98 Elazar, *Exploring Federalism*, pp. 34–38, 170–173.
99 Fritz Scharpf is most identified with this concept. See, for example, Scharpf *et al., Politikverflechtung.*
100 For a review of the different stages of postwar German federalism as reflected in the terms used to describe the system, see Hartmut Klatt, "Forty Years of German Federalism: Past Trends and New Developments," *Publius: The Journal of Federalism* 19, no. 4 (Autumn 1989), pp. 185–202.
101 Feuchte, "Die rechtliche Ordnung," p. 148.
102 Gerhard Lehmbruch, "Institutional Linkages and Policy Networks in the Federal System of West Germany," *Publius: The Journal of Federalism* 19, no. 4 (Autumn 1989), p. 222.
103 Fritz W. Scharpf, "Die Politikverflechtungs-Falle: Europäische Integration und deutscher Föderalismus im Vergleich," *Politische Vierteljahresschrift* 26, no. 4 (1985), pp. 346–350; see also an English version of this article: "The Joint-Decision Trap: Lessons from German Federalism and European Integration," *Public Administration* 66 (Autumn 1988), pp. 239–278.
104 This section is based on the chapter by Willi Blümel, "Rechtsprechungs-zuständigkeit," in *Handbuch des Staatsrechts der Bundesrepublik Deutschland*, vol. IV, edited by Josef Isensee and Paul Kirchhof (Heidelberg: C. F. Müller, Juristischer Verlag, 1990), pp. 966–983. See also Christoph Degenhart, "Gerichtsorganisation," in *Handbuch des Staatsrechts*, vol. III, pp. 859–878, and, by the same author, *Staatsrecht I*, 14th revised edn (Heidelberg: C. F.

Müller Verlag, 1998), pp. 65–66 and 219–220; for useful general discussions, see Reuter, *Föderalismus*, pp. 64–67 and Laufer, *Das föderative System*, pp. 91–92; for a discussion of the German court system in English, see Wolfgang Heyde, *Justice and the Law in the Federal Republic of Germany* (Heidelberg: C. F. Müller, 1994), pp. 7–15.

105 *Marbury* v. *Madison* 1 Cranch 137; 2 L. Ed. 60 (1803).

106 Philip M. Blair, *Federalism and Judicial Review in West Germany* (Oxford: Clarendon Press, 1981); and by the same author, "Federalism, Legalism and Political Reality: The Record of the Federal Constitutional Court," in *German Federalism Today*, edited by Charlie Jeffery and Peter Savigear (New York: St. Martin's Press, 1991), pp. 63–83.

3

Administrative structures in Germany

Administration after 1945

To some extent the Allies, especially the British,[1] tried after the war to break older administrative traditions in Germany, but the Americans and French looked for guidance at the pre-Nazi administrative structures in their occupation zones. Nineteenth-century organizational structures were largely reinstated under the formula, "a new beginning, but not a fundamentally new organization."[2] But there was a focus on localizing administration, in part as a consequence of the Potsdam Agreement that called for "decentralization" in post-war Germany.[3] The reconstruction of administration from the bottom up helped strengthen and stabilize local self-government.[4] In the nineteenth century it was said that "the state ends with the *Landrat* [county administrator]."[5] After May 1945 one could say that in the Western zones of Germany "the state only just begins with the *Landrat*."[6]

The Germans carried out wide-ranging territorial reorganizations and administrative reforms in the late 1960s and 1970s,[7] but these efforts were not conceived as a deep-seated political change comparable to the administrative transformations in Prussia after 1870. Rather, they took the form of adjustments of the administrative organization to long-ignored changes in social and economic developments.[8]

Today the sixteen *Länder* are divided between thirteen territorial states (*Flächenstaaten*) and three city states (by size of population: Berlin, Hamburg, and Bremen). There are four large territorial states (by size of population: North-Rhine Westphalia, Bavaria, Baden-Württemberg, and Lower Saxony), eight medium-sized states, and one small territorial state (the Saarland). There is a remarkable unity in the basic structure of most of the territorial *Länder*; the most obvious difference lies in the lack of a "middle instance" in six small-to-medium *Länder*. The city states are different in principle, because they make no distinction between "state" and "local" administration (with some modifications regarding Bremen and Bremerhaven).[9]

Some principles and concepts

Although Article 83 of the Basic Law speaks only of the *Länder* executing federal laws on their own responsibility, there is a constitutional presumption that there are three administrative arenas in the Federal Republic: federal, *Land*, and local. While there are various interconnections among these arenas, they remain more or less separate and autonomous. Nevertheless, Articles 30 and 83 make reference only to the federation and the *Länder*,[10] and the basic constitutional structure, as in the United States, consists of these two levels.[11] Unlike the United States, however, where the local governments are not even mentioned in the Constitution and are creatures of the states, counties and municipalities are singled out for protection by Article 28 of the Basic Law. This protection does not extend to individual local governments but rather to the institution of the county and the municipality. Their organizational structure and boundaries are matters for the *Länder* to determine. As constituent parts of the *Länder*, the local governments are also responsible for administration and, therefore, they execute federal as well as *Land* laws along with their own ordinances.[12]

In the discussion of levels of administration below, several distinctions should be kept in mind. One is between *direct* administration, which is generally the "own" administration (*Bundeseigene, Landeseigene Verwaltung*) by state agencies discussed above in Chapter 2 on the constitutional framework – for example, the federal crime office or air controllers; and *indirect* administration, which includes the "delegated" administration – for example, federal highway administration delegated to the *Länder* or the federal health insurance program delegated to regional sickness funds. At the *Land* level, there is direct *Land* administration of the schools and police and indirect administration of a large majority of "state" (federal and *Land*) laws mostly by the semi-autonomous counties and cities but also by numerous non-governmental institutions. Another distinction is between *general* administration, exemplified best by the mid-level government districts and German rural counties and large county-free cities versus *specialized* administration by a wide variety of special authorities (*Sonderbehörden*).

Federal administration

Federal administration differs significantly from *Land* administration in two ways: the federation has no general administrative agencies, only specialized agencies; and, with some exceptions discussed below, the federation has only high authorities with no substructures.[13] As at the *Land* level, a distinction is made between the supreme authorities (*oberste Behörden*) and the high authorities (*Bundesoberbehörden*). A distinction is also made between direct and indirect administration.

Federal supreme authorities include the Chancellor and his office, the federal ministers, the Federal Accounting Office, and the *Bundesbank.*[14] The federal president, the presidium of the *Bundestag* and *Bundesrat*, and the Federal Constitutional Court are sometimes given also as examples of supreme federal authorities,[15] but they are not parts of the state administrative organization.[16]

The high federal special authorities answer to the federal ministries, i.e., to the supreme authorities from which they emerged as semi-autonomous agencies. They generally have no substructures, but they can set up branches. Examples of high federal authorities are the Press and Information Office of the federal government, the Federal Statistical Office, the Federal Crime Office, the Federal Cartel Office, the Patent Office, the Office for Constitutional Protection, and the Federal Environmental Office.[17] Other examples of direct federal administration are technical and research institutions (*Bundesanstalten*) that answer to the ministries, for instance, the air controllers under the Ministry of Transportation,[18] or the Federal Insurance Office under the Ministries of Labor and Health that supervises the hundreds of public corporations that provide retirement, health, accident, and nursing care insurance in conformity with federal law.[19]

Subnational direct federal administrative structures exist only in the foreign service; federal waterways administration, which falls under the Ministry of Transportation and is organized at the middle as well as at lower levels;[20] military and border control administration; and finance administration (see below). The federal railways and postal services had multiple levels until they were privatized in 1993–94;[21] however, the federal government still has certain supervisory and other responsibilities.[22] The twenty-two high finance authorities (*Oberfinanzdirektionen*) are mid-level agencies that are a peculiar example of joint federal–*Land* administration, i.e., they serve simultaneously as agencies of the *Länder*. The head of such an office is both a federal and *Land* civil servant who directs both federal and *Land* sections. Lower- level agencies that answer to the high finance authorities include federal customs offices, federal property offices, and federal forest offices. As one can see from figure 3.1, the *Länder* also have their own finance offices that answer to the high finance authority.[23]

While less common, indirect administration also exists at the federal level. There is, for example, the Federal Employment Office in Nuremberg which has its own lower *Land-* and local- level structures. There is also the *Deutsche Welle,* which provides radio and television broadcasts for foreign listeners and viewers, while *Deutschlandfunk,* now *Deutschlandradio,* serves the domestic audience based on a contract with the *Länder.* The *Bundesbank* is also an example of indirect federal administration, but it is completely autonomous, as are its branches in the *Länder* (*Landeszentralbanken*).[24] A variety of social insurance agencies are also included in indirect federal administration.

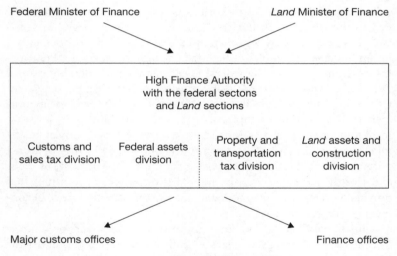

Figure 3.1   **The joint high finance authority**

Administration in the territorial *Länder* and the city-states

The *Länder* are responsible for their own administrative organization. Some *Länder* provide for their organizational structure in a single law, others have it contained in several laws. In spite of a number of differences, there are certain common principles of organization based on

general and special administrative agencies organized at three levels: the
Land government (cabinet) or ministry level; the government district
(*Regierungsbezirk*); and the rural county and city-county (or county-free
city). Exceptions to the common principles are the three city-states and
the Saarland, Schleswig-Holstein, Rhineland-Palatinate, Brandenburg,
Mecklenburg-Vorpommern, and Thuringia (which has a *Land* Administrative Office as a substitute), all small-to-medium sized *Länder* that do
not have the middle-level *Regierungsbezirk*.[25]

Administration in the federation and the *Länder* is separate in principle. *Land* administration is not *under* the federation but rather is an
autonomous arena next to the federation.[26] "Mixed administration" is
supposedly not permitted by the Basic Law, for example, in that a *Land*
agency reports to a federal agency or that the federation must approve
Land measures or exercise some power of co-decision. In fact there are
numerous examples of some form of mixed administration,[27] although
these depend in part on what is meant by the term.[28] Examples of federal
involvement in *Land* administration are the federal legal supervision of
laws delegated to the *Länder* for administration and the joint tasks under
Articles 91a and 91b described later in this chapter and in Chapter 2 on
the constitutional framework of German federalism. An example of a
joint agency is finance administration mentioned briefly above. The federation and the *Länder* have their own finance administration, but the
twenty-two high finance authorities serve as joint agencies at the middle
level of *Land* administration. Joint agencies also exist among the *Länder*.
For example, the Film Assessment Office in Wiesbaden determines which
movies should receive public subsidies based on a contract among the
Land ministers of education and culture. Finally, there are coordinating
agencies among the *Länder,* for example, the Conference of Education
and Culture Ministers (*Kultusministerkonferenz* [*KMK*]); the Conference
of Ministers of Justice; and the University Rectors Conference.[29]

The three levels of Land *administration*

The high level
The first of the three levels is called the high or central level (*Oberstufe*)
which, as in the case of the federation above, consists of two parts: the
supreme *Land* authorities (*oberste Landesbehörden*) and the high *Land*
authorities (*Landesoberbehörden*). The supreme *Land* authorities are the
Land government (cabinet), the prime minister (*Ministerpräsident*), and
the cabinet ministers. Some would add the speaker of the *Land* parliament

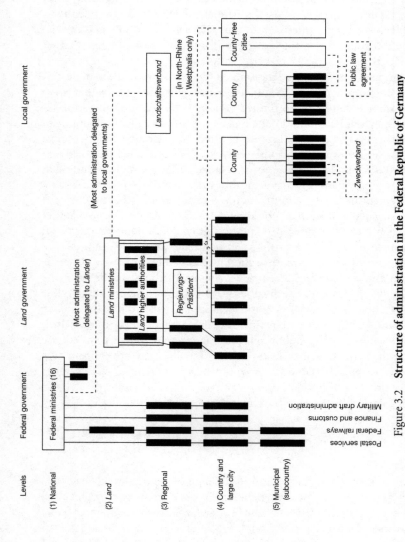

Figure 3.2 **Structure of administration in the Federal Republic of Germany**

Source: Adapted from Frido Wagener, "Äusserer Aufbau von Staat und Verwaltung," in *Öffentliche Verwaltung in der Bundesrepublik Deutschland,* edited by Klaus König, H. J. von Oertzen, and Frido Wagener (Baden-Baden: Nomos Verlagsgesellschaft, 1981), p. 80.

and the *Land* accounting office.[30] Unity is maintained by the guideline authority (*Richtlinienkompetenz*) of the prime minister and the principle of collegiality in the cabinet.

As indicated above, the prime minister is more than first among equals in the cabinet; he exercises the "guideline authority" or leadership of the government. Thus, in spite of the strong traditions of responsibility of ministers for their subject areas (*Ressortprinzip*) and collegiality, the prime minister is the boss (*Kanzlerprinzip*); but this is less true in the city-states. The prime minister represents the *Land's* interests *vis-à-vis* the other *Länder* in the prime ministers' conference and the federation in the *Bundesrat*, where he or she can exercise considerable influence on federal legislation. In this regard he is far more influential nationally than a typical American governor. He or she is assisted in leadership responsibilities by a staff (*Staatskanzlei*) responsible to the prime minister; in Baden-Württemberg, the staff is called *Staatsministerium*, in the city-states, *Senatskanzleien*. The prime minister's political staff has grown over the years along with the increasing role of the prime minister as dominant *Land* politician and *Landesvater* or "*Land* prince," a designation that reflects the prime minister's additional role as ceremonial head of state.[31] The staff's first and permanent task is to coordinate the work of the ministers, to support the prime minister, to manage information, and to be innovative in initiating and conceptualizing policy proposals. Coordinating *Land* policy in the committees and plenary sessions of the *Bundesrat* is also a major activity.[32] In addition, the chiefs of staff organize the meetings of *Land* prime ministers, which take place about every three months (about every six months with the Federal Chancellor). For a while, especially in the late 1960s and early 1970s, the prime minister's staff was engaged in development planning activities, but these have since been turned over to the ministries.[33] On the other hand, political planning remains an important staff activity.[34]

As a rule the prime minister's staff is organized into offices that are responsible for areas such as parties and organizations; local governments; information and analyses; and preparation of legislation, speech writing, and setting the prime minister's calendar. The organization of the staffs in the city-states is considerably more modest, but press and public information offices are found everywhere. Some staffs house the office of the *Land* representative in Bonn (now Berlin), who usually also is head of the *Land* mission in the capital. Some staffs also have a special representative for European, i.e., EU, affairs.[35]

In most *Länder* there are from seven to nine ministries. These include the six core ministries (Interior, Education and Culture (*Kultus*), Finance,

Economics, Social, and Justice) and others that have been added and eliminated over the years. For example, since the 1970s a Ministry of Science that has been given responsibility for the universities has been carved out of the older Ministry of Education and Culture[36]

The specific tasks of the ministries vary from *Land* to *Land*. Thus transportation is located in the Ministry of Interior in Baden-Württemberg but in the Ministry of Economics elsewhere. Sports may be in the ministries of education, interior, or social welfare. Variation is especially great regarding land use and environment, since it can be problematic to place environment and agriculture in one ministry. The most important ministry traditionally has been the Ministry of Interior, which has been a kind of "umbrella agency" for tasks not assigned to more specialized agencies. Therefore, it is the ministry with a certain unity of command function.[37]

Ministers are members of the government (cabinet) and heads of subject ministries. Thus they are responsible for central leadership and direction as well as for the personnel and functional supervision of lower-level authorities and institutions in their area. They develop general regulations and rules for administrative execution at lower levels and do *Land*-wide planning. They draft legislation and regulations and deal with the *Land* parliament in areas under their responsibility. On the other hand, they make individual decisions only rarely.[38]

These activities lead to the dual function of the ministry serving as the highest administrative authority and at the same time as a political organ of the cabinet. This dual function is more apparent at the *Land* level than at the federal level, because the *Land* ministries have a complete subject area and an administrative structure to which they can give some unity and direction. This does not lead to a dualism between politics and administration so much as to the function of gearshift (*Umschaltfunktion*) between politics and administration. Thus the *Land* ministries more than their federal counterparts are "simultaneously lawmaking and administrative ministries." That is, the experience and information gained from administrative practice can be taken into account in the program development and policy making process in the ministry.[39]

In actual practice the above distinction between the political and administrative functions is difficult to make, because of the growth of *Land* ministries over the years resulting from demands on central direction and coordination activities. Growth in the ministries is also due to an increasing interaction with the *Land* parliaments in the number of written and oral questions raised and the close contact with parliamentary committees and with governing party group committees. Ministries have also borne the burden of an increasing tendency toward a concern with sets of single issues, such as the construction of an autobahn or federal highway, airport, or nuclear power plant. This gets ministries very much involved in planning activities which, in turn, tend to become politicized. In practice, then, it is difficult to develop a clear picture of the multiple functions of the ministries. They are program development agencies, but they also exercise supervision and control over subordinate units.[40]

In contrast to the supreme *Land* authorities (*oberste Landesbehörden*), the high *Land* authorities (*Landesoberbehörden*) are, like their federal counterparts, specialized agencies responsible to a minister. They tend to be technically demanding offices with extensive information-gathering responsibilities and data analysis and research capabilities. Examples include *Land* statistical offices, *Land* crime offices, and *Land* offices of constitutional protection.[41] They also include specialized agencies such as the *Land* geological office and offices for environmental protection, earth research, plant protection, agricultural development, and so forth. A completely unique high authority is the *Land* Administrative Office in Lower Saxony which combines ten formerly autonomous high authorities without any particular connecting principle[42]

The middle level (Mittelstufe *or* Mittelinstanz)
At this level one finds the director (*Regierungspräsident*) of the district government (*Bezirksregierung*) of the government district (*Regierungsbezirk*). This is where the important Continental administrative principle of unity of command (*Einheit der Verwaltung*) has been applied most clearly in the German administrative tradition. It is where "state" (federal and *Land*) policies are "bundled" for implementation and where the director (similar to the classic example of the French *prefect*) serves as a coordinator and mediator between the high and the low levels of administration. The director of the government district is a political appointee and the general representative of the *Land* government in the district, and he or she ensures that the goals of the government are realized in the district. This, of course, is a political function; however, the director is also a special counsel for the concerns of the region *vis-à-vis* the *Land* and federal governments. Thus he may see himself as an "honest broker" between the "state" and local governments, as a representative of the *Land* in the district and of his district to the *Land*.[43]

The director is responsible especially to the *Land* Minister of the Interior but also to the other ministers for the proper administration of their policies and laws. But as an agent of "bundling" and coordination, the director is the most important counterweight against an otherwise dominant tendency toward specialization. The director attempts to counter specialization through a variety of means, including co-signature, discussions with section chiefs, coordinating units and through his involvement in various planning activities. However, some observers argue that vertical relationships (in the United States, "picket-fence" federalism) are so strong today in the organization of the government district along ministerial lines and between groups of subject experts at different levels that horizontal coordination is more difficult than in the past.[44]

There is a strong tradition in German administration – and on the Continent in general – that holds that specialized agencies such as those at all levels of American administration, especially the ubiquitous special districts at the local level, should be discouraged in principle if not always in fact. Where it is not feasible to integrate various functions in one administrative unit, there should be at least an attempt to have the function administered in one territory.[45] This tradition today does not deny that there are some advantages to specialized administration, for example, administration by subject specialists, better performance by focusing on specific tasks, subject neutrality and nonpartisan implementation, and sometimes greater efficiency of administration. But disadvantages include "selective attention," narrowness of view and blindness to other factors, isolation within the general administrative structures, lack of coordination with other agencies, exaggeration of the importance of own area, and perfectionist tendencies among the administrators. This is reflected in the "vertical brotherhood of experts"[46] that exists between higher and lower levels in German administration. Special administrative agencies tend to be removed from politics; yet they are subject to capture by the clientèle they serve and special interest groups. They tend also to be less transparent, often less accountable, and removed from citizen input.[47]

The director of the government district has the function of guaranteeing the legal and uniform conduct of administration throughout the territory of the district through his functional and personnel supervision of subordinate state authorities. In some *Länder* (Bavaria, Lower Saxony, North-Rhine Westphalia) this includes the supervision of school teachers, who are *Land* civil servants. In other *Länder*, e.g., Baden-Württemberg, there is a separate and special hierarchical organization for schools. In a more general and traditional sense, the director provides legal supervision of local governments in their areas of autonomous self-government. This usually involves consultation and advice, but repressive measures are available to the director in extreme cases. Related to this function is the review of grant applications by local governments. The director also provides legal supervision of other public corporations, such as schools. He is responsible for the legal *and* functional supervision of delegated state tasks carried out by local governments as well as by special authorities under the authority of the district government.[48]

While the government districts are in principle institutions of general administration, they also carry out specialized administration on behalf of the ministries. This relieves the ministries of certain administrative burdens that for certain reasons cannot be included in the area of responsibility of local governments. The number and kind of specialized functions performed by the district government, and/or supervised by it at the local branch level, varies among the *Länder*, but they tend to require special expertise or involve common standards. Examples include the administration of technically complicated emission controls, traffic planning, protection of nature areas, management of public property, regional planning, and planning and taking certain measures in the areas of water management and agriculture.[49]

In spite of the theory of unity of command and the efforts to combine as many tasks as possible in the district governments, counties and cities, there are special authorities at the middle level that can be found at least to some extent outside the confines of the district governments. Lower Saxony differs from the other *Länder* in that it has a *Land* Administrative Office at the high level that combines several functional agencies outside of the middle-level district governments but is not a "bundling" office.[50] Thuringia and Rhineland-Palatinate have also created *Land* administrative agencies that perform some of the functions found in the district governments in other *Länder*. Nevertheless, even in Lower Saxony there are special agencies that answer directly to the ministries and do not fall under the supervision of either the district governments or the *Land* Administrative Office. An unusual example of an activity that is not included in the government districts is finance administration, where the high finance office is both a federal and a *Land* middle-level agency directed by a head who is both a federal and *Land* official. Salaries and appointments of the public employees as well as functions are divided between the federal and *Land* officials. Below the middle-level agency are branch offices in the municipalities. The territory served by these local branches does not always conform with county boundaries.[51]

Following the territorial and administrative reforms of the 1960s and 1970s and the re-establishment of five new *Länder* in the East, there were thirty-two government districts which differed significantly in size of population and area. No other administrative institution has been called into question so often since 1945; the government districts were almost eliminated by Baden-Württemberg in the early 1970s. In the late 1990s they were being considered for elimination by Rhineland-Palatinate, and in 1999 a law was introduced in the *Land* parliament which did, indeed, replace the three government districts as of 1 January 2000 with "structure and licensing directions" in Koblenz and Neustadt/Weinstraße and a "supervisory and service center" in Trier.[52] During the discussions regarding the territorial reforms of the late 1960s and early 1970s mentioned above, some critics argued that the functions of the district governments could be divided in part by the ministries and the counties, and, especially, that they could be replaced by integrated planning and administrative and financing agencies at the regional level. At least in the larger territorial *Länder*, in contrast to the Rhineland-Palatinate, the view prevailed that they were necessary, and regional planning today is in effect mostly planning by the government district but in some *Länder* by the counties. The government districts appear now to be firmly established in the larger *Länder*;[53] however, as noted above, there is no middle level in six of the smaller territorial *Länder*: the Saarland; Schleswig-Holstein; Rhineland-Palatinate; Mecklenburg-Vorpommern; Brandenburg; and Thuringia, which has a substitute in the form of a *Land* administrative office.[54] North-Rhine Westphalia, which is a large territorial state with the largest population, is in the process of reforming and reorganizing its government districts.

A nonpartisan administration in the government districts is assumed; however, given the politicization of much of the higher levels of administration in *Land* and local governments in recent decades, some concern has been expressed about the tradition of political neutrality at the middle level of administration. Certain voices have called for a district government that is "closer to the people," a more "democratized" or "parliamentarized" or less bureaucratized administration. But there is no reason why the middle level should be "political" just because the higher and lower levels are. Indeed, the difficult job of serving as a mediator and coordinator between *Land* and local governments, which often have different partisan colors, cannot be performed well by a partisan district government.[55] Besides, any parliamentarization at the government district level would subtract proportionately from the authority of the *Land* parliaments and elected county and local government councils (figure 3.3).[56]

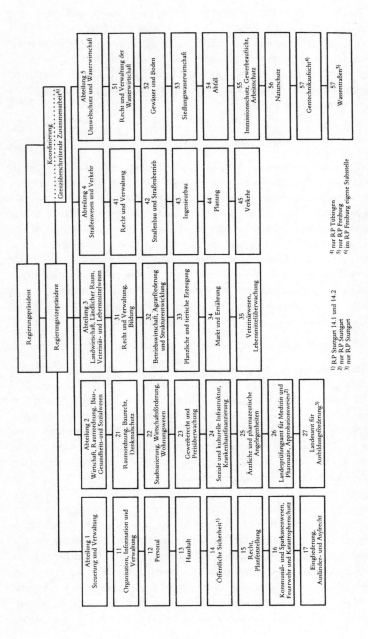

Figure 3.3 **Organization plan for the government districts of Baden-Württemberg**

Lower Saxony was mentioned at the end of the previous section as having a unique high authority in the form of a *Land* Administrative Office in addition to government districts. Thüringia, in contrast, differs from all other *Länder* in having established a single *Land* Administrative Office at the middle level in place of government districts. The Rhineland-Palatinate, as noted above, has just replaced its three government districts with three other regional offices.

The lower level: direct state administration

In all of the *Länder* there are varying numbers and kinds of offices that in some cases are directly responsible to high *Land* special authorities but mostly answer to the government districts (in the *Länder* with no government districts, some local state offices are directly responsible to the supreme *Land* authorities, i.e., the ministries). Typical examples of the former are weights and measures, autobahn, road construction, and finance offices. The far more numerous examples of state offices that are supervised by the government districts include the police, and land registry, agriculture, and business regulation offices, and in most, but not in all, cases, school administration and forestry (figures 3.4 and 3.5).

The lower level: indirect administration by local governments

Public administration *on behalf of the state* is also carried out by local governments. Indeed, it is estimated that 75–80 percent of all federal and *Land* laws are implemented by local governments. The most important units in this regard are the counties, of which there are two kinds: the "rural county" (*Landkreis*), which may be in fact rather densely populated owing to the size and number of municipalities that constitute the county; and the "city-county" (*Stadtkreis*),[57] a larger city usually referred to as the county-free city (*kreisfreie Stadt*).

The lower level: rural county government   German rural counties are territorial public corporations consisting of municipalities, their surrounding territory, and their citizens (thus *Gemeindeverband*). There is very little unincorporated territory in Germany; examples would be certain forests and lakes. The counties' purpose is to administer those matters that are "above" or beyond the reach or capability of the municipalities that constitute the county. Matters of county self-government include the voluntary establishment and maintenance of social and cultural institutions

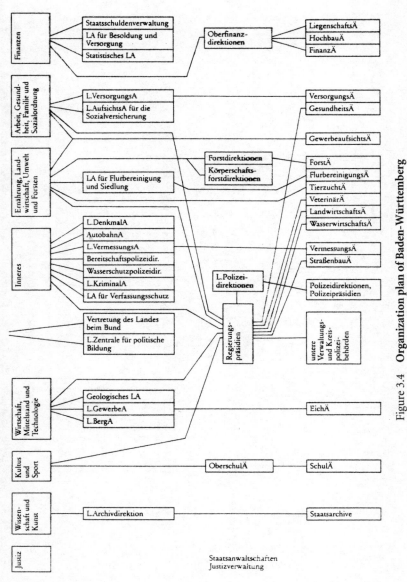

Figure 3.4 Organization plan of Baden-Württemberg

Source: Rainer Wahl, "Die Organisation und Entwicklung der Verwaltung in den Ländern und in Berlin," in Deutsche Verwaltungsgeschichte, Band 5: Die Bundesrepublik Deutschland, edited by Kurt G. A. Jeserich et al. (Stuttgart: Deutsche Verlagsanstalt, 1987), p. 243.

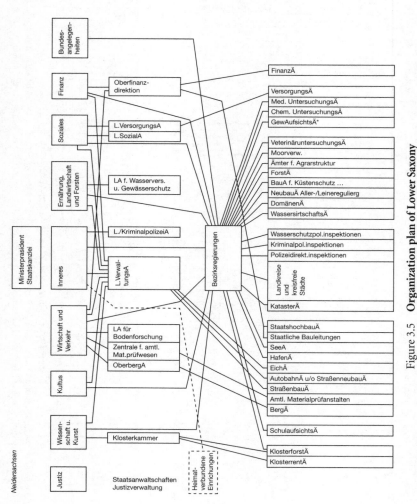

Figure 3.5 **Organization plan of Lower Saxony**

Source: Rainer Wahl, "Die Organisation und Entwicklung der Verwaltung in den Ländern und in Berlin," in Deutsche Verwaltungsgeschichte, Band 5: Die Bundesrepublic Deutschland, edited by Kurt G. A. Jeserich et al. (Stuttgart: Deutsche Verlagsanstalt, 1987), p. 243.

such as concert halls and museums; the construction and maintenance of general schools, retirement and nursing homes; hospitals and ambulance services, etc. Mandated tasks may include fire protection; vocational schools; county roads; waste disposal; and last-resort public assistance (*Sozialhilfe*). Delegated tasks include the administration of student subsidies for promoting education; rent subsidies (*Wohngeld*); health and veterinary offices; office for foreigners; building supervision; monument maintenance; dam supervision; and hunting and fishing licenses. The rural county can delegate some functions to its municipalities.[58]

The *Landrat* (until the second half of the 1990s a mostly ceremonial figure in North-Rhine Westphalia and Lower Saxony, see map 3.1) is the chief administrative officer responsible for the administration of both "state" and local affairs – that is, he combines the two at the rural county level and is the "connecting link between state administration and self-government in the county." As such he falls under the legal and functional supervision of the government district.[59] Germans therefore sometimes speak of the county's "loaning" the *Landrat* to the state (*Land*) for the

Map 3.1   **Counties and county-free (independent) cities in Lower Saxony**

administration of state (both federal and *Land*) laws;[60] however, in Lower Saxony the county government has been "communalized" as a result of the pressure of British occupation authorities after the war to remove the "state" from local government. Thus the county manager in Lower Saxony (now also called *Landrat*) performs delegated tasks on behalf of the *Land,* but as a local official.[61] In the other *Länder* the *Landrat* can be seen as an agent of direct state administration, even though he is a local government official. But there are no state administrative offices within the jurisdiction of the cities, towns, and villages that make up the county, so their administration of state laws is indirect administration under the legal supervision of the *Landrat*. Of course, the specific responsibilities of the *Landrat* vary rather significantly among the *Länder*.

The lower level: municipal governments   The cities, towns, and villages (*Gemeinden* in German; *communes* in French) are territorial public corporations which have the right of self-government as guaranteed by Article 28, para. 2, sent. 1 of the Basic Law (see map 3.2). They are responsible for the entire range of public administration in their territory, which is in conformity with the principle of unity of command (*Einheit der Verwaltung*) that stands in sharp contrast to the functional fragmentation

Map 3.2   **The municipalities (*Gemeinden*) in the county of Göttingen**

of local government administration in the United States. They have different political and administrative structures, depending on the respective *Land*-wide charter law (*Gemeindeordnung*).[62] There was a change in the *Länder* in the 1990s to direct election of the mayor as chief executive officer (even in the North German city manager systems), which has always been a feature of the South German Council form found in Baden-Württemberg and Bavaria. With its adoption by the five new *Länder* in the East, the South German Council form of local government is now the most common in Germany.[63]

German municipalities are responsible for two kinds of administration: matters of self-government (*Selbstverwaltungsangelegenheiten*), also called "own area of responsibility" (*eigener Wirkungskreis*); and delegated matters (*Auftragsangelegenheiten*), also called delegated area of responsibility (*übertragener Wirkungskreis*). In matters of self-government, the principle of general powers (*Allzuständigkeit*) applies.[64] According to this principle, which is somewhat comparable to home rule in the United States, the municipalities (and counties) in Germany have the authority to do anything they wish so long as it is within the framework of and does not conflict with a *Land* or federal law (Article 28, para. 2). In theory at least it stands in sharp contrast to the American *ultra vires* rule, according to which American municipalities may engage only in those activities authorized by their charters. In practice the *Länder* have not left their cities and towns all that much room to maneuver, so that the general powers rule, like Articles 30 and 70 of the Basic Law regarding the powers of the *Länder* and the federation, is somewhat misleading.

Matters of self-government include voluntary (*freiwillige Aufgaben*) and mandated tasks (*Pflichtaufgaben*). Voluntary tasks may in fact be required in the sense that they are needed and cannot be ignored. Or, on the other hand, voluntary tasks may not be performed owing to a lack of financial means or a lack of administrative capability. The focus of voluntary tasks is the provision of social, cultural, and economic public facilities and services. Examples of voluntary tasks are the construction and maintenance of swimming pools, athletic fields, lecture halls, libraries, museums, and, in larger cities, theaters; support of cultural associations and music schools; the provision of parks and green areas; the construction and maintenance of nursery schools, youth centers, retirement and nursing homes, hospitals, and so forth. Mandated tasks include, for example, waste collection; sewerage; public playgrounds; street construction and maintenance; fire protection; zoning; maintenance of elementary schools, and, for the city-counties, maintenance of secondary schools.[65]

Delegated matters are responsibilities that must be carried out by the municipalities because there are no general and direct state agencies at the municipal level for such purposes. Municipalities carry out fewer delegated tasks than the counties, but they are involved to some extent in this area of responsibility. There are no special authorities in municipalities. Delegated matters include passport administration; local registration of inhabitants and the provision of personal identity cards, which in turn is connected to registration for the military draft (or alternative civilian service); building supervision; care of the homeless and of refugees and asylum seekers. On the other hand various welfare tasks and the promotion of economic development and culture are mostly in the category of self-government matters.[66]

In their administration of matters of self-government, German municipalities are responsible for their actions, that is, they must operate within the law. For municipalities in the counties, this means they are subject to the *legal* supervision of the *Landrat* (or county manager) for the self-government activities and to his or her functional supervision for the delegated activities. The *Landrat*, in turn, is supervised by the director of the government district who in turn answers to the various ministries. In those smaller territorial *Länder* without government districts, supervision is by the Minister of Interior. Supervision is carried out informally through routine consultation. The next stage usually takes the form of requests for information. In cases of noncompliance, the supervising authority can order compliance, arrange to implement measures at the cost of the municipality, or, finally, replace the local authorities with a state commissar, which was done on numerous occasions during the last difficult years of the Weimar Republic but only rarely in the Federal Republic. To prevent such extreme actions, there are various approval procedures, for example, for selling public property, borrowing money, etc. In cases of disagreement, municipalities can contest the decision of the supervisory authority before an administrative court.[67]

The lower level: the county-free cities In all of the *Länder*, there is city-county separation (found as a rule in the United States only in Virginia) for the largest cities; therefore, as we have already seen, they are referred to as city-counties (*Stadtkreise*) or, more commonly, as county-free cities (*kreisfreie Städte*). The county-free cities are responsible for administering all local affairs and serve also as substitutes for lower state administrative authorities. The responsible organ is the governing mayor (or city manager until the 1990s) who, however, is not "on loan" to the state. Rather, he administers state laws as "delegated matters" of local government on his own responsibility. Again, there are no state administrative offices within the jurisdiction of the county-free cities, so that indirect state administration takes place here also.[68] In both the rural counties and the county-free cities, then, the *Land* is relieved of establishing its own local agencies, and the administration of state tasks is carried out by those who are familiar with the local conditions and the people. At the same time local governments gain some understanding for the concerns of higher levels via contact with their agents. "[T]he leading and deeper idea behind the organization of the lower level is not that of a clean separation between two arenas, but communication, mutual exchange of information, and a balancing of state and local interests."[69]

Administration of delegated state functions by the county-free cities falls under the functional supervision of the district government (see above); supervision of all matters of local self-government is legal only. In some *Länder* larger cities that are not county-free have been given similar rights and responsibilities.[70]

An especially important example of county and county-free city administration of delegated tasks is the public assistance (*Sozialhilfe*) that is provided by federal law to those who have exhausted their unemployment benefits or have no other source of income. This includes not only the handicapped and blind but also refugees and asylum seekers. This law has been delegated to the *Länder*, which in turn have given the actual administration of payments for living expenses to the rural counties and county-free cities as a matter of self-government. Since these local governments are responsible not only for administrative costs but also for providing the actual funds for payments, and since there has been relatively high unemployment in recent years among Germans and even higher rates among the many foreigners that have come to Germany, the financial stress of local governments has been exacerbated significantly by this responsibility.

The result has been considerable conflict between the different levels over current arrangements. Federal guidelines leave the local governments little room for maneuver, because benefits are supposed to be standard throughout the country. When the Public Assistance Act was revised in 1961, it was assumed that its importance would decline steadily owing to economic growth and affluence. The restrictions placed on local government autonomy in administering the program were therefore not taken very seriously. With the rise of long-term unemployment and the large numbers of refugees and asylum seekers, public assistance has become a major bone of contention between federal, *Land*, and local authorities. The dilemma facing the localities is that they do not have the revenues to assume responsibility for public assistance, and even if they did there are strong ideological and practical reasons for having a federal program with nation-wide standards.[71]

Youth and family assistance is also a delegated function that is a matter of self-government for the rural counties and county-free cities. This involves subsidies for nursery schools (*Kindergarten*); programs for music, sports, international understanding, youth consultation, etc.; and a variety of family social services and youth homes. Family promotion has been added in recent years in the *Länder* in the form of one-time payments for bearing children (*Babygeld*). This is in addition to monthly child support payments (*Kindergeld*) for all families. Educational promotion funds, for example, funds to pay for board and room costs of some higher school and university students (tuition is free) based on family income, are regulated nationally, but some *Länder*, for example, Lower Saxony, have added supplements for pupils attending higher secondary schools (*Gymnasien*) who cannot live at home because of the distance of the school from their place of domicile.[72]

There have been many complaints in Germany – as in the United States – about the growing influence of "the state" at the local level, especially in terms of mandated functions. A recent example is the federal law – approved by the *Bundesrat* – that requires all municipalities to provide nursery schools for all children whose parents want them but without providing the funding for the schools. Thus some observers see the work of local governments as consisting more or less of administering state-mandated and delegated tasks. This has also had a significant influence on the financial situation of the municipalities, and it raises constitutional questions about the guarantee of local self-government.[73] It also raises questions about the extent to which the *Bundesrat* reflects the interests of local governments as opposed to broader party interests.

The lower level: special inter- and intramunicipal associations Some *Länder*, e.g., Lower Saxony, Rhineland-Palatinate, Baden-Württemberg, and Schleswig-Holstein, also have subcounty associations of villages and towns, somewhat like a local federation of small municipalities (called, respectively, *Samtgemeinden*, *Verbandsgemeinden*, *Verwaltungsgemeinschaften*, and *Ämter*). In other cases some former villages or towns (*Ortsschaften*) that were consolidated into larger municipalities during the territorial reforms of the 1960s and 1970s were given certain limited responsibilities in compensation for their loss of autonomy. They are modeled to some extent on the intra-municipal city districts of certain large cities. Some special-purpose administrative associations have been formed in Bavaria, Saxony-Anhalt, and Thuringia; Bavaria, North-Rhine Westphalia, and Rhineland-Palatinate have higher- level multiple-county associations.[74]

In addition, many municipalities and counties have formed special districts (*Zweckverbände*), usually for a single purpose such as provision of drinking water, regional planning, constructing a swimming pool, regulating a river separating two political units, maintaining a common school bus, etc.[75] While these are common features of local government in Germany, they are not as ubiquitous as in the United States.

The lower level: special supra-municipal associations   In some *Länder* associations of municipalities have been created at a regional level in order to carry out certain functions that cannot be administered effectively at the municipal or county levels. The best examples are the two regional associations (*Landschaftsverbände Rheinland* and *Westfalen-Lippe*) in North-Rhine Westphalia, which are in the process of being reformed and replaced; the seven districts in Bavaria; and the *Bezirksverband Pfalz* in the Rhineland-Palatinate. There are also *Land* welfare associations in Baden-Württemberg, Hesse, and Saxony as well as the regional planning associations in Baden-Württemberg. An innovative regional association was formed by Stuttgart and five surrounding counties in 1994, and it has a wide range of planning and coordination functions.[76]

Administration in the city-states

Unlike any other existing federation, Germany has three city-states: Bremen, Hamburg, and Berlin. The first two have their origins in the Holy Roman Empire as trading cities that were important participants in the Hanseatic League, while Berlin's status is the result of the city's division during the Cold War, its unification in 1990, and the failure of a referendum in May 1996 that, if successful, would have led to a consolidation of Berlin and Brandenburg.

Bremen is not a simple city-state, but rather a two-city state. Unlike Hamburg and Berlin, which are unitary cities, Bremen consists of the cities of Bremen and Bremerhaven, separated by 65 km with territory from Lower Saxony in between. The governmental organs (*Senat*) and parliament (*Bürgerschaft*) of the *Land* Bremen also serve the city of Bremen, but Bremerhaven has its own city government and council in addition.[77]

In Bremen and Hamburg the high-, middle-, and lower-level *Land* functions are combined to a considerable extent. The advantage, of course, is less distance between the citizen and government officials and administrators; the disadvantage is the resulting complexity of city administrative organization. In all three city-states neighborhood or district offices have been created, but they have fewer powers in Bremen than in Hamburg or Berlin.

In Hamburg there is no separation between the "state" and "municipal" administration. The city, like Bremen, has a lord mayor as head of government (*Senat*) and a parliament (*Bürgerschaft*). The city is divided into districts which are not autonomous but do provide "deconcentrated administration." The districts have elected assemblies and an administration that implements measures that do not require a larger area.[78]

Unlike the other two city-states, Berlin has two administrative levels, but it is different from the territorial *Länder* that have two levels (e.g., Schleswig-Holstein and Saarland). It is not a traditional city-state like Bremen and Hamburg, which were city-states before the war and the division of Germany after 1945. Berlin became a divided city-state under Allied occupation during the Cold War; it was reunited in the summer of 1990, and in June 1991 the *Bundestag* decided by a close vote to make it the national capital again. In 1994 the city completed a constitutional and administrative reform that was to prepare it for its future responsibilities at least until consolidation with Brandenburg; however, the referendum that was to bring this about failed in May 1996, so that Berlin's new legal framework may last longer than many expected.

As in the other city-states, there is no difference between state and local government administration. The tasks of the city as municipality, county and *Land* are met by the parliament (*Abgeordnetenhaus*), government (*Senat*), and administration, including administration by the twenty-three districts into which Berlin was divided (In 1999 the twenty-three districts were reduced to twelve). There is, then, a high or main administration and a district administration. These two levels have existed since 1920, when Berlin annexed eight cities, fifty-nine towns and villages, and twenty-seven estates. The division of the city into the then twenty districts was designed in part to compensate the incorporated areas for their lost status.[79]

There are three categories of tasks or responsibilities in Berlin: the tasks of the main administration; the tasks delegated to the districts under the supervision of the city; and district tasks. The 1994 Berlin constitution enumerates the powers of the main administration and those that can be delegated. What is not enumerated belongs to the districts. Federal laws that are delegated to the *Länder* are divided in Berlin between the main administration and the districts which, like local governments in the territorial *Länder*, implement these laws as matters of their own responsibility. The districts are responsible for such matters as schools, adult education, hospitals, libraries, swimming facilities, youth homes, athletic fields, parks, and music schools. Delegated matters under supervision include building plans, street maintenance and lighting, elections, and property issues. The districts can make their own zoning plans, and they enjoy some fiscal autonomy. The main administration is responsible for general law and order, constitutional protection, relations with the federal government, asylum seekers, citizenship issues, money and credit, city-wide planning, public housing, etc.[80]

Unlike the typical territorial *Land* described on p. 87, the "chancellor principle" does not apply to the city-states. According to this principle, the prime minister is elected by the *Land* parliament and then appoints his cabinet members. In each of the three cities, however, the lord mayor is elected by the city parliament which also elects the members of the cabinet. The city parliament can also remove cabinet ministers in a vote of no-confidence. In practice, of course, the parliament elects the cabinet nominees already selected in negotiations within the majority party or majority coalition. In any case the lord mayor does not have the power to set the guidelines of policy as do his counterparts in the territorial *Länder*, that is, the principles of collegiality and ministerial responsibility are stronger in the city-states.[81]

Special agencies

As noted above, a distinction is made in Germany as in the United States between general- purpose and special-purpose administration. We have seen that there are a good many special agencies in Germany. At the federal and *Land* levels special offices are common. These serve at the federal level in place of missing substructures, but they are subunits of the various ministries at the *Land* level.[82] They are seen usually as means of relieving the ministry of an administrative burden in favor of greater decentralization, but sometimes they are also seen as centralizing agents. They are usually at the higher level of administration, that is, below the supreme and above the middle levels; however, some are also at the middle level, where they may be to some extent in competition with the district government. They tend to be technically demanding, e.g., statistical offices, or responsible for certification functions, e.g., geological offices. The *Gewerbeaufsichtsämter* can be found between the middle and lower levels.[83] These are special authorities established for the purposes of supervising business operations regarding workplace health and safety standards, noise levels, temperature conditions, radiation, abuse of workers or animals, and protection of nature, and so forth.

At the lower level there is considerable administrative fragmentation, in spite of unity of command in the rural counties and county-free cities. This is more evident in the south (Baden-Württemberg, Rhineland-Palatinate, Bavaria) than in the north (North-Rhine Westphalia, Hesse). Examples of special authorities that are not easily integrated into the rural counties and county-free cities because of the territory they cover or their specialization are weights and measures (*Eichämter*); mountain and forest offices; and cultural and road construction offices. Regional development and environmental protection can also be difficult to integrate within a local unit of general administration.[84]

Indirect administration by nongovernmental public bodies and private persons

Direct administration by "state" (*Land* and federal agencies at various levels) and indirect administration by self-governing local governments do not exhaust the forms and instruments of administration in Germany. Indirect administration by self-governing nongovernmental public corporations, institutions, and foundations is also important. Public territorial corporations have members – those living in the territory – and autonomy, for example, municipalities and counties. Universities, on the other hand, are personnel corporations. Public institutions (*Anstalten*) have the function of carrying out a particular purpose. They have no members, only users; examples would be the *Sparkassen*, which have a monopoly as savings and loan associations, or public radio and television networks[85] sponsored by the *Länder*. Public foundations are institutions that have a continuing purpose set by a founder with funding provided by an endowment from public and/or private sources. All of these legal forms of service providers share a degree of autonomy or the right of self-government of their affairs, subject only to the legal supervision of ministries.

Social insurance agencies[86]

Next to the local governments, social insurance is the most important area in which *indirect* state administration is carried out. The Federal Employment Office in Nuremberg is responsible for providing unemployment compensation as well as employment counseling and other services such as child support payments for *all* children in Germany. It is a semi-autonomous federal institution (*Anstalt*) with branches at *Land* and local government levels.[87] Social insurance agencies that provide health and retirement benefits with responsibilities above the *Land* level are federal bodies (that is, special public corporations carrying out federal law), of which there are several examples.

Social insurance for health, accident, retirement, and, most recently, nursing care programs is provided by federal law, but administration is not by government agencies. All employees who earn less than a certain amount per month – 90 percent of the employed – are required to join a health insurance provider. In the past there were insurance providers restricted to special occupations or groups of employees as well as providers for the general population. Since the beginning of 1996, employees may select their provider; however, each provider must offer a uniform system of services and quality standards, and no one may be refused admission. Therefore, the price competition among the different providers will be based primarily on the efficiency of their operations, although there is some concern that the effect of this reform will work to the disadvantage of the rapidly growing older population.[88]

The public corporations that provide insurance are semi-autonomous institutions that implement the social insurance law as matters of their own responsibility. In most cases an assembly and executive committee are elected with equal representation for both employers and employees; social insurance funds for miners, where the insured make up two-thirds of the self-governing organs, are an exception. Eligible voters for the assembly elections are the insured employees.

In the early 1990s there were about 1,235 sickness funds organized in a variety of forms. The largest number of insured are with 274 regional funds (*Ortskrankenkassen, AOK*). There were also 747 funds organized by companies (*Betriebskrankenkassen*), 176 funds offered by vocational groups (*Innungskrankenkassen*), twenty-one funds for farmers, one for seamen, one for miners, and fifteen voluntary "substitute" funds. By the end of 1999, these numbers had been reduced sharply to seventeen regional funds, 354 company funds, thirty-nine vocational funds, and nineteen substitute funds.[89] Minimum numbers of insured are required; e.g., 100,000 for the company funds, 1,000 for a vocational fund.[90] All public sickness funds are supervised by the district governments and *Land*, while private funds are supervised by the federal insurance office.

Retirement programs are divided among three large branches. The first is for manual workers, which is organized into *Land* insurance institutions and institutions for federal railway workers and seamen. The second is for white-collar or salaried workers which is run by the Federal Insurance Agency for Employees in Berlin. And the third is the Retirement Insurance Agency for Mine Workers. Farmers were added in 1957, their family members in 1985. Independent journalists and artists were added in 1981, and as of 1986 mothers receive credit for retirement insurance based on the number of years they were engaged in child-rearing activities.[91]

Other significant institutions in the area of social insurance are the nongovernmental "free providers and associations." The most important of these are churches and religious societies as well as groups of private welfare providers. These are engaged in the "workers' welfare assistance," or the German Red Cross, German Caritas, the Jewish Central Welfare Center, and so forth, located at different levels of government. German Christian – especially Catholic – social doctrine focuses on the principle of *subsidiarity*, according to which public policies should be carried out at the lowest level possible. This principle has been adopted to a considerable extent by federal law makers, who have delegated to or authorized private, nongovernmental agencies to carry out numerous social welfare functions with considerable public financial support. Thus before unification private welfare providers (*freie Wohlfahrtsverbände*) sponsored 40 percent of the hospitals for acute treatment, about 60 percent of the retirement homes, about 70 percent of facilities for youth, and 60 percent of the facilities for handicapped persons. Continuing education, especially in the form of adult education, is also a major activity. In the 1980s there were about 900 adult education centers (*Volkshochschulen*) which were being turned over increasingly to local governments which provided about two-thirds of their funding.[92]

Chambers

There are numerous self-governing nongovernmental public corporations, or chambers, in the *Länder* that are designed in part to relieve the ministries, to which they are responsible, of some administrative tasks. In the process, they are performing indirect *Land* administrative functions. They all have certain common characteristics: required membership; an assembly, directly elected by the members as defined by law; a board elected by the assembly and a professional manager; and a president elected to represent the concerns of the chamber in the broader community.[93]

The chambers can be broken down into various categories. In the economic area, for example, one finds chambers of industry and commerce, chambers of tradesmen/craftsmen, and agricultural chambers. In the area of free professions, there are chambers of attorneys, somewhat comparable to state bar associations in the United States; and chambers of physicians, dentists, pharmacists, architects, and so forth. The chambers see themselves more as agencies assisting the state in numerous administrative tasks than as typical interest groups.[94]

Especially well-known chambers are found in the economic area. Every *Land*, for example, has at least one agricultural chamber, membership in which is required of all farmers. This chamber is financed in part by a modest assessment on the members based on the value of their property and collected by the tax authorities. Some income is received from fees, and at least half to two-thirds of the income comes from the *Land*. The chamber is governed by a policy making assembly, elected by the members, a ceremonial president, and a professional director and his staff. Traditional tasks of promoting agricultural interests are joined by other tasks delegated by the *Land*. The chamber administration has sections for agricultural technology, animal husbandry, training and continuing education, plant and seed protection, forestry, and so forth. It also operates numerous vocational schools and experimental farms.[95]

Two other examples of well-known economic chambers that work with the Ministry of Economics are the Chamber of Tradesmen/Craftsmen and the Industry and Commerce Chamber. Membership in both is required and is represented by an elected assembly and officers. The Chamber of Tradesmen/Craftsmen is responsible for training programs for apprentices and for the examinations that lead to certification as journeymen (*Gesellen*) and master craftsmen. The territory covered by such a chamber usually conforms to that of a government district. The Industry and Commerce Chamber consists of natural persons, commercial enterprises, and legal persons that operate a business in the territory of the chamber. The chamber is financed by set contributions and by assessments based on the volume of sales. Small business members pay no assessment and only one-half of the set contribution. The task of the chamber is to represent the interests of the members as a whole. It provides reports on the status of businesses, sets ethical standards, establishes mediating boards for disagreements among members, takes measures against unfair competition, regulates conditions of sales, and handles consumer complaints. It engages in numerous other activities as well, such as registering business enterprises, certifying various activities, inspecting grocery stores, and providing consulting services. Like the agricultural chambers and the chambers of tradesmen/craftsmen, it is also responsible for training programs and vocational education.[96]

Chambers of the free professions are numerous but not all-encompassing, given the differences that exist among the wide variety of practicing groups. Free professions form chambers because of the special relationship they have with clients or patients, a nonmaterial relationship of trust involving a special responsibility to society. Free professions, in spite of their "freedom" and self-determination, are bound by certain obligations and rules, e.g., formal admission procedures, fee structures, and prohibitions on advertising. All free professions are organized in chambers, membership in which, again, is required. Nevertheless, not all groups are included. Thus in the health professions, there are chambers for physicians and pharmacists, but not for homoeopaths, midwives, dental technicians, and physical therapists. There are chambers for attorneys, notaries, tax advisers, and accountants, but not for business consultants, salesmen, or driver training instructors. Nor are there any chambers for scientific, artistic, educational or journalistic professions.[97]

Universities and specialized schools of higher education (Fachhochschulen)

Institutions of higher education enjoy academic freedom as a constitutional right and have the right of self-government "within the framework of the laws." In general these are *Land* laws, but these reflect the provisions of the Federal University Framework Law of 1976 in the creation of which the *Länder* participated. Thus, while laws vary by *Land*, they share many common features. In Lower Saxony, for example, the Senate, the organ responsible for routine academic affairs, including hiring of faculty, consists of the deans of the schools as a consulting group and four groups who have the decision making powers: professors; students; academic assistants, research aides, etc.; and employees in the technical and administrative services. Actual representation in this "group university" takes place in the proportion of seven professors, two students, two academic aides, and two "others." The concept of the "group university" originated during the late 1960s, when students engaged in a general revolt against older academic structures. At first there were three "groups": faculty, broadly defined; students; and "others," including administrative and technical personnel. Each group had an equal voice. The Federal Constitutional Court ruled in 1973 that the professors must have a majority of the votes in matters involving teaching and research, and the system described briefly above emerged as a result.[98]

The highest official of the university is the president, elected by the *Konzil*, a central university organ consisting of more than 100 faculty, for a term of six years. The *Konzil* also elects the chief administrative officer, the chancellor. Other institutions of higher education, such as the art schools and the specialized colleges (*Fachhochschulen*), are led by a rector, who is elected from the faculty for two years.

The next level of university administration consists of the general subject areas (*Fachbereiche*), roughly similar to schools in the United States, headed by an elected dean who serves a two-year term. Students are automatically members of the "student body" which is represented by a student parliament and a general student committee (*AStA*) that provides a number of student services.[99]

Public radio and television[100]

Since the electronic media fall under the concept of "culture," programming and broadcasting are the responsibility of the *Länder*; however, the federation is responsible for technical matters. Until the mid-to-late 1980s, when private satellite and cable television were introduced after considerable controversy over their potential effects,[101] all radio and television in Germany was public, which meant sponsored by the *Länder*. Each of the individual *Länder* has the right to create its own network, and many have done so. Thus Bavaria, Berlin, Brandenburg, Bremen, Hesse, North-Rhine Westphalia, and the Saarland have their own radio and television networks operated by autonomous boards. The other *Länder* have joined in various combinations to form a joint network. The North German Network consists of Lower Saxony, Hamburg, Schleswig-Holstein, and Mecklenburg-Vorpommern, and the Central German Network is composed of Saxony, Saxony-Anhalt, and Thuringia. In the south of Germany a part of one *Land* (Württemberg) sponsors the South German Network and another part (Baden) has joined with the Rhineland-Palatinate to form the Southwest German Network.[102] In April 1997 these two networks agreed to join into one Southwest German Network.[103] There are ten public broadcasting networks (legally, "institutions") sponsored by the *Länder*. Each network offers its own radio programming over two–eight channels, and each has one regional television channel which it may share in part with other networks.

In 1950 the public broadcasting institutions in the *Länder* formed the Working Group of Broadcasting Institutions (ARD), an "umbrella institution" that runs a nationwide television network known as "the first program" and regional networks referred to collectively as "the third program." A second network for television only is called in German "the second program" (ZDF); it was created in 1961 on the basis of contracts with all of the *Länder* after an attempt by the Adenauer Government to form a federal network was ruled unconstitutional by the Federal Constitutional Court.[104]

All of these networks are financed largely – more than 80 percent – by nonvoluntary fees paid initially via the post office and since 1976 to the License Fee Office (GEZ) operated by the ARD and ZDF. The fees are set by the *Land* parliaments of all the *Länder* and amounted in the late 1990s to DM 28.25 per month (after 2001, DM 33.33) per household for television and radio. The fees are divided by a ratio of 64:36 between the ARD and ZDF. The ARD then transfers funds to the various *Land* networks based on their size. Commercials also provide some income, but they are subject to restrictions; for example, they are limited to 20 minutes a day and are not allowed after 8.00 p.m. or on Sundays and holidays and not at all on the "third program."[105] The financing of the public radio and television networks is a major theme at the prime ministers' conferences.[106]

The networks are operated by a director and supervised by an administrative council of usually eight–ten members and by a larger board consisting of up to fifty representatives from the parties in parliament, arts and sciences, religious groups, management and labor, and social organizations. This internal pluralism is supposed to ensure nonpartisan, comprehensive programming. Just how nonpartisan the politically oriented programs really are is subject to considerable debate, because some are obviously slanted to the left or right. While political parties normally have no more than one-third of the membership, their influence is reflected by other group representatives as well.[107] Nevertheless, "there is obviously a systematic confrontation and counterbalance of political orientations" in the public systems, that is, "*no single political party* has ever enjoyed undue influence over the entire public-service broadcasting system."[108] Therefore, there seems to be little doubt that the networks are basically independent.[109]

ARD and ZDF together offer a cable network, SAT 3, for an additional fee, and they have begun new channels for children and news-oriented programming. They also joined with a French network to offer ARTE, which is more culturally oriented. Networks across Europe have joined in a European Broadcasting Union (EBU) to offer "Euronews" as an alternative to CNN.

There is another public broadcasting network at the national level which is operated by the national government under its authority for foreign affairs. Thus radio and television programs are broadcast to foreign listeners, and while German Radio (*Deutschlandradio*) can be heard also in Germany, the television broadcasts (*Deutsche Welle*) are available only outside the country.

As noted above, private television and radio broadcasting was introduced only in 1984. This created the "dual system" of public and private stations in Germany today.[110] Rather than "peaceful coexistence" between the two systems, controversy has arisen over several issues. In the first place, the public networks, ARD and ZDF, are required to offer complete, high-quality programming. Private channels offering specialized programming or little more than entertainment have attracted large numbers of viewers, and they have also attracted most of the money for commercials. Competition has also led to a dramatic increase in the costs of broadcasting, for example, for major sporting events and movies. These rising costs have placed the public networks at a serious disadvantage

Thus, Radio-Television-Luxemburg (RTL), based in Cologne, appeals especially to younger people and is now the most-watched German television network, with more than 16 percent of market share.[111] Together with SAT 1, which features movies and sports and operates 24 hours a day, these two private channels have as many viewers as the public networks. Indeed, private commercial television now has about 60 percent of the total viewership.[112]

Public savings and loan associations (Sparkassen)
Sparkassen were established in Germany to encourage savings and to provide credit to the local community with particular focus on the middle classes and weaker social groups. The responsible sponsors are larger municipalities and rural counties. They are governed by a council, members of which come from the local elected city or county council, and by a two-member management board elected by the council. They are supervised by the district governments. Together the various *Sparkassen* form a *Land* association under the supervision of the *Land* Minister of Finance.[113]

Foundations
Foundations exist under public, civil, and private law. An example of a private law foundation would be the VW Foundation which promotes research in science and technology. A well-known public foundation under federal law is the Foundation for Prussian Cultural Treasures, which maintains libraries, archives, museums, etc., that belonged to the state of Prussia. An example of a *Land* foundation is the Lower Saxony Foundation that provides financial support for cultural activities that the *Land* does not or cannot finance, in part due to lack of funds. Its endowment comes

from an initial bloc of money received from the *Land*, from gifts from certain large businesses and banks, and from private persons. Foundations are most common with respect to the maintenance of certain churches, monasteries or convents, and to the provision of funds for cultural activities. They were much more common in the past than today.[114]

Water and ground associations

In Lower Saxony, as an example of one *Land*, there are about 2,000 associations that deal with water and ground issues, including drainage, sewerage, and water supply. There are numerous dike associations of which all land owners in certain areas are required to be members. Costs for the dikes and their maintenance are covered by the *Land*; the federal government by way of the federal–*Land* "joint task" responsibility for improving agricultural structures and coastal protection (Article 91a of the Basic Law); and by the property owners. Forestry associations and hunting and fishing associations are supported by the rural counties.[115]

"Borrowed" instruments ("Beliehene")

Certain institutions, groups, or individuals can also be engaged in administration due to some kind of expertise. Chimney sweeps report on fire and building conditions, emissions, and energy use in making their required periodic checks of heating systems in homes and businesses, and property owners are required to correct defects that have been detected. The private technical inspection service (*TÜV*) performs the required biennial inspections of safety conditions of all cars and trucks. And, owing to the nature of their positions, ship captains and airplane pilots can exercise certain state responsibilities for maintaining safety and order.[116] Other examples include game wardens, bankruptcy administrators, some notary publics (specialized attorneys who offer certain key legal services), certified private schools, private welfare providers, and so forth.[117]

Planning in the *Länder*

General

Given the recent experience of the Nazi regime and the then current example of the communist system in East Germany, there was a certain amount of suspicion in the first years of the Federal Republic against planning beyond zoning and budgetary plans. But some planning did exist, for example, in agriculture (*Grüner Plan*), youth affairs (*Bundesju-gendplan*), and with respect to roads, sports, and some other matters. The *Länder* also engaged in some planning, especially for refugees and education. The main characteristics of this first planning phase were isolated sectoral planning; individual infrastructure planning with unsophisticated methodologies and little consideration of financial resources; and little federal–*Land* cooperation.[118]

In the period 1966–69, there was a dramatic change in the attitudes and practices in Germany regarding planning. This was reflected, for example, in the Federal Law of 1967 on the promotion of stability and growth of the economy. This led to framework planning for the entire economy, or "global direction," on the basis of medium-term goal projections and multi-year financial planning at the federal, *Land*, and local levels. It also produced coordinating agencies, such as the financial planning council and the economic cycle council and, finally, the corporatist "concerted action" at the federal level involving consultations among state officials, large firms, and unions.[119]

The Finance Reform of 1969, which brought about several major changes in the Basic Law, included two articles dealing with "joint tasks." Article 91a deals with federal–*Land* cooperation in university construction, improvements in regional economic structures, and improvements in agricultural structures and coastal protection, each of which involves a joint planning committee, medium-term framework planning for investments, and/or subsidies and joint financing. In 1970 a federal–*Land* commission for educational planning was created under Article 91b.

A federal territory planning program was started, and planning staffs and planning groups were established in all of the ministries and in the Chancellory. In the *Länder* work began on "*Land* development plans" and numerous functional and regional plans. In larger cities there were city development plans. Characteristic of this phase was the intensification and perfection of already existing planning efforts, e.g., federal highway planning and *Land* development planning; the introduction of a qualitative new role for financial planning and direction of the economy, and new planning units in the general administration; the securing by legislation of middle-range planning in the areas of finance and joint tasks; and the belief that joint federal–*Land* planning was necessary under "cooperative federalism."[120]

After 1975 there was a period of critical distance from planning, due in part to the oil crises of 1973 and 1980 and rising unemployment. This called more for short-term crisis management than for long-term planning, and it undermined plans already made. Revenues were now below projections and indebtedness rose. New problems, including demographic changes, rising health costs, and environmental concerns led to more skepticism toward planning, and planning staffs were reduced in size and their tasks limited. Planning continued as a routine activity, but ambitious systems of development planning were dropped. Crisis management with narrower concerns and a shorter range of planning became especially prominent at the local level. This has led to a renaissance of functional planning with a reduction in expectations of vertical and sectoral coordination. But in comparison to 1965 there is functional planning in more policy areas than before; it is methodologically more sophisticated; and there is more areal, financial and procedural coordination.[121]

Types of planning

At the federal level, the Basic Law requires or authorizes five kinds of planning: budget planning; finance planning, which is *above all* resource planning but also functional planning; defense planning; framework planning under Article 91a; and educational planning under Article 91b. The latter two will be discussed below, since they involve the federation and the *Länder*.

The *Länder* also engage in budget planning and five-year finance planning by the Minister of Finance. More specific to the *Länder* is functional or sectoral planning for responsibilities such as roads and education (projections of pupils, teachers, building needs) and regional land-use planning. Municipal building and zoning plans must conform to these plans, but local officials have a voice in the process before it is completed.[122]

Regional land-use planning is one of the most important examples of *Land* planning, and it is probably the best example of attempts to coordinate and integrate various sectors of planning sometimes involving federal, *Land*, regional, and municipal efforts.[123] EU planning regulations are also of growing importance, e.g., in highway and railway planning, in nature preservation and the environment in general.[124] An American study of land-use planning in Germany has noted the crucial importance of the constitutional principle of "uniformity [*Einheitlichkeit*] of living conditions" found in Article 72 of the Basic Law for an understanding of such planning.[125] Article 72 is the basis for the federal concurrent legislative authority to pass the federal framework law on land use (*Raumordnungsgesetz* (*ROG*)) of 1997.[126] But land-use planning is also based on the German concept of the "social state."[127]

The ROG provides for vertical coordination of land-use planning among the federal ministry for regional planning and construction, *Land* ministries, and local governments, and for horizontal coordination between the latter two levels. Another means of cooperation and coordination is through various committees and councils, including the conference of *Land* ministers of regional planning. Implementation of the goals of the ROG is the responsibility of the *Land* planning process. *Land* law provides for the organization of planning at the *Land* and local levels. Individual land-use plans established by the *Länder* determine long-term goals and include data on population, employment, economic development, education, transportation, etc. The ROG places particular focus on the environment, including nature preservation. *Land* officials also review local county and city plans and encourage coordination and cooperation.[128]

The most important elements of regional planning today focus on the "central places," i.e., cities and towns that have been selected by the *Länder* as service providers and communication centers for their surrounding areas.[129] These centers are key instruments in achieving the goal of "equivalent" living conditions, because they provide the surrounding areas with the necessary economic, financial, medical, educational, cultural, and other services and opportunities.[130] A somewhat related activity is regional municipal planning, such as that established by Baden-Württemberg in 1994 for the city of Stuttgart and five surrounding counties. Its activities include regional territorial planning, traffic and commuter planning, regional economic and tourism planning, and waste disposal planning. It can require municipalities to formulate local zoning plans in conformity with regional plans. The agency has been given some popular legitimacy via an elected regional assembly consisting of eighty delegates.[131]

The ROG provides for the development of the territory of the Federal Republic so that, among other goals, "uniform" or "equivalent" living conditions will be achieved. As noted in Chapter 2 on the constitutional framework of German federalism, "uniform"– it was changed to "equivalent" in 1994 – did not mean equality in the sense of some kind of leveling process.[132] Rather, these terms meant then and still mean today providing the necessary infrastructure, environmental conditions, employment opportunities, educational and cultural services, etc., that are required of a "social state."[133] Nevertheless, there was misunderstanding of "uniformity," in that some politicians and others interpreted the term too literally.[134] After unification and the recognition of dramatic differences in the living conditions of the eastern and western parts of Germany, it became evident that "uniformity" was misleading at best and that the conditions in the eastern part of united Germany required new thinking.[135] For all of these reasons, the term "uniform" was changed in the constitutional reform process of 1994 to "equivalent," but it is not clear that this change will have much effect. In the meantime there is less emphasis on either term today and increasing use of the concept of "comparable living conditions" for the eastern *Länder*. This discussion has led to considerable controversy, however, because it raises the question of more federal assistance to achieve "equivalent" living conditions at the cost of *Land* autonomy.

Joint task planning

A continuing example of federal–*Land* planning, which is an otherwise generally discouraged example of "mixed administration," can be found in the "joint tasks" provisions of Article 91a and 91b that were described briefly above and in Chapter 2 on the constitutional framework of German federalism.[136] Article 91a and 91b were added to the Basic Law in 1969 as part of the larger Finance Reform of that year, because of the consensus in the German parties that a strict separation between the federation and the *Länder* in a number of areas was no longer appropriate and constitutional reality required cooperation. Article 91a permits the federation to participate in the construction of university facilities, including medical clinics; in the promotion of regional development; and in making improvements in agriculture and coastal protection. It provides for federal financing of 50 percent of university construction and regional development and 50 percent or more of agriculture improvements and coastal protection. In practice the federation's share has been 60 and 70 percent, respectively, for these latter two areas.[137]

This cooperation requires joint planning between the federal and *Land* governments, the procedures for which are provided in three federal implementation laws passed by the *Bundestag* and *Bundesrat*. Each of the three areas designated as a joint task has a planning committee. The members are the federal and *Land* cabinet ministers responsible for the subject matter of each committee, together with the federal finance minister. The federation has sixteen votes, which must be cast as a bloc, and each *Land* has one vote. A majority consists of the votes of the federation and a majority of the *Länder*. The plans developed and approved are, however, framework plans; detailed planning is left to the *Länder*, as are all other executive functions connected with the joint task in question.[138]

Once the joint framework plans have been approved, the governments in effect are bound to include the measures in their next budget. This, of course, presupposes parliamentary approval. Approval can be denied, but there is a common trust that each government will be able to abide by the bargain. On the other hand, a *Land* can refuse to implement the actions in its territory, or it can go beyond the agreed plan as long as its actions are not in conflict with the provisions of the plan. Budgetary autonomy is upheld in that the amounts approved are decided by the parliaments, but they cannot in good faith cut off funds to the extent that action is undermined. Once the budget is approved, the *Land* or federation is committed. Problems can arise when municipalities have plans that are not in conformity with the general plan, in which case the *Land* may be required to interfere based on its right of legal supervision of local actions.[139]

While Article 91a *mandates* federal–*Land* cooperation, Article 91b *authorizes* it in the areas of educational planning and in the promotion of research institutions and plans that are of general or national importance. As in the case of Article 91a, Article 91b provides a constitutional foundation for cooperative practices (*zusammenwirken*) that were already taking place. For example, the German Education Council (*Bildungsrat*) was formed in 1965, while the Science Council (*Wissenschaftsrat*) was created as early as 1957.[140]

Article 91b was added to the Basic Law at a time when there was a great deal of confidence in and enthusiasm for planning in general. A Federal–*Land* Commission for educational planning and promotion of research was formed in 1970, and it set about to create a "joint long-term framework plan for a coordinated development of the entire educational system" together with a joint educational budget.[141] For a variety of reasons, including conflicts between the national government and *Land* governments, partisan conflicts, and financial considerations, the planning process proved to be more complicated than had been anticipated in 1970. While there was agreement on a Framework Plan in 1973, it did not result in exercising any "significant influence in controlling and coordinating the political activities of the individual *Länder*."[142] In the meantime economic conditions had changed in Germany, partisan conflict in various areas increased, and general educational planning under Article 91b ended altogether in 1982, largely for partisan and financial reasons. Once the more conservative Christian Democrats and Liberals replaced the more planning-oriented Social Democrats in the national government in October 1982, the downsized Commission began serving as a forum for discussion between the national government and the *Länder* rather than as an agency for planning.[143]

In the case of Article 91b, federal–*Land* educational planning may have failed,[144] but cooperation continues in other areas. Cooperation in scientific research, which would normally be a *Land* responsibility, has an important national purpose and continues unabated, as is seen, for example, in joint support efforts for the Max-Planck Institutes and the German Research Association (*Deutsche Forschungsgemeinschaft*).[145] Indeed, a so-called "Blue List" contains the names of about fifty research institutions and museums that fall under Article 91b.[146]

As was noted in Chapter 2 on the constitutional framework of German federalism and will be noted in Chapter 5 on finances, there has been a good deal of criticism of Article 91a and 91b and the joint tasks they authorize. Probably the most fundamental and certainly the best known is the criticism by Fritz Scharpf, who notes that there is a tendency in joint programs which are based on unanimous or near-unanimous decision making to involve a "joint-decision trap" which leads to a number of undesirable consequences, including increased expenditures.[147] Other criticisms include the argument that the *Land* parliaments are too little involved; that the federation has too much say in the financing of projects; and that the "mixed administration" involved violates the principle of division of powers between responsibility for legislation by the federation and for administration by the *Länder*. In reaction to these and other criticisms, the argument can be made that planning is in principle an executive function in which the parliaments are not well equipped to participate but can, instead, control to some extent; on the other hand, the *Länder* now give their framework plans to their parliaments before presentation in the joint commissions, and at the federal level the Ministry of Agriculture shows its plans to the Agriculture Committee of the *Bundestag* during the planning process so that questions regarding the framework plan can be raised in time for some parliamentary control. One response to the criticism that mixed administration violates the Basic Law is that the constitution does not require a strict separation of functions between the federation and the *Länder*.[148]

Public employees

Classification

In 1997 there were about 4.6 million public employees in Germany in direct administration and excluding former employees of public enterprises, e.g., railway workers (Tables 3.1, 3.2). This represents a little more than 12 percent of the total work force. Public employees are divided into two general classifications. One is the long-established division among civil servants (*Beamte*); salaried employees (*Angestellten*); and blue-collar workers (*Arbeiter*). The other classification is the division of the above categories into the simple (*einfachen*), the middle (*mittleren*), the elevated (*gehobenen*), and the higher (*höhere*) service levels. For the higher service level a university background is required, usually a law degree but increasingly a degree in economics;[149] for the elevated service, the selective secondary school degree (*Abitur*) and, increasingly, a special- ized college background (*Fachhochschule*) is the normal precondition. The middle level usually requires the *mittlere Reife*, roughly equivalent to an average American high school degree. There are no special educational

Table 3.1 **Basic categories of public employees in direct administration in Germany, 1999**

	Federation	*Länder*	Municipalities	Special counties	Total districts
Full-time					
Civil Servants/Judges/					
Soldiers[a] (*Beamte*)	316,064	1,025,346	158,625	2,430	1,502,465
Salaried employees					
(*Angestellte*)	84,005	615,739	652,396	33,614	1,385,754
Blue-collar workers					
(*Arbeiter*)	79,049	125,284	251,163	17,547	473,043
Part-time					
Civil servants/Judges/					
Soldiers (*Beamte*)	6,914	231,239	17,206	170	255,529
Salaried employees					
(*Angestellte*)	19,231	286,600	307,539	12,474	625,844
Blue-collar workers					
(*Arbeiter*)	4,956	27,895	150,450	6,441	189,742
Total full and part-time					
Beamte					1,757,994
Total full- and part-time					
Angestellte					2,011,598
Total *Arbeiter*					662,785

Note: [a] Career and longer-serving soldiers only (c. 60 per cent of total Federal *Beamte*).
Source: Adapted from Federal Statistical Office, *Statistical Yearbook 2000* (Stuttgart: Metzler-Poeschel, 2000), p. 516.

Table 3.2 Classification of basic categories of public employees in Germany, 1998

Full and part time (%)	Federation		Länder		Municipalities/ counties		Special districts		Total	
	FT	PT	FT	PT	FT	PT	FT	PT	FT	PT
Civil Servants/Judges/ Soldiers[a] (*Beamte*)	318,925	4,859	1,038,010	218,418	160,653	15,428	2,415	145	1,520,003	238,850
Higher service	30,486	867	293,799	46,615	24,869	1,635	617	39	349,771	49,156
Elevated service	61,867	2,332	492,274	151,834	81,464	8,727	1,204	61	636,809	162,954
Middle service	184,447	1,587	243,190	19,770	53,641	5,046	554	45	481,832	26,448
Simple service	42,125	73	8,747	199	679	20	40	–	51,591	292
Salaried Employees (*Angestellte*)	88,018	17,443	661,169	228,009	684,833	262,324	31,394	9,260	1,465,414	517,036
Higher service	5,422	1,008	136,757	43,914	49,512	6,623	3,785	254	195,476	51,799
Elevated service	15,296	1,247	201,675	70,368	169,957	34,726	8,022	1,206	394,950	107,547
Middle service	65,282	14,610	309,116	110,226	445,322	212,772	18,628	7,451	838,348	345,059
Simple service	2,018	578	13,621	3,501	13,818	8,203	959	349	30,416	12,631
Blue-collar workers (*Arbeiter*)	81,767	3,913	134,265	24,309	270,367	115,389	16,765	3,948	503,164	147,559

Note: [a] Career and longer-serving soldiers only.
Source: Based on Federal Statistical Office, *Statistical Yearbook 2000* (Stuttgart: Metzler-Poeschel, 2000), p. 517.

requirements for the simple service levels, but previous training in an apprenticeship (*Lehre*) in a practical subject may be an expectation. Continuing education courses are increasingly common, especially in the first two categories.[150] There is little opportunity for promotion without having met the educational requirements, regardless of the quality of performance on the job – although this has changed somewhat in recent decades. This is not much different from the private sector, where "certification" is also very important in determining opportunities for advancement. It is one reason for the enormous increase in student numbers in Germany since the late 1960s. Since the numbers of university graduates has multiplied, there are far more applicants than available positions in the higher service, so that graduates have moved into the elevated and even the middle levels since the 1970s. By the 1980s a trend could be seen toward an increase in the numbers of the two higher levels, while the middle level stagnated and the lower level was declining. Only then were efforts undertaken to place more limits on the previously generous promotion policies within the top two levels.[151]

On the other hand the proportions of civil servants, salaried employees, and workers have been relatively constant over the past decades if one counts the blue-collar workers in the federal railway and postal services before they were privatized in the mid-1990s. Both civil servants and salaried employees can be in the higher, elevated, and middle services. For example, police employees, firemen, and even locomotive engineers are civil servants, as are teachers, professors and bureaucrats in higher administrative positions; however, these civil servants vary in status and pay by level of service.

The Basic Law divides the authority for regulating civil servants and the other public employees between the federation and the *Länder*. If in the federal service, civil servants are regulated by federal law; otherwise, the federation has only framework powers under Article 75, para. 1. In 1971 the Basic Law was amended (Article 74a) to permit the federal government to pass legislation regulating the pay and benefits of all civil servants. This was done with the approval of the *Länder* in the *Bundesrat*, because they were interested in reducing the salary competition that had emerged among the *Länder* in spite of the federal civil service framework law of 1957 which left the *Land* parliaments little leeway in regulating their civil servants.[152] This action is cited often as an example of the *Länder* giving up voluntarily certain important powers that they once possessed.

There has been considerable discussion during the past decades and again today about the rationale for preserving the difference between civil servants and salaried employees.[153] Some politicians and others, especially on the left of the political spectrum, would like to change the status of certain classes of *Beamten* to *Angestellten*.[154] Others defend the current system and for a variety of reasons are strongly opposed to any basic changes.[155] Owing to their exercise of "autonomous public functions" (*hoheitsrechtlicher Befugnisse*), the civil servants are said to have certain characteristics that, taken together, distinguish them from other public servants:

- The civil servants have no right to strike, which is important in times of crisis. Civil servants may be called upon to substitute for personnel in the other levels if and when they go on strike.
- The civil servants, owing to their positions of trust, must not demonstrate any disloyalty to the constitutional order.
- Civil servants are life-time public servants, whose career status provides them with independence; this does not exclude probationary periods to determine suitability for office. Temporary positions also exist, but they are of questionable legality or appropriateness.
- Civil servants may be expected to work overtime and must observe certain rules of behavior in their private lives.[156]

Loyalty expectations

Today the second characteristic noted above is much less relevant than before the collapse of communism in East Germany and throughout eastern Europe. Loyalty expectations have always existed in the German civil service as they have in other countries, but during the Weimar Republic of 1919–33 the democratic state was confronted by many civil servants who were not loyal to the Constitution. As a result the Basic Law specifies in Article 5, para. 3, that while "art and science, research and teaching are free," the "freedom to teach does not release one from loyalty to the constitution." And Article 33, paras 4 and 5, have been interpreted to mean that those who enter the civil service must be loyal to the Federal Republic. Thus federal laws regulating the civil service have stated that only persons may become civil servants "who can be depended upon at all times to stand up for the free, democratic basic order in terms of the Basic Law." Although there was some controversy after the establishment of the Federal Republic concerning the employment of persons alleged to have served the Nazis,[157] it was not until the late 1960s and early 1970s that these provisions became an important public issue. It was then that student radicals, heavily influenced by Marxist thought, began to threaten to "march through the institutions" of the Federal Republic and bring about some form of revolutionary change. To keep extremists from the right and – especially – left from entering the civil service, Chancellor Willy Brandt and the prime ministers of the *Länder* agreed in 1972–73 to a set of principles that called for a review by the *Land* offices of constitutional protection of every applicant for a civil service position, including teachers. These procedures caused a great deal of controversy among the attentive public and politicians at the federal and *Land* levels, criticism from abroad,[158] and massive opposition by students, very few of whom were actually rejected.[159] By the time the Wall fell in November 1989, some of the *Länder* governed by the SPD had ceased participating in the reviews entirely or in part.[160] Since the collapse of communism in the East, the reviews have been dropped and the issue practically forgotten. It is not surprising, then, that new questions have been raised about maintaining the differences between civil servants and salaried employees.

Political patronage

Another controversy of much longer duration and relevance today is political patronage. The model civil servant is often seen as the competent, loyal, and allegedly neutral Prussian bureaucrat in the nineteenth century and before the First World War. It has been pointed out, however, that civil servants at that time were recruited with a strong bias toward social class and conservative, pro-monarchist sentiments.[161] Complaints about party patronage in the Weimar Republic after 1919 tended to ignore the issue of loyalty of many public officials to the monarchy rather than to the new republic.[162]

In the United States the Hatch Act of 1939 prevents civil servants from participating actively in partisan politics, and there is a long tradition of a nonpartisan civil service in Great Britain. This has not been the German tradition. Civil servants not only participate actively in partisan politics, they are one of the most important groups from which elected officials are recruited. (One should keep in mind that teachers and professors are also civil servants in Germany, and, as in France, a large proportion of the civil servants in German legislative assemblies at all levels are teachers.) The involvement of German public employees in politics also raises questions about the neutrality of the civil service. Since the 1950s, there have been complaints about the importance of a "party book," i.e, membership in a political party, for securing higher-level civil service as well as salaried employee positions in federal, *Land*, and local administrative structures, including local government commercial enterprises, public radio and television boards, local savings and loan associations, and, of course, city government.[163] On the other hand,

> [p]arty patronage in the immediate post-war years had both moral and very practical functions. It could be regarded as the best indicator of regime loyalty in bureaucratic recruitment and promotions . . . [Parties] had already emerged as undisputably the most 'reliable' institutions, and membership of a party licensed by the Allies was the most tangible sign of democratic commitment.[164]

Some German authors have also pointed to the positive binding of the civil service to society and to democratic parties after 1945 as one reason for politicization of the bureaucracy.[165]

Some critics accuse the German parties of being "patronage parties" rather reminiscent of the American Tammany Hall model.[166] However, there are several important differences. First, the alleged corruption in Germany is of a very different order and extent from the American model. Another difference is that there was little ideology involved in the American spoils system, whereas ideology has been an element of patronage politics in Germany. A third difference is that "the career principle was modified (not displaced) in the interests of party control" in Germany, that is, "neither side expects administrative rules to be broken solely for reasons of political pressure or expediency."[167]

The Tammany Hall analogy suggests itself because there is probably more patronage at the local level than elsewhere,[168] although the higher *Land* levels are hardly exempt.[169] Evidence suggests, however, that the patronage at the federal level is modest in comparison to American practices. As Renate Mayntz has noted, "In Germany most high-level vacancies continue to be filled by career civil servants even though it is understood that political criteria can play a legitimate role in recruiting outsiders to high positions in the federal bureaucracy."[170]

While there is little disagreement that party membership can be a factor in gaining higher- level civil service positions at the federal, *Land*, and local levels, there is disagreement about whether party patronage is really a new phenomenon, the reasons why it exists, the extent to which it exists, and whether this is so very objectionable. As noted above, the argument that the Prussian bureaucracy was strictly neutral is a myth. In contrast to the many voices condemning party patronage at the federal, *Land*, and especially local levels and the argument by some constitutional lawyers that it is unconstitutional under Article 33,[171] other scholars have noted that there are good reasons for the practice. As noted above, civil servants in Germany, in contrast to their American and British counterparts, may and do participate actively in politics as members of parties, as candidates, and as elected officials.[172] Defenders also point out that while there may be some abuses, civil servants have an advantage in information and knowledge that can make it difficult for elected politicians to control them. To compensate for this advantage, politicians seek to gain control over the bureaucracy by insuring that persons friendly to them are appointed to key positions. They also need cooperative civil servants in drafting policy initiatives in conformity with their party programs, i.e., promises made to their voters. This is in part a result of the fact that political executives in Germany do not have large personal staffs and must rely on the civil servants for help.[173] Questions can also be raised about the imprecision of the concept of patronage, and it has been noted that there is little empirical evidence for many of the general complaints made about patronage.[174]

Where evidence does exist about federal- and *Land*-level patronage, it applies above all to the highest civil service levels which consist largely of so-called "political officials" (*politische Beamte*) who are mostly career civil servants who occupy key positions and may be forced to accept temporary retirement for political reasons; however, only a small minority of about 10 percent are actually dismissed. Another, much smaller category, consists of the parliamentary state secretaries, who are members of the *Bundestag* and may answer questions for their minister at question time and perform other, more political, functions. They have existed only since 1967, in contrast to the "political officials," who go back to mid-nineteenth-century Prussia.[175]

Public sector unions

As we saw above, civil servants, regardless of service level, are not allowed to strike due to their status under public law as persons serving the state in special positions of authority that require trust and loyalty. Salaried employees and workers may strike and have done so on several occasions since the 1950s. The significant gains made in benefits, salaries, and employment conditions for these two groups have, of course, affected the civil servants as well. The result was a steady increase in personnel costs in proportion to total public expenditures and GNP. Today personnel costs in the old *Länder* average around 40 percent of their budgets. With growing financial stress in the public sector since the 1980s, however, the real increase in salaries and benefits has been more modest. Nevertheless, the resistance of the public service unions to privatization efforts suggests that public employees are still relatively well off in comparison to the private sector, especially in terms of job security.[176]

Federal and state civil servants do have their own union: the German Civil Servants Federation (*Deutscher Beamten Bund, DBB*). The DBB may not exercise the strike weapon, but it has excellent contacts with legislators at the *Land* and federal levels, many of whom are themselves former civil servants, e.g., school teachers, university employees, judges, police, various bureaucratic staff, etc., and have the right to return to their old positions if they give up their seats for whatever reason. This represents a striking difference to the United States, where civil servants are not allowed to engage openly in partisan politics or hold public office. Of course some civil servants in Germany would not be considered to be part of the civil service in the United States, e.g., school teachers and university employees.

The salaried employees (*Angestellten*) are represented by the German Salaried Employees Union (*Deutscher Angestellten Gewerkschaft, DAG*)or by several unions organized in the Federation of German Unions, i.e., the Public Transportation Union (*Öffentliche Transport und Verkehr, ÖTV*); the postal union; the railway workers union; or one of several competing teachers' unions, the Union for Education and Science. In 1961 the DAG and ÖTV negotiated the Federal Salaried Employees Compensation Contract (BAT) with the federal government, the Joint Salary Commission of the German *Länder*, and the Association of Local Government Employers.

This contract, which still generally applies today, set salary schedules and provided for various benefits that closed considerably the gap between salaried employees and civil servants. For example, civil servants can be relieved of their positions only for cause, and according to this contract the same protection applies to salaried employees after fifteen years.[177] In July 2001 the largest union in the world, the united services union, or "ver.di", was formed by joining five separate unions: the DAG; ÖTV; the Union for Commerce, Banks, and Insurance; the postal union; and the media union.[178]

In addition to traditional union representation, civil servants and salaried employees also have the right to elect representatives to the "personnel councils"(*Personalräte*) of their agencies or offices which are comparable to the "works councils"(*Betriebsräte*) in the private sector that were introduced by a federal "codetermination" (*Mitbestimmung*) law in the coal and steel industry in the 1950s. These councils are important bodies, because they must be consulted by management in all personnel matters. This, of course, places certain constraints on the ability of managers in the public and private sectors to make personnel decisions, but the experience in most cases seems to be that relationships are based more on cooperation rather than confrontation.

Conclusion

The "state" in Germany is either the federation or the *Land,* depending on the context in which the term is used. Either can administer policies directly. For example, the federal government is involved in administration directly and "on its own" through a number of special agencies, such as the Federal Statistical Office and the Federal Criminal Investigation Office. It shares with the *Länder* the direct administration of finances. The *Länder* also have direct "own" administration through their special agencies, such as criminal investigation offices, statistical offices, and finance offices along with many others that fall under the direct authority of a *Land* ministry. Either state may also delegate policies to different bodies for indirect administration. Thus the federal government has the *Länder* administer the autobahns and numerous other federal tasks; but the federal government also turns over to the *Länder* many more tasks that they then administer on their *own* responsibility, not merely as delegated federal responsibilities. The *Länder* on their part delegate some tasks to the local governments for administration and turn over a great many other functions to the local governments for "indirect" administration on their own responsibility as self-governing units. As a result it is estimated that the local governments administer 75 percent or more of all laws in Germany. But the federation and the *Länder* also turn over many responsibilities to nongovernmental bodies, such as institutions, chambers, universities, and other agencies for indirect administration.

If the policy is delegated, the "state" exercises functional and personnel supervision over those actually implementing it. If the policy has been turned over to others as matters of their own responsibility, only legal supervision by higher authorities takes place. The most common example of legal supervision is that by the *Länder* over their local governments, which have the constitutional right of self-government.

The legal persons that administer "state" functions indirectly are various kinds of public corporations, such as local governments, social insurance providers, and numerous chambers; institutions, such as the public savings and loan associations and public radio and television networks; and foundations, such as those that administer certain cultural facilities or activities.[179]

Indirect administration can also be carried out by private persons, as, for example, by chimney sweeps and the technical inspection service (TÜV). Indirect administration works against the ideal of unity of command, but centrifugal forces are countered by many formal and informal centripetal forces.[180]

Even though Germany is a two-tier federation, one can speak of three levels of administration: the federal, *Land,* and local levels. But most of the *Länder* also have three levels – high, middle, and local – whereas Berlin and five of the generally smaller territorial *Länder* have two levels and Bremen and Hamburg have basically only one. To complicate matters further, one should note that the rural counties and their towns and villages constitute two levels, so that the larger *Länder* have four levels: *Land,* middle, county, and municipalities that constitute the counties. With the federation, this brings the total number of levels to five, unless one wants to count as separate levels the supreme and high levels, respectively, of the federation and the *Länder,* which is not normally done.[181]

In spite of the apparent complexity of administrative structures, administration in Germany is based on certain fundamental principles along with numerous exceptions that apply for mostly pragmatic reasons. The first principle is that the federal state is responsible for most legislation, the *Länder* for most administration. A second principle is unity of command, i.e., the attempt to combine administrative functions in one unit. At the supreme levels of the federation and the *Länder,* the Ministry of Interior bundles together numerous functions, while the government districts at the middle level in eight *Länder* serve as classic examples of unity of command. Other classic examples are the rural counties and, especially, the county-free cities. A third principle is decentralized administration based on the principle of self-government subject only to legal supervision by the state. Here the classic examples are administration by the *Länder* of numerous federal laws and administration by the local governments of most federal and *Land* laws, many of which are based on federal laws. Examples of nongovernmental institutions carrying out federal and *Land* laws on their own responsibility are social insurance providers and chambers. A fourth principle might be seen in the *Allzuständigkeit,* the general powers, of the municipalities, in contrast to the limiting principle of *ultra vires* in the United States; however, the general powers of the local governments have in fact been circumscribed by federal and *Land* laws. In any case it is possible to speak of a "system" of administration in federal Germany – as in unitary France – to a much greater extent than in the United States.

Notes

1 A friend of UK Prime Minister Attlee's, Professor William A. Robson (*Political Quarterly* 16, 1945), asserted that traditional German local government had a number of undemocratic features and therefore needed radical reform. The result of his criticism was the North German Council form of local government with city and county managers appointed by the local elected councils after the manner of the English chief clerk. It is not a little ironic that this system was largely abandoned in the mid-1990s, because it was not deemed sufficiently democratic by German critics. See Georg-Christoph von Unruh, "Die Lage der deutschen Verwaltung zwischen 1945 und 1949," in *Deutsche Verwaltungsgeschichte*, vol. 5, edited by Kurt G. A. Jeserich, Hans Pohl, and Georg Christian von Unruh (Stuttgart: Deutsche Verlags-Anstalt, 1987), p. 79. See also Wolfgang Rudzio, *Die Neuordnung des Kommunalwesens in der Britischen Zone* (Stuttgart: Deutsche Verlag Anstalt, 1968), pp. 43–45 and Arthur B. Gunlicks, *Local Government in the German Federal System* (Chapel Hill: Duke University Press, 1986), p. 28.
2 Rainer Wahl, "Die Organisation und Entwicklung der Verwaltung in den *Ländern* und in Berlin," in Jeserich *et al.*, *Deutsche Verwaltungsgeschichte*, vol. 5, p. 216.
3 Potsdam Agreement, sec. 2, para. 9.
4 Wahl, "Die Organisation und Entwicklung," p. 217.
5 In the nineteenth century the *Landrat* was the appointed chief administrative officer of the Prussian county. See Herbert Jacob, *German Administration since Bismarck: Central Authority versus Local Autonomy* (New Haven: Yale University Press, 1963), pp. 15–16.
6 Von Unruh, "Die Lage," p. 71.
7 Gunlicks, *Local Government*, Ch. 4, and, by the same author, "The Reorganization of Local Governments in the Federal Republic of Germany," in *Local Government Reform and Reorganization: An International Perspective*, edited by Arthur B. Gunlicks (Port Washington: Kennikat Press, 1981), pp. 169–181. In the same publication, see also Raymond C. McDermott, "The Functions of Local Levels of Government in West Germany and their Internal Organization" in ibid., pp. 182–201.
8 Wahl, "Die Organisation und Entwicklung," p. 217.
9 Ibid., p. 213.
10 Lerche in Theodor Maunz *et al.*, *Kommentar zum Grundgesetz* (München: C.H. Beck'sche Verlagsbuchhandlung, 1989), Article 83, Rdnr 14.

11 Albert von Mutius, "Kommunalverwaltung und Kommunalpolitik," in Jeserich *et al.*, *Deutsche Verwaltungsgeschichte,* vol. V, pp. 328–329.

12 Ibid., p. 329.

13 Hartmut Maurer, *Allgemeines Verwaltungsrecht* (12th edn; München: C. H. Beck'sche Verlagsbuchhandlung, 1999), p. 543.

14 Ibid.

15 Walter Rudolf, "Verwaltungsorganisation," in *Allgemeines Verwaltungsrecht,* edited by Hans-Uwe Erichsen (10th edn; Berlin and New York: Walter de Gruyter, 1995), pp. 722–723.

16 Maurer, *Allgemeines Verwaltungsrecht,* p. 544.

17 Ibid., p. 544 and Rudolf, "Verwaltungsorganisation," pp. 722–723.

18 Rudolf, "Verwaltungsorganisation," pp. 723–724.

19 Fred Schneider, "Das Bundesversicherungsamt und seine Aufgaben," *Die Sozialgerichtsbarkeit* 43, no. 2 (February 1996), pp. 45–48.

20 Rudolf, "Verwaltungsorganisation," pp. 723–726.

21 These privatizations were, in German terms, organizational, not material, i.e., the federal government became the only stockholder. Short-distance routes of the German railroads have already been divided into regions, with local governments as owners, while the long-distance trains remain for the time being under the ownership of the federal government. There are plans to transfer after 2003 all mail services except for letters up to 50 g to the private sector.

22 Maurer, *Allgemeines Verwaltungsrecht,* p. 544.

23 Ibid., p. 548.

24 Rudolf, "Verwaltungsorganisation," pp. 726–727.

25 Maurer, *Allgemeines Verwaltungsrecht,* p. 535–536.

26 Ibid., p. 545.

27 Willi Blümel, "Verwaltungszuständigkeit," in *Handbuch des Staatsrechts der Bundesrepublik Deutschland,* edited by Josef Isensee and Paul Kirchhof, vol. IV, pp. 935–938.

28 Maurer, *Allgemeines Verwaltungsrecht,* p. 546.

29 Ibid., pp. 548–549.

30 Rudolf, Verwaltungsorganisation," p. 727.

31 Alfred Katz, *Politische Verwaltungsführung in den Bundesländern* (Berlin: Duncker & Humblot, 1975), p. 94.

32 For a discussion of the coordination activities of the prime ministers' staffs, see Klaus-Eckart Gebauer, "Zur Optimierung von Koordination und Planung in einer Regierungszentrale," *Verwaltungs-Archiv* 85, no. 4 (1 October 1994), pp. 485–506.

33 Wahl, "Die Organisation und Entwicklung," p. 226.

34 Gebauer, "Zur Optimierung," pp. 507–519.

35 Manfred König, "Leistungsorganisation der Verwaltung," in *Öffentliche Verwaltung in Deutschland,* edited by Klaus König and Heinrich Siedentopf

(Baden-Baden: Nomos Verlagsgesellschaft, 1996), pp. 604–605.

36 Wahl, "Die Organisation und Entwicklung," p. 223.

37 Ibid., pp. 224–225.

38 Burckhard Nedden, "Verwaltungsorganisation," in Heiko Faber and Hans-Peter Schneider (eds), *Niedersächsiches Staats- und Verwaltungsrecht* (Frankfurt/M.: Alfred Metzner Verlag, 1985), p. 124.

39 Wahl, "Die Organisation und Entwicklung," pp. 219–220.

40 Ibid., pp. 221–222.

41 Maurer, *Allgemeines Verwaltungsrecht*, pp. 536–537.

42 Wahl, "Die Organisation und Entwicklung," pp. 237–238.

43 Ibid., p. 228 and Theodor Elster, "Die Verwaltung," in *Verfassung und Verwaltung des Landes Niedersachsen*, edited by Heinrich Korte, Bernd Rebe, *et al.* (2nd edn; Göttingen: Vandenhoeck & Ruprecht, 1986), p. 369.

44 Wahl, "Die Organisation und Entwicklung," pp. 228, 230.

45 Elster, "Die Verwaltung," pp. 325–327.

46 Frido Wagener, "Milderungsmöglichkeiten nachteiligen Folgen vertikaler Politikverflechtung," in *Politikverflechtung im föderativen Staat*, edited by Joachim Hans Hesse (Baden-Baden: Nomos Verlagsgesellschaft, 1978), pp. 149–165 and "Gemeinsame Rahmenplanung und Investitionsfinanzierung," *Die Öffentliche Verwaltung* 30, no. 16 (August 1977), p. 588.

47 Wahl, "Die Organisationund Entwicklung," p. 236.

48 Elster, "Die Verwaltung," pp. 369, 470–471.

49 Ibid., p. 370 and Wahl, "Die Organisation und Entwicklung," p. 229; for lists of the numerous special authorities at the district government and local levels in Lower Saxony, see Nedden, "Verwaltungsorganisation," pp. 131–133.

50 Elster, "Die Verwaltung," pp. 382–383; Wahl, "Die Organisation und Entwicklung," pp. 237–238.

51 Ibid., pp. 385–408.

52 Gesetzentwurf: Landesgesetz zur Reform und Neuorganisation der Landesverwaltung, 31 March 1999, Drucksache 13/4168 (Rheinland-Pflalz).

53 Wahl, "Die Organisation und Entwicklung," pp. 227–230.

54 Rudolf, "Verwaltungsorganisation," p. 728.

55 Wahl, "Die Organisation und Entwicklung," p. 231.

56 Elster, "Die Verwaltung," p. 371.

57 The *Stadtkreis* should not be confused with the *Kreisstadt*, which is the county seat.

58 Elster, "Die Verwaltung," pp. 424–425, 440–441.

59 Rudolf, "Verwaltungsorganisation," p. 736.

60 Maurer, *Allgemeines Verwaltungsrecht*, p. 539 and Rudolf, "Verwaltungsorganisation," p. 730.

61 Elster, "Die Verwaltung," pp. 372–373.

62 For a description in English of the South German Council, the Mayor, the Magistrat, and the North German Council forms of municipal government,

see Gunlicks, *Local Government,* pp. 73–81; see also Maurer, *Allgemeines Verwaltungsrecht,* pp. 556–560 and Rudolf, "Verwaltungsorganisation," pp. 732–734; for diagrams of the forms of local government, see Bernd Becker, *Öffentliche Verwaltung: Lehrbuch für Wissenschaft und Praxis* (Verlag R. S. Schulz, 1989), pp. 344–350 and Joachin Jens Hesse and Thomas Ellwein, *Das Regierungssystem der Bundesrepublik Deutschland, vol. 2: Materialien* (7th edn; Opladen: Westdeutscher Verlag, 1992), pp. 467–470.

63 Rudolf, "Verwaltungsorganisation," p. 734 and Maurer, *Allgemeines Verwaltungsrecht,* pp. 558–559. Franz-Ludwig Knemeyer, "Verfassung der kommunalen Selbstverwaltung," in König and Siedentopf, *Öffentliche Verwaltung in Deutschland,* pp. 208 and 213, suggests that the South German Council form, now the most common in Germany, should be called the Dual Council–Mayor form.

64 Maurer, *Allgemeines Verwaltungsrecht,* p. 567.

65 Ibid., pp. 567–568; Elster, "Die Verwaltung," pp. 415–416.

66 Ibid. and ibid., pp. 416–419.

67 Maurer, *Allgemeines Verwaltungsrecht,* pp. 571–573.

68 Ibid., pp. 539–540 and Elster, "Die Verwaltung," p. 730; Wahl, "Die Organisation und Entwicklung," p. 233.

69 Wahl, "Die Organisation und Entwicklung," p. 232.

70 Rudolf, "Verwaltungsorganisation," p. 732.

71 Ursula Münch, *Sozialpolitik und Föderalismus: Zur Dynamik der Aufgabenverteilung im sozialen Bundesstaat* (Opladen: Leske & Budrich, 1997), pp. 232–246.

72 Ruland, Franz, "Sozialrecht," in *Niedersächsisches Staats- und Verwaltungsrecht,* edited by Heiko Faber und Hans-Peter Schneider (Frankfurt/M.: Alfred Metzner Verlag, 1985), pp. 507–508; Günter Happe, "Jugend- und Familienhilfe," in *Deutsche Verwaltungsgeschichte,* vol. V, pp. 596.

73 Elster, "Die Verwaltung," p. 418.

74 Rudolf, "Verwaltungsorganisation," pp. 734–735; Maurer, *Allgemeines Verwaltungsrecht,* pp. 575–576.

75 Maurer, *Allgemeines Verwaltungsrecht,* pp. 575–576.

76 Frido Wagener and Willi Blümel, "Staatsaufbau und Verwaltungsterritorien," in König and Siedentopf, *Öffentliche Verwaltung in Deutschland,* pp. 118–119.

77 Wahl, "Die Organisation und Entwicklung," pp. 283–284; Reinhold Roth, "Bremen," in *Handbuch der deutschen Bundesländer,* edited by Falk Esche and Jürgen Hartmann (Frankfurt: Campus Verlag, 1990), p. 171.

78 Wahl, "Die Organisation und Entwicklung," pp. 289–292 and Roth, "Bremen," p. 187.

79 Peter Massing, "Berlin," in Esche and Hartmann, *Handbuch der deutschen Bundesländer,* p. 134 and Karsten Sommer, "Die Berliner Verwaltung nach Vereinigung, Hauptstadtbeschluß, und Verwaltungsreform," *Juristische*

Rundschau, no. 10 (October 1995), p. 397.

80 Sommer, "Die Berliner Verwaltung," pp. 399–402.

81 Massing, "Berlin," p. 148; Roth, "Bremen," p. 185; Falk Esche and Jürgen Hartmann, "Hamburg," in Esche and Hartmann, *Handbuch der deutschen Bundesländer*, p. 213.

82 For a list by *Land* of special nonministerial organizational units, see Becker, *Öffentliche Verwaltung in Deutschland*, pp. 325–327.

83 Wahl, "Die Organisation und Entwicklung," pp. 237–238.

84 Ibid., pp. 239–240.

85 Walter Krebs, "Verwaltungsorganisation," *Handbuch des Staatsrechts der Bundesrepublik Deutschland*, vol. III, edited by Josef Isensee and Paul Kirchhof (Heidelberg: C. F. Müller Juristischer Verlag, 1988), pp. 585–587.

86 For a brief overview of social insurance administration, see Dieter Schimanke, "Selbstverwaltung außerhalb der Kommunalverwaltung, insbesondere: Selbstverwaltung in der Sozialversicherung," in König and Siedentopf, *Öffentliche Verwaltung in Deutschland*, pp. 257–268. For a description in English by Alfred Pfaller of "The German Welfare State After National Unification," which includes a discussion of the current fiscal crisis and alternatives, see www.armoninstitute.org/welfarestate.htm; also Christian Toft, "German Social Polic," in *The Politics of Social Policy in Europe*, edited by Maurice Mullard and Simon Lee (Lyme, NH: Edward Elgar Publishing, 1997), pp. 144–169. For a comprehensive description of the German welfare state, see Johannes Frerich and Martin Frey, *Handbuch der Geschichte der Sozialpolitik in Deutschland*, (2nd edn; München: R. Oldenbourg Verlag, 1996).

87 Elster, "Die Verwaltung," p. 521; Jochen Schmitt, "Arbeits- und Sozialversicherung einschließlich Sozialversicherung und Sozialversorgung," *Deutsche Verwaltungsgeschichte*, vol. 5, p. 570.

88 Martin Pfaff, "Funktionsfähiger Wettbewerb innerhalb und zwischen den gesetzlichen und privaten Krankenkassen," *Arbeit und Sozialpolitik* 49, no. 9/10 (1995), pp. 12–13; and Wolfgang Rüfner, "Das Gesetz zur Sicherung und Strukturverbesserung der gesetzlichen Krankenversicherung (Gesundheitsstrukturgesetz)," *Neue Juristische Wochenschrift* 46, no. 12 (24 March 1993), p. 756.

89 VDAK/AEV, *Ausgewählte Basisdaten des Gesundheitswesens 2000* (Siegburg, 2000), p. 20.

90 Bertram Schulin (ed.), *Handbuch des Sozialversicherungsrechts, vol. I, Krankenversicherungsrecht* (München: C. H. Beck, 1994), pp. 1193, 1197, 1201.

91 Schmitt, "Arbeits- und Sozialversicherung," pp. 570–584; also Wolfgang Rüfner, "Daseinsvorsorge und soziale Sicherheit," in *Handbuch des Staatsrechts der Bundesrepublik Deutschland*, vol. III, pp. 1079–1082.

92 Günter Püttner and Bernhard Losch, "Verwaltung durch Private und in privatrechtlicher Form," in Jeserich *et al.*, *Deutsche Verwaltungsgeschichte*,

vol. V, pp. 376–77.

93   Elster, "Die Verwaltung," pp. 529–530.

94   Maurer, *Allgemeines Verwaltungsrecht*, pp. 577–578.

95   Klara van Eyll, "Berufständische Selbstverwaltung," in Jeserich *et al.*, *Deutsche Verwaltungsgeschichte*, vol. V, pp. 355–356.

96   Ibid., pp. 358–360.

97   Ibid., pp. 362–363.

98   Franz Letzelter, "Die wissenschaftliche Hochschulen und ihre Verwaltung," in Jeserich *et al.*, *Deutsche Verfassungsgeschicte*, vol. V, pp. 659–664.

99   Elster, "Die Verwaltung," pp. 509–513; Ernst Gottfried Mahrenholz, "Schul- und Hochshulrecht," in *Niedersächsisches Staats- und Verwaltungsrecht*, pp. 540–541.

100 Much of the discussion below is based on Hermann Meyn, *Massenmedien in der Bundesrepublik Deutschland* (Berlin: Edition Colloquium, revised edn, 1994), pp. 117–162; see also Peter J. Humphreys, *Media and Media Policy in Germany: The Press and Broadcasting since 1945* (2nd edn; Oxford/Providence: Berg, 1994). A good overview of the electronic media in Germany from the late 1940s to the late 1990s can be found in Ansgar Diller, "Öffentlich-rechtlicher Rundfunk," in *Mediengeschichte der Bundesrepublik Deutschland*, edited by Jürgen Wilke (Bonn: Bundeszentrale für politische Bildung, 1999), pp. 146–166.

101 Winand Gellner, "Federalism and the Controversy over the New Media in West Germany," *Publius: The Journal of Federalism* 19, no. 4 (Autumn 1989), pp. 133–145.

102 Humphreys, *Media and Media Poicy*, pp. 298–299.

103 *Frankfurter Allgemeine Zeitung* (16 April 1997), p. 2.

104 Diller, "Öffentlich-rechtlicher Rundfunk," pp. 153–158.

105 Hans J. Kleinsteuber and Barbara Thomass, "TV in Deutschland," *Deutschland: Magazine on Politics, Culture, Business and Science*, no. 2 (April 1998), pp. 24–30.

106 Klaus-Eckart Gebauer, "Interessenregelung im föderalistischen System," in *Grundrechte, soziale Ordnung und Verfassungsgerichtsbarkeit*, edited by Eckart Klein (Heidelberg: C. F. Müller Juristischer Verlag, 1995), p. 75.

107 Humphreys, *Media and Media Policy*, pp. 140–147, 176–177, 320–321.

108 Ibid., p. 321, emphasis in the original.

109 Hesse and Ellwein, *Das Regierungssystem, vol. 1*, p. 140.

110 Humphreys, *Media and Media Policy*, pp. 255, 260, 265.

111 Kleinsteuber and Thomass, "TV in Deutschland," p. 27.

112 Ibid., pp. 27–28; German Information Center, *Deutschland Nachrichten*, 13 June 1997, p. 6; and Humphreys, *Media and Media Policy*, pp. 271–273. According to an article in the *Frankfurter Allgemeine Zeitung* (25 June 1999), p. 24, the public stations had 41.3 percent of the viewing public in 1998.

113 Elster, "Die Verwaltung," pp. 525–527.

114 Mauerer, *Allgemeine Verwaltungsrecht*, p. 591.

115 Elster, "Die Verwaltung," pp. 534–536.

116 Ibid., pp. 538–539; Mauerer, *Allgemeine Verwaltungsrecht*, p. 592.

117 Püttner and Losch, "Verwaltung durch Private," vol. V, p. 374.

118 Heinrich Mäding, "Verwaltung und Planung," in Jeserich *et al.*, *Deutsche Verwaltungsgeschichte*, vol. IV, pp. 1046–1047.

119 Ibid., p. 1048.

120 Ibid., p. 1049.

121 Ibid., pp. 1051–1052.

122 Mauer, *Allgemeines Verwaltungsrecht*, pp. 402–403.

123 Gottfried Schmitz, "Räumliche Planung," in König and Siedentopf, *Öffentliche Verwaltung in Deutschland*, p. 405.

124 Rainer Wahl, "Europäisches Planungsrecht Europäisierung des deutschen Planungsrechts," in *Planungs–Recht–Rechtschutz*, pp. 617–646.

125 Clifford Larsen, "What Should be the Leading Principles of Land Use Planning? A German Perspective," *Vanderbilt Journal of Transnational Law* 29, no. 5 (November 1996), pp. 967–1021.

126 Carl Sartorius, *Verfassungs- und Verwaltungsgesetze der Bundesrepublik Deutschland, vol. I* (München: C. H. Beck'sche Verlagsbuchhandlung, 1999), ROG 340.

127 Larsen, "What Should be . . . ?," p. 981.

128 Ibid., pp. 996–1006.

129 Schmitz, "Räumliche Planung," p. 405.

130 Larsen, "What Should be . . . ?," pp. 1006–1008.

131 Frido Wagener and Willi Blümel, "Staatsaufbau und Verwaltungsterritorien," in König and Siedentopf, *Öffentliche Verwaltung in Deutschland*, p. 119.

132 Münch, *Sozialpolitik und Föderalismus*, p. 149.

133 Larsen, "What Should be . . . ?," pp. 993–996.

134 Münch, *Sozialpolitik und Föderalismus*, pp. 149–152.

135 Larsen, "What Should be . . . ?," pp. 1012–1013.

136 For a detailed discussion of joint framework planning under Article 91a, see Erwin Kalinna, *Die Rahmenplanung und der Rahmenplan nach Artikel 91a GG*, Dissertation, University of Munich, 1985; see also Blümel, "Verwaltungszuständigkeit," pp. 952–953.

137 Bruno Schmidt-Bleibtreu and Franz Klein, *Kommentar zum Grundgesetz* (8th edn; Neuwied: Luchterhand Verlag, 1995), pp. 1187, 1203.

138 Ibid., pp. 1201–1202; Arthur Benz, "Verflechtung der Verwaltungsebenen," in König and Siedentopf, *Öffentliche Verwaltung in Deutschland*, p. 176.

139 Schmidt-Bleibtreu and Klein, *Grundgesetzkommentar*, Article 91a, pp. 1202–1204.

140 Maunz *et al.*, *Kommentar zum Grundgesetz*, Article 91b, Rdnr 1-3.

141 Heinrich Mäding, "Federalism and Education Planning in the Federal Republic of Germany," *Publius: The Journal of Federalism* 19, no. 4 (Autumn

1989). p. 120.

142 Ibid., p. 126.

143 Ibid., pp. 125–131; see also the discussion by Blümel, "Verwaltungszuständigkeit," pp. 954–956.

144 Blümel, "Verwaltungszuständigkeit," pp. 943, 954–956.

145 Paul Feuchte, "Die rechtliche Ordnung der Verwaltung im Bundesstaat und ihre Entwicklung," in Jeserich *et al.*, *Deutsche Verwaltungsgeschichte*, vol. 5, pp. 141–142.

146 Blümel, "Verwaltungszuständigkeit," pp. 956–958.

147 Fritz W. Scharpf, "The Joint-Decision Trap: Lessons from German Federalism and European Integration," *Public Administration* 66 (Autumn 1988), pp. 255–271.

148 Schmidt-Bleibtreu and Klein, *Grundgesetzkommentar*, Article 91a, pp. 1189-1190; Kalinna, *Die Rahmenplanung*, pp. 156–159.

149 Christoph Hauschild, "Aus- und Fortbildung für den öffentlichen Dienst," in König and Siedentopf, *Öffentliche Verwaltung in Deutschland*, p. 581.

150 Ibid., pp. 582–589.

151 Günter Püttner, "Der öffentliche Dienst," in Jeserich *et al.*, *Deutsche Verwaltungsgeschichte*, vol. 5, p. 1131; Hans Mommsen, "Wohlerworbene Rechte und Treuepflichten," in *Wozu noch Beamte? Vom starren zum schlanken Berufsbeamtentum*, edited by Peter Grottian (Reinbeck: Rowohlt Taschenbuch Verlag, 1996), pp. 19–36.

152 Püttner, "Der öffentliche Dienst," p. 1138.

153 Helmut Lecheler, "Der öffentliche Dienst," in *Handbuch des Staatsrechts*, vol. III, p. 721.

154 Heide Simonis, "Beamte oder nicht – das ist nicht die Frage," in Grottian, *Wozu noch Beamte?*, pp. 107–121 and also "Verwaltungsreform: Jetzt oder nie?" *Verwaltung und Management* 1, no. 2 (1995), pp. 68–73.

155 Detlef Merten, "Das Berufsbeamtentum als Element deutscher Rechtsstatlichkeit," in *Staat und Verwaltung: Fünfzig Jahre Hochschule für Verwaltungswissenschaften Speyer*, edited by Klaus Lüder (Berlin: Duncker & Humblot, 1997), pp. 145–168.

156 Detlef Merten, "Beamtenrecht und Beamtenverfassungsrecht," in *Planung–Recht–Rechtschutz*, pp. 342–346, 350.

157 There was, of course, controversy in Germany over the question of civil servants who had served the Nazi regime, but there was little concern that these officials would try consciously to undermine the new democratic system after 1949.

158 For criticism by one American scholar among others, see Gerard Braunthal, *Political Loyalty and Public Service in West Germany: The 1972 Decree against Radicals and its Consequences* (Amherst: University of Massachusetts Press, 1990).

159 Schmidt-Bleibtreu and Klein, *Grundgesetzkommentar*, Article 33, p. 667.

160 Ibid., pp. 665–673; Lecheler, "Der öffentliche Dienst," pp. 754–756.

161 Renate Mayntz, "German Federal Bureaucrats," *Bureaucrats and Policy Making: A Comparative Overview*, edited by Ezra N. Suleiman (New York: Holmes & Meier, 1984), p. 176.

162 Hans-Ulrich Derlien, "Politicization of the Civil Service in the Federal Republic of Germany: Facts and Fables," in *The Politicization of Public Administration*, edited by François Meyers (Brussels: International Institute of Administrative Sciences, 1985), pp. 3–4.

163 For a devastating criticism of local party patronage practices in Cologne, see Ervin K. and Ute Scheuch, *Cliquen, Klüngel und Karrieren* (Reinbeck: Rowohlt Taschenbuch Verlag, 1992); sharp criticisms of party patronage, particularly at the *Land* level, can be found in the writings of Hans Herbert von Arnim. See, for example, his *Staat als Beute: Wie Politiker in eigener Sache Gesetze Machen* (Munich: Knauer, 1993), Ch. 6 and *Staat ohne Diener* (Munich: Kindler Verlag, 1993), Ch. 4.

164 Kenneth Dyson, "The West German 'Party-Book' Administration: An Evaluation," *Public Administration Bulletin* 25 (December 1977), p. 4.

165 Jörg Auf dem Hövel, "Politisierung der öffentlichen Verwaltung durch Parteien? Ursachenforschung und normative Debatte," *Zeitschrift für Parlamentsfragen* 27, no. 1 (January 1996), pp. 82–95; Everhard Holtmann, "Politisierung der Kommunalpolitik und Wandlungen im lokalen Parteiensystem," in *Aus Politik und Zeitgeschichte* B 22-23/92 (22 May 1992), p. 20.

166 "Tammany Hall" was a corrupt party "machine" that controlled New York City under "Boss Tweed" after the Civil War.

167 Dyson, "The West German 'Party-Book' Administration," p. 20.

168 For a brief discussion in English of *Filzokratie*, a mixing of private and public interests in certain large cities, see Dyson, "The West German 'Party-Book' Administration," pp. 8–12; Scheuch, *Cliquen, Klüngel und Karrieren*.

169 Von Arnim, *Staat als Beute*, Ch. 6.

170 Renate Mayntz, "The Higher Civil Service of the Federal Republic of Germany," in *The Higher Civil Service in Europe and Canada*, edited by Bruce L. R. Smith (Washington: The Brookings Institution, 1984), p. 65.

171 For example, Schmidt-Bleibtreu and Klein, *Grundgesetzkommentar*, Article 33, p. 659, and Ulrich Battis in Michael Sachs (ed.), *Grundgesetz Kommentar* (München: C. H. Beck'sche Verlagsbuchhandlung, 1996), p. 870, insist that party patronage in civil service appointments is unconstitutional. See also Merten, "Das Berufsbeamtentum," pp. 161–166, for a detailed analysis of constitutional and other objections.

172 Mayntz, "German Federal Bureaucrats," pp. 183–184.

173 Mayntz, "The Higher Civil Service," pp. 56–57.

174 Some empirical evidence, which is not necessarily representative of the whole and, in addition, is rather dated, can be found in Wolfgang H. Lorig,

"Parteipolitik und öffentlicher Dienst: Personalrekrutierung und Personal-patronage in der öffentlichen Verwaltung," *Zeitschrift für Parlamentsfragen* 25, no. 1 (January 1994), pp. 94–107; for different meanings of patronage, see Derlien, "Politicization in the Civil Service," pp. 5–6.

175 Mayntz, "The Higher Civil Service," pp. 61–62.

176 Püttner, "Der öffentliche Dienst," p. 1134.

177 Ibid., p. 1138.

178 See the website at www.verdi.de/verdi/index.php3.

179 Burckhard Nedden, "Verwaltungsorganisation," pp. 110–111.

180 Krebs, "Verwaltungsorganisation," pp. 578–581.

181 Wagener and Blümel, "Staatsaufbau und Verwaltungsterritorien," p. 118; Gerhard Wittkämper, "Die Landesverwaltung," in *Nordrhein-Westfalen: Eine politische Landeskunde*, edited by Landeszentrale für politische Bildung (Köln: W. Kohlhammer Verlag, 1984), p. 156. For a detailed description in English of the complexities of the overall administrative structures in Germany, see McDermott, "The Functions of Local Levels," pp. 182–188.

4

The *Land* constitutions

Introduction

For almost forty years after the federal Constitution went into effect, little attention was paid to state (*Land*) constitutions in Germany. Amendments were made on numerous occasions, but these were almost always rather minor changes or technical corrections and did not arouse much controversy. At the end of the 1980s and the beginning of the 1990s, this changed dramatically for two major reasons. A scandal in Schleswig-Holstein in 1987 involving allegations that the prime minister (*Minister-Präsident*) had been guilty of a serious abuse of power (the Barschel/Pfeiffer affair) led to a thorough revision of that *Land*'s Constitution which included both far-reaching plebiscitary (direct democracy) features and provisions strengthening the parliament's control over the government (cabinet). The reforms contained in this Constitution have since had a significant impact not only on the new *Länder* in the East but also on Bremen, Hamburg, Lower Saxony, and Rhineland-Palatinate in the West.

The second cause of a strong interest in *Land* constitutions was, of course, the collapse of the Wall, the re-emergence of five *Länder* which had ceased to exist in 1952, and the unification of Germany in October 1990. The result was a third generation of *Land* constitutions following the first generation before the Basic Law went into effect in 1949 and the second generation which followed that event during the 1950s. The Schleswig-Holstein Constitution of 1990 became an inspiration for the five new *Länder* in the East, and their constitutions, in turn, encouraged several of the old *Länder* in the West to revise their constitutions. In addition to Schleswig-Holstein, the old *Länder* had provided the new *Länder* in their constitution making with model structures and practices proven by time; now the new *Länder* were providing their western counterparts with innovative "modern" ideas for constitutional changes.[1]

The Basic Law and the *Länder*

The Constitution of the Federal Republic, called the "Basic Law" (*Grundgesetz*) owing to its presumed provisional nature until unification was achieved, not only reintroduced a democratic and federal state in the western part of Germany but also forbade in Article 79 any amendments "affecting the division of the Federation into *Länder*, the participation on principle of the *Länder* in legislation or the basic principles laid down in Arts. 1 [concerning human dignity] and 20 [concerning democratic principles and the rule of law]."

Like the Bismarck Constitution but unlike the Weimar Constitution, the *Länder* constituting the Federal Republic are listed by name. This does not mean, however, that the component parts of the federation are constitutionally guaranteed. The reorganization of the *Länder* through consolidation, annexation, or redrawing of boundaries is constitutional; however, such changes are subject to Article 29 of the Basic Law, which presently requires popular referenda in such matters.

As in the Weimar Republic, the *Länder* are represented in the Federal Council (again called *Bundesrat*, as in the Bismarck Reich) by delegates appointed by the *Land* cabinets. However, with Prussia's demise after 1945, four new "large" *Länder* emerged, two each in the North and South of the country. These *Länder* were given 5 votes each in the Federal Council; medium-size *Länder* with populations between 2 and 4 million received 4 votes and small *Länder* 3 votes (all cast as a block).[2] Government bills are introduced in the *Bundesrat* before going to the *Bundestag*. All bills require the approval of the *Bundestag*. The *Bundesrat* has a suspensive veto and an absolute veto, the latter regarding legislation affecting the *Länder* (approximately 60 percent of all bills). Bills affecting the *Länder* are those in particular that call for *Land* administration in accordance with the German federal tradition. Constitutional amendments require a two-thirds vote in both houses of parliament.[3]

Origins and legal framework of *Land* constitutions

At the Potsdam Conference in July and August 1945, the Four Allied Powers called for a "decentralization of the political structure and the development of local responsibility."[4] This provision applied to local and regional structures. In the American, Soviet, and French zones of occupation, *Länder* were created and constitutions adopted in 1946 and 1947. The British delayed constitution making in their zone until the federal constitution had been adopted.

Constitutional passage

Thus, the Constitution of Hesse, the oldest of the still existing postwar *Land* constitutions, was passed by a constitutional assembly in October and by a popular referendum in December 1946. Bavaria's Constitution was passed in June 1946 by a constitutional assembly and also in December by a popular referendum. A constitutional assembly passed the Constitution of the Rhineland-Palatinate in April, which was approved by a popular referendum in May 1947. Bremen's Constitution was passed by the parliament (*Bürgerschaft*) in September 1947 and by a referendum in October. While the Saarland did not join the Federal Republic until 1 January 1957, its Constitution was passed by a constitutional assembly in November and accepted by the French military government in December 1947.[5]

With the passage of the Basic Law in May 1949 by all of the *Land* parliaments except Bavaria's, the British-occupied *Länder* began their constitution making. *Land* "by-laws" were passed by the parliament in Schleswig-Holstein in December 1949. Perhaps not surprisingly, given the British skepticism regarding plebiscitary processes, there was no popular referendum. Nevertheless, the Constitution of North-Rhine Westphalia, which also was located in the British Zone, was passed by a bare majority of the parliament in June 1950, followed by a popular referendum the same month. But in Lower Saxony, the "temporary" Constitution was passed by the parliament in April 1951 with no referendum, and the Constitution of Hamburg was passed in June 1952, also with no referendum. In both of these cases, however, approval in parliament was overwhelming.

The most recent of the "original" West German constitutions is that of Baden-Württemberg, adopted in November 1953 by a constitutional assembly but without a referendum, after it was agreed to consolidate Baden, Württemberg-Baden, and Württemberg-Hohenzollern. The first Constitution of Berlin in 1946 was the work of the Allied command. Following the East–West split, a new Constitution for West Berlin was prepared by Germans and approved by the West Berlin parliament and Western Allies in 1950.

Once the five reconstituted *Länder* of the former GDR joined the Federal Republic in October 1990, their parliaments adopted temporary constitutions and, except for Thuringia, established constitutional commissions to draft new permanent constitutions. They then devoted much of their efforts between 1991 and 1995 to debating, drafting, and approving new constitutions. By the end of August 1992, Brandenburg, Saxony, and Saxony-Anhalt had completed their constitution making.[6] Saxony and Saxony-Anhalt relied on a two-thirds vote in their parliaments for final approval of their constitutions, while Brandenburg and the new *Länder* that followed held referenda. Mecklenburg-Vorpommern's constitution went into effect in May 1993, although a popular referendum that approved it was not held until June 1994. Thuringia followed at the end with its constitution in October 1993, but a confirming referendum was not held until a year later at the time of the federal parliamentary election. A new Constitution for Berlin, which, because of the prior existence of West Berlin, is not considered to be among the "five new *Länder*," was approved by referendum in October 1995. Given the strong possibility of a merger between Berlin and Brandenburg, this Constitution was expected to be short-lived; however, the failure in 1996 of the referendum proposal to consolidate the two *Länder* has changed that assumption.

The strong focus on constitution making in the East, together with the impact of the new Schleswig-Holstein Constitution of 1990, led to considerable discussion of constitutional issues throughout Germany, at least among legal experts, so that several of the "old" West German *Länder* began considering revisions or even new constitutions. Thus, Lower Saxony implemented, in effect, a new constitution in May 1993, and several other old *Länder* began considering constitutional changes thereafter.

To summarize the constitution making processes used by the sixteen German *Länder* in the fifty years after 1945, it can be seen that four procedures were used for accepting constitutions: first, approval by a constitutional assembly followed by a referendum (Bavaria, Hesse, and Rhineland-Palatinate); second, approval by the *Land* parliament followed by a referendum (Berlin, Brandenburg, Bremen, Mecklenburg-Vorpommern, North-Rhine Westphalia, and Thuringia); third, approval by a constitutional assembly only (Baden-Württemberg and Saarland); fourth, approval by the parliament only (Hamburg, Lower Saxony, Saxony, Saxony-Anhalt, and Schleswig-Holstein). Thus, all of the constitutions were passed first either by a constitutional assembly or by the parliament, and nine of the sixteen constitutions were approved as well in popular referenda.[7]

Basic differences and similarities

Perhaps more significant than the ratification procedure was the "generation" of the constitution. The five *Länder* that passed the constitutions before the Basic Law went into effect in 1949 wrote "full constitutions" containing organizational structures as well as the whole array of political and social provisions, including basic human rights. Three of these constitutions – those of the Rhineland-Palatinate, Bavaria, and the Saarland – were influenced strongly by Christian thought in reaction to the value-neutral Weimar Constitution and the total disregard of Christian principles by the Nazi regime. The other two *Länder* – Bremen and Hesse – were affected more by socialist ideas that rejected the economic concentration that allegedly bore some responsibility for the rise of the Nazis.

The second generation of constitutions prepared after 1949 in Baden-Württemberg, Hamburg, Lower Saxony, North-Rhine Westphalia, and Schleswig-Holstein, consisted of documents that were focused more on organizational principles, since the Basic Law provided for basic human and individual rights. The third generation of constitutions in the new *Länder* followed the western models in large part, but they were also far more influenced by "modern" values, including social rights and state goals.[8] The old *Länder* that have changed their constitutions since 1990 could also be said to have been influenced by the third- generation "modern" values.

In spite of these generational differences, there is a fundamental constitutional "homogeneity" between the federation and the *Länder* and among the latter. As in the United States, they all provide for the same basic political system – in this case, a single-chamber parliamentary system (Bavaria's Senate was eliminated by referendum in 1998). They all must abide by the fundamental rights provided by the Basic Law. They tend to react to the same underlying societal trends, as in the case of demands for certain state goals such as environmental protection. And, above all, they are under the influence of national political parties that are generally well organized, disciplined, programmatic, and in control of *Land* governments and parliaments.[9]

Amendments

All of the older *Land* constitutions were amended between 1946 and 1995, ranging from three times in Hesse to thirty-two times in the Rhineland-Palatinate. From the beginning of 1995 through 1997, there were one or more amendments to the constitutions of Baden-Württemberg, Bavaria,

Berlin, Brandenburg, Bremen, Hamburg, Rhineland-Palatinate, and the Saarland. The Basic Law has been amended fifty times.[10]

There is no common method of amendment among the *Länder*; however, no amendments are possible without action by their parliaments. Some *Länder* follow the example of the federal Basic Law which calls for an amendment process requiring a two-thirds vote of the *Bundestag* and *Bundesrat*, with the difference that the *Länder* have only one legislative chamber. In others, voters at large are involved in the amending process through initiatives and/or referenda. No *Land* constitution gives the people sole authority to amend. Legal challenges to amendments can be taken to the *Land* constitutional court before a referendum is held.

The focus of amendments has been on adjusting *Land* law to federal law, just as most amendments to the Basic Law have been concerned with German federalism. Amendments to *Land* constitutions have served to bring their texts into conformity with Federal Constitutional Court decisions. However, several *Land* constitutions contain provisions which are not in conformity with the federal Basic Law and, therefore, have been superseded by the Basic Law's supremacy clause in Article 31.

Many changes in *Land* constitutions have been responses to demands to strengthen the parliament through petition committees, investigative committees, or through other means of parliamentary control. Some more recent amendments reflect newer concerns, such as protecting the environment or personal privacy and liberty by restricting the dissemination of data.[11]

The legal framework for Land constitutions

According to German legal theory, the *Länder* are "states" that enjoy considerable legal autonomy within the German federal system. They are not derived from the federation but rather are recognized by it.[12] They are not "states" in the sense of international law,[13] even though they do have limited powers in certain areas of foreign policy.[14] As states, the *Länder* have constitutional autonomy, namely, the right to create their own constitutions.[15] But this autonomy is exercised within a legal framework provided by the *federal* Basic Law;[16] that is, *Land* autonomy exists simultaneously with the necessity of federal "homogeneity."[17] Thus, Article 28, para. 1, requires the constitutional order in the *Länder* to conform to the principles of a republican, democratic, and social state of law. While federalism and, therefore, multiple *Länder* are guaranteed by Article 79, para. 3, individual *Länder* are not. Thus Article 29 provides for boundary changes, which could include the consolidation of *Länder,* but only by federal law that is confirmed by a popular referendum in the areas affected. In contrast to the American Constitution, at least until 1925 and after, the *Länder* are also required by Article 79, para. 3, to accept as their own all federally protected basic rights contained in Articles 1–20. They may, however, add new or other rights that do not violate the federal constitutional rights. There is also, of course, a federal supreme law-of-the-land clause, Article 31, which can serve as a barrier to *Land* constitutional provisions. Finally, Article 93, para. 1, sentence 4a, provides for an individual constitutional complaint before the Federal Constitutional Court which could be used to challenge a *Land* constitution.[18]

While these various restrictions are rather formidable, but hardly surprising in their content, they do not prohibit the *Länder* from engaging in some degree of experimentation and, as we shall see below, creating some controversy.

Land parliaments and legislation

Land *parliaments*

Since a referendum in 1998 eliminated Bavaria's corporative Senate, which was composed of various professions, crafts, and social groups, all parliaments in the German *Länder* have one house. These are called the *Landtag* in the territorial states, *Abgeordnetenhaus* in Berlin, and *Bürgerschaft* in Bremen and Hamburg. Seven *Land* constitutions prescribe the size of the parliament, which varies from fifty-one members in the small territorial *Land* of Saarland to 231 in the most populous *Land,* North-Rhine Westphalia. The *Land* parliaments are now mostly elected for five years; however, in Bremen, Hamburg, Hesse, Mecklenburg-Vorpommern, and Saxony-Anhalt the term is for four years. Except for Baden-Württemberg and Bremen, the parliamentary period can end earlier by self-dissolution or, in a few cases, by popular referendum at the inititative of the prime minister or parliamentary president.

Most voters probably look to the *Land* parliaments as the major instrument for reflecting the public will. All elections to the *Land* parliaments must be "general, direct, free, equal and secret," in accordance with the Basic Law. In all *Länder* elections are based on a system of proportional representation with a minimum of 5 percent of the total vote required in order to obtain seats in parliament. This strongly favors political parties, which are mentioned explicitly in Article 21 of the Basic Law and in some *Land* constitutions.

Parliamentary law making

While *Land* parliaments are responsible for law making, the extent of their legislative powers depends largely on the powers granted to them by the federal Basic Law. At first glance, these powers appear to be extensive. As we saw in Chapter 2, Article 30 (somewhat like the US Constitution's Tenth Amendment) states that the *Länder* are responsible for the exercise of government powers unless the Basic Law provides otherwise. Article 70 also confers legislative powers on the *Länder* except where such powers are given to the federation. Federal powers are then listed in Article 73, concurrent powers in Article 74. The federal parliament also has the right to pass framework or skeleton laws that the *Länder* must then "fill in." Given that the federal government has acted in virtually all areas of concurrent powers, thus excluding *Land* actions through the federal supremacy clause in Article 31, and has also taken advantage of its framework powers, there is not a great deal of legislative activity left for the *Länder* to pursue independently. They do retain autonomy in the areas of culture (e.g., education, electronic media, museums, and support for the performing arts, etc.), police, and local government law, and they engage in numerous economic activities including various activities abroad.[19] Of course, where they have some leeway, they adapt federal laws, including especially framework laws, to local regional conditions for administration by the *Land* bureaucracy.

In 1992 and 1993 a Joint Constitutional Commission met to discuss proposals for changes in the Basic Law as a result of unification. One focus was German federalism. With respect to the legislative powers of the *Länder*, Article 72, which deals with concurrent powers, was made more precise in order to limit federal preemptions to specific laws rather than to allow the federation to absorb a broad function based on a partial preemption. Another change was to alter the language of Article 72, para. 2, to grant the federation power to pass legislation for the maintenance of *equivalent* rather than *uniform* living conditions in the country. Article 75, which provides for federal framework laws, was revised to make more precise the language that grants the federation powers to pass framework legislation regarding higher education.

Other changes relevant to German federalism were made in Articles 24 to grant the *Länder* the right to transfer with approval of the federal government certain sovereign powers to transnational border authorities for the purpose of dealing with common problems. Also Article 28 was changed to provide local governments with more autonomous financial responsibility[20] and to grant voting rights in the local elections to citizens of member states of the EU living in Germany.

Direct democracy[21]

All German constitutions declare the people sovereign, as in "[a]ll state [government] authority derives from the people" (Article 20, para. 2 of the Basic Law). But this provision of the Basic Law continues to state that "[i]t shall be exercised by the people by means of elections and referenda and by specific legislative, executive, and judicial organs." There is no provision for referenda in the federal Basic Law, except in Article 29 which refers to the reorganization of *Land* boundaries. There was a heated discussion about the old Article 146 of the Basic Law and whether it required a referendum on a new or revised federal constitution before or after unification (in fact, there was no referendum, and the five new *Länder* joined West Germany by accession under the old Article 23). However, with these exceptions, the Federal Republic's Basic Law, like the United States Constitution, provides for a *representative* republic.

In contrast, most of the *Länder* provided from the beginning for some form of popular initiative and referendum. In accordance with British tradition, Hamburg, Schleswig-Holstein, and Lower Saxony did not (but Schleswig-Holstein's new Constitution of June 1990 now contains the most far-reaching plebiscitary features of any "old" Constitution). By 1997 all *Länder* had constitutional provisions for referenda.[22]

One of the most vigorously discussed features of the new constitutions in the East following unification has been their provisions for direct democracy, although this exists in the old *Länder* as well. One reason for the debate was the effort by the political left to introduce some plebiscitary features into the federal Basic Law. These efforts were rejected in 1993 by the government coalition parties, the Christian Democrats (CDU and CSU) and the Free Democrats (FDP), and were dropped as a result.[23] (An attempt by the SPD–Green coalition government to gain a two-thirds majority in the *Bundestag* and amend the Basic Law to allow direct democracy failed in the summer of 2002, owing the opposition by the CDU/CSU and a majority of the FDP.)[24] But another reason has to do with the low thresholds in the East for initiating petitions and referenda and for approval of the latter.

There are two-step and three-step procedures in the *Länder* that have plebiscitary features. The older constitutions generally had two steps only: the *Volksbegehren* (petition for a referendum) and the *Volksentscheid* (referendum). The new constitutions in the East, except Thuringia, follow the thoroughly revised 1990 Constitution of Schleswig-Holstein by providing for three steps. First, there is a provision for a "people's initiative" (*Volksinitiative* or, in Saxony, *Volksantrag*, and, in Thuringia, *Bürgerantrag*), a petition to place certain items or a specific proposal on the *Land* parliament's agenda for consideration. The new Schleswig-Holstein Constitution requires only 20,000 signatures for an initiative, or slightly less than 1 percent of the eligible voting population, which is considered to be very low. This set the stage for Brandenburg's identical requirement of 20,000, Saxony's requirement of 40,000, and Mecklenburg-Vorpommern's requirement of 15,000 signatures, the latter two of which constitute slightly more than 1 percent of the population. Saxony-Anhalt's requirement of 35,000 signatures is about 1.6 percent of its population.[25] These low requirements have been criticized by some for their potential abuse by extremist groups or even by opposition parties.

If the parliament does not act on the proposal within a certain period (e.g., three–six months), interested citizens may complete a petition (*Volksbegehren*) for a popular referendum on a specific bill. Here the signature requirements are much higher (though still considerably lower than in most West German *Land* constitutions, where they are generally between 10 and 20 percent), ranging from 80,000 in Brandenburg (about 4 percent of eligible voters) to 450,000 or 12.5 percent in Saxony. If the parliament does not accept the proposal within a set period (e.g., two months), then, third, a referendum will be held on the bill (an alternative bill might be added by the parliament). In striking contrast to the United States, qualified majorities are required for approval of legislative referenda (e.g., a majority of those voting but at least one-fourth of eligible voters in Brandenburg and Saxony-Anhalt, a majority and one-third in Mecklenburg-Vorpommern and Thuringia, but only a majority of those voting in Saxony). In the western constitutions, approving majorities for referenda must constitute typically one-fourth or one-third of the eligible electorate.

It should also be noted that in contrast to the United States, no petitions or referenda are permitted that deal with judges, constitutional decisions, the bureaucracy, or with budgets, taxes, public employee salaries, political finance, or other financial matters. It has been argued that it is hypocritical to deny the people the right to vote in a referendum on questions of finance, since most public policy issues today involve public finances. Some voices are also skeptical of direct democracy in general, because of the belief that most issues of public policy are too complicated to be settled by public referenda.[26]

Others suggest that the provisions for direct democracy in the constitutions of the *Länder* really have the effect of encouraging the political parties to take up the issues raised and place them on the parliamentary agenda. According to this view, plebiscitary features serve to promote public discussion. Some fears have been expressed that plebiscitary features may also lead politicians to avoid difficult decisions in favor of referenda, thus undermining the representative system. There is no evidence so far, however, that this is likely to happen.[27]

Legislative control

Some observers argue that a more important function than law making exercised by *Land* parliaments today is control of the executive, in particular the government (cabinet). The nature and extent of this control vary by *Land* constitution.

In the city-states the parliament elects the entire cabinet: in Berlin, first the lord mayor, then the cabinet; in Bremen and Hamburg, first the *Senat* (cabinet), which then elects the lord major. In six *Länder* the parliament elects only the minister-president (prime minister), whose cabinet appointees then require parliamentary approval. In seven *Länder* the parliaments do not control the prime minister's formation of the cabinet, which is also the case at the federal level. In all of the *Länder,* the governments can call for a vote of confidence. Except in Bavaria, the parliaments can also initiate a vote of no-confidence by majority vote of the members. In such cases a government falls only if a majority of parliament can select a new minister-president. This is called a "constructive" vote of confidence, which applies at the federal level as well. In Schleswig-Holstein the government can dissolve parliament if it calls for and fails to receive majority support. Berlin, Hesse, the Rhineland-Palatinate, and the Saarland have a "destructive" vote of confidence, that is, the parliament must provide an alternative within a certain period or be dissolved. Bavaria makes parliamentary control of the government difficult in that the parliament can force the minister-president to resign only indirectly through the state constitutional court.

Of course, routine control of the executive also exists through parliamentary scrutiny of the budget (a key control device), question time for ministers, petition committees, and investigative committees. However, the strong party discipline in German parliaments can frustrate efforts, especially by the opposition, to control government actions. This occurs despite the fact that all German constitutions proclaim parliamentary delegates to be free in their decisions and not subject to mandates.

Land executives, judiciaries, and social institutions[28]

The executive

Governments (cabinets) stand at the apex of the executive branch in the German *Länder*. In seven *Länder*, for example, the prime minister alone appoints and dismisses the other cabinet ministers. In contrast to the general bureaucracy, the ministers have political leadership responsibilities. The constitutional powers of the minister-president are weakest in the three city-states and stronger in the territorial states, especially Schleswig-Holstein. In that *Land* and in Berlin, the head of government may also continue in office beyond the legislative term, although in practice the lord mayor of Berlin resigns at the end of that period. In twelve *Länder* the minister-president is constitutionally responsible for general policy guidelines (*Richtlinienkompetenz*); in the other four *Länder* the principle of ministerial responsibility and collegiality obtains.

Constitutional provisions regarding administration of the *Länder* are generally brief. In Bavaria ministries of the cabinet are listed; in other *Länder* ministries are determined by law or need. As noted above, the *Länder* administer most federal laws on their own responsibility. While this aspect of German federalism is outlined in some detail in the federal Basic Law, the *Land* constitutions are silent on the subject. Most constitutions contain brief, general provisions regarding the rule of law, democracy, obligations of public servants, salary, and the like, and the constitutions of all territorial states have sections that guarantee the right of local self-government. They also contain provisions regarding *Land* finances, including the financing of local governments.

The judiciary[29]

Land constitutions do not say much about the organization of courts. This has been left to legislation. The major exception concerns rather detailed provisions regarding the *Land* constitutional courts (*Staatsgerichtshof* or *Verfassungsgerichtshof*).[30] All courts of first instance, excepting the Federal Patents Court, are *Land* courts. These are divided among local and regional courts, labor courts, administrative courts, finance courts, and social courts (for various social insurance and welfare cases). *Land* courts of appeal on the facts exist for regular courts as well as for labor, administrative, and social courts. Federal courts for each of these general categories of law are courts of final appeal on points of law. The most important and best known is the Federal Constitutional Court in Karlsruhe, which has decided many cases dealing with German federalism.[31] In accordance with the Continental tradition, virtually all judges in Germany are career judges, or, in some federal courts and *Land* constitutional courts, professors of law rather than former attorneys as in Anglo-Saxon countries.

Institutions of society

All of the new constitutions contain the traditional protection of certain institutions of society (*Einrichtungsgarantien*), such as marriage and family; churches and religion; and vocational training, education, schools, and universities. In some constitutions these are included in the sections on basic rights, in others they are contained in separate sections.

Although constitutional references to institutions of society are usually routine and noncontroversial, Brandenburg insisted on provisions protecting both marriage and the family as well as "other permanent forms of common living arrangements."[32] The new Constitution of Berlin also contains this clause.[33] Some critics have argued that this creates a legal contradiction and probably violates the Basic Law, which protects marriage and the family,[34] while others, though recognizing problems of definition, were more positive in their assessment. This dispute seems to have been resolved in July 2002, when the Federal Constitutional Court upheld the law passed by the SPD–Green coalition government in 2001 allowing homosexual marriages.

Basic rights, social rights, and state goals

Classical basic rights

As indicated above, the *Länder* are bound by the basic rights contained in Articles 1–20 of the federal Basic Law. For that reason some *Länder* have not bothered to include these rights in their constitutions and have merely indicated that the rights of the federal Constitution apply to them as well. Thus, Article 4 of the Mecklenburg-Vorpommern Constitution states that "Law making is bound by the Basic Law for the Federal Republic of Germany," and there is no list of conventional basic rights. The other new *Länder* and Berlin have more or less repeated the rights listed in the Basic Law.

While the *Länder* are bound by the Basic Law, they are not prohibited from adding to the list of federal rights.[35] Examples can be found in all the new constitutions in the eastern *Länder*, the most common of which are data protection and protection of the environment. Environmental protection was added recently to the federal Constitution, while data protection is provided by federal statute law and constitutional interpretation.

In Article 39 of the Brandenburg Constitution, which deals with the environment in considerable detail, the final paragraph states that Brandenburg will work toward preventing the development, manufacture, or storage of chemical, biological, or nuclear weapons. In Article 40, para. 5, the Constitution commits Brandenburg to working toward returning military installations to civilian use. These are questionable provisions, given that the federal government has legislative responsibility for such activities.[36] Several other rights have also been added by individual *Land* constitutions, such as equality provisions for the handicapped or for those who have a different "sexual identity" (Brandenburg) or "sexual orientation" (Thuringia).[37] Some constitutions also protect animals against inhumane treatment or avoidable suffering, and Brandenburg even mentions plants as worthy of respect.[38] Not only are art, science, research, and teaching mentioned in all of the constitutions as objects of protection; art and culture, as well as sport, are to be promoted by public funds.

While additions to the basic rights provided by the federal Constitution are clearly acceptable in principle, the weakening of federal rights is more problematic. An example is provided in the Constitution of Brandenburg, which contains a provision (Article 31, para. 2) that permits statutory restrictions on research that is injurious to human dignity or destructive of the natural foundations of life. This implies restrictions on gene technology and nuclear research and probably violates Article 5, para. 3 of the Basic Law.[39]

Social rights and state goals

The most controversial provisions of the constitutions in the new *Länder* concern social rights and state goals.[40] Both can be found in the Basic Law and in constitutions of the old *Länder*, but the vigor with which they were pursued in the East raised numerous questions.[41] Social rights, both in the old and the new constitutions include, for example, the right to employment; the right to unemployment compensation; the right to worker protection; the right to education and training; the right to public support in case of illness, old age, or emergency; the right to social security; and the right to housing.

Some combination of these social rights can be found in all of the new constitutions; however, in contrast to the older constitutions of the West, they are often expressed as "state goals." The two can thus be distinguished more easily in form than in content.[42] However, some provisions are more obviously state goals than social rights, such as the right to death with dignity[43] and the protection against physical or psychological force in marriage, in the family, and in other living arrangements (Brandenburg Constitution).

Social rights and state goals, unlike the classical basic rights, are not generally enforceable in a court of law.[44] To the extent that the new constitutions, Brandenburg's in particular, did not make this clear,[45] some legal experts have predicted that the courts will be busy in the future trying to decide what is and is not legally enforceable. This carries with it the potential of turning over policy making to judges and removing it from the legislatures.[46]

As can be seen from the examples above, social rights concern entitlements of the modern welfare state that must be included in state budgets (which will remain critically tight in the East for decades to come) and paid for from taxes. These are matters for governments and legislative bodies, not for the courts.[47] State goals usually consist of social rights as well; but they may also refer to other matters, in particular protection of the environment, gender equality, culture, and the aged and handicapped. If expressed as state goals, the new constitutions sometimes qualify their implementation by wording indicating that the *Land* "is obligated, within the limits of its ability, to realize (or bring about or promote)" (Brandenburg); "contributes toward" (Mecklenburg-Vorpommern); "recognizes the right of each person to" (Saxony); "works within the limits of its powers" (Saxony-Anhalt); or "has the obligation, according to its abilities and within the limits of its powers, to bring about the state goals listed in this constitution" (Thuringia).

Social rights and state goals – and even classical rights – are often mixed together; however, in some constitutions (e.g., Mecklenburg-Vorpommern and Saxony-Anhalt), the first two are clearly separated from classical rights.

As noted above, the constitution of Brandenburg in particular has been criticized severely by legal experts for failing to make a clear distinction between the enforceable classical "negative" rights and, according to their supporters, the "more modern" "positive" rights.

Some critics dismiss social rights and state goals as mere populist rhetoric to make people feel good. More serious criticisms are that they are too vague, that they ignore the supremacy of federal law, that they are left-wing efforts to make good real or imagined deficits in the Basic Law, and, above all, that they raise unrealistic expectations by making promises that cannot be kept.[48] Pointing to Brandenburg's guarantee of the right to employment, one constitutional expert shows how difficult and unrealistic this promise is in a free-market society. He argues that such state goals are "time bombs" waiting to explode when the promissory note comes due, and he refers to them as "current fashions" that have the effect of weakening the responsible legislative bodies.[49]

However, some commentators have been very sympathetic to these social rights and state goals. One common view is that in spite of the inadequacy of the actual services and benefits promised in the German Democratic Republic (GDR) constitutions, often provided at below standard if at all, many East Germans after unification longed for the security which they felt they enjoyed under the communists. Huge job losses and growing claims for the return of property confiscated or appropriated by the communists in particular led to demands for the right to employment and housing. The new *Länder* emphasized more than their western counterparts social rights and state goals in order to deal with the concerns and calm the fears of their populations[50] and, in the process, bring the constitutions closer to the people.[51] Another view is that the modern state has to deal with new challenges, such as environmental protection, that were ignored in the past,[52] and it must focus on more than the classical rights that grant freedom from the state; instead, the state today helps to create and secure the conditions of freedom. Regarding the right to employment, for example, "so long as appropriate work cannot be found, there is a claim to job training, further education, and financial support. All of the provisions of the Brandenburg Constitution make clear without illusions that the state has no power to create jobs and that there exists no individual legal claim . . . against the state."[53]

One problem with this view is that there are indeed people who have illusions about social rights and state goals. In both Mecklenburg-Vorpommern and Thuringia, the reformed Communist party (PDS) led a campaign against the Constitution before the popular referendum on the grounds that it did not guarantee sufficiently the right to employment and housing.[54] In Mecklenburg-Vorpommern 40 percent of those voting (65 percent of eligible voters) cast their ballots against the Constitution,[55] and in Thuringia about 30 percent of those voting (75 percent of eligible voters) opposed the Constitution.[56]

Other rights and duties

Alongside rights provided by *Land* constitutions are provisions concerning *duties*. Citizens have the duty to attend school, raise their families, seek employment, lend assistance in emergencies, serve on juries, be loyal to the democratic state, and, in some cases, serve the common good while participating in the economy.

The role of the *Länder* in cultural, economic, and welfare activities is also reflected in *Land* constitutions. Provisions concerning primary, secondary, higher education, and adult education can be found in some constitutions. Religious instruction is usually protected. Performing arts are to be protected and promoted in some *Länder*. Several constitutions devote a section to the economic and social order. While economic liberty is guaranteed, there may be provisions protecting the middle class and agriculture. Socialization and land reform are also mentioned in some constitutions.

Constitution making in the new Länder

In spite of the focus in the constitutions of the new *Länder* on social rights and state goals, their constitutions are similar to those of the "old" western *Länder*. All provide for democratic, parliamentary systems. The one-house legislature is elected every five, rather than four, years in Brandenburg, Saxony, and Thuringia. These same states mention explicitly the opposition, as did Schleswig-Holstein when it revised its Constitution in 1990. The Brandenburg constitution also calls for public meetings of its committees, which is not typical in German parliamentary bodies, and it provides for a minimum committee membership for all party groups in the parliament. In Brandenburg a majority of deputies can withdraw confidence in any minister, whom the minister-president must then remove from office. This and other provisions of the Brandenburg constitution have been criticized by West German legal scholars.[57]

Conclusion

Just as all American state constitutions provide for a similar political system with a directly elected governor and a two-house legislature (with the exception of Nebraska, which has a unicameral legislature), all of the German *Länder* have provided for single-chamber parliamentary systems. In some *Länder* the constitution was approved by a qualified vote of the parliament, in others by a referendum, and in still others by both a parliamentary vote and a referendum. In the first generation of *Land* constitutions before the Basic Law "full constitutions" were written, while in the second generation after 1949 less attention was paid to the basic rights which had been provided by the Basic Law and which included the *Länder*. The third generation of constitutions in the five new *Länder* were influenced more by "modern" values such as social rights and state goals, which aroused a good deal of controversy at least among constitutional scholars in the West. While direct democracy was authorized in several of the older *Länder*, this alternative has become more available since the revisions of the constitution of Schleswig-Holstein in 1990 and the passage of the constitutions of the five new *Länder* which largely followed the Schleswig-Holstein model. As a result more "plebiscitary" democracy, whether in the form of referenda, the direct election of mayors, or other applications, has become a focus of discussion and controversy since the beginning of the 1990s. Some other differences are less dramatic. For example, just as in the American states the powers of the governors vary, in Germany the heads of government of the city states have somewhat fewer powers than their counterparts in the territorial *Länder*. In some German *Länder* elections are held every four years, in others every five years. The number of cabinet ministers varies, as do their titles and areas of responsibility. In spite of all these and other differences, the autonomy the *Länder* possess is exercised within a legal framework provided by the Basic Law, which requires a considerable degree of "homogeneity."

Notes

Somewhat different versions of this chapter have been published in *Publius: The Journal of Federalism* 28, no. 4 (Autumn 1998), pp. 105–125, and the *Rutgers Law Journal* 31, no. 4 (Summer 2000), pp. 971–998.

1 Andrea Stiens, *Chancen und Grenzen der Landesverfassungen um deutschen Bundesstaat der Gegenwart* (Berlin: Duncker & Humblot, 1997), pp. 308–310.

2 Article 51, Basic Law.

3 For a discussion in English of the Bundesrat, see Hans-Georg Wehling, "The Bundesrat," *Publius: The Journal of Federalism* 19, no. 4 (Autumn 1989), pp. 53–64.

4 Potsdam Agreement, sec. 2, para. 9.

5 For a review of the origins of the *Land* constitutions, see Sven Hölscheidt, "Die Praxis der Verfassungsverabschiebung und der Verfassungsänderung in der Bundesrepublik", *Zeitschrift für Parlamentsfragen* 26 (February 1995), pp. 58–84.

6 For a detailed discussion of the constitutions of these three *Länder*, see Hans von Mangoldt, *Die Verfassungen der neuen Bundesländer* (Berlin: Duncker & Humblot, 1993).

7 Hölscheidt, "Die Praxis," p. 81.

8 Stiens, *Chancen und Grenzen der Landesverfassungen*, pp. 314–315.

9 Ibid., p. 317; see also the more provocative reasons suggested by Brun-Otto Bryde, "Verfassungsreform der Länder unter bundesverfassungsrechtlichem Unitarisierungsdruck," 50 Jahre Verfassung des Landes Hessen: Eine Festschrift, edited by Hans Eichel and Klaus Peter Möller (Wiebaden: Westdeutscher Verlag, 1997), pp. 433–444.

10 Ibid., pp. 59 and 63.

11 Mattias Niedobitek, *Neuere Entwicklungen im Verfassungssrecht der deutschen Länder* (Speyer: Forschungsinstitut für öffentliche Verwaltung der Hochschule Speyer, 1994), pp. 38–40.

12 Albert von Mutius and Thomas Friedrich, "Verfassungsentwicklung in den neuen Bundesländern – zwischen Eigenständigkeit und notwendiger Homogenität," *Staatswissenschaft und Staatspraxis* (1991), p. 247.

13 See, for example, Niedobitek, *Neuere Entwicklungen*, p. 2.

14 Klaus Otto Nass, "The Foreign and European Policy of the German Länder," *Publius: The Journal of Federalism* 19, no. 4 (Autumn 1989), pp. 165–184,

15 Siegfried Magiera, "Verfassunggebung der Länder als Gliedstaaten der Bundesrepublik Deutschland," *Zur Enstehung von Landesverfassungen in den neuen Ländern der Bundesrepublik Deutschland*, edited by Klaus Stern (Köln: Carl Heymanns Verlag, 1992), pp. 141–163.

16 Christian Starck, "The Constitutionalisation Process of the New Länder: A Source of Inspiration for the Basic Law?," *German Politics* 3, no. 3 (December 1994), pp. 118–119.

17 Von Mutius and Friedrich, "Verfassungsentwicklung," p. 248.

18 Johannes Dietlein, "Die Rezeption von Bundesgrundrechten durch Landesverfassungsrecht," *Archiv des öffentlichen Rechts* 120, no. 1 (March 1995), pp. 2–3.

19 For foreign activities of the Länder, see Nass, "The Foreign and European Policy," pp. 165–184.

20 Arthur B. Gunlicks, "German Federalism After Unification: The Legal/Constitutional Response," *Publius: Journal of Federalism* 24, no. 2 (Spring 1994),

pp. 90–91.

21 The following section is based on Arthur B. Gunlicks, "The New Constitutions of East Germany," *German Politics* 5, no. 2 (August 1996), pp. 262–275; see also the excellent discussion on direct democracy at the local and Land levels in Germany today in Susan E. Scarrow, "Party Competition and Institutional Change," *Party Politics* 3 (October 1997), pp. 451–472.

22 For a table showing the date of acceptance of referenda at the local and *Land* levels into the constitutions of the *Länder* from 1970 through 1996, see Scarrow, "Party Competition," pp. 462–463.

23 Wolfgang Luthardt, *Direkte Demokratie: Ein Vergleich in Westeuropa* (Baden-Baden: Nomos Verlagsgesellschaft, 1994), pp. 113–118.

24 *Frankfurter Allgemeine Zeitung* (8 June 2002), p. 4.

25 For an excellent overview of the Land requirements for various kinds of referenda, see Hans-Herbert von Arnim, *Vom schönen Schein der Demokratie* (München: Droemer Verlag, 2000), pp. 304–311 (cloth edn).

26 Detlef Merten, "Grundgesetz und Verfassungen der neuen deutschen Länder," in *Verfassungen im vereinten Deutschland*, edited by Willi Blümel, Siegfried Magiera, Detlef Merten, and Karl-Peter Sommermann (2nd edn; Speyerer Forschungsberichte 117, Forschungsinstitut für öffentliche Verwaltung, 1993), pp. 58–59. See also on this point, Arthur B. Gunlicks, "Elections in Germany and the United States at Local, State and National Levels: Too Much or Too Little Democracy?," *Amerikastudien* 39, no. 3 (1994), pp. 407–414.

27 Johannes Rux, "Die Verfassungsdiskussion in den neuen Bundesländern – Vorbild für die   Reform des Grundgesetz?," *Zeitschrift für Parlamentsfragen* 23, no. 2 (June 1992), pp. 304–305.

28 For a very useful review of Land constitutional provisions regarding the institutions of government, citizen rights, and other aspects of government, see Christian Pestalozza, "Introduction," *Verfassungen der deutschen Bundesländer* (5th edn; München: C.H. Beck [dtv], 1995), pp. E1–E52.

29 Ibid., p. E24.

30 For detailed analyses of the jurisprudence of the *Land* constitutional courts, see Christian Starck and Klaus Stern (eds), *Landesverfassungsgerichtsbarkeit*, 3 vols (Baden-Baden: Nomos Verlagsgesellschaft, 1983).

31 See, for example, Gunter Kisker, "The West German Federal Constitutional Court as Guardian of the Federal System," *Publius: The Journal of Federalism* 19, no. 4 (Autumn 1989), pp. 30–52. See also Donald P. Kommers, *The Constitutional Jurisprudence of the Federal Republic of Germany* (Durham: Duke University Press, 1989), pp. 69–120; Philip Blair, *Federalism and Judicial Review in West Germany* (Oxford: Clarendon Press, 1981) and, by the same author, "Federalism, Legalism and Political Reality: The Record of the Federal Constitutional Court," *German Federalism Today*, edited by Charlie Jeffery and Peter Savigear (New York: St. Martin's Press, 1991), pp. 63–83.

32 Brandenburg Constitution, Article 26, para. 2.

33 "Bestimmte Lebenswirklichkeiten," *Frankfurter Allgemeine Zeitung* (16 June 1995), p. 14.

34 Otmar Jung, "Landesverfassungspolitik im Bundesstaat: ein listiger Umweg der Geschichte?" *Zeitschrift für Parlamentsfragen* 26 (February 1995), p. 56; Johannes Dietlein, "Die Verfassunggebung in den neuen Bundesländern," *Nordrhein-westphälische Verwaltungsblätter* 7 (1 November 1993), pp. 402–403, and "Der Schutz nichtehelicher Lebensgemeinschaften in den Verfassungen und Verfassungsentwürfen der neuen Länder," *Deutsch-Deutsche Rechtszeitschrift*, no. 5 (1993), pp. 136–141; and Gerhard Deter, "Frauenrechte in den Verfassungsentwürfen der neuen Länder," *Zeitschrift für Rechtspolitik*, no. 1 (1993), pp. 22–29.

35 Dietlein, "Die Rezeption," p. 10.

36 Detlef Merten, "Über Staatsziele," *Die öffentliche Verwaltung* 46 (May 1993), p. 375.

37 Brandenburg Constitution, Article 12, para. 2; Thuringian Constitution, Article 2, para. 3. The difference in language is potentially important. "Sexual identity" refers to individuals; "orientation" could refer to others, thus raising questions about sexual abuse of children. See "Bestimmte Lebenswirklichkeiten," *Frankfurter Allgemeine Zeitung* (16 June 1995), p. 14.

38 Thuringian Constitution, Article 32; Brandenburg Constitution, Article 39, para. 3.

39 Rux, "Die Verfassungsdiskusion," p. 298; Ute Sacksofsky, "Landesverfassungen und Grundgesetz am Beispiel der Verfassungen der neuen Bundesländer," *Neue Zeitschrift für Verwaltungsrecht*, vol. 3 (1993), p. 238.

40 The discussion about social rights and state goals in the East was influenced by the proposals for a new East German Constitution made by "the Roundtable" in the winter of 1990, before the results of the March parliamentary elections which made clear that a large majority of the population wanted unification with West Germany, not a new East German Constitution. See Bernd Guggenheimer and Tine Stein (eds), *Die Verfassungsdiskussion im Jahr der deutschen Einheit* (München: Carl Hanser Verlag, 1991), Section IV; Christoph Fedderson, "Die Verfassunggebung in den neuen Ländern: Grundrechte, Staatsziele, Plebiszite," *Die öffentliche Verwaltung* (December 1992), p. 990.

41 D. Franke and R. Kneifel-Haverkamp, "Die brandenburgische Landesverfassung," *Jahrbuch des öffentlichen Rechts der Gegenwart* NF, vol. 42, Peter Häberle (ed.) (Tübingen: J. C. B. Mohr, 1994), p. 112.

42 Siegfried Jutzi, "Staatsziele der Verfassung des Freistaats Thüringen – zugleich ein Beitrag zur Bedeutung landesverfasungrechtlicher Staatsziele im Bundesstaat," *Thüringischer Verwaltungsblätter* 4 (3 February 1995), p. 26.

43 Hans von Mangoldt, a leading constitutional expert, has expressed strong criticism of such provisions as being mere vague declarations without any practical effect. See his *Die Verfassungen*, p. 14.

44 Peter Häberle suggests that while the distinction between enforceable and

nonenforceable rights needs to be maintained, the traditional dualism may not be all that convincing anymore. Peter Häberle, "Die Verfassungs-bewegung in den fünf neuen Bundesländern Deutschlands, 1991–1992," *Jahrbuch des öffentlichen Rechts* NF vol. 42, Peter Häberle (ed.) (Tübingen: J. C. B. Mohr (Paul Siebeck), 1994), p. 159.

45 Dietlein, "Die Verfassunggebung," p. 402.

46 Karl-Peter Sommermann, "Die Diskussion über die Normierung von Staatszielen," *Verfassungsprobleme im vereinten Deutschland*, p. 79. Christian Starck is especially critical in his article, "The Constitutionalisation Process," pp. 127–128.

47 Von Mangoldt, *Die Verfassungen*, p. 33.

48 Ibid., pp. 17–18, 42–43; Merten, "Über Staatsziele," pp. 371, 375 and "Grundgesetz," pp. 61–62.

49 Merten, "Über Staatsziele," p. 376. See also Dietlein, "Die Verfassunggebung," pp. 403–404. For a view that these concerns are "exaggerated," see Siegfried Jutzi, "Staatsziele der Verfassung des Freistaats Thüringen," *Thüringischer Verwaltungsblätter* 4 (3 März 1995), p. 59.

50 Karl-Peter Sommermann, "Die Diskussion," pp. 78–79, 85. For a view that the focus on various rights was a reaction against almost six decades of dictatorship, see Dietlein, "Die Verfassunggebung," p. 402.

51 Konrad Hesse, "Der Beitrag der Verfassungen in den neuen Bundesländern zur Verfassungsentwicklung in Deutschland," *Kritische Vierteljahresschrift zur Gesetzgebung und Rechtswissenschaft* 76, no. 1 (1993), pp. 8 and 12.

52 Ibid., p. 9 and Sommermann, "Die Diskussion," pp. 78–79.

53 Rosemarie Will, "Die Grundrechtsgewährleistungen und die staatssorganisationsrechtlichen Regelungen der neuen Verfassungen im Vergleich," *Kritische Vierteljahresschrift für Gesetzgebung und Rechtswissenschaft* 76 (1993), pp. 469, 482.

54 Klaus Walter, "Volksabstimmung über Landesverfassung," *Das Parlament* (27 May/3 June 1994), p. 10; "Die PDS sieht sich as Sieger der Wahlen und der Volksabstimmung," *Frankfurter Allgemeine Zeitung* (14 June 1994), p. 5.

55 Hölscheidt, "Die Praxis der Verfassungsverabschiedung," p. 77.

56 Ibid., p. 79.

57 See, for example, Christian Starck, "Verfassunggebung in den neuen Ländern," *Zeitschrift für Gesetzgebung* 7, no. 1 (1992), p. 17.

5

Financing
the federal system

Introduction

According to the official English translation of Article 20, para. 1, of the
Basic Law, the Federal Republic of Germany is a "democratic and social
federal state." A better translation might be "a democratic and federal
social welfare state." "Social" in German usually means socially fair, or
just, and generally equal. Therefore, this concept provides a constitutional basis for the German welfare state. A European-type welfare state
is under strong unitary pressures, because government programs for old
age pensions, disability, medical insurance, nursing home care, unemployment insurance, child support, and other social services must be
offered on a national basis in order to avoid regional differences and meet
nation-wide expectations of fairness and equality. Even such programs as
public assistance (*Sozialhilfe*), which is implemented and financed by
local governments, is regulated by federal law so that there are hardly any
differences among the localities. The Basic Law still speaks of preserving
or securing "uniformity of living conditions" in Article 106, para. 3. This
goal was modified somewhat in the 1994 constitutional reform process to
read "equivalency of living conditions" in Article 72, para. 2 (Article 106
was not changed, because it was anticipated that it would be replaced by
a new section on financial arrangements). In any case these "conditions"
are not only those provided by the welfare state but also include a variety
of services such as education, cultural activities, youth services, police
protection, hospitals, sports facilities, etc. They also include the infrastructure that goes with such services, such as schools, roads, bus, and rail
services. Total expenditures for all of these and other public services and
facilities amounted to 50.8 percent of GDP in 1995 and 50.6 percent in
1996, but declined to 48 percent in 1998 (United States = 31.6 percent

in 1997). Taxes for all levels were 22 percent and various social insurance charges 18.5 percent for a total of *40.5 percent of GNP* (however, *individual* social insurance charges in 1998 were 41.8 percent of wages and salaries, which is significantly higher than in the United States).[1] It is clear that pressures are strong for a national welfare and tax system that can raise efficiently and effectively the revenues needed to support the many state functions in Germany.

On the other hand, the Basic Law provides for a federal system that, along with the concept of the "social" state, is guaranteed in Article 79, para. 3. How to secure and preserve a highly developed social welfare state with a variety of public services available to all citizens and simultaneously maintain a functioning federal system with autonomous *Länder* is a question Germans have had to wrestle with since the Basic Law went into effect in 1949. To put it somewhat crassly, "power is where the money is." If the federal government has control over revenues, it is going to be difficult to sustain a meaningful federal system. As we will see below, the federal *government* does not "control" the tax system, but the *federation* does. What this means is that the government and its majority in the *Bundestag* can pass tax legislation that also binds the *Länder*, but the *Bundesrat*, which represents the *Land* governments, must approve such legislation as long as the tax revenues accrue at least partially to the *Land* or local governments. The result is that the *Länder* – that is, the *Land* governments that make up the *Bundesrat* majority – have about as much power collectively as the federal government and its majority in the *Bundestag* in passing finance legislation, but the individual *Länder*, especially if they are in the minority, have little influence. The *Land* parliaments, which are not represented in the *Bundesrat*, have even less to say.

Historical development[2]

In the Bismarck Reich of 1871, the Constitution gave the federation the right to collect customs duties and revenues derived from postal and telegraph services as well as various excise taxes on salt, tobacco, and sugar. The states (they were not called *Länder* until the Weimar Republic) were given the general power to pass tax legislation, and the Reich was dependent on the states for contributions based on population. These contributions were approved annually by the *Bundesrat*, which then as now is composed of unelected delegates from the states. They were not adequate to meet the needs of the federation, which had to borrow heavily as a result.

The Weimar Republic that emerged after the First World War brought about fundamental changes in the tax system. The constitution gave the federation general authority for tax legislation, and the *Länder* had little power to shape federal tax policy. The only limitation on the federation was that it had to preserve the capacity of the *Länder* to survive, which was a nebulous restriction at best. The new constitution provided the basis for a uniform Reich administration of finances and for the finance and tax reform introduced by Finance Minister Matthias Erzberger shortly after 1918. The separate taxes of the previous Reich were replaced by a system of joint taxes. The most important taxes, the income tax, corporation tax, and turnover (sales) tax, were assumed by the federation, which then transferred a certain percentage of each to the *Länder*. Since the revenues the *Länder* received from the income and corporation taxes depended on the local yield, considerable differences in tax resources emerged among the *Länder*. These were made up to some extent by transfers among the *Länder* and federal grants.

If the Weimar Republic became more like a decentralized unitary state than a federal state, the Third Reich of Adolf Hitler was a centralized state with no pretense of regional autonomy. In January 1934, a year after Hitler took power, a law was passed according to which the *Länder* ceased to exist as meaningful federal units, and the local administrative units that came into being were financed by grants from the central government.

During the occupation in West Germany after 1945, politically active German finance experts debated the future of their country's tax policy. They divided basically into two camps: one oriented strongly by principle toward a federal solution that favored the *Länder* more or less along the lines of the Bismarck Reich, and one that was more unitary in orientation for pragmatic and largely economic reasons. Those who focused on economic and social policies, especially the Social Democrats, tended to support the more unitary solution, but federalists and centralists could not always be identified with any particular party.

In the years immediately following the 1945, significant differences emerged among the newly created *Länder* in their fiscal capacities, with those receiving the largest numbers of refugees from the East suffering the most. Controversy developed among the *Länder* over some kind of fiscal equalization measure which demonstrated their desire to arrive at a resolution of the issue; however, this was hardly possible without some kind of central authority. The "poor" and "rich" *Länder* were divided among themselves, sometimes in spite of common political party ties. As we shall see, the Basic Law and its provisions for tax legislative authority at the federal level brought about a dramatic change of the situation.

The issue of taxes in the drafting of the Basic Law[3]

In June 1948 the Western Allies encouraged the Germans in their three zones to draft a democratic and federal Constitution and to call for a constitutional convention by 1 September 1948. Though many Germans were reluctant to take a step that was sure to exacerbate tensions between the Western Allies and the Soviets and therefore place unification at risk, a group of constitutional experts was invited to participate in a conference in August at Herrenchiemsee, a palace on a lake island in Bavaria. The Bavarians introduced a draft constitution that was basically confederal in nature and which gave the *Länder* taxation powers modeled after the Bismarck Reich. Other participants looked more at the Weimar Constitution as a more unitary model for a federal state. After the opening debates about confederation versus federation, this issue was turned over to committee for further deliberation.

Given these two very different positions on the nature of the future political system, it is not surprising that the participants of the Herrenchiemsee Conference were provided with some dramatically different models of financing. They were also ambivalent about which alternatives to follow, because of the uncertainty over the future financial needs of the federal, *Land,* and local governments. The result was a set of rather disappointing recommendations for the Parliamentary Council, which was to draft the official document.

The Parliamentary Council met on 1 September 1948 as the first parliamentary-like body to include representatives of all three Western zones. The political parties generally sent their leading members, some of whom were also constitutional experts. Although the majority of votes was controlled by the middle-class parties – CDU/CSU, FDP, and DP – the SPD was confident of victory in the coming elections and decided to concentrate on broad legislative powers for the *Bundestag* rather than attempting to have certain economic and social provisions included in the new Constitution. The middle- class parties, in turn, focused on a federal system that could serve as a barrier to future socialist economic policy that might be introduced by a social democratic government.

When the finance committee of the Parliamentary Council met, the discussions were dominated by an expert, Hermann Höpker-Aschoff from the FDP, rather than the representatives of the large parties. The committee did not follow the American example of fiscal autonomy for the states, because this allowed for differences in tax systems, revenues, and thus public services that the Germans thought they could not afford. Dr. Höpker-Aschoff explained that

[o]ur poverty and the high level of our tax rates will not permit us the luxury of an entirely unregulated scramble for tax sources between two competitors. In the United States it may be possible for the federation to levy and collect its own income tax and the states to levy and collect their income taxes – the same with inheritance taxes and so on. For us, it would be entirely unworkable.[4]

The goal was to create a system of finances in which neither the federal nor the *Land* level would be dependent on the other, as was the case, respectively, in the Bismarck Reich and the Weimar Republic. The solution presented was to have certain taxes set aside for each level but to have the two levels share the most important taxes. Statutory law would then provide for a distribution of the shared or joint taxes in such a way that the needs of the poorer *Länder* would be addressed. It was also agreed that the *Länder* via the *Bundesrat* would have the right to veto the tax legislation proposed by the federal government. Only the administration of the finances remained unsettled. Unfortunately for the finance committee, however, the Allies – in particular, General Lucius Clay – indicated they would not accept these provisions, because they were not sufficiently federal.[5]

The Allies insisted that the Constitution provide for a dual tax system in which the federation and *Länder* each had legislative authority over only those taxes it needed to meet its responsibilities.[6] The Allies also rejected the proposed system of fiscal equalization payments by the richer to the poorer *Länder*, which not even the Germans in the Economic Council in the Bizonia had approved at that time. They saw a system of grants-in-aid on the American model as a better solution that would not make the *Länder* so dependent on the federation for their taxes. The *Land* governments, on the other hand, took the opposite position that their autonomy would be threatened by a system of federal grants but protected by the proposal to require approval of finance legislation in the *Bundesrat*.

While Konrad Adenauer and the CDU seemed willing to compromise with the Allies, the SPD leader, Kurt Schumacher, and his party were adamant in insisting on tax legislation authority for the federation. The SPD believed that a strong welfare state in West Germany would be attractive to East Germany and discourage communist elements in their efforts to undermine the West German republic. Only a financially strong federation could meet this challenge. Too great a focus on federal principles would make it more difficult to offer the necessary social services equally and nation-wide.

It is not a little ironic that just as the Allies notified the Parliamentary Council toward the end of April that they would accept a broad federal legislative authority in tax matters and a joint administration of finances, the SPD was also indicating its willingness to compromise with the Allies on various issues. Agreement on the constitutional draft between the Allies and Germans was therefore reached without much difficulty. Turnover (sales) taxes were given to the federation, and the income and corporation taxes were given to the *Länder*; however, the right of the federation to tap into these taxes made them in effect joint taxes, in spite of the fact that the Allies had rejected the proposal for federal–*Land* joint taxes. Concurrent powers were broadened so that the SPD no longer feared the federation would not have sufficient authority to pass the kind of economic and social legislation it desired. Though not provided for directly, the constitutional draft also made it possible to create a system of fiscal equalization among the *Länder*. The constitution, called Basic Law because of its alleged temporary nature until unification, went into effect on 23 May 1949.

The finance reforms of 1955 and 1969[7]

Once the Basic Law went into effect, much, but not all, of the German system of finance had been determined. The proportions of the income and corporation taxes that were to go to the federation and *Länder* had to be set each budget year, and each year the federal government and the *Länder* struggled over these in the *Bundesrat*. That this was more a federalism issue and not just a partisan struggle could be seen in the fact that the CDU/CSU-dominated federal government, which had a majority in both chambers, could not count on all of the CDU-governed *Länder* to support it. Connected to the question of the proportions of the income and corporation taxes that each level would receive was the issue of fiscal equalization and the transfer of funds to the poorer *Länder*. The first law passed by the *Bundestag* and *Bundesrat* regulating the proportions each level was to receive gave the federation 27 percent for the fiscal year 1951; between 1951 and 1954 the federal share was raised to 38 percent. The demands of the federal government for a still larger share led to considerable tension between the federal government and the *Länder* and demonstrated clearly that the finance provisions in the Basic Law were unsatisfactory, especially for the poorer *Länder*.

A second continuing controversy raged between the poorer and richer *Länder* over the issue of fiscal equalization payments among them. The poorest *Länder*, Schleswig-Holstein, Lower Saxony, and Bavaria, in that order, were especially burdened by large proportions of refugees; these same *Länder* were more rural than industrial and simply did not have the tax resources enjoyed by the more industrialized territorial *Länder* and city-states; and some *Länder*, for example, those in the French zone, had higher occupation costs. The richer city-states of Hamburg and Bremen had suffered severe bomb damage and were reluctant to share their *relative* wealth with their neighbors because of their own burdens; the richer territorial states, especially North-Rhine Westphalia, insisted on the importance of maintaining *Land* autonomy in a federal system. Based in part on a study commission's recommendations, a modest fiscal equalization law was passed in February 1951. It was promptly challenged before the Federal Constitutional Court by two of the richer *Länder*, but the law was upheld. Nevertheless, the poorer *Länder* remained frustrated in their efforts to pursuade their richer counterparts to approve a law that would provide meaningful transfers of funds.

In the meantime the federation and the *Länder* had become committed by a change in the Basic Law to pass a finance reform act by the end of 1955. Two bills were involved: one was in effect an amendment to the Basic Law specifying which major taxes were to belong to which level and distributing the proportions of the income and corporation taxes between the federation and the *Länder*; the other concerned the transfer payments among the *Länder* designed to achieve more fiscal equality. The conflict over the provisions of this legislation between the federal government and, to a considerable extent, the poorer *Länder*, on the one hand and the richer *Länder*, on the other hand was severe, and it revealed fundamental differences between these two groups about the federal order. For the majority of *Länder*, especially for the richer *Länder*, their ability to manage their own affairs and their essential autonomy were at stake, while for the poorer *Länder* their ability to provide essential services and meet the constitutional requirement of uniform living conditions required assistance from the federal and other *Land* governments. In the meantime the federal government continued to demand a greater share of total revenues in order to meet its needs, which now included a newly established military force.

Finally, in December 1955, a compromise was reached and approved by both chambers. The turnover (sales) tax was retained as a federal tax, and the income and corporation taxes remained with the *Länder* with federal shares set at first at 33.3 and then at 35 percent after 1958. The new provisions for transfers among the *Länder* and federal supplementary grants were to bring the fiscal resources of the poorer *Länder* to within 87.5 percent of the *Länder* average. As in the period of the late 1940s and early

1950s noted above, the conflict over the finance reforms in 1955 was not partisan, although party loyalty had some relevance.

Unfortunately, the Finance Reform of 1955 did not bring about the stability that everyone had hoped to achieve. The federation became more intrusive in its dealings with the *Länder*, gaining ever more authority via federal grants to the *Länder*, a process that was occurring also in the United States. At the same time the *Länder* were required to administer – and to finance – more and more federal legislation. In theory the *Bundesrat* could have been more of a barrier against these federal activities, but partisan considerations combined with the fact that most of the *Länder* thought it politically unwise to reject federal help usually made it difficult to oppose the government.[8] Criticism grew that *Land* tasks were being financed by the federation and federal policies by the *Länder*, that federal grants were undermining *Land* autonomy, and that there was too much imbalance in the development of federal and *Land* budgets.[9]

On the other hand, the law on fiscal equalization among the *Länder* which was debated and changed in 1959, brought considerable relief to the *Länder*. The amounts by which the resources of the poorer *Länder* were to be raised were increased to 90 percent of the average of all the *Länder* in 1958 and 91 percent after the beginning of 1959. *Länder* with above-average fiscal capacity were to transfer 75 percent of the amount between 100 and 110 percent to the pool for the poorer *Länder*. In general these changes were to the advantage of the poorer *Länder* and came largely at the expense of North-Rhine Westphalia and Hamburg.[10]

In March 1964 the government of Chancellor Ludwig Erhard and the *Land* prime ministers agreed to form a commission to recommend a comprehensive finance reform. This became known as the Troeger Commission, named after its chairman, a former minister of finance in Hesse.[11] Both the SPD and CDU/CSU were represented, which was necessary because any constitutional amendment to reorganize the system of finances would require a two-thirds majority in the *Bundestag* and *Bundesrat*. The Commission issued its final report in March 1966. The concept of "cooperative federalism," borrowed from the American term that suggested cooperation rather than competition or conflict between the federal and subnational levels, was a theme that ran throughout the comprehensive recommendations of the report. This implied a reduction of *Land* autonomy in favor of joint tasks. Later this positive view toward cooperation was given particular expression in Article 104a, para. 4, which authorizes federal grants in very broad language, and in the "joint tasks" of Article 91a and 91b, which called for the federation to participate in the financing and planning of three areas that had been *Land* responsibilities.[12]

In the meantime the Erhard government was severely weakened by eroding economic conditions and strains between the two partners in the government coalition, the CDU/CSU and the FDP. When this coalition fell apart, a Grand Coalition of CDU/CSU and SPD was formed in December 1966. One of its announced goals was a finance reform that the previous government under Chancellor Erhard had begun but not completed. Dissatisfaction with the Finance Reform of 1955 remained high: severe conflict remained over fiscal equalization; there had been an increase in "mixed financing" that was in a constitutional "gray zone"; and federal grants for various projects were a tempting "golden harness" (*Goldener Zügel*) that led to distortions in *Land* priorities, which meant that tasks not aided by federal government were neglected.[13] But the *Länder* demonstrated again that they were unable to come to an agreement among themselves without the intervention of the federal government.[14]

The new government introduced a bill in March 1967 based closely on the Troeger Commission report. It asserted in its draft legislation that the people no longer accepted significant differences in services and burdens as the price of a general autonomy for the *Länder* in policy making.[15] But federation–*Land* differences arose immediately and threatened to undermine the reform even though the Grand Coalition government had an overwhelming majority in both legislative chambers. The underlying problem in efforts to achieve any kind of finance reform was that the federal government and the rich and poor *Länder*, respectively, always agreed that someone else should pay. For the poor *Länder*, dependence either on their richer counterparts or on the federation was unsatisfactory.[16] For the rich *Länder*, their autonomy was at stake. The federation always claimed to need more funds.

But there was agreement that the uncontrolled growth (*Wildwuchs*) of commonly financed programs should be straightened out by placing them into separate areas. For example, the federation should restrict itself to programs, including joint tasks, that involved responsibilities that crossed *Land* borders and were expensive. In such programs there should be joint financing and planning. However, controversy emerged regarding the number of joint tasks that should be included in the reform package. In the end three were accepted, and it was agreed that as a rule the federation would provide 50 percent of the funding.[17] The localities should share in the joint taxes, partly from the Value-Added Tax (VAT) and partly from the personal income tax. In the case of the income tax, the federal government wanted to give localities the right to set different rates. But it did not push for a general local government finance reform at that time.[18]

An important debate occurred over the taxes that were to become joint taxes – that is, the income, corporation, and turnover (sales) taxes. In 1968 the VAT was introduced as a new European Community-wide turnover tax. Conflict arose immediately over the distribution of its revenues, over joint taxes, need-based distributions, and *Land* autonomy.[19]

In March 1968 the federal government introduced a draft of a finance reform bill that went to the *Bundesrat* in April. It proposed several changes in the previous system of finance, including the addition of Article 91a and 91b and Article 104a to the Basic Law. Joint taxes were to consist of the VAT as well as the income and the corporation tax. The business tax for the local governments was in effect – though not officially – a joint tax, because 40 percent of the revenues were to be shared with the *Land* and federal levels. The localities would participate in income tax revenues, but they would not set tax rates.[20] After considerable controversy, especially between rich and poor *Länder*, final agreement was reached and a considerable number of important changes in the system of finance, usually referred to as the Finance Reform of 1969, went into effect on 1 January 1970.

Fiscal equalization measures in 1970 brought about a range in the adjusted fiscal capacity of the *Länder* from 95.6 percent to 104.7 percent of the average. Article 104a and the joint tasks put an end to the uncontrolled growth of federal grants. The federation now sat in committees with all the *Länder*, and bilateral agreements ceased. Federal grants were now based on *Bundesrat* approval. In federal–*Land* planning committees for joint tasks, each *Land* was given one vote and the federation was given votes equal to the total number of *Länder*; decisions were made with a three-fourths majority. The "supply-side dictatorship" (*Angebotsdiktatur*) created by federal grants basically disappeared. The federation no longer had the option of offering a single *Land* funds or of withdrawing an offer.[21]

The expert whose book on German finance from 1948 to 1990 has been the source for this historical review concluded, among other things, that the constitutional finance reform of 1969 which

> strengthened the trend toward a broader unitary system under the slogan of "cooperative federalism" did not lead to a strengthening of the federation vis-à-vis the *Länder* in general. On the contrary, as a result of the increase in central decision-making at the federal level with a strengthened participation of the *Bundesrat*, or, in other words, through more "joint and intertwined decision-making" (*Politikverflechtung*), the *Länder* as a whole gained additional influence in federal policy-making. One should not overlook the

fact, however, that the individual *Land* more likely lost an autonomous room for maneuver.[22]

The Finance Reform of 1969 did not, of course, resolve all of the conflicts between the rich and poor *Länder* and between these and the federation. Significant changes in the fiscal capacity of *Länder* took place in the 1970s. As a result of the oil crises in the early and late 1970s, Lower Saxony benefited strongly from its oil production. To the great annoyance of the *Länder* that had to transfer equalization funds to Lower Saxony, these oil revenues were not counted in fiscal equalization. Owing to the steel and shipbuilding crises, North-Rhine Westphalia, Bremen, and Hamburg became much less affluent, and the Saarland became even poorer. On the other hand, Bavaria rose to about average in fiscal capacity. It was alleged with some reason that the CDU/CSU–FDP coalition government favored the CDU/CSU *Länder* in financial matters. Several SPD *Länder* took the fiscal equalization law to the Federal Constitutional Court, which ruled much of it unconstitutional in 1986 and set the criteria for a new law. One of these criteria concerned changing the basis of the calculations for transfers from the richer to the poorer *Länder* to fiscal capacity rather than tax capacity. Thus, Lower Saxony could not exclude its oil revenues after 1986.[23]

No sooner was the reform implemented in response to the 1986 decision of the Federal Constitutional Court than several SPD *Länder* complained again before the Court in 1988. In the meantime a new conflict arose over federal grants for public assistance, for which the *Länder* and their localities are responsible. This conflict was resolved in December 1988 via a compromise that was to provide the *Länder* with DM 2.5 billion in "structural funds" grants over a ten-year period.[24] This change had barely gone into effect when the Wall came down in November 1989. German unification, which came eleven months later, meant that new and far-reaching changes in the German system of public finance were now required. But while experts were wrestling with these challenges, the Federal Constitutional Court's decision in 1992 in response to the SPD challenge in 1988 led to the provision of additional federal funds for the purpose of reducing the debt of Bremen and the Saarland.

Basic principles of German fiscal federalism[25]

All constitutional provisions regarding finances are contained in Section X of the Basic Law, which consists of Articles 104a to Article 115. These

Articles and legislation dealing with finances are called the "financial con-stitution" (*Finanzverfassung*). They are supplemented by Article 28, para. 2, which provides certain guarantees of fiscal autonomy to local governments, and Article 91a and 91b which provide for federal–*Land* "joint tasks."

The federation, that is, the federal government (cabinet) *together* with the *Bundestag* and *Bundesrat*, has most of the taxing authority (Article 105). It has exclusive jurisdiction over some taxes and concurrent legisla-tive powers over most other taxes. In German constitutional law, the exer-cise of a concurrent power by the federation excludes any *Land* legislation on the matter. The *Länder* have the authority to pass legislation concern-ing local excise and consumer taxes, but this legislation usually allows their local governments to raise the taxes.

The term used by German economists to reflect the distribution of rev-enues between the units of the German federal system is *Finanzausgleich*. It has a basic meaning of fiscal balance among levels of government and is perhaps best translated as "fiscal equalization." Nevertheless, it can have somewhat different specific meanings. "Vertical fiscal equalization" (*ver-tikaler Finanzausgleich*) refers to the distribution between different *levels*, while "horizontal fiscal equalization" (*horizontaler Finanzausgleich*) refers to transfers within the level.

The five stages of fiscal equalization[26]

Stage one: vertical distribution of separate and joint tax revenues

Article 106, discussed below, deals with vertical fiscal equalization, some-times also referred to as "primary fiscal equalization." The vertical fiscal equalization goes a long way toward providing the federation and *Länder* with the funds necessary to carry out their responsibilities. Indeed, Article 106, para. 3, says that the federation and *Länder* have an equal claim to cur-rent revenue to cover their necessary expenditures and that necessary expenditures of each level are to be coordinated in such a manner as to achieve a fair balance, avoid an overburdening of taxpayers, and provide uniformity of living conditions in the territory of the federation. Never-theless, given the differences in the economies of the German *Länder* and the autonomy of their governments, vertical or primary distributions of revenues do not bring about equality of resources.[27]

The Germans distinguish between a *Trennsystem*, or separate taxes accruing to one or another level, and a *Verbundsystem*, joint taxes shared by the various levels. The American practice which is mostly one of sepa-rate taxes for each level but which allows the different levels to tap the same source, as in the case of federal *and* state income taxes or federal *and* state gasoline or tobacco taxes, is unknown in Germany. The general rule is that any one source of funds can be taxed by only one level.[28] However, there is some discussion today of allowing the *Länder* and their local governments to set their own rates on the income tax within certain limits.

Separate federal taxes are listed in Article 106, para. 1.[29] They include taxes on the "finance monopolies," now only brandy; customs duties, most of which go to the EU; excise taxes, such as tobacco, sparkling wine, coffee, and gasoline taxes; income and corporation surtaxes for expenses attributed to unification; and taxes raised within the framework of the EU. Separate taxes for the *Länder*, provided by Article 106, para. 2, include a wealth tax (no longer being raised); inheritance tax; motor vehicle tax; property acquisition tax; beer tax; and betting and casino gambling taxes. They also have a tax for the purpose of fire protection, and they raise additional revenues through lotteries.[30]

Local governments are included in Article 106 of the Basic Law, but most of the details regarding their limited tax authority are provided by federal and *Land* statutory law. Separate local taxes include consumer or user taxes on such items as entertainment, nonalcoholic beverages, dogs, hunting and fishing, and licenses for the sale of beer. These are minor taxes that account for around 1–4 percent of local revenues,[31] about the same proportion as in the United States. The most important separate taxes are the *Realsteuern*, which include taxes on municipal property (*Grundsteuer* B) and agricultural land and forests (*Grundsteuer* A). The latter consist of most of the land that surrounds the village or town and is included within its jurisdiction,[32] that is, there is little land in Germany that is not incorporated. Property taxes accounted for about 12 percent of local tax revenues, or DM 11.1 billion, in 1994.[33] *Realsteuern* also include the *Gewerbesteuer*, a tax on business enterprises in the municipality. This tax used to be divided into three kinds: a tax on gross profits, a tax on capital assets, and a payroll tax. The latter two taxes were eliminated in 1998 and 1979–80, respectively. The remaining business tax (*Gewerbeertragssteuer*) is a tax placed usually on around 5 percent of net profits. The municipalities are allowed within limits to set their own assessment rates on the different *Realsteuern*.[34] The *Gewerbesteuer* is an important tax for most municipalities; however, it varies widely in yield based on the rate assessed by the localities and on the nature and location of the business enterprises.[35] In the 1970s the localities shared 40 percent of their business tax revenue with their *Land* and the federation; today the amount assessed is about 20 percent in the old *Länder*, about 25 percent of which goes to the federation. The assessment in the new *Länder*, which do not pay a supplementary contribution to the German Unity Fund, is about 10 percent.[36]

The most important taxes in Germany are not the separate taxes listed in table 5.1, but the joint, or shared, taxes authorized in Article 106, para. 3. These are the income tax, the corporation tax, and the turnover tax (since 1968 the VAT, a sales tax applied to each stage of production). Together they make up about 72 percent of total tax revenues and about 88 percent of *Länder* revenues.[37] The local governments receive 15 percent of the income tax and since 1998 2.2 percent of the VAT after the federation has received 5.63 percent for old age pensions. The federation and the *Länder* each receive 42.5 percent of the income tax and 50 percent of the corporation tax. The proportion of the VAT received by each level is set by federal law and can change when developments in revenues and expenditures at the federal and *Land* levels so demand. In 1998 VAT revenues – the VAT was set at 16 percent of the sale of goods and services in 1998 – were divided between the federation, *Länder*, and municipalities as indicated in table 5.1.

Stage two: horizontal distribution of joint tax revenues[38]
Article 107, para. 1, first grants the *Länder* their "primary" revenue share yielded from the personal income tax and corporation tax according to the residency principle, the same "local yield" (*örtliches Aufkommen*) principle that is applied to the municipalities' share of the income tax. In other words, the revenues from personal income taxes go to the municipality (up to an amount specified by law) and *Land* in which the taxpayer has his or her residence. The corporation tax revenues go to the location of production facilities, not to where the firm headquarters are located. The "local yield" principle has always been a source of controversy between the "richer" and "poorer" *Länder*. The former see the right to keep revenues generated in their own territory as a function of their autonomy, while the poorer *Länder* argue that funds should be distributed on the basis of need or population.

In contrast to the "local yield principle," the distribution of 75 percent of the *Land* share of the VAT is based on population. This provides for an element of equalization of revenues based on an "abstract" general need[39] and, more technically, according to certain assumptions of "final consumption."[40]

Table 5.1   **Own source taxes/revenues and distribution of joint tax revenue, 1999**

Federation	Länder	Localities
Insurance premium tax	Personal wealth tax[a]	Real property tax A
Bill of exchange tax a	Motor vehicle tax	Real property tax B
Domestic investment tax[a]	Beer tax	Second home tax
Road freight tax[a]	Inheritance tax	Licensing tax
Capital transfer/	Property acquisition tax	Entertainment tax
transaction tax[a]	Racing and lottery tax	Hunting & fishing tax
Customs duties	Casino gambling tax	Dog tax
Gasoline tax	Fire protection tax	Local beverage tax
Coffee tax		Business tax[b]
Sparkling wine tax		
Tobacco tax		
Brandy tax		
Solidarity tax surcharge		

Joint taxes %

Turnover tax (VAT = a form of sales tax)[c]	Special Distribution	Federation earmarked for old age pensions	5.63
		Municipalities compensation for elimination of capital business tax	2.2
	Remainder (92.17)	Federation	50.5
		Länder	49.5
Corporation tax		Federation	50
		Länder	50
Personal Income tax and payroll tax		Federation	42.5
		Länder	42.5
		Municipalities	15
Local business tax (*Gewerbesteuer*)b		This is a municipal tax, but some of it is shared with the *Land* and federal governments. The amounts shared depend on a number of factors that make it difficult to generalize.	

Notes: [a] These taxes are authorized but are no longer being raised; [b] The business tax is legally a local tax, but *de facto* it is a joint tax; [c] figures for 1999.
Sources: "Unsere Steuern von A-Z," Ausgabe 1997 (Bonn: Bundesministerium der Finanzen), pp. 44–45; Thomas Lenk, "Länderbericht Bundesrepublik Deutschland" in *Föderalismus – Hält er noch, was er verspricht?* edited by Hans Herbert von Arnim, Gisela Färber, und Stefan Fisch (Berlin: Duncker & Humblot, 2000), pp. 241–248; BMF, *Finanzbericht 1999*, 144.

Stage three: horizontal distribution based on tax capacity
At the third stage those *Länder* whose total share of revenues from the
personal income tax, corporation tax, business tax, the 75 percent of the
VAT distributed on the basis of population, and *Land* tax revenues is
below the *per capita* average receive supplementary funds from the
remaining 25 percent of the *Länder* share of the VAT. This "secondary"
distribution brings the poorer *Länder* up to 92 percent of the average *per
capita* revenue of all *Länder*.[41]

Stage four: horizontal fiscal equalization among the Länder
Same-level transfers from richer to poorer *Länder* are designed to provide
more differentiated assistance.[42] These transfers are sometimes called fiscal equalization "in a narrower sense."[43] The federal law that provides for
transfers among the *Länder* requires approval by the *Bundesrat*.

Horizontal fiscal equalization among the *Länder* is a further refine-
ment with the purpose of giving all *Länder* the means to provide virtually
the same services. This is derived from the "federal principle of standing by
one another,"[44] which in turn is a form of federal comity. The further
adjustments to produce even more equalization are considered necessary
to secure for the poorer recipient *Länder* the budget autonomy they
need and to meet the goal of equivalent living conditions throughout the
country.

Horizontal fiscal equalization is based on a complicated scheme that
contrasts the tax revenues a *Land* should have (fiscal needs) with those it
actually has (fiscal capacity). Both indicators are calculated on the basis of
average tax revenues, including 50 percent of the municipal tax revenues
(excluding their minor taxes), but each is subject to certain modifications.

Fiscal needs include consideration of the size and density of population
of municipalities. In accordance with the so-called "Brecht–Popitzsches
principle" first enunciated in the 1920s, it has been assumed that the larger
the population and the greater the population density of a municipality,
the higher are the *per capita* expenditures. Thus, the population of a town
of 5,000 is factored in at 100 percent, but for a city of 500,000 it is 130
percent; density figures of 1,500–2,000 inhabitants per km2 are worth
2 percent, while for 3,000 inhabitants per km2 they are worth 6 percent.
In recent years questions have been raised in the literature and in the
Federal Constitutional Court about the empirical evidence for this
principle.[45]

Another adjustment is made for the city-states, Bremen, Hamburg, and
Berlin. Their real populations are multiplied by 135 percent, with the result

multiplied in turn by the fiscal capacity of the city-state. Thus, by this procedure in 1993 the population of Hamburg (1,690,000) was increased to 2,280,000, which then raised Hamburg's equalization index figure from DM 7.161 billion to DM 9.347 billion (see table 5.2). The justification for this adjustment is that the city-states provide many services for people in the metropolitan area who live outside the city-state boundaries.[46]

Fiscal capacity includes the total tax revenues of the *Länder*, special levies (e.g., on oil production in Lower Saxony), 50 percent of the total volume of municipal revenues based on the average assessment rate for property and business taxes, and harbor burdens. Thus the federal Fiscal Equalization Law allows Bremen, Hamburg, Mecklenburg-Vorpommern (Rostock), and Lower Saxony (Emden) to deduct from their fiscal capacity DM 142 million (Hamburg) to DM 18 million (Lower Saxony).[47] If the financial need is greater than the fiscal capacity, the *Land* receives transfer funds. If the fiscal capacity is greater than the fiscal need, the *Land* must transfer funds to the recipient *Länder*.

As table 5.2 demonstrates, the calculation of the amounts to be transferred from and to the various *Länder* begins with the fiscal capacity of the individual *Länder*. This figure is then multiplied by the proportion of the *Land* population to total population in Germany to produce the equalization index figure. The fiscal capacity figure is then divided by the equalization index figure which results in a percentage indicating whether the *Land* is above or below average. The equalization index is subtracted from the figure for fiscal capacity to arrive at the surplus or deficit of each *Land* in comparison to the average.

The next step is for the *Länder* that are above average (payer *Länder*) to transfer to the recipient *Länder* 37.5 percent of any missing amount between 92 and 100 percent; this brings their fiscal capacity to 95 percent of the average. The *Länder* that have a higher figure for fiscal capacity than for their equalization index must transfer 15 percent of their "surplus" that lies between 100 and 101 percent, 66 percent of their surplus that lies between 101 and 110 percent, and 80 percent of any surplus above 110 percent. In case these transfers do not achieve their purpose of bringing all of the recipient *Länder* to 95 percent of the average, additional transfers might take place from the surpluses above 101 percent.

The *Länder* that are above average and transfer funds to the poorer *Länder* have varied over the years. In the first decades of the Federal Republic, for example, Bremen and North-Rhine Westphalia were later joined by Baden-Württemberg as perennial "payers," whereas Schleswig-Holstein, Lower Saxony, Bavaria, and Rhineland-Palatinate were recipients. In the

Table 5.2 **Fiscal equalization in the old *Länder*, 1993**

	NW	BY	BW	NI	HE	RP	SH	SL	HH	HB	Total
Fiscal capacity measure (FC)	74358.00	50113.00	44705.00	29148.00	28020.00	14646.00	10662.00	3893.00	9170.00	2931.00	267646.00
Compensation measure (CM)	74542.00	49157.00	42404.00	31717.00	24790.00	16223.00	11171.00	4537.00	9347.00	3758.00	267646.00
CM/actual inhabitants	4216.00	4176.00	4178.00	4186.00	4186.00	4180.00	4169.00	4185.00	5535.00	5479.00	4240.00
FC in proportion to CM in %	99.75	101.94	105.43	91.90	113.03	90.28	95.44	85.81	98.11	78.01	100.00
Surplus/Deficit	−185.00	956.00	2301.00	−2569.00	3230.00	−1576.00	−509.00	−644.00	−177.00	−826.00	0.00
Fiscal equalization (FE)	69.00	0.00	−1009.00	983.00	−2122.00	765.00	191.00	417.00	66.00	639.00	0.00
FC after FE	74427.00	50113.00	43696.00	30131.00	25898.00	15412.00	10853.00	4310.00	9236.00	3570.00	267646.00
FC after FE in proportion to CM	99.84	101.94	103.05	95.00	104.47	95.00	97.15	95.00	98.82	95.00	100.00
FC in DM/inhabitants	4210.00	4258.00	4306.00	3976.00	4373.00	3971.00	4050.00	3976.00	5469.00	5205.00	4240.00
in % of average	99.28	100.40	101.54	93.77	103.12	93.65	95.51	93.76	128.98	122.75	
in DM/weighted inhabitants	4210.00	4258.00	4306.00	3976.00	4373.00	3971.00	4050.00	3976.00	4051.00	3856.00	4185.00
in % of weighted average	100.59	101.73	102.87	95.01	104.48	94.88	96.77	94.99	96.80	92.13	
Inhabitants (millions)	17680.00	11770.00	10150.00	7580.00	5920.00	3880.00	2680.00	1080.00	1690.00	690.00	63.12
Weighted inhabitants	17680.00	11770.00	10150.00	7580.00	5920.00	3880.00	2680.00	1080.00	2280.00	930.00	63.95

Source: Dieter Carl, Bund–Länder–Finanzausgleich im Verfassungsstaat (Baden–Baden: Nomas Verlagsgesellschaft, 1995), p. 64.

1970s and 1980s the decline of smokestack industries had a very negative effect on North-Rhine Westphalia and the Saarland, and the decline of ship-building hurt Bremen. In the meantime Hesse and Baden-Württemberg prospered, and for the past few decades there has been a North–South gap in Germany that began to include Bavaria in the fiscally stronger group in 1989. Populous North-Rhine Westphalia returned to the payer or provider column in 1989 but was a recipient of transfer funds in 1993 and 1994. It has since returned to the provider column. With the accession of the five new *Länder* in the East, an even greater East–West gap has been superimposed on the North–South gap.[48] Data for 1995–2000 are provided in table 5.3.

Stage five: federal supplementary grants[49]
After the transfer of funds from the richer to the poorer *Länder*, which bring the poorer *Länder* to 95 percent of the average fiscal capacity of all

Table 5.3 **Fiscal equalization among the Länder, 1995–2000 (million DM)**

	1995	1996	1997	2000
Transfer Payment Länder (-)				
North-Rhine Westphalia	3,449	3,132	3,033	2,201
Bavaria	2,532	2,862	3,079	3,749
Baden-Württemberg	2,803	2,521	2,423	3,873
Hesse	2,153	3,240	3,130	5,354
Hamburg	117	482	264	1,099
Schleswig-Holstein	141	–	5	–
Recipient Länder (+)				
Lower Saxony	452	553	672	1,113
Rhineland-Palatinate	229	231	305	780
Schleswig-Holstein	–	16	–	358
Saarland	180	234	203	329
Bremen	562	635	351	872
Berlin	4,222	4,336	4,425	5,521
Saxony	1,773	1,965	1,896	2,328
Saxony-Anhalt	1,123	1,241	1,162	1,407
Thuringia	1,019	1,127	1,110	1,320
Brandenburg	864	1,035	976	1,263
Mecklenburg-Vorpommern	771	856	835	983
Total	+11,195	+12,229	+11,934	+16,274

Sources: BMF, *Finanzbericht 1999*, p. 154; for 2000, *Das Parlament* 21 (18 May 2001), p. 11.

Länder, the federation again enters the picture with federal supplementary payments (*Bundesergänzungszuweisungen, BEZ*) designed to raise the average fiscal equalization deficits from 95 percent to 99.5 percent. In this process, special burdens carried by the recipient *Länder* may be considered. These include federal payments for above-average costs of operating the political system, e.g., legislative and executive salaries. These payments range from DM 219 million for Berlin and Rhineland-Palatinate to DM 126 million for Bremen. Other *Länder* receiving such funds are Brandenburg, Mecklenburg-Vorpommern, Saarland, Saxony-Anhalt, Schleswig-Holstein, and Thuringia. Special burdens grants also go to eastern *Länder* for municipalities with especially low fiscal capacity and for burdens associated with the division of Germany. Berlin and the five new *Länder* receive funds that range from DM 3.658 billion for Saxony to DM 1.479 billion for Mecklenburg-Vorpommern. These payments are to be continued until 2004. In recognition of disproportionate burdens, several western *Länder* also receive federal grants which ranged in 1995 from DM 507 million for Lower Saxony to DM 80 million for Bremen and the Saarland. Rhineland-Palatinate and Schleswig-Holstein also received DM 451 and DM 227 million, respectively. These grants are to be reduced 10 percent each year after 1995. In addition Bremen and the Saarland received DM 1.8 billion and DM 1.6 billion in 1995–98 for the purpose of debt reduction and important investments designed to improve the economies of these *Länder.*[50] They will receive decreasing amounts until 2003.

While from an American perspective fiscal equalization measures in Germany may appear to reduce the autonomy of the poorer *Länder* by making them partially dependent on the federation and the richer *Länder,* the German view, especially in the poorer *Länder,* has been that it is precisely the general fiscal equalization among the *Länder* that makes it possible for them to carry out all of their functions autonomously and to meet the constitutional requirement of providing equivalent or uniform living conditions (Article 72, para. 2, and Article 106, para. 3). Equivalent living conditions do not mean the elimination of all differences in living conditions throughout Germany, but the concept does suggest generally equivalent public services and standards that only an adequate funding of all government units throughout the country can provide. The goal of equivalent living conditions is anchored in the principle of the *sozialer* (social welfare) state, the state of law (*Rechtsstaat*), and the federal state (Article 20, para. 1). Its specific application, however, is subject to interpretation.[51]

Unification and the Solidarity Pact of 1993

When it became increasingly clear in the months following the opening of the Berlin Wall on 9 November 1989 that Germany would be united again after more than forty years (but without the eastern territories lost to Poland and Russia after 1945), some attention began to be paid to the many financial problems that unification would bring – although these were underestimated. One of the most difficult of these was the question of providing "uniform" living conditions in a country that now had a huge gap in productivity, housing standards, infrastructure, and general standard of living between East and West. Two very different social and economic systems were to be integrated, although the eastern part had less than one-third of the *per capita* GDP of the western part. This was then reflected in a statistical reduction of about 15 percent in average *per capita* income for the united Germany. The result was that "from a state which had become poorer, more services were now demanded."[52]

Beginning in 1990, huge transfers of funds have flowed from West to East. The annual amounts have generally been estimated at around DM 150 billion annually; however, there is disagreement about the calculations of the transfers. Depending on what is counted, they range for 1992 from DM 100 billion to DM 234 billion. One expert suggests after a careful analysis that the net transfer in 1992 was between DM 162.5 and DM 183 billion, or about 6 percent of the West German GDP. This represented about 60 percent of the GDP of East Germany.[53]

In May 1990 the two Germanies signed a treaty in preparation for the currency, economic, and social union to go into effect on 1 July 1990. In order to finance the anticipated East German deficits through 1994, a "German Unity Fund" was created. At that time it was thought that this deficit could be financed one-third each by East Germany, the federation, and the old *Länder*. The German Unity Fund was to contain DM 115 billion for payments through 1994, with the federation commiting DM 20 billion through savings from previous expenditures connected to the division of the country (e.g., subsidies for border areas and West Berlin) and the federation and the old *Länder* providing DM 47.5 billion each from loans. Although it was argued that the federation was fiscally responsible for unification costs, the old *Länder* agreed to assume a heavy loan burden to avoid having to meet the demand by the federation that its share of VAT revenues be increased dramatically.[54]

At the end of August 1990, the East and West Germans signed the Unification Treaty. Article 7 of this Treaty dealt with the financing of united

Germany from 1991 through 1994. In principle the East was to be integrated into the system of public finance in the Federal Republic. Thus, the provisions of Article 91a and 91b, which provided for certain grants to the *Länder* based on mixed financing, and the provisions of Article 104a that authorized the federation to give grants to the *Länder* for a variety of purposes, were to be applied to the five new *Länder* as of 1 January 1991. It was soon apparent, however, that the investments derived from these provisions were inadequate to meet the needs in the East that were proving to be much greater than had been anticipated. This led to an agreement between Chancellor Kohl and the prime ministers of the new *Länder* to establish an investment fund (*Aufschwung Ost*), that provided an additional DM 12 billion each for the years 1991 and 1992. Another investment program (*Aufbau Ost*) providing DM 6.6 billion annually was established in 1993 that went into effect in 1995 and is to expire in 2004.[55]

Until 1994 there were also some important exceptions in the East to the general rules of the financial system of the Federal Republic. The distribution scheme of VAT revenues to the *Länder* was not applied at first in the eastern *Länder*, and they did not participate in the transfer of funds from richer to poorer *Länder*. The eastern *Länder* were so much poorer that all of the recipient *Länder* in the West except Bremen would have had to make sizable transfers to the East.[56] This was, of course, unacceptable to the old *Länder*. The "German Unity Fund," which was originally established to cover East German debts but was revised in the Treaty on German Unity to provide the new *Länder* with transfer funds based on population, was to serve as a substitute for these exceptions. But it soon became apparent that these measures were inadequate as well. The budget pressures in the new *Länder* forced them to borrow heavily, and it was clear they needed additional funds. After 1 January 1991, the new *Länder* began receiving their full share of VAT revenues based on population, and the contributions of the old *Länder* were increased. The federation gave up the 15 percent portion of the German Unity Fund that it planned to use for "central purposes" and turned it over to the new *Länder*. As a result of these actions, the new *Länder* received an additional DM 10 billion, and the German Unity Fund was increased from DM 115 billion to DM 161 billion.[57] By the end of 1991 the VAT on goods and services was increased from 14 to 15 percent (in part because of the EU) and the *Länder* share of VAT revenue was increased from 35 to 37 percent. A 7.5 percent temporary surcharge on income and corporation taxes was also imposed between 1 July 1991 and 30 June 1992.

In 1991 and 1992 the federation as well as the old and new *Länder* were borrowing so heavily that many observers became alarmed. This was not only because of conventional economic arguments regarding the accumulation of excessive debt, but also because of the convergence criteria set by the EU for qualifying for the common currency, the "Euro." It became apparent that the financial arrangements for meeting the fiscal challenges of unification were inadequate and would have to be changed significantly when these arrangements elapsed at the end of 1994. Voices were heard demanding an overall finance reform that would be incorporated into the package of constitutional changes being considered in 1993 and 1994 by a joint committee of the *Bundestag* and *Bundesrat*. However, a comprehensive finance reform was not taken up by this committee for several reasons, including the fact that there was no consensus on a general framework or concept of reform and, as a result, a lack of will to spend so much time and effort on a reform that would interfere with and delay other deliberations on constitutional change.[58]

The result of the strong pressures for revision of the fiscal equalization system was the Federal Consolidation Program ("Solidarity Pact") of 1993 that provided the changes in the system of finances that have applied with only minor alterations since 1 January 1995. Change of some kind was made absolutely necessary by the fact that the temporary measures described above were to elapse at the end of 1994. Given the economic conditions in the East, the heavy burdens on the federation, and the realization by the old *Länder* that admitting the new *Länder* to the West German system of fiscal equalization would have devastating consequences for them, it became clear that a new financing system would have to be devised before 1995, when the new *Länder* were scheduled to join the the equalization system as regular members. As a result of these pressures, the finance ministers of the sixteen *Länder* formed in September 1991 a working group, "Finance Reform 1995." This group met regularly until the spring of 1993, during which time the larger, mostly richer, *Länder* proposed reforms generally opposed by the mostly smaller, poorer, *Länder*. The new *Länder* were, of course, interested in being included as soon as possible in the fiscal equalization measures, but no model of reform could garner a majority.

Disagreements between the federation and the *Länder* were also a barrier to reaching consensus on a reform model. This encouraged the *Länder* to work together in order to counter the federal government's efforts to push through reforms that the *Länder* saw as disadvantageous to them. After many months of wrangling between the federal government and the *Länder* and among these as well, agreement was reached in May 1993.

Starting in 1995, the Solidarity Pact provided annual transfers of DM 56 billion for ten years to the East along with billions in loans for housing construction, infrastructure, environmental cleanup, and business promotion. It also provided DM 40 billion for old Eastern debts. The federation's contribution is financed as of January 1995 in large part by a 7.5 percent "solidarity surcharge" on personal income taxes and corporation taxes, a tax which had gone into effect briefly after unification but dropped again in 1992. By the late 1990s it had become very unpopular and politically controversial, at least in western Germany, owing in part to the incorrect belief held by many West Germans that East Germans do not have to pay the surcharge. The five new *Länder* were included in the horizontal equalization scheme, which, as we saw above, requires large transfers from the old to the new *Länder*. In compensation, the *Länder* share of VAT revenues was raised from 37 to 44 percent. In 1996 this was changed again to 49.5 percent for the *Länder*.[59] The federation accepted the burden of giving up a large chunk of its share of VAT revenue and at the same time agreed to transfer large sums to the eastern *Länder* in order to bring their fiscal capacity up to 92 percent (stage three) and then, finally, from 95 percent to 99.5 percent of the average (stage five).

When compared to what the federal government had proposed initially for the solidarity pact, the *Länder* appeared to emerge as the victors in the struggle over a revised system of finances.[60] Others argue that if one considers the costs incurred before the Solidarity Pact, the old *Länder* come up short.[61] The federation conceded that it was responsible for most of the burdens of unification, although the *Land* share, which is only about 10 percent, is still very sizable. On the other hand, the new *Länder* have become far more dependent on the fiscal equalization procedures and on federal grants than the poor *Länder* in western Germany ever were. This adds fuel to the argument that the *Länder* have too little fiscal autonomy and need more own source revenue. Nevertheless, the solidarity pact represents incremental reform; it is not a major departure from the system in operation since the Finance Reform of 1969.

Other federal grants to the *Länder*

One could easily conclude that the large federal transfers to the *Länder* within the framework of the fiscal equalization scheme might exhaust the possibilities for revenue distribution. But outside this scheme the federation has the constitutional authority to provide numerous other grants for investments in the *Länder*. Article 104a, para. 4, permits federal grants to the *Länder* and local governments (municipalities and counties) for "especially important investments" designed "to avert a disturbance of the overall economic equilibrium or to equalize differing economic capacities within the federal territory or promote economic growth." Details must be provided by statutory law subject to approval by the *Bundesrat*.

Article 104a, para. 4, does not give the federation a general right to provide direct grants to the *Länder* and indirect grants to localities, but the Article's provisions are not very specific. After all, determining what "a disturbance of the overall economic equilibrium" is cannot be based on precise calculations but rather on whether there is a stagnating or declining economy in the region. Any investments that would seem to help counter this decline would be appropriate. In contrast to this Article, Article 91a and 91b provide for more long-term aid. Some of the goals of Article 104a, para. 4, and Article 91a are the same or similar, but Article 91a is more "specialized," because it calls for the participation of the federal government in a particular planning procedure and a predetermined financial scheme. But above and beyond the provisions of these Articles, the federal government has no right to participate in the selection of individual projects. It can only exclude projects that do not fit the provisions of the federal law.[62]

The *Länder* and especially their local governments are responsible for about 80 percent of all investments, which have a strong impact on the economy as a whole. The federation was therefore given indirectly a good deal of responsibility for the economy when Article 104a was introduced in the Finance Reform of 1969. In the case of federal financial grants under Article 104a, para. 3, if 50 percent or more of the project to be funded is paid from federal funds, the project is administered by the *Länder* on behalf of the federation. If the *Länder* contribute more than 25 percent, the program must be approved by the *Bundesrat*. Grants must be for projects with a broad purpose, not just for local or regional concerns. In 1994 federal aid included urban renewal (federal share = 33 percent); public housing (about 50 percent); local public transportation (60–75 percent); local streets (90 percent); public commuter transportation (90 percent); and others.[63] A special investment program for the eastern *Länder* (*Aufbau Ost*) was established in 1995 under Article 104a as well. This program includes project grants worth DM 6.6 billion annually for ten years. The federation may not interfere in the *Land* or local planning for these measures, nor is it responsible for the way the money is spent. It can, however, determine whether the funds are spent according to the law.[64]

Article 91a and 91b, also introduced by the Finance Reform of 1969, provide the *Länder* with additional funds for investing in "joint tasks." Thus, the federation may participate in *Land* responsibilities when these are important for the general population and federal participation is necessary to improve living conditions. Three such areas are listed in Article 91a: expansion and construction of university buildings, including university clinics; improvement of regional economic structures; improvement of agricultural structure and coastal preservation. Joint tasks are regulated by federal law approved by the *Bundesrat*. The laws include provisions for joint planning for grants that must have the approval of the *Länder* to which they apply. For the construction of university buildings and for regional economic structures, the federation provides one-half of the funding for the project; for improvement of agricultural structure and coastal preservation the federation covers at least half of the cost for each *Land*. For universities and university clinics, plans called for DM 1.8 billion for the period 1998–2001; for regional economic structures, plans included investments of DM 5.7 billion in the new *Länder* and of DM 700 million in structurally weak regions of western Germany, with each level contributing 50 percent. For improving agriculture and preserving coastal regions, the plans called for a total of DM 3.22 billion, with the federation paying 60 percent for agricultural improvements and 70 percent for coastal preservation.[65]

Article 91b provides for cooperation between the two levels in the area of educational planning and in promotion of research institutions and research projects with broad impact. Educational cooperation exists, but it is not nearly as widespread or intrusive as originally planned during the "planning euphoria" of the late 1960s and early 1970s when the Finance Reform of 1969 was being debated. In the area of research institutions and research projects, including the Max-Planck-Gesellschaft scientific institutes and the German Research Association (DFG), federal assistance has become essential.

Fiscal equalization within the *Länder*

Horizontal fiscal equalization takes place not only among the *Länder* but also between them and their local governments. Article 106, para. 7, requires the *Länder* to share a percentage of their joint tax income with their local governments. *Land* laws are also to determine whether and to what extent the *Land* taxes are to be shared with the localities in order to equalize to a considerable degree the finance capacity of the local governments. The percentage shared varies by *Land*, but in 1996 the total of all grants by the *Länder* to their counties, cities, towns, and villages was DM 95.3 billion.

There are two general categories of grants: general-purpose formula grants and special-purpose categorical or project grants. General-purpose grants are designed to provide local governments with the financial means to meet their general obligations and are not tied to any specific tasks.[66] Most general-purpose grants are provided in the form of formula grants, distributed primarily on the basis of population; however, some general-purpose grants are provided on the basis of need. "Need" can apply to towns that have been designated "central places" that provide many services for surrounding towns, or they can be towns that have spas or military installations. Special needs may also result from the amount of public assistance the municipalities are providing to those who do not qualify for unemployment compensation.[67] Population size is determined not only by a real count but also by size of municipality. Thus, the larger the municipality, the more each person "counts," e.g., the population of a town of 5,000 may be multiplied by 100 percent, while the population of a town of 10,000 may be multiplied by 110 percent.[68] As noted earlier, this practice is based on the view that larger towns and cities provide many services to the region and on the theory mentioned in an earlier section that the greater the population density, the higher the *per capita* costs.[69]

Special-purpose grants are designed to finance all or part of certain functions. These include grants that compensate local governments for implementing specific delegated tasks, including grants that pay for various direct transfers of money and grants that help pay for schools, streets, and commuter transportation. Investment grants for infrastructure, like project grants in the United States, are awarded on the basis of application from the local units of government. They normally require financial participation by the applying unit. As in the United States, they are frequently criticized for distorting the priorities of local governments and thus limiting to some extent their local autonomy. But they make up only a small part of the total income of the localities and hardly play a significant role, so that, at least in the view of some experts, any measurable effect of *Land* investment grants on local priorities is unlikely.[70]

Even in comparison to the *Land* and municipal governments, the counties have few taxes of their own; indeed, only about 1 percent of their income is from their own tax sources.[71] On the other hand, as noted at the beginning of this section, the *Länder* are required by the Basic Law to provide their local governments, which include the counties, with a proportion of their joint tax income, the percentage to be determined by each *Land* parliament. These revenues are then shared with the counties through formula grants as described above.[72]

In addition to the formula grants received by the counties, they also receive transfer payments from the towns and villages that comprise the county (there is very little unincorporated territory in Germany) via a county assessment (*Kreisumlage*). Originally conceived as a complementary source of funds for the counties, the county assessment funds are now their most important source.[73] The details of the county assessment procedures are found in *Land* legislation. As in the case of the fiscal equalization procedures for transfers between the *Länder*, the assessment is based largely on the fiscal capacity of the municipalities within the county. This consists of their income from property taxes and business taxes, i.e., *Realsteuern*; their share of the income tax; and the formula grants they received from the *Land*. The county council then decides on the standard rate to be assessed against the municipalities that make up the county. In some cases this rate might be made more progressive for the more affluent municipalities. Some *Länder* also take into consideration financial advantages or disadvantages that accrue to a municipality owing to certain facilities located in its jurisdiction.[74] There seems to be agreement that the assessment rate is not to exceed 50 percent of the fiscal capacity of the municipalities, since a higher rate would undermine municipal autonomy. Some experts argue that 25 percent is the maximum that should be allowed,[75] but a few *Länder* are above even the 50 percent level.

Current pressures for reform

As we have seen from the sections above, conflict between the federation and the *Länder* and between the rich and poor *Länder* has accompanied the German system of public finance from the beginning. The growing centralization of taxing powers over the decades has left the *Länder* with virtually no tax autonomy and the municipalities with a limited autonomy derived basically from their right to set assessment rates for property and business taxes. Almost 80 percent of *Land* expenditures are financed by federally regulated taxes and grants over which the *Länder* have no influence except in the *Bundesrat*.[76] The federation is always demanding more funds for its needs, while at the same time the poorer *Länder* are never satisfied with the financial resources available to them for meeting the constitutional requirement of uniform or equivalent living conditions for their inhabitants. The richer *Länder,* on the other hand, remain frustrated in their attempts to retain a larger proportion of the revenues they receive from their above-average fiscal capacity. In spite of several legislative reforms and some important decisions of the Federal Constitutional Court, the system of vertical and horizontal fiscal equalization has never been organized to everyone's satisfaction.

Today perhaps even more than in previous decades this system is being challenged from a number of directions. The most general argument is that from the beginning, a majority of postwar Germans who were in positions of authority were confronted by the alternative of more autonomy for the *Länder* and thus the acceptance of regional differences, or a focus on uniform or equivalent living conditions and thus the demand for a degree of egalitarianism throughout the country.[77] The second position prevailed. But as an American observer has noted, "independence" or autonomy for an American state usually means being "left alone." In Germany autonomy has tended to mean giving the *Länder* the *ability* to achieve the goal of equivalent living conditions through a "fair" distribution of total tax revenues and not being forced to turn over tasks to the federation because of insufficient fiscal capacity.[78]

Nevertheless, one especially common argument is that the current system serves to reduce or weaken the fiscal autonomy of the *Länder* and therefore weakens the federal system. While the *Länder* do participate in the *Bundesrat* in passing most financial legislation, they can still be said to lose autonomy when they are a minority in the *Bundesrat* or when they prefer a certain action and cannot act on their own owing to their lack of legislative power in raising own source revenues. In other words, the *Länder* have no autonomy for raising taxes or experimenting with new tax sources, because they do not have what the Germans call "the right to find taxes" (*Steuerfindungsrecht*). This means among other things that the *Land* governments and parliaments cannot raise or lower their most important taxes in order to pursue policies that may have popular support, i.e., they are not "fiscally responsible" for their actions. In the meantime there has been increased discussion among many prominent Germans, including former Federal President, Roman Herzog,[79] about the need to secure for the *Länder* and local governments some fiscal autonomy and ability to engage in some degree of "competitive federalism."[80]

While they have little autonomy on the revenue side, the *Länder* do enjoy considerable autonomy on the expenditure side. But here, too, there is a strong federal presence in many social policies, such as individual rent subsidies or the federal regulations pertaining to public assistance which is financed by *Land* and local governments.[81] There is also a common complaint that the federal grants provided under Article 104a and the funds for joint tasks under Article 91a and 91b sometimes have the effect of manipulating or distorting *Land* plans and projects. This also produces more uniformity in expenditure policy, because the federal grants tend to be for more general than for narrower *Land*-specific purposes. Further-more, the *Länder* agreed in 1971 to a constitutional amendment (Article 74a) to give the federation the concurrent legislative power to regulate the salaries of all civil servants (*Beamte*) in order to prevent differences in salary scales that could lead to a self-destructive salary competition (which was a problem at the time). The local governments, in turn, add to this list of complaints by noting that the federation – as well as the *Land* governments – continue to devolve various activities to them without providing the funds. The latest example is children's nursery schools, which federal law now requires and regulates but for which it provides no financial support.[82] This issue is, of course, virtually identical to the issue of federal mandates in the United States that led in 1995 to passage of the Unfunded Mandates Reform Act.[83]

Another set of arguments concerns the transfer payments from the richer to the poorer *Länder*. We have seen in the brief historical review presented above that even in the late 1940s there was tension between the *Länder* that had above- and below-average financial strength. Since unifi-cation, with the addition of five new *Länder* which all share extraordinary fiscal weaknesses, the gap between the rich and poor *Länder* has grown significantly. If one takes seriously the constitutional command regarding equivalent living conditions, there has to be a massive transfer of funds to the new *Länder*. This is in fact occurring, but, one can argue, at a high cost of dependency of these *Länder* on the federation and richer *Länder*. In contrast to the original optimistic predictions that took as a model for the new *Länder* the "economic miracle" of West Germany in the late 1940s and early 1950s, it now looks as though the eastern *Länder* will lag behind western Germany for a long time, probably several decades. What effect during this time the dependency of the eastern *Länder* on transfers from the western *Länder* and federation will have remains an open question. If it becomes a permanent condition, it is not difficult to predict increasing conflict among the *Länder*.

In the meantime stage three of the fiscal equalization process which distributes 25 percent of the VAT to the poorer *Länder* to bring them to 92 percent of the average of *per capita* revenues, the horizontal transfers in stage four between the *Länder* that raise their capacity to 95 percent, and, finally, the supplementary federal grants in stage five that bring the poor *Länder* to 99.5 percent of average fiscal capacity, taken together, have come under increasing criticism. Article 107, para. 2, speaks of an "appropriate" equalization of the different fiscal capacities of the *Länder*. Critics argue that 99.5 percent is not just inappropriate, it is egalitarian "leveling" which the Federal Constitutional Court has rejected.[84] The practical results, among other things, are said to include continuing tensions between the richer and poorer *Länder*, disincentives for the poorer *Länder* to govern more frugally and efficiently, and disincentives for the richer *Länder* to introduce cost-saving measures. Thus neither the provider nor the recipient *Länder* will do much to increase their own source revenues.[85]

Indeed, conflict has been apparent. Bavaria and Baden-Württemberg, the latter a permanent "provider" of transfer funds over the decades, decided in 1997 to go to the Federal Constitutional Court with a complaint which they filed in July 1998 that the current system of fiscal equalization is unconstitutional.[86] Hesse joined them several months later. The Bavarian minister of finance suggested somewhat provocatively that the recipient *Länder* enter negotiations with the provider *Länder* in order to avoid the uncertainties of a Court ruling against them;[87] however, as noted in an earlier section, the *Länder* among themselves have never been able to agree on a major reform of the distribution of tax revenues.[88] The federal government and the Federal Constitutional Court have always been necessary elements in financial reform efforts. The question arises, however, whether German politicians do not turn too often to the Court to resolve what are really political questions.[89]

The finance ministers of Bavaria and Baden-Württemberg[90] argued that the current system has gone beyond the constitutional requirement of an "appropriate" fiscal equalization (Article 107, para. 2) to an excessive "leveling" and that it is "absurd" that these two financially strong *Länder* and Hesse end up at the bottom of the ranking of *Länder* fiscal capacity (positions 16th, 15th, and 12th, respectively, at the time they brought their case to the Court) after all of the transfers of funds from the federation and richer *Länder* have been completed. The complaint asked that the richer *Länder* be allowed to retain at least half of their "surplus" above the general *Land* average of fiscal capacity. It alleged that the current system serves to penalize those richer *Länder* which, because of their supposedly more cautious spending habits and efforts to promote economic development, have higher fiscal capacity. It also implied that the system serves to permit "big-spender" *Länder* with bloated bureaucracies and ineffective economic development policies to continue their behavior while others pay the bills but have no voice.[91]

It is important to note that some experts reject the implications of table 5.4 and believe that the charges leveled by Bavaria and Baden-Württemberg are spurious, because the funds received by the recipient *Länder* include grants for special burdens that the provider *Länder* do not have.[92] The best example is the special burdens carried by the new *Länder* for the costs related to unification.[93] But there are also funds that are not counted in the determination of fiscal capacity, e.g., 50 percent of the revenues of

Table 5.4 **Comparison of *per capita* fiscal capacity before and after fiscal equalization transfers among the *Länder* and federal supplementary equalization grants (*BEZ*), 1995**

	Per capita tax revenues of the Länder in 1995, % of the *Länder* average	Ranking	*Per capita* fiscal capacity in 1995 afterfiscal equalization between the *Länder* and *BEZ*, % of the *Länder* average	Ranking
Hamburg	236	1	120	7
Hesse	132	2	89	16
Bremen	125	3	197	1
North-Rhine Westphalia	120	4	91	12
Baden-Württemberg	116	5	90	15
Bavaria	112	6	90	14
Berlin	98	7	141	2
Schleswig-Holstein	91	8	94	10
Saarland	90	9	135	3
Rhineland-Palatinate	86	10	94	11
Lower Saxony	83	11	91	13
Brandenburg	43	12	120	8
Saxony	40	13	117	9
Saxony-Anhalt	36	14	121	5
Mecklenburg-Vorpom.	36	15	122	4
Thuringia	35	16	120	6

Source: Heinz Laufer and Ursula Münch, *Das föderative System der Bundesrepublik Deutschland* (Bonn: Bundeszentrale für politische Bildung, 1997), p. 174.

the local governments and the financial burdens associated with harbors.[94] One critic suggests that the complaint by the south German *Länder* is analogous to the millionaire who, after taking all of his numerous tax deductions, gives his taxable income as the standard for his wealth.[95]

Another powerful argument is that expenditures for public assistance, which is provided to those whose unemployment insurance payments have expired or to those who do not qualify for unemployment compensation, vary significantly among the *Länder*. Most public assistance is paid by local governments from their share of funds distributed by the *Länder*. Differences among the *Länder* are not due to profligate spending habits but rather are based on federal law, which the municipalities must implement. These expenditures amount to as much as 20 percent of the fiscal capacity of Bremen and 14 percent of the Saarland but to only about 7.5 percent of the fiscal capacity of Baden-Württemberg and Bavaria. A similar case could be made for the financial consequences of implementing other federal laws as well.[96]

Needless to say, the recipient *Länder* do not accept the critical analysis of their situation and have rejected the attempt to negotiate a settlement between richer and poorer *Länder*.[97] They argue that the assumption that the poorer *Länder* are somehow responsible in part for their condition owing to wasteful spending habits, inappropriate economic development policies, or other shortcomings conveniently ignores the reality of fundamental economic factors over which the poorer *Länder* have virtually no control. For example, the decline of smokestack industries, the shipbuilding crisis, changes in agricultural conditions, or the collapse of whole industries in the eastern *Länder* have little to do with *Land* economic policies. In their view federalism in Germany cannot consist merely of competitive elements. Of course the *Länder* have policies designed to attract business from other *Länder* and therefore do engage in competitive practices. But this requires fair starting chances, e.g., in infrastructure, that are now provided by the current system of fiscal equalization.[98] Some experts argue it is "absurd" to speak of competition among the *Länder* when the gap between eastern and western *Länder* is as great as at present. A serious decline in fiscal transfers that would bring about real differences in living conditions could be socially explosive.[99]

In spite of such arguments, the Kohl government reacted positively to the initiative by the two southern *Länder*, suggesting that it had warned in the past against too much egalitarian leveling (*Nivellierung*). On the other hand, a spokesman for the SPD said the initiative was an attack against the new *Länder*, which receive 87 percent of the funds transferred to the

poorer *Länder*. Some other *Länder* accused the southern *Länder* of attack-
ing the fiscal equalization system for partisan election campaign purposes, while still others rejected the implication that Germany should
return to a hodge-podge of separate, little independent states.[100]

In the summer of 1998 the federal minister of finance proposed a number of potentially far-reaching changes in the system of fiscal equalization.[101] He suggested that the responsibilities or tasks of the federation
and *Länder* be redistributed along with the system of vertical financial
equalization. The numerous examples of "mixed financing" should be
reduced sharply; this could be accomplished by ensuring that each level
has it own tax autonomy. This might occur by giving the federation the
revenues from the VAT, while the *Länder* would receive the income and
corporation taxes.[102] This was a rather remarkable proposal in that it
seemed to offer a return to what was once thought to be an unsatisfactory
tax distribution scheme that existed before the Finance Reform of 1969.
Another alternative offered by the finance minister was to grant the *Länder* the right to set their own rates for the income and corporation taxes
they share with the federation.[103]

The proposals raised suspicions among some *Land* finance ministers
that one of the goals of the federal minister was really to provide the federation with a greater share of funds. After all, one of the reasons for the
introduction of joint taxes in the Finance Reform of 1969 was the idea
that the risks of rising and declining revenues from the different taxes
would be shared. Thus, the revenues from the VAT are not affected nearly
as much by the state of the economy as are the revenues received from
income and corporation taxes. It is not surprising, then, that the federation wants to keep the VAT for itself in redistributing the various taxes
between the federal and *Land* levels.[104] Another criticism of the reform
proposals by the federal government rests on the fear that tax autonomy
for the *Länder* would lead to a competition to set the lowest rates; this
would put the new *Länder* at a strong disadvantage, because they need all
the revenue they can get to meet their obligations. Furthermore, the federal government has insisted on more tax conformity in the EU in order
to prevent unfair tax competition among the member states. This is a
position that seems at odds with the advocacy of more tax autonomy
for the *Länder*.[105]

These proposals and reactions became major news items in the late
1990s, but they were not new in principle. For many years there has been
a discussion of changes that would give the *Länder* taxing powers, even if
this might mean less focus on uniform or equivalent living conditions.[106]

Some observers, however, suggest that a general financial autonomy would probably not be acceptable, because of the problems that would arise between *Länder*, particularly in border areas, over tax avoidance schemes. This problem already exists in the EU and is considered a major nuisance. It is for this and other reasons, e.g., the relatively small yield of the taxes that might be raised, that led some critics to argue that such taxes could not pass any cost-benefit test. Owing to these and other problems, it does not seem to be very realistic to advocate a comprehensive tax autonomy for the *Länder*.[107]

Another proposal that has been made many times in the past and was repeated by the federal finance minister at the beginning of August 1998 is to give the *Länder* and local governments the right to decide themselves within certain limits on the taxes they want to raise. More concrete proposals have been to allow them to set assessment rates on the income tax or VAT within a range set by federal law.[108] This would avoid dramatic differences among the *Länder* while making it possible for *Land* and local politicians to take somewhat more responsibility for taxes. This, it is alleged, would also make the people more aware of the consequences of public spending policies and make the elected officials more cautious in their spending proposals.[109] It would also serve to strengthen the role of *Land* parliaments and to reduce the dependence on the federation for various investments and "mixed financing."[110] Yet another benefit would be a slight reduction of the exaggerated leveling that occurs in the fiscal equalization process.[111]

The fear has been expressed that more fiscal autonomy and competition might lead to as a "race to the bottom" in order to attract investment,[112] as has often happened in the United States.[113] One reaction to this argument is that there are already differences among the *Länder* in tax breaks, e.g., the opportunities for major tax deductions for investing in the eastern *Länder* or different tax assessment rates for the local business tax; or, in the past, one could point to special tax breaks for investing in West Berlin and in the border regions between East and West Germany. These measures seem not to have had a major impact in influencing private investment strategies. Nor does it seem likely that there would be a strong temptation for individual tax payers to change residency from one *Land* to another, any more than to change residency from one country to another, except perhaps in the cases of the very wealthy.[114]

A "race to the bottom" in the area of services also seems unlikely in Germany, because of general ethnic and cultural homogeneity and the strong tradition of equality which leads to such constitutional requirements as "uniform living conditions" and the highly developed social welfare state. The immediate reaction by many Germans that differences of almost any kind are "unsozial" and therefore really unacceptable is probably an important check on too much *Land* autonomy. This set of attitudes in the political culture makes it very difficult to believe that most Germans would be comfortable with conditions in the various *Länder* that differ by more than a small margin from the average.[115] Thus, more competition among the *Länder* in any serious sense might become as or even more controversial than the status quo. On the other hand, numerous voices, for example, former Prime Minister Kurt Biedenkopf of Saxony, have urged that Germans learn to accept more differences among the *Länder* in order to strengthen the idea of federalism and ease the pressure to provide uniform living conditions.[116]

All of these arguments, of course, revolve around the issue of "competitive federalism," which would necessarily lead to a de-emphasis on equivalent living conditions. The FDP made a major point of promoting competitive federalism in a report produced by its Friedrich-Naumann Foundation in the summer of 1998.[117] This may come as no surprise for a classical liberal party, but a special committee associated with the SPD also called for separate taxes and functions for the federal and *Land* levels.[118] In response to the growing intensity of the discussion about fiscal federalism, the newly elected government of Chancellor Gerhard Schröder agreed on 17 December 1998 with the prime ministers of the sixteen *Länder* to form a commission to study a reform of the German system of fiscal equalization after the current system elapses in 2005.[119]

This commission came under even more pressure to offer reform proposals after the Federal Constitutional Court decided in November 1999 that in the case brought before it in 1998 by Bavaria, Baden-Württemberg, and Hesse the current system of fiscal equalization had to be changed in its broad principles by the end of 2002 and in its legislative details by the end of 2004. The Court ruled that German legislators and the *Bundesrat* must decide just what changes should be made, but it indicated that the regular equalization payments may not exceed 95 percent of the average, in contrast to the current 99.5 percent; nor may the recipient *Länder* end up with a higher rank order in their financial capacity than the provider *Länder* after all transfers have taken place.[120] While many observers seemed to think that this decision would force the politicians to come up with some creative changes in the system of fiscal equalization and quite possibly encourage a meaningful devolution of powers to the *Länder*, a careful analysis of the decision and its implications for change suggested caution and even skepticism that German federalism would look very different after 2005.[121]

The commission's deliberations did not lead to a consensus among the *Länder*, and by the third week in June 2001 it looked as though the sixteen prime ministers would not be able to come to an agreement. But on June 23 Chancellor Schröder stepped in to break the Gordian knot by offering to have the federation pay the price for agreement. The maximum payment the richer *Länder* make of 80 percent of above-average tax revenues to the equalization fund will be reduced to 72.5 percent, and *Länder* that enjoy an increase in tax revenues over the previous year will be able to set aside 12.5 percent before it is counted in the amount owed for the fiscal equalization transfer. These changes will cost the federation DM 1.5 billion annually, and they will save the richer *Länder* between DM 200 and 400 million (102–204 million Euros) annually.[122]

In addition the new *Länder* will continue to receive heavy subsidies under a new solidarity pact that goes into effect in January 2005 following the expiration of the ten-year pact negotiated in 1993. The federation agreed to pay two-thirds of the DM 306 billion package the East is to receive between 2005 and 2019 in installments that are to be reduced every year after 2009. This means that the payments in the first years will be considerably higher than the current DM 20.6 billion. In 2020 special aid to the East is supposed to cease for good, but the unpopular solidarity surcharge on German tax payers will have to continue until then.[123]

The issue of *Länder* consolidation

The system of fiscal equalization in Germany has probably produced more uniform living conditions throughout the country than in any other major European state, including unitary states such as Great Britain and France. Even the new *Länder*, whose *per capita* income is about half of the average of the old *Länder*, are able today to provide a level of services and infrastructure that is not significantly lower than in the western *Länder*. This is the obvious strength of the system. But criticism and dissatisfaction are growing, and the demands for change are strong.

It seems apparent that the major problem in the fiscal equalization system lies in the gap in fiscal capacity between the richer and poorer *Länder*. With the exception of Lower Saxony, the poorest *Länder* – Bremen and the Saarland in the West and Berlin and the five new *Länder* in the

East – are the smallest in population. Hamburg is the exception among the richer western *Länder*. One of the arguments against more autonomy for the *Länder* in their present form is that the small and poor *Länder* are simply in no position to take advantage of greater fiscal autonomy. If they are to continue to offer reasonably uniform or equivalent living conditions, they must have financial support from the federation and/or their richer counterparts. Thus, there is really little prospect of granting the *Länder* real fiscal autonomy. This is precisely why, according to some German critics, Article 29, para. 1, of the Basic Law says that the *Länder* "can" be consolidated (before 1976, Article 29 read: "The federal territory is . . . to be newly constituted") in order to guarantee that they have the size and capacity to carry out their tasks effectively. Some experts who are opposed to the excessive emphasis on egalitarian leveling through increased centralization of tax legislation and fiscal transfers argue that if the *Länder were* to be given more fiscal autonomy, their populations would soon notice the difference in the ability of the *Land* government to provide the services they want and would, as a result, be amenable to a consolidation of their *Land* with a richer neighbor.[124] A federal system with seven–ten *Länder* would mean the creation of *Länder* that would be more autonomous fiscally; would have lower costs *per capita* for numerous services, personnel, and institutions, e.g., ministers, parliaments, and courts; and also be able to provide the equivalent living conditions that the public apparently demands.[125] A "Europe of the Regions," in which the EU Commission and Council of Ministers can devolve certain activities according to the subsidiarity principle, also requires fiscally and administratively strong *Länder*.[126]

The pro-consolidation case thus presents a persuasive argument which draws on discussions that reach back to the early days of the republic;[127] on the analogy of comprehensive county and municipal boundary reforms that were carried out in all of the territorial *Länder* in the late 1960s and early 1970s in the western *Länder* and took place the new *Länder* in the the 1990s;[128] on the results of a comprehensive, highly detailed expert commission report in 1973[129] on reorganizing *Land* boundaries; and on a massive scholarly literature that has appeared over the decades.[130] But Bernhard Vogel, the former prime minister of Rhineland-Palatinate and the current prime minister of Thuringia, noted in 1990 that "now is the time," and if action to consolidate the *Länder* does not take place early after unification, it will be far more difficult to act later.[131]

Unfortunately for the advocates of *Land* boundary reform, there are also persuasive arguments against their position as well as practical difficulties of achieving reform.[132] Article 29, para. 1, speaks not only of reorganizing *Land* boundaries in order to guarantee that they have the size and capacity to carry out their tasks effectively; it also says that in the process due regard shall be given to regional identities, historical and cultural ties, economic expediency, and the requirements of regional and *Land* planning. Thus, any large scale redrawing of boundaries would inevitably be rejected by large numbers of people who have developed feelings of identity with their *Land*.[133] Even the people in the former East Germany, who lived in a highly centralized state that eliminated any pretense of being a federation in the early 1950s, apparently preferred creating five new *Länder*,[134] which had at least some historical basis, to continuing to live in one territory that would have been roughly equivalent in population to North-Rhine Westphalia in the West. A related argument is that smaller *Länder* are "closer to the people" and perhaps therefore more responsive to the political and cultural wishes of the population.[135] The small states, provinces, and cantons in the United States, Canada, and Switzerland, respectively, are not constantly targeted as obsolete and in need of being consolidated with surrounding neighbors, so why should small *Länder* in Germany be considered so dysfunctional? Of course, the proponents of reform in Germany would argue, among other things, that the *Länder* have functions unique to German federalism, i.e., implementing with their local governments most federal legislation with the responsibility of financing most of the expenditures incurred.[136]

Perhaps even more formidable in overcoming the resistance to boundary change are the provisions of the Basic Law. Article 29, para. 2-8, that call for a complicated referendum process. This process begins with a federal law which must be approved by a majority vote in a referendum in all of the *Länder* whose territory is affected. If a majority in one *Land* does not approve, it can be overridden by a two-thirds vote in the territory that is directly affected (unless a two-thirds majority of the *Land* reject the referendum). Based on the American experience with referenda on the consolidation or annexations of local government units, these provisions probably make *Land* boundary changes unlikely if not impossible. An obvious example already exists in the defeat in May 1966 by voters in Brandenburg of the proposal that was approved by Berliners – at least West Berliners – and all of the major political elites in the two territories to merge the City of Berlin with the surrounding *Land* of Brandenburg. Again, proponents of reform may argue that this referendum was affected by too many extraneous matters, such as resentment by Easterners against their former capital city and the much richer West Berlin. But others would suggest that if a fusion of these two obvious candidates cannot pass, there is little hope for other efforts. In any case, there are no current efforts to consolidate any *Land* territory in any part of Germany.

Conclusion

We have seen that several themes have been prominent in the discussions in Germany about fiscal federalism since the late 1940s. One theme has been the locus of the major taxing powers, i.e., the states, as in the Bismarck Reich, or the national government, as in the Weimar Republic. A system of shared taxes, which was finally adopted officially in the Finance Reform of 1969, seems to be a perfectly reasonable compromise; however, no clear consensus has ever developed over the proper distribution of the tax revenues. A second theme has been the richer vs the poorer *Länder*. From the period of Allied Occupation to the present time, the poorer *Länder* have expressed their dissatisfaction with their fiscal status, in spite of very significant transfers of funds to them from both the federation and the richer *Länder*. This suggests a third theme, which is the fiscal equalization payments made by the more affluent to the less affluent *Länder*. Tinkering with the amounts and procedures for equalization has been a preoccupation of some public finance experts and politicians over the years, especially from the poorer *Länder*. And, finally, a theme running throughout the discussion has been the proper relationship between the *Länder* and the federation.

The highly complex, systematic – and even perfectionist – nature of German fiscal equalization measures that have emerged from these years of controversy and compromise stands in sharp contrast to the far more *laissez-faire* and ad hoc American practices. Dual federalism in the United States, according to which the federal and state governments operated separately in different functional areas until the "cooperative federalism" of the New Deal, did not lead to the expectation that the states would have to pay for their own programs. Indeed, there are relatively few program areas today in which the federal, state, and/or local governments do not share financing, a practice which in Germany is generally frowned upon and authorized only to a limited extent under Articles 91a and 104 of the Basic Law. We have seen that in Germany the process begins with a vertical equalization that involves the distribution of joint taxes between the federal and *Land* levels. To ensure more balance in fiscal capacity, the federation distributes 25 percent of the revenues derived from the VAT to bring the financially weaker *Länder* up to 92 percent of the average *per capita* revenues among the *Länder*. To reduce this gap even further, there is a horizontal transfer of funds from the richer to the poorer *Länder*, so that the poorer *Länder* are brought up to 95 percent of average *per capita* revenues. The federation then steps in to provide even more equity by distributing supplementary grants that raise the fiscal capacity of the poorer *Länder* to within 99.5 percent of average *per capita* revenues. The *Länder* are then required to share their portion of joint tax revenues with their local governments, i.e., counties, cities, towns, and villages. The various municipalities receive these funds in the form of general-purpose formula grants and special-purpose categorical or project grants. The counties receive general-purpose formula grants from the *Länder*, but an even more important source of income is the transfer of funds to them from the towns and villages that constitute the county. As we have seen on numerous occasions, the basic reason for this elaborate system of finance is the general idea of uniformity or equivalence of living conditions throughout the country, the individual *Länder*, among the cities, and throughout the counties. A 1998 OECD report raises the question whether this goal of equivalent living conditions has assumed a higher place in the scale of values than economic incentives;[137] others ask whether it has not weakened the autonomy of the *Länder* and municipalities and served to undermine German federalism. Indeed, some experts have noted over the years that those who believe everything ought to be equal everywhere should be honest enough to admit that they have no interest in a federal organization of the country.[138]

A decision by the Federal Constitutional Court in November 1999 led to some important, but not fundamental, changes in German fiscal federalism that were worked out by a special commission. These changes, beginning in 2005, will come largely at the expense of an already financially strapped federal government and do not deal to the satisfaction of many critics with the issue of "competitive federalism" and more autonomy for the *Länder*.

Notes

A somewhat different version of this chapter was published in *German Studies Review* 23, no. 3 (October 2000), pp. 533–555.

1 *Zahlen zur wirtschaftlichen Entwicklung der Bundesrepublik Deutschland* (Köln: Institut der Deutschen Wirtschaft, 1999), pp. 84, 86, 94, and 150.

2 The following section is based on Wolfgang Renzsch, *Finanzverfassung und Finanzausgleich* (Bonn: Verlag J. H. W. Dietz Nachf., 1991), pp. 20–53; see also, by the same author, "Neuordnung des bundesstaatlichen Finanzausgleichs. Finanzverfassung und Föderalismus, Probleme und Perspektiven," *Gegenwartskunde* 4 (1986), pp. 499–533.

3 Renzsch, *Finanzverfassung*, Ch. II.

4 Cited in John Ford Golay, *The Founding of the Federal Republic of Germany* (Chicago: University of Chicago Press, 1958), p. 76.

5 Ibid., p. 77.

6 Peter Merkl, *The Origin of the West German Republic* (New York: Oxford University Press, 1963), pp. 73–74.

7 Renzsch, *Finanzverfassung*, Chs III, IV, V.

8 Ibid., p. 170.

9 Ibid., p. 172.

10 Ibid., pp. 180–182.

11 Kommission für die Finanzreform (Troeger Kommission), *Gutachten über die Finanzreform in der Bundesrepublik Deutschland* (Stuttgart: Verlag W. Kohlhammer and Deutscher Gemeindeverlag, 1966).

12 Renzsch, *Finanzverfassung*, pp. 214–215.

13 Ibid., pp. 209–210.

14 Ibid., p. 208.

15 Cited in Dieter Carl, *Bund-Länder-Finanzausgleich im Verfassungsstaat* (Baden-Baden: Nomos Verlagsgesellschaft, 1995), p. 21.

16 Renzsch, *Finanzverfassung*, p. 207.

17 Ibid., pp. 223–229.

18 Ibid., pp. 221–223.

19 Ibid., pp. 231–232.

20 Ibid., pp. 232–234.

21 Ibid., pp. 257–259.

22 Ibid., p. 259.

23 For an analysis of the federal government's legislative response to the Court's decision and the reaction of the *Länder*, see Wolfgang Renzsch, "Unbefriedigende Lösung für die 'armen' *Länder*," *Die demokratische Gemeinde* 2 (1988), pp. 20–22.

24 Renzsch, *Finanzverfassung*, pp. 269–273; see also Rüdiger Voigt, "Financing the German Federal System," *Publius: The Journal of Federalism* 19, no. 4 (Autumn 1989), pp. 11–112.

25 Very little has been written in English about German public finances. However, an excellent current overview and assessment can be found in Clifford Larsen, "States Federal, Financial, Sovereign and Social: A Critical Inquiry into an Alternative to American Financial Federalism," *The American Journal of Comparative Law* 47 (Summer 1999), pp. 429–488. Several brief overviews can also be found in Arthur B. Gunlicks, *Local Government in the German*

Federal System (Durham: Duke University Press, 1986), Ch. 7; "Financing Local Governments in the Federal System," in *Intergovernmental Relations and Public Policy*, edited by J. Edward Benton and David R. Morgan (New York: Greenwood Press, 1986), pp. 77–92; and "German Federalism After Unification: The Legal/Constitutional Response," *Publius: The Journal of Federalism* 24, no. 2 (Spring 1994), pp. 81–98.

26 Carl, *Bund-Länder-Finanzausgleich*, p. 25. Bernd Huber, "Der Finanzausgleich im deutschen Föderalismus," *Aus Politik und Zeitgeschichte* B24/97 (6 June 1997), p. 23, speaks of four stages. Still others speak of three.

27 Klaus Vogel, "Grundzüge des Finanzrechts des Grundgesetzes," in *Handbuch des Staatsrechts der Bundesrepublik Deutschland*, vol. IV, edited by Josef Isensee and Paul Kirchhof (Heidelberg: C. F. Müller Juristischer Verlag, 1990), pp. 19–20, 25–26.

28 Herbert Fischer-Menshausen, in Ingo von Münch and Philip Kunig (eds), *Grundgesetz-Kommentar*, vol. 3, 3rd edn (München: C.H. Beck'sche Verlagsbuchhandlung, 1996), p. 960.

29 For a useful figure showing the distribution of taxes among the federal, *Land*, and local levels, see Heinz Laufer and Ursula Münch, *Das föderative System der Bundesrepublik Deutschland* (Bonn: Bundeszentrale für politische Bildung, 1997), p. 160.

30 Fischer-Menshausen, *Grundgesetz-Kommentar*, pp. 990–991.

31 Michael Inhester, *Kommunaler Finanzausgleich im Rahmen der Steuerverfassung* (Berlin: Duncker & Humblot, 1998), pp. 97–99; Fischer-Menshausen, *Grundgesetz-Kommentar*, p. 963.

32 German cities, towns, and villages receive revenues from rural properties, because they include within their municipal limits virtually the entire land area of the Federal Republic; that is, there is very little unincorporated territory. Legally, then, a German rural county is a territorial corporation (*Gebietsverbnd*) that contains the combined area of a number of smaller territorial corporations called cities, towns, and villages (*Gemeinden*). Larger cities, usually with populations in excess of 100,000, may form city-counties or county-free cities (*Stadtkreise* or *kreisfreie Städte*). In the United States, only Virginia has city–county separation on a state-wide basis.

33 Inhester, *Kommunaler Finanzausgleich*, pp. 93–94.

34 In a long list of selected cities, the assessment rate varied from 600 per cent to 375 percent for the urban property tax and 515 percent to 320 percent for the business profits tax. Hanns Karrenberg and Engelbert Münstermann, "Gemeindefinanzbericht 1998," *Der Städtetag* 3 (1998), p. 159.

35 Inhester, *Kommunaler Finanzausgleich*, p. 95.

36 "Unsere Steuern von A-Z," Ausgabe 1997 (Bonn: Bundesministerium der Finanzen), n. 3, pp. 44–45. For details, see Karrenberg and Münstermann, "Gemeindefinanzbericht 1998," p. 240.

37 Fischer-Menshausen, *Grundgesetz-Kommentar*, p. 992.

38 Carl, *Bund-Länder-Finanzausgleich*, pp. 34–39.

39 Ibid., p. 39.

40 Interview with Gisela Färber, German Postgraduate School of Administrative Sciences, 14 July 1999.

41 Carl, *Bund-Länder-Finanzausgleich*, pp. 44–46.

42 Fischer-Menshausen, *Grundgesetz-Kommentar*, p. 982.

43 Huber, "Der Finanzausgleich," p. 25.

44 BVerfGE 72, 330 (386).

45 Inhester, *Kommunaler Finanzausgleich*, pp. 167–170.

46 Carl, *Bund-Länder-Finanzausgleich*, pp. 62–63.

47 Fiscal Equalization Law, *BGBl* 1993, *Teil* 1, p. 978.

48 For data from 1980 to 1994, see the tables in BMF, *Finanzbericht 1998*, p. 145.

49 Carl, *Bund-Länder-Finanzausgleich*, p. 68.

50 Fiscal Equalization Law, *BGBl* 1993, *Teil* I, pp. 980–981.

51 Carl, *Bund-Länder-Finanzausgleich*, p. 20.

52 For a review in English of financial developments in the period 1990 to 1995, see Wolfgang Renzsch, "Financing German Unity: Fiscal Conflict Resolution in a Complex Federation," *Publius: The Journal of Federalism* 28, no. 4 (Autumn 1998), pp. 127–146. A lengthy chapter by the same author in German provides an excellent and detailed review of financial and budgetary developments in Germany from 1989 to 1996: "Budgetäre Anpassung statt institutionellen Wandels. Zur finanziellen Bewältigung der Lasten des Beitritts der DDR zur Bundesrepublik," in Hellmut Wollmann *et al.*(eds), *Transformation der politisch-administrativen Strukturen in Ostdeutschland* (Opladen: Leske & Budrich, 1997), pp. 49–118; see also Peter Selmer, "Finanzverfassung im Umbruch," in Jörn Ipsen *et al.* (eds), *Verfassungsrecht im Wandel* (Köln: Carl Heymanns Verlag, 1995), pp. 231–250.

53 Renzsch, "Budgetäre Anpassung," pp. 51–52. Others calculated a transfer of 6.6 percent of the West German GDP amounting to a total of DM 1.4 trillion by the end of 1997. See Ulrich Heilemann and Hermann Rappen, *The Seven Year Itch? German Unity from a Fiscal Viewpoint*, AICGS Research Report 6 (Washington, DC: American Institute for Contemporary German Studies, 1997), p. 2.

54 Renzsch, "Budgetäre Anpassung," pp. 54–55.

55 Ibid., pp. 56–61, p. 92.

56 Rolf Peffekoven, "Deutsche Einheit und Finanzausgleich," *Staatswissenschaften und Staatspraxis* 1, no. 4 (1990), p. 497.

57 Renzsch, "Budgetäre Anpassung," pp. 61–66.

58 Ibid., pp. 110–111.

59 The struggles that led to the solidarity pact are described in detail in many German publications, e.g., Wolfgang Renzsh, "Föderative Problembewältigung: Zur Einbeziehung der neuen Länder in einen gesamtdeutschen Finanzausgleich ab 1995," *Zeitschrift für Parlamentsfragen*, no. 1 (1994), pp. 116–138. For a

brief overview in English, see Gunlicks, "German Federalism after Unification," pp. 84–88.

60 Renzsch, "Föderative Problembewältigung," p. 138; *Frankfurter Allgemeine Zeitung*, 24 April 1993, p. 3; for an interesting review in English of the negotiations that led to the Solidarity Pact, see Razeen Sally and Douglas Webber, "The German Solidarity Pact," *German Politics* 3, no. 1 (April 1994), pp. 18–46.

61 Gisela Färber, "Reform des Länderfinanzausgleichs," *Wirtschaftsdienst* VI (1993), pp. 305, 307.

62 Theodor Maunz, *Grundgesetz-Kommentar*, Article 104a, para. 4, Rdnr 43-51.

63 For the amounts of aid available for these programs, see BMF, *Finanzbericht 1998*, pp. 138.

64 Fischer-Menshausen, *Grundgesetz-Kommentar*, pp. 914–915, 923, 930.

65 BMF, *Finanzbericht* 1998, p. 136.

66 Inhester, *Kommunaler Finanzausgleich*, p. 164.

67 Ibid., p. 180.

68 Ibid., pp. 165–166.

69 Ibid., pp. 166–167.

70 Ibid., p. 183.

71 Ibid., p. 184.

72 Ibid., p. 179.

73 Ibid., p. 187.

74 Ibid., pp. 194–197.

75 Ibid., p. 191.

76 Fischer-Menshausen, *Grundgesetz-Kommentar*, p. 942.

77 Selmer, "Finanzverfassung im Umbruch," p. 232; Renzsch, *Finanzverfassung und Finanzausgleich*, pp. 54–56.

78 Larsen, "States Federal," pp. 434–435.

79 See, for example, *Frankfurter Allgemeine Zeitung*, 10 August 1998, p. 4.

80 Klaus-Dirk Henke, "Möglichkeiten zur Stärkung der Länderautonomie," in Der Präsident des Niedersächsischen Landtages (ed.), *Die Stärkung der Finanzautonomie im föderativen System der Bundesrepublik Deutschland* (Hannover, 1995), pp. 38–39. A very similar version of this chapter, with the same title, can be found in *Staatswissenschaften und Staatspraxis* 6, no. 4 (1995), pp. 643–657.

81 Ibid., pp. 46–47 and 651–654, respectively.

82 Horst Zimmermann, "Stärkung der kommunalen Finanzautonomie," in *Die Stärkung der Finanzautonomie im föderativen System der Bundesrepublik Deutschland*, pp. 18–19.

83 Paul L. Posner, "Unfunded Mandates Reform Act: 1996 and Beyond," *Publius: The Journal of Federalism* 27, no. 2 (Spring 1997), pp. 53–71.

84 BVerfGE 72. 398. For a detailed critical analysis of the perfectionism in fiscal equalization, see the report to the finance ministers of Baden-Württemberg and Bavaria by Hans-Wolfgang Arndt, *Finanzausgleich und Verfassungsrecht*, pp. 12, 36–42.

85 This is a very common complaint in the literature. See, for example, ibid., pp. 25–26; Rolf Peffekoven, "Reform des Länderfinanzausgleichs tut not," *Wirtschaftsdienst*, no. II (1998), p. 81; a report by the "Reform Commission on the Social Market Economy" also makes this point: *Frankfurter Allgemeine Zeitung*, 17 August 1998, p. 10.

86 While the constitutional complaint was not brought officially before the Federal Constitutional Court until the last week of July 1998, these two *Länder* made public their intention to sue in October 1997. See German Information Center, *Deutschland Nachrichten* (24 October 1997), p. 2.

87 *Frankfurter Allgemeine Zeitung*, 25 July 1998, p. 2.

88 The Bavrian Finance Minister has complained that the majority of *Länder* rejected the Bavarian and Baden-Württemberg proposals for reform in the January 1998 conference of finance ministers. See Erwin Huber, "Länderfinanzausgleich: Grenzen der Solidarität," *Wirtschaftsdienst*, no. 2 (1998), p. 73.

89 Selmer, "Finanzverfassung im Umbruch," p. 233.

90 Not surprisingly, the Federation of Taxpayers in Baden-Württemberg is also critical of the fiscal equalization sytem. See Bund der Steuerzahler Baden-Württemberg, *Der Finanzausgleich oder Der geschröpfte Steuerzahler Baden-Württembergs*, Finanzwirtschaftliches Institut, 1998.

91 *Frankfurter Allgemeine Zeitung*, 31 July 1998, pp. 1–2.

92 Some experts are not persuaded by these rankings, because they do not reflect accurately enough the real financial situation of the *Länder*. Bremen, for example, receives large transfers of fund for a variety of "special needs" that Hesse does not have. See Stefan Homburg, "Im Gewirr der Kompetenzen," *Frankfurter Allgemeine Zeitung*, 31 October 1998, p. 15.

93 Hartmut Perschau, "Es geht um Aufholchancen! Zehn Thesen zum bundesstaatlichen Finanzausgleich," *Wirtschaftsdient*, no. 2 (1998), pp. 74–75. See also Peffekoven, "Reform des Länderfinanzausgleichs tut not," pp. 82–83.

94 Peffekoven, "Reform des Länderfinanzausgleichs tut not," p. 81.

95 Gisela Färber, "Finanzverfassung," in *50 Jahre Herrenchiemseer Verfassungskonvent – Zur Stuktur des deutschen Föderalismus*, edited by Bundesrat (Nördlingen: Beck'sche Buchdruckerei, 1999), pp. 89–131.

96 Gisela Färber, *Probleme der Regionalen Steuerverteilung im Bundesstaatlichen Finanzausgleich: Gutachten im Aufrag der Saarländischen Landesregierung*, Speyer, January 1999, pp. 20–21.

97 *Frankfurter Allgemeine Zeitung*, 31 July 1998, p. 2.

98 Ibid., 11 August 1998, p. 13; see also the arguments by Hartmut Perschau that the current system of *Länder* transfers is not nearly so bad as many critics suggest. "Es geht um Aufholchancen!," pp. 73–76.

99 Carl, *Bund-Länder-Finanzausgleich*, p. 25.

100 *Frankfurter Allgemeine Zeitung*, 31 July 1998, p. 2.

101 A discussion among public finance experts concerning the initiative of

Bavaria and Baden-Württemberg was published in July 1998 under the title *Die Reform des Finanzausgleichs – Föderale, ökonomische und verfassungsrechtliche Aspekte, Expertengespräch*, edited by Finanzministerium Baden-Württemberg and Bayerisches Staatsministerium der Finanzen.

102 A similar proposal was made by the chairman of the finance committee of the parliament of Baden-Württemberg, Professor Dieter Puchta. See *Frankfurter Allgemeine Zeitung*, 28 June 1997; see also Homburg, "Im Gewirr," p. 15.

103 *Frankfurter Allgemeine Zeitung*, 5 August 1998, pp. 1–2. These proposals are rather similar to the recommendations and comments made by the OECD in a report issued in August 1998. See *Frankfurter Allgemeine Zeitung*, 7 August 1998, p. 13.

104 Some experts, however, argue that the income tax revenue is just as stable as the VAT revenues. See Homburg, "Im Gewirr," p. 15.

105 *Frankfurter Allgemeine Zeitung*, 11 August 1998, p. 13.

106 See, for example, the five proposals suggested by Reinhard Hendler, "Finanzverfassungsreform und Steuergesetzgebungshoheit der Länder," *Die öffentliche Verwaltung*, no. 7 (April 1993), pp. 292–299.

107 Henke, "Möglichkeiten," p. 40 and p. 646, respectively; Wolfgang Renzsch, Finanzausgleich und die Zukunft des Föderalismus," unpublished manuscript, October 1998.

108 Henke, "Möglichkeiten," pp. 40–41 and 647–649, respectively.

109 Fischer-Menshausen, *Grundgesetz-Kommentar*, p. 942.

110 Henke, "Möglichkeiten," pp. 39–40.

111 Ibid., p. 44.

112 Ibid., p. 42.

113 Larsen, "States Federal," p. 477.

114 Henke, "Möglichkeiten," pp. 42–44.

115 See the data cited in Franz Gress, "Similarities and Differences in the Development of American and German Federalism: Theory and Practice" (paper presented at the American Institute for Contemporary German Studies, Washington, DC, 1997), p. 7, also cited in German in "Aktuelle Probleme und Perspektiven des Föderalismus in der Bundesrepublik Deutschland und den USA," in *Krise und Reform des Föderalismus* (edited by Reinhold C. Meier-Walser und Gerhard Hirscher) (München: Olzog Verlag, 1999), pp. 136–139.

116 *Frankfurter Allgemeine Zeitung*, 30 April 1993, p. 1.

117 "Föderaler Leistungswettbewerb auf getrennte Rechnung," *Frankfurter Allgemeine Zeitung*, 22 August 1998, p. 14.

118 "Der SPD-nahe Managerkreis fordert eine Reform des Föderalsystems," *Frankfurter Allgemeine Zeitung*, 31 October 1998, p. 13.

119 *Das Parlament* (25 December 1998), p. 1; some public finance experts have already made their comprehensive reform proposals. See, for example, Färber, "Finanzverfassung," pp. 127–131.

120 *Frankfurter Allgemeine Zeitung*, 12 November 1999, p. 1 and 13 November

1999, p. 1; *Die Zeit*, 18 November 1999, p. 25; and *Das Parlament* (26 November 1999), p. 9.

121 Wolfgang Renzsch, "Finanzausgleich und die Modernisierung des Bundesstaates: Perspektiven nach dem Urteil des Bundesverfassungsgerichts" (FES-Analyse Verwaltungspolitik) (Bonn: Friedrich-Ebert-Stiftung), February 2000.

122 *Süddeutsche Zeitung*, 25 June 2001, pp. 1, 2, and 24.

123 Ibid. and *Das Parlament* 27 (29 June 2001), p. 1.

124 For example, see Fischer-Menshausen, *Grundgesetz-Kommentar*, p. 883; Henke, "Möglichkeiten," p. 651.

125 For a strong argument for various reforms of German federalism, with territorial reform serving as "the key for the protection of German federalism against deformation," see Uwe Leonardy, "Deutscher Föderalismus jenseits 2000: Reformiert oder deformiert?," *Zeitschrift für Parlamentsfragen* 30, no. 1 (February 1999), p. 162.

126 Hartmut Klatt, "Ländr-Neugliederung: Eine staatspolitische Notwendigkeit," *Zeitschrift für Beamtenrecht*, no. 5 (1997), p. 149.

127 Lower Saxony, North-Rhine Westphalia, and Hesse were created after 1945 by the British and Americans, by consolidating several older territories, and Baden-Württemberg was created by the Germans in the early 1950s by consolidating three former territories.

128 For descriptions and analyses in English of the local government territorial reforms in the western *Länder*, see Gunlicks, *Local Government*, Ch 4; "The Reorganization of Local Governments in the Federal Republic of Germany," in *Local Government Reform and Reorganization: An International Perspective*, edited by Arthur B. Gunlicks (Port Washington: Kennikat Press, 1981), Ch. 10; and "Restructuring Service Delivery Systems in West Germany," in *Comparing Urban Service Delivery Systems*, edited by Vincent Ostrom and Frances Bish (Beverly Hills: Sage, 1977), pp. 173–179.

129 Bundesministerium des Innern, *Bericht der Sachverständigenkommission für die Neugliederung des Bundesgebietes*, Bonn, 1973 (Bericht der Ernst-Kommission).

130 For a recent comprehensive review of the literature, developments, and need for *Länder* consolidation, see Klatt, "Länder-Neugliederung," pp. 137–149.

131 Bernhard Vogel, "Mehr Länder, weniger Föderalismus," *Staatswissenschaft und Staatspraxis*, no. 2 (1990), pp. 129–131.

132 A strong critique of *Land* boundary reform based on financial considerations can be found in Gisela Färber, "Finanzverfassung," p. 126.

133 Klatt points out that feelings of identity have much to do with the times. Thus, the artificial *Länder* created by the Allies after 1945 seem to have become a source of identity for most of their citizens. Klatt, "Länder-Neugliederung," p. 149. Hans-Wolfgang Arndt, on the other hand, suggests that a strong identity of people with the *Länder* never developed after the war and that the small *Länder* have no right to exist indefinitely at the expense of

the others. See "Finanzverfassungsrechtlicher Reformbedarf – vom uni-tarischen Föderalismus zum Wettbewerbstföderalismus," *Wirtschaftsdient*, no. 2 (1998), pp. 77, 80.

134 See, for example, Peter Badura, "Die Finanzverfassung im wiedervereinigten Deutschland," in *Verfassungsrecht im Wandel*, edited by Jörn Ipsen *et al.* (Köln: Carl Heymanns Verlag, 1995), p. 20.

135 Larsen, "States Federal," p. 464.

136 Making this point with disapproval: Gisela Färber, "Finanzverflechtungen von Bund, Ländern und Gemeinden," manuscript, 1997, p. 44.

137 *Frankfurter Allgemeine Zeitung*, 7 August 1998, p. 13.

138 Horst Zimmermann, in Der Präsident des Niedersächsischen Landtages (ed.), *Die Stärkung der Finanzautonomie im föderativen System der Bundesre-publik Deutschland* (Hannover, 1995), p. 32.

6

The German *Land* parliaments (*Landtage*)

Historical development

In the Kaiserreich of 1871–1918, the Constitution gave the central government only a brief catalogue of powers, with all other powers reserved for the states; however, the central state also had concurrent powers and implied powers. Over time the national government assumed more powers through constitutional changes and legislation which also had to be passed by a second chamber, the *Bundesrat*, that represented the mostly monarchical governments in the states. The state parliaments had no voice in these developments or in the many cooperative agreements signed by the state governments to bring about more uniformity in the country.[1]

In the Weimar Republic of 1919–33, the monarchical governments in the states (now called *Land* (singular) and *Länder* (plural)) were replaced by governments dependent on majorities in the *Land* parliaments (*Landtage*). But these democratically legitimated governments now faced a central government with more domestic powers than its predecessor had enjoyed. In contrast to 1867 and 1871, the state parliaments had no role in approving the Constitution in 1919. Rather, a nationally elected National Assembly ratified the Constitution after having given the central government a much longer list of powers, including concurrent powers, than under the Reich Constitution of 1871. The reordering of public finances also had a unitary effect, made necessary in part because of the heavy burdens of the First World War. As a result, the budgetary powers of the *Länder* were almost completely undermined. In the *Reichsrat*, which replaced the *Bundesrat* of the Kaiserreich, the *Land* governments acted on the basis of political party policy, not on views expressed by the *Land* parliaments (although, of course, the governments had to have majorities in the parliaments). Conferences of various *Land* officials with the goal of providing for more uniform *Land* legislation also helped undermine the *Land* parliaments.[2]

With the accession of Adolf Hitler to power in January 1933, the *Land* governments were soon authorized to bypass the *Land* parliaments by passing laws through "simplified legislative procedures." Following the national elections of 31 March 1933, first Communist, then Socialist, seats were denied in all parliamentary bodies. In April the *Land* parliaments lost the right to pass votes of no-confidence, and in October 1933 the state parliaments were dissolved along with the national parliament, the *Reichstag*. Exactly one year after Hitler came to power, 31 January 1934, the *Land* parliaments were officially disbanded.[3]

The *Land* parliaments as legislatures today

Land *parliaments and the Basic Law*

Local and *Land* governments were the first to be established after the Second World War. The first elections were held in 1946 and 1947, depending on the occupying power. The governments and legislatures formed then became the building blocks for the establishment of the Federal Republic in 1949, and then as now they were important training and recruiting grounds for national office. From the beginning, all of the *Länder* have had only one chamber, called the *Landtag* in the thirteen territorial *Länder*, *Bürgerschaft* in Bremen and Hamburg, and *Abgeordnetenhaus* in Berlin. The one exception was Bavaria, which had a corporatist *Senat* as a second chamber with limited powers until it was eliminated by a popular referendum in 1998.

We have seen in previous chapters that according to Article 30 of the Basic Law, the *Länder* are responsible for "governmental powers" unless the Basic Law provides otherwise. Article 70 then states that "the Länder have the right of passing legislation insofar as this Basic Law does not grant legislative authority to the federation." The Basic Law provides for three kinds of national legislation: exclusive, concurrent, and framework. Article 73 enumerates exclusive legislation, including defense and foreign affairs, currency, customs, citizenship, immigration, postal services, etc. Areas of concurrent legislation are found in Article 74 and include civil and criminal law, public welfare, economic affairs, nuclear energy, labor relations, transportation, etc. An especially controversial provision is found in Article 72, which gives the federal government the right to pass concurrent legislation in favor of promoting equivalent living conditions throughout the country "if required." This very general provision, which covered a wide range of activities,[4] was tightened somewhat in the constitutional amendments of 1994 by substituting "if required" for "if needed." Unlike concurrent legislation in the United States, where the national government prevails only in cases where specific national and state provisions are in conflict, federal concurrent legislation in Germany preempts all *Land* legislation in the area of regulation.

Framework legislation is the third area, and it concerns regulation of all public employees, general principles of higher education, regional planning, registration of residence, etc. Federal laws in this category are supposed to leave details to the *Land* parliaments, which are obliged to act within a reasonable period of time. In general, however, the provisions of the framework laws do not leave the *Land* parliaments much leeway.[5]

As a result of these many exceptions to Article 30 and Article 70, the national organs, i.e., government, *Bundestag*, and *Bundesrat*, are responsible for most legislation, while the *Länder* are generally responsible for administration under Article 83. This is "the essential characteristic of German federalism"[6] and is generally what is meant when references are made to "dual federalism" in Germany.

This does not mean that the *Länder* have no influence on federal legislation. We have seen that the *Bundesrat*, the chamber of the *Länder*, has an absolute veto over more than half of the legislation passed by the *Bundestag* and a suspensive veto over the rest. The influence exerted by the *Länder* in the *Bundesrat* is, however, exercised by the *Land* governments, not the *Land* parliaments.

The party group

The party group (*Fraktion*) or parliamentary party (in the United States, "caucus"), is legally a parliamentary organ and is publicly financed.[7] It the key institution for the German office holder at all levels of government. It is his or her "home" in parliament, and little can be accomplished unless one is a member of a party group. The introduction of bills requires the support of a certain number of deputies, which is the same as the minimum number of deputies required to form a party group. Thus bills are introduced through the party group, which also determines the speakers in debates. The party groups decide among their own members who will serve on the various committees, including investigative committees. The leaders of the party groups form an executive committee to determine the agenda of the parliamentary meetings and the time for debate.[8] Party groups form working groups based on committee assignments, and most of the parliamentary work done by the deputies is done in or for these groups. Thus parliamentary activity is primarily party group activity.[9]

A minimum number of deputies, usually 5 percent of the total membership, is required in order to form a party group. This is generally not a problem, because in the German proportional representation system a party normally needs 5 percent of the total vote in order to enter parliament. The exception is for candidates who win a direct seat in a single-member district. In this case the candidate would enter parliament, but unless he or she joined a party group, the deputy would be a lone figure unable to participate effectively in the affairs of parliament. Since Germany is a "party state," independent candidates are rare, and they have no chance of winning a direct seat. At the federal level a party may secure representation in the *Bundestag* and even benefit from the features of proportional representation in spite of failing to meet the 5 percent vote requirement by winning three or more direct seats. Not until the Party of Democratic Socialism (PDS), the successor to the East German Communist Party (SED), won four direct seats in East Germany in the federal elections of 1990 and 1994, did any party enter the federal parliament under this rule.

German party groups, like their counterparts in most other European parliamentary systems, demonstrate a high degree of unity in both committees and in the plenary meetings. Normally the party group takes a position in support of the recommendations of its working groups. *Fraktionszwang*, or coercion, is not allowed under Article 38 of the Basic Law for the federal level or under similar provisions in the *Land* constitutions for the *Land* parliaments and local councils. But *Fraktionsdisziplin*, or discipline, is assumed, and members of the party group rarely deviate from the "party line," which is really the party group position based on deliberations among the members of the party group.[10] On important issues the leadership, of course, exercises a good deal of influence. This is especially the case if the party is supporting the government and feels obligated to back its own ministers in their actions and policies. Sometimes a deputy may find it difficult to maintain unity, as in the case of territorial reforms of local government boundaries that were introduced in the late 1960s and 1970s throughout the West German *Länder*.[11] In such cases, which are rare, the deputies may be allowed to abstain.[12]

The party groups are, of course, closely related to the extra-parliamentary political party, but they are part of the parliament, that is, they are "state" institutions that receive generous funding from the *Land* budget.

They are not allowed to use these funds for campaigns or other strictly party purposes, but the line may be difficult to draw on occasion. They are supported by the parliamentary advisory service staff, and they may hire additional staff at their own expense. As is the case with committee staff members in the United States, the parliamentary advisory staff assist party group members in many ways and are an important part of the working groups, committees, and the legislative process in general.[13]

The party group leader is usually the most prominent member and the spokesperson for the party in parliament. He or she may be overshadowed by the prime minister or some ministers if the party is supporting the government, but if the party is in opposition the party group leader is in effect the Leader of the Opposition and a probable candidate for prime minister in the next election. The party group leader is also responsible for maintaining unity in the group, since any evidence of disunity is seen by opposing groups as a sign of weakness and disarray. Everyone in the party group knows that the group's effectiveness depends in part on unity, which encourages discipline all the more.[14] The party group leader is assisted by a general manager, who may or may not be a member of the parliament. As a kind of chief of staff, this person may gain considerable influence and use the position as a springboard for high positions in the future.[15]

The decline of Land legislative powers

Before one begins any discussion of a decline of *Land* legislative powers, it should be noted that complaints about loss of powers have existed since the Basic Law was promulgated; however, it would not be correct to conclude that the *Land* parliaments were not given or have not retained some important legislative powers of their own. These include responsibility for their own organization, including such areas as electoral law and budgets; cultural areas, including not only the arts but also universities, schools and training facilities; church law; much of police law, including construction and water rights; planning and nature conservation; local government law (but within limits of the guarantee of local self-government); radio and television (excluding technical aspects); and a few concurrent powers not assumed by the federal government.[16] It can certainly be argued, though, that the *Land* parliaments had their days of glory in the period between 1946 and early 1950s,[17] before the national government existed[18] or had begun to act in areas of concurrent legislation that the *Länder* had already dealt with. The last great hurrahs of the western *Land* parliaments may have been the educational reforms and territorial reorganizations[19] of the late 1960s and early-to-mid-1970s, while for the new *Länder* in the East important legislation was passed after unification in the mid-1990s. One can also point today to various administrative reorganization schemes and reforms being discussed or carried out that are designed to increase efficiency and reduce personnel (*Schlanker Staat*). Attention is also being given to changes in the budget process and control instruments.

But for several decades it has been a kind of conventional wisdom that there has been a decline of *Land* legislative powers, and those making this case are informed and knowledgable observers.[20] On the other hand, there have been some dissenters and others who suggest that the standard complaint begs the question. Thus a few voices have suggested that based on statistics on *Land* legislation, there has been no loss of legislative functions – either in number or in importance.[21] Others have suggested that the *quantity* of *Land* legislation has not really declined so much as its *quality*.[22] In another line of argument, Alois Glück, the party group leader of the CSU in the Bavarian *Land* parliament, has rejected in parliament and elsewhere the thesis that the *Land* parliaments are less important today due to a loss of legislative powers, because new tasks have been added.[23] The assertion that they have been reduced to the level of local governments is "absurd."[24] Indeed, one recent study suggests that the conclusion that there has been a loss of legislative powers depends on the issue area and/or on particular legislative functions (legislative, articulation, control, and public information) as performed separately by the government parties and Opposition. For example, if one does a careful *empirical* examination of *Land* legislation concerning illegal drug policies, one finds that over the years since 1968 the *Land* legislatures were active in varying degrees in performing articulation, control, public information, and innovation functions but were barely active in the lawmaking arena. Thus government parties were more engaged in information functions and the Opposition in control, and, to a lesser extent, innovation functions.[25] Still another view is that the focus on *Land* legislative powers seems to confuse the greater legislative functions of a *legislature* in a presidential-type system and the different functioning of a *parliament* in a parliamentary system which is based more on the relationship between the government and its supporting majority in parliament versus the Opposition. The government majority carries the responsibility for the exercise of power, including legislative initiatives of the cabinet, and the Opposition has the role of controlling that power in public.[26]

Nevertheless, most observers continue to argue that the legislative powers of the *Land* parliaments have been weakened dramatically over the years for a variety of reasons. One simple explanation is that the most important laws have been passed, and today the *Länder* are concerned above all with modifying and amending their earlier legislation, filling in the details of federal framework legislation, and providing for the implementation of federal laws that the *Länder* administer.[27]

It is frequently noted that the constitutional amendments passed since 1949 which enhanced federal powers were approved by the *Länder* in the *Bundesrat*, and that they did so voluntarily.[28] A common reason given for the willingness of the *Länder* to approve such changes from the early 1950s to the mid-1970s, including the preemption of *Land* legislative powers through federal concurrent legislation, the joint tasks under Article 91a and 91b, and the financing arrangements under Article 104a, has been the pressure by the media, the political parties, and various interest groups for more uniform living conditions throughout the country.[29] In the meantime there has been much criticism of this justification, not only because of the growing difficulty of financing measures deemed appropriate to promote more uniformity but also because of the undermining of federalism that it implies. As noted in Chapter 2, Article 72 was amended in 1994 in order to make its provisions less sweeping. Thus the "need" to pass concurrent legislation was changed to "essential" or "required" in order to promote "equivalent" rather than "uniform" living conditions. But the tradition and generally strong popular acceptance of the welfare state, and the public expectations related to a wide variety of public services, make it difficult to maintain differences in these policy areas.[30] While this has always been a challenge since the Second World War in the West, unification in 1990 with the former and much poorer Eastern territories has helped create severe strains in the welfare state. This has implications for federalism, because there is little support in the East for differences in service levels in the name of *Land* autonomy.

Not only have the *Land* parliaments lost powers to the federation. The focus of attention is on the prime minister and his government,[31] and in virtually all legislative bodies, especially in parliamentary systems, complaints have long been heard about the dominance of governments over the legislatures in the legislative process.[32] Executive dominance over the parliament is a common theme in almost every textbook on French and British government, and even in the United States, where the national and state legislative bodies are comparatively powerful, it is frequently observed that "the Administration proposes and the legislature disposes."

In a parliamentary system, the governments usually control the agenda, even if – as in the United States – they cannot always control the results. But in a parliamentary system with strong party discipline, which is typical of Germany, the parliamentary majority is generally bound to follow the proposals of the government. Internal disagreements within the majority party or coalition may lead to compromises or changes of various kinds, but the government usually prevails in a parliamentary vote. The result, of course, is a weakening of the parliament *vis-à-vis* the government and an undermining of separation of powers; in effect, separation of powers exists in the relationship between the government and its majority in parliament on the one hand and the Opposition on the other. It is the role of the parliamentary Opposition or sometimes of groups outside of parliament, such as the student protest movements and the citizens' initiatives in Germany in the 1970s, to criticize the government openly and offer alternatives. Some German *Land* deputies may complain about the restrictions imposed by party discipline when they are in the majority and about the general futility of their criticisms when they are in the Opposition, but these conditions seem inherent in a functioning parliamentary system.

A more complicated explanation for the weakening of *Land* parliaments is the development of cooperative federalism. Though Konrad Hesse pointed to the emergence of a "unitary federal state" in Germany at the beginning of the 1960s,[33] cooperative federalism did not begin "officially" until after the Finance Reform of 1969, which provided for joint taxes as the most important sources of revenue; for joint planning and financing of a variety of activities that were formerly the sole responsibility of the *Länder* (Article 91a and 91b); and for federal grants under Article 104a, paragraph 4, that required *Land* financial participation. Especially from the 1950s to the 1970s, the federal government assumed increasing legislative powers through constitutional change and preemption of *Land* powers through concurrent legislation. The *Länder* were compensated to the extent that the *Land* governments had the right to joint decision making in these legislative arenas in the *Bundesrat* (at least if they were in the majority) and in their authority in many cases to issue regulations that bypassed the *Land* parliaments. The *Land* governments also engaged increasingly in numerous cooperative arrangements with other *Länder* through a wide variety of conferences and committees ranging from the conferences of *Land* prime ministers, *Land* ministers – e.g., the Conference of Education and Culture Ministers (KMK) – and numerous conferences and meetings of bureaucrats that produced much pressure for uniformity throughout the country, in large part through model legislation.[34] The governments' majorities in the *Land* parliaments are reluctant to reject decisions made in these conferences,[35] so the governments generally have a free hand unless there are disagreements within the majority party or coalition. (Though rare, there have been instances when a majority party did reject a government's decision made at a conference with officials of other *Länder*, thereby forcing changes to be made.[36]) The concept of *Politikverflechtung* – roughly equivalent to the American concept of intergovernmental relations – reflects this web of joint planning, joint decision making, and shared financing between the federal and *Land* governments and the wide-ranging voluntary cooperation and coordination among the *Länder* themselves that have been characteristic of German federalism since at least the late 1960s.[37] Indeed, some observers believe that cooperation and coordination between the federation and the *Länder* and among the latter via the numerous conferences and meetings raise a question of whether the practical effect is not an unconstitutional undermining of *Land* parliament powers.[38] In any case the political weight of the *Länder* is based more on the *Land* governments than on the parliament, which is one reason why some observers speak of "executive federalism" in Germany.[39]

Another important reason for the loss of legislative powers by *Land* parliaments that is rarely mentioned in the literature is the accumulation of large debts by the *Länder*. The high interest payments, not to mention the principal, have lessened considerably the parliamentary room to maneuver in various policy arenas. In some *Länder*, such as the Saarland and Bremen, the parliaments can hardly think responsibly of new policy initiatives.[40]

In addition to the various domestic pressures that have served to weaken the *Land* parliaments, the EC/EU has enacted numerous regulations affecting *Land* powers. Indeed, the federal government was able in the past under the old Article 24 of the Basic Law to transfer sovereign powers, including *Land* powers, to international organizations. This meant that the federal government could vote on measures in the EC Council of Ministers in Brussels affecting exclusive *Land* powers, such as education, training, and culture, over which it had no authority in Germany.[41] For this and other reasons, the *Länder* insisted on and finally, in the late 1980s and early 1990s, succeeded in gaining rights of consultation and participation via the *Bundesrat* in decisions affecting their powers (see Chapter 7).

In constitutional terms, the weakening of the *Land* parliaments can only go so far, even though some observers would argue that the limits have been reached. Article 20, para. 1, of the Basic Law says that Germany is a "democratic and socially conscious *federal* state," and Article 79, para.

3, prohibits amendments "affecting the division of the Federation into *Länder*." The *Länder* are considered to be "states" – though not in the sense of international law – which means they must retain an essential core of responsibilities. These include *Land* parliaments with a minimum of exclusive legislative powers.[42] It is sometimes argued that the *Länder* have been compensated for losses of parliamentary powers by increased participation of the *Land* governments in the *Bundesrat* and various forms of cooperation with the federal government and other *Land* governments. Most constitutional scholars reject this view, pointing out that the *Land* parliaments have no right to direct the governments in their decisions in the *Bundesrat*, which is a *federal* organ, and they note that the parliaments are generally ignored in decisions made in the wide variety of conferences between their governments and the federal and other *Land* governments.[43] On the other hand, modest changes were made in the Basic Law in 1994 which should help to protect the *Land* parliaments from further erosions of their powers, and the consultation and participation rights gained by the *Länder* via the *Bundesrat* with respect to the EU might even serve to strengthen the *Länder* in the process of European integration. But any further loss of *Land* legislative powers, which has been an issue since the early years of the Federal Republic,[44] could affect the legitimacy of the German federal system.[45]

Functions of the Land parliaments today

Walter Bagehot and Max Weber suggested long ago that parliaments have multiple functions besides legislation, and it is no surprise that close observers of the *Land* parliaments also see them as performing several functions.[46] In addition to the legislative function, one can distinguish among an electoral and recruitment function, that is, the election of the prime minister and his or her cabinet (only in seven *Länder* can the prime minister select his or her cabinet without parliamentary approval); a political control function, which serves as a check on the executive branch and overlaps with a public information function; a debating function, which has to do with educating the public as well as with information and communication; and a representation and articulation function, which serves as a means of expressing a plurality of public wishes, expectations and concerns in the policy making process. Finally, perhaps as a part of the previously named function, one can point to a service function, which is so important in the United States but sometimes ignored in the German literature on *Land* parliaments.

Legislative functions

Given the strong role of legislative bodies in the United States, most Americans naturally think of these as having legislation as their main function. But even in the United States legislatures have other functions, such as controlling the executive through legislative oversight, confirming the appointments of various officials, and performing numerous representation and service functions. In parliamentary systems governments depend on majority support in parliament in order to remain in office, but there is also a strong tendency, especially in disciplined political party systems such as the German and British, for the majority party or coalition to support government policies with relatively little open criticism. Legislative initiatives come largely from the government, and though some changes in government bills may be made in committee or behind the scenes, the parliamentary majority is expected to support the government's agenda. Nevertheless, laws cannot be passed without the parliaments, so that at least formally they retain ultimate power in the legislative process.[47]

According to one close observer of *Land* parliaments, legislation today takes up little time in the *Landtage* – about one-sixth of the plenary sessions.[48] As noted above, their legislative powers have been weakened during the past decades by constitutional changes, cooperative administrative arrangements with the federal government and other *Länder*, and encroachments by the EU. As a result, many critics have suggested that the *Land* parliaments are largely superfluous bodies with only limited powers of any significance. Even in those areas over which they have retained some powers, the majorities are constrained by the need to support the government, and the Opposition forces have little or no chance to prevail. At best they may exercise some influence in committee deliberations hardly noticed by the general public.[49] As noted above, this view is not accepted by all observers.

Electoral and recruitment functions

In a parliamentary system the electoral and recruitment functions are often more important than the legislative function. The prime minister as well as the Opposition candidate for chief executive in the previous election usually emerge from the *Land* parliament[50] or a previous *Land* cabinet (or, sometimes, from a federal cabinet post), and he or she generally has the strongest role in selecting the cabinet ministers. This is especially the case in the seven *Länder* where the prime minister appoints individual cabinet members without parliamentary interference, but even then the wishes of and pressures from the parliamentary party and/or coalition partner must be taken into consideration. Pre-election agreements can also limit the prime minister's influence.[51]

There are some differences among the *Länder* in the role of the parliament in selecting cabinet ministers. For example, in the city-states the parliament elects the entire cabinet: in Berlin, first the lord mayor, then the cabinet; in Bremen and Hamburg, first the *Senat* (cabinet), which then elects the lord mayor. In six of the territorial states, the parliament elects only the minister-president (prime minister), whose cabinet appointees then require parliamentary approval. In seven *Länder* the parliaments do not control the prime minister's formation of the cabinet, which is also the case at the federal level. But in almost all cases ministers are recruited from the parliaments. "Outsiders" do become ministers on occasion, but they usually have some political experience elsewhere if not in the parliament.[52] Only in Bremen and Hamburg is there a rule of incompatibility between executive and legislative office.[53] The parliamentary majorities are also involved in the appointment of key civil service positions, such as state secretaries, possibly some department section chiefs (who, however, are usually career civil servants), and directors of government districts (*Regierungsbezirke*) who are considered to be "political bureaucrats." Parliamentary deputies sometimes seek these positions themselves. In the city- states leadership positions in public enterprises are also important patronage posts, and there are frequent complaints about the party patronage (*Filzokratie*) that is often associated with them.[54] Finally, *Land* deputies elect judges to their state constitutional courts, and every five years they select – mostly from among their own members – half of the electors of the Federal Assembly which elects the Federal President as ceremonial head of state.

Political control functions

A third major function of the *Land* parliaments is control of the government and bureaucracy. Indeed, given the importance of the *Länder* in administering most laws,[55] this is seen in much of the literature as their most important function.[56]

The instruments of control include parliamentary questions, both oral and written; the right to demand that responsible ministers respond to questions personally and that ministers submit reports to the parliament (*Zitierrecht* and *Berichtsersuchen*), which may be taken up either in the plenary meeting or by committees; the current-issues question time (*Aktuelle Stunde*) for short questions and answers; resolutions, which can deal with a general question without specifying a particular address, for example, the *Land* parliament condemns the actions of skinheads against asylum seekers, or demands that are legally nonbinding calling on the *Land* government take certain actions; a vote of no-confidence, which, of course, is the sharpest control instrument but is rarely used;[57] control via committees of various kinds, including investigative committees; parliamentary control commissions, e.g., the commission responsible for overseeing the office of constitutional protection, and special persons, such as the personal data protection commissioner; informal controls, e.g., discussons in cabinet meetings, majority party group meetings which are also attended by a minister, or meetings between leaders of coalition parties, etc.; parliamentary control via the courts, where the minority parties have the right to bring matters before the *Land* or federal constitutional courts to determine the constitutionality of some action; and parliamentary control of government actions, such as review of state contracts, *Bundesrat* matters, EU questions, results of subject minister conferences, and planning decisions.[58] Of course the quality of the review of government actions taken in horizontal conferences of prime ministers and subject ministers ("third level") and in vertical conferences of bureaucrats ("fourth level") depends on the relationship between the government, the majority and minority parties; the time and information available; the feasibility of taking action when informal commitments have already been made, etc.[59] Such conferences are what Frido Wagener was referring to when he spoke of *vertikale Ressortkumpanei* and *vertikale Fachbrüderschaften* (vertical ministerial cliques and vertical subject brotherhoods, respectively).[60] While Wagener's terms carried critical and negative connotations, it has also been noted that such conferences are important mechanisms of coordination and information management between and among levels.[61]

As in the British House of Commons, legislative control activities, for example, through the increasing number of written and oral questions, now take up far more time in plenary sessions than legislation. Indeed, one former *Land* prime minister suggested to the author that too many deputies see their active participation in question time as a means of keeping busy and of justifying their full-time status at the expense of the time and energy of the civil servants who serve the government ministers and must gather the information to answer the questions.

As the above suggests, it is useful to distinguish among various kinds of control. Herbert Schneider, for example, has divided types of controls into policy direction, administrative performance, and specialist categories. In the question times set aside in parliament, "major questions" (*Große*

Anfragen) are usually reserved for sessions devoted to policy issues; "small questions" (*Kleine Anfragen*) and individual questions from deputies are generally associated with administrative performance; and the more routine specialist control is exercised mostly in parliamentary committees.[62]

Other authors have noted the distinction between formal controls, e.g., those performed especially by the Opposition in public sessions through question time, and those that take place behind the scenes in the cabinet, internal party group meetings, party committees, etc.[63]

Parliamentary controls have different functions. The three most important are securing information,[64] exercising influence on government actions and proposals, and promoting critical publicity. In addition, one can see control functions as serving to occupy a theme, to set the stage for a government pronouncement, to demonstrate to the public that the *Land* parliament is acting on some matter, and to make points against the other parties.[65]

Germans often distinguish between "working parliaments, " e.g., American legislatures, and "talking parliaments," e.g., the British House of Commons. German parliaments are both, but the "working" function is stronger. This is reflected above all in the time and effort devoted to committee work.[66] Ministers and high-level civil servants spend a good deal of time in committee meetings, and the result is that deputies can develop considerable expertise in the subject matter and gain respect and influence in return. The committees meet usually from Tuesday through Thursday – except in Bavaria, Brandenburg, Rhineland-Palatinate, and Berlin usually in closed meetings – during special weeks set aside for that purpose, while plenary meetings of the parliament are held generally on the same days during one week a month for seven–ten months per year. While closed meetings may be problematic in terms of the transparency of committee actions, most German legislators are convinced that confidentiality is necessary to ensure serious work rather than public posturing and to limit interest group influence.[67] Another problem arises, however, when some committee actions or deliberations in the mostly nonpublic meetings are not communicated in plenary sessions of the parliament, so that noncommittee members may not be as well informed as they should be and there is less public information about the committees.[68] The case for opening committee meetings to the public and press is often made, but it has not had much impact.[69] On the other hand, it should be noted that the parliamentary petition committee in each *Land* receives all kinds of citizen complaints and requests and serves an ombudsman function quite effectively.

Parliamentary control of finances is limited, as in most other parliamentary bodies, by the large proportion of expenditures that are fixed by law and not subject to political manipulation. In practice joint task expenditures made under Article 91a and 91b or Article 104a, para. 4, of the Basic Law are also not subject to revision by the *Land* parliamentary majorities because of their reluctance to refuse federal matching funds or reject actions of their own government. On the other hand, the deputies do receive reports of the Minister of Finance, and they can rely to a considerable extent on the *Land* general accounting office for ensuring cost-effective administration, the director of which is named by the *Land* government.[70]

As noted in other chapters, most federal laws are administered by the *Länder*. One of the problems *Land* parliaments face in their control of the administration of these laws is the lack of information. The best-informed civil servants may be in the federal ministries that drew up the legislation, and neither they nor their ministers can be made to appear before the *Land* parliaments to answer questions.[71] The *Land* civil servants who actually implement the federal laws can always point to their federal origin (on the other hand, much legislation is changed to some extent in the *Bundesrat*, which is the domain of *Land* civil servants). Nevertheless, some questions raised in the *Land* parliaments refer to federal actions, sometimes even including foreign and defense policy. Of course these have no legal effect.[72]

A common complaint heard for the last few decades is that cooperative federalism – and more specifically, the joint and interlocking decision making by experts associated with the *Politikverflechtung* concept – largely removes the *Land* parliaments from a good deal of decision making and opportunities for control. Decision making in parliaments is more transparent than in governments, and when *Land* ministers and bureaucrats meet together in a wide variety of specialized conferences, and *Land* and federal officials meet to engage in joint planning efforts under the joint tasks of Article 91a and 91b, increased transparency and public information levels are not the result. Yet effective parliamentary control should result in making political responsibility visible. In cooperative federalism, however, decisions are largely the result of negotiated compromise by governments with little opportunity for parliamentary participation.[73]

The debating function

This function is concerned with political education, but even more with communication with constituents and party supporters. Debates are far less a means of persuading deputies on the other side than of scoring

points and of confirming the views and wishes of and speaking to supporters with the aid of the media that report on activities in the *Land* parliament. This is especially important as elections approach.

Debates follow government declarations, major questions raised in
question time, and bills that have been introduced. The Opposition has the
obligation of pointing to contradictions, weaknesses in conception, problems of financing, and alternative provisions. Speakers for the majority
party or coalition parties reflect the views of the government and not necessarily the real divisions that may exist internally. This, of course, can
make the debates all too predictable and therefore boring.[74] Some issues,
such as the education and territorial reforms of the late 1960s and early
1970s already mentioned, enjoy considerable public interest. Most, however, do not. Even the introduction of the "Current-Issues Discussion"
(*Aktuelle Stunde*) has done little to arouse public interest, perhaps in part
because of the style and nature of the debates as well as the lack of public
information and often limited press coverage.[75] There is probably little difference, however, between *Land* parliaments and state legislatures in the
United States in the generally low level of public interest in their activities.

Debates are usually not as sharp in the *Land* parliaments as in the *Bundestag*, because their smaller size makes it possible for the delegates to
know one another personally, and because *Land* parliaments enjoy a
more collegial atmosphere.[76] On the other hand, this does not prevent
occasional sharp exchanges based on both ideological and personal differences.

Representation and articulation function

Representation can take on different meanings, depending on the context
in which it is used. Alan Rosenthal, in his book on American state legislatures, distinguishes between *political* representation, *deliberative* representation, and *descriptive* representation.[77] Political representation refers to
such factors as reapportionment and redistricting of representative single-
member districts in order to provide equality and fairness. Deliberative
representation has to do with the legislative process, information-gathering, legislative skills, linkage between issues, bargaining and compromise,
and responsibility for decisions made. Descriptive representation suggests
a mirror image of the voters in terms of income, occupation, age, race or
ethnic group, and gender. No legislative body in the democratic world conforms to this image of representation, which would be achieved better by
drawing lots than by holding elections. This is not to say that the increases
in representation of women and minorities or changes in occupational

backgrounds of legislators are not important or do not make a difference. But these new members are also not typical of the electorate they serve. Whether they can be said to "refine and enlarge the public views," as claimed by James Madison in *Federalist* no. 10 (1787), may depend on the time, place, issue, and perspective of the observer. Finally, a fourth kind of *participatory* representation, based on citizen initiatives, legislative initiatives and referenda, recall, etc., along with a greater focus on public opinion polls, is another alternative which has aroused great controversy in both the United States and Germany.[78]

In Germany parliament reflects the diversity of interests in the *Land* better than the prime minister or the cabinet, which is one reason why the argument is made that the weakening of parliaments *vis-à-vis* the governments must be resisted.[79] This does not, of course, prevent some groups from maintaining that they are not represented. A good example is the environmentalists in the 1970s, who formed citizen initiatives in competition with elected bodies at both the local and *Land* levels. Since the early 1980s, however, these elements have formed and have been generally absorbed by the Greens, who have gained representation in all of the *Land* parliaments in the West (but none in the East!) and large numbers of local governments.[80] Environmental concerns have also been picked up to a much greater extent than before by the older, established parties.

Parliamentary debating and articulation functions are closely related. Debating functions are shared with the media, and articulation functions are shared with interest groups. Group interests are, of course, also reflected in debates, and they are articulated in nonpublic committee meetings.[81] The petition committees, mentioned above, should also be noted as instruments for connecting public concerns and demands with the *Land* parliaments.

Service function

This is a key function in the United States, where it involves a wide variety of constituency services. The amount and nature of service provided varies among the states, based largely on the amount of staff support the legislator has at his or her disposal.[82] In Germany the service function is often ignored in the literature as a specific function of legislators, probably because *Land* legislators generally do not have staff other than perhaps a part-time secretary to assist them with such activities. On the other hand, they do have office hours in their constituencies or home towns, and they are often visited or contacted by individuals, groups, and local government officials who have various requests and concerns.[83] They also receive numerous telephone calls in their homes from constituents, some of whom seem to pay little regard to the timing of their call. Furthermore, deputies would point to the many group meetings, festivals, ceremonies, etc., that they are expected to attend back home. The petition committee mentioned above should also be mentioned as a means of providing service functions.

"Laboratory" function

The German *Länder* are not in as strong a position as American states to perform a laboratory function in terms of new policy initiatives, such as the experiments carried out by several American states in the 1990s in the area of welfare reform. On the other hand, elections in the *Länder* may be seen at times as tests for the parties at the federal level, as in the case of Hesse in February 1999 where the CDU and FDP won an unexpected victory only months after the federal election in September 1998 which the SPD and Greens won clearly. *Land* elections also offer opportunities for new parties to demonstrate their seriousness and potential. Examples on the left would be the Greens in the 1980s and, after unification, the PDS in the eastern *Länder*; on the the far right, parties such as the *Republikaner* in the late 1980s and the German People's Party (DVU) in the 1990s have had some limited success. The formation of new *Land* government coalitions in the 1990s, such as the SPD and the Greens in Hamburg, Bremen, and Hesse, could be seen as the precursor of the SPD–Green coalition in Bonn in September 1998; whether the SPD and the PDS coalition in Mecklenburg-Vorpommern will become any kind of model for future coalitions in other *Länder* and perhaps even for the federal level remains to be seen. These examples in addition to the introduction of personal data protection procedures in Hesse and the vote for sixteen-year-olds in local elections in Schleswig-Holstein, Lower Saxony, and Hesse (changed again to age eighteen by the new CDU/FDP government in Hesse in summer 1999) have led some to conclude that "the *Land* level today is in spite of all unitary tendencies within certain limits a field for political experimentation."[84]

Land *parliaments and governments*

As noted above, there is a tendency in all democratic systems, and especially in parliamentary democracies, for the executive to take major responsibility for setting the legislative agenda and for pushing its budgetary, fiscal and other policy proposals through the legislature.[85] In all

democratic systems the broader agenda is the result of increased governmental responsibilities in social, economic, transportation, environmental, educational, and other policy areas, while the success rate in passing
agenda items is based on varying degrees of party discipline and size of
the majority. In parliamentary systems it is also due to the interconnection between the government and the majority party or coalition in the
parliament and the reluctance of this majority to challenge government
policy and therefore weaken the government or even force the calling of
new elections which would be difficult for the majority to contest if it was
itself responsible for the downfall of its own government.

In Germany the institution of the *Bundesrat*, a *federal* organ which
allows *Land* governments to participate in the federal legislative process,
has contributed to what some observers call a system of "executive federalism." This is a system in which the federal government and its majority
in the *Bundestag* can pass a majority of its legislative proposals – and
usually the more important ones – if the *Bundesrat*, composed of *Land
government* representatives, grants its approval. We have noted above that
the federal government has assumed major responsibility for legislation
in the German federal system as a result of a series of constitutional and
other changes since the Basic Law was adopted in 1949. As will be seen in
Chapter 11, the influence of the *Land* governments has also increased in
recent years as a result of constitutional reforms providing the *Bundesrat*
with additional powers in decision making concerning the EU. It is also
clear that the influence of the *Land* governments increases under conditions of divided government, as in the 1990s and since 2000.

The problem with these developments from the perspective of the *Land*
parliaments is that they have not benefited from the increased participation
of their governments in federal decision making; indeed, the increase in
Bundesrat legislative initiatives in the past few decades is in part a reflection
of the loss of legislative powers in the *Land* parliaments.[86] While *Land* governments do have an obligation to keep their parliaments informed, and
parliaments may make recommendations to their governments, proposals
to make *Land* government votes in the *Bundesrat* dependent on approval by
Land parliaments have been rejected as both unconstitutional and impractical. They are unconstitutional because the *Bundesrat* is a *federal* organ
over which the *Land* parliaments have no authority, and impractical
because of time pressures and information levels. This results in the widespread complaint that the *Land* parliaments have been the real losers in the
increased legislative powers of the federal government and the growth in
participation of the *Länder* in many federal decisions via the *Bundesrat*.[87]

Not only are the *Land* parliaments left out of decision making in the *Bundesrat*; they have also been bypassed when the federal government passes concurrent legislation that calls on the *Land* governments to issue regulations for implementation without parliamentary action,[88] a practice that was revised somewhat in favor of the *Land* parliaments in the constitutional amendments in 1994.[89] The horizontal meetings of the *Land* prime ministers and of subject ministers (the so-called "third level") also lead to numerous agreements that, in theory, are subject to parliamentary scrutiny and approval; however, in fact the parliamentary majority is unlikely to reject its own government's actions, not only because of party discipline but also because of a lack of information.[90] Model legislation may also emerge from such meetings. In addition, hundreds of specialized meetings involving higher civil servants of the *Länder* and meetings of federal and *Land* experts result in a large number of recommendations that are not legally binding but that in fact lead to a high degree of cooperation and coordination. These may be formally subject to *Land* parliament approval, but they have a unitary effect. Meetings of federal and *Land* bureaucratic officials (sometimes referred to as "the fourth level") may also lead to federal–*Land* agreements that can have an effect on laws or create bodies that do not affect the *Land* parliaments directly.[91] It is not clear, however, just what the "proper" role of the *Land* parliaments should be in these circumstances, given the logic of the parliamentary system which calls for support of the government by the majority party or coalition parties.

The role of Land parliaments

In summary, the complaint that the *Land* parliaments have been weakened over the last few decades is, at least to some extent, a questionable proposition. If one looks only at the legislative functions they perform, they surely have been weakened; however, if one looks at other functions, their weakness is not so apparent.

Even if the *Land* parliaments have been weakened in their legislative function, it can be argued that they continue to perform other important functions, such as the election and recruitment, control, debating, representation, and service functions discussed above. Part of the problem the *Land* parliaments face in exercising these functions, however, is that their exercise often requires considerable expertise on the part of individual deputies, they take place in relative obscurity, and they appear generally to be less interesting to both the media and the public. The fact that it s above all the role of the Opposition to exercise effectively many of the control functions – and in the process usually be easily defeated – makes it more difficult to keep the media and public interested in routine legislative sessions.

Also when compared with parliamentary systems in other countries, it might be argued that it is not really so clear that German *Land* parliaments have lost significantly more power in general terms than parliamentary bodies elsewhere. If one looks at the role of governments in Great Britain or in any number of parliamentary systems in setting the agenda and relying on party cohesion to push through their policy initiatives, one could also point to a relatively passive law making role as performed by the parliament. One can also point to the general weakness of the French National Assembly or even the British House of Commons for comparative purposes. A strong legislature, after all, suggests an ability to defy the government in committees and in plenary sessions, to set its own agenda, and to act independently in general, not only in cases of divided government but even when the same party controls both the executive and legislative branches, as in the United States. But these are characteristics of a presidential or separation of powers system, not a parliamentary system in which the government and its supporting party or coalition parties are interconnected. The highly individualistic American model might mean that the legislature is more "responsive,"[92] but it also suggests a less "responsible" party system and a less "responsible" government, because the voters cannot generally hold weak parties, divided government, or government with uncertain party support as such accountable for their actions. Even some *Land* parliament deputies who have complained to the author about the inability of their institution to act more independently of the government seemed unaware of the change to a system of separation of powers and weakened parties that a powerful *Land* parliament would imply.

This raises the question of whether at least some of the concern expressed about the weakening of *Land* parliaments is based on a misunderstanding of the parliamentary system. As one observer of the political scene in Germany has noted, the "loss" of power to the federal level and, increasingly, to the EU level, seems inevitable, and it helps little to whine about it; besides, the *Länder* are primarily concerned with administration, which is a key concern of the people, and therefore it is important for the *Land* parliaments to focus on control functions. This observer also notes that in a party democracy, such as Germany's, the natural obligation of the majority party in parliament is to support the government in implementing its proposals and program, but this calls for control measures both within and outside of parliament, e.g., the press.[93] Another observer suggests that a parliamentary system "is basically a flagrant violation of the separation of powers, because the parliament and government . . . are connected in a special way that is important to the functioning of parliament . . . Therefore, in answering the question of what the *Land* parliaments can and should do, the principle of separation of powers has little relevance."[94] Studies have shown, however, that most Germans believe that separation of powers is or should be a characteristic of their parliamentary system and that there is a widespread misperception of the roles of government and opposition parties in supporting and opposing the government and the leading role of the government in the legislative process.[95] These studies are not very different in principle from studies that show that many Americans also do not understand their state legislatures, and, like many Germans, have unrealistic and contradictory expectations regarding legislators and the policy making process. It is no surprise that, as a result, they are supercritical.[96]

The organization of the *Land* parliaments

Like legislative bodies in the American states, each *Land* parliament has an administrative staff to assist the deputies in various aspects of their work. This administration is supervised by the President of the *Landtag* and led by a *Landtagsdirektor*. It is not a part of the executive branch; the staff are *Land* civil servants appointed by the President. From small numbers of higher-level civil servants and lower-level employees in the early 1950s, the total staff has grown to several hundred in the larger *Länder*. About half of the higher civil servants are employed by the parliamentary advisory service, which is concerned with numerous technical legislative services such as legislative bill drafting.

As in the United States, the size of the administrative staff has increased over the years as a result of improvements made in the levels and kinds of services provided; the increased work of the parliaments; the addition and growth of professional legislative services, due in part to the growing complexity of legislation; and the addition of press and information as well as visitors' services.[97] The staff has the responsibility of supporting the parliament, its President, the committees, the party groups, and the deputies. It is divided into two sections: one concerned primarily with the preparation, implementation, and assessment of plenary, committee or commission meetings and the parliamentary petition office and public

information; the other section is involved primarily with classic administration, such as payroll and record keeping.

The parliamentary services section[98]

Legal services
The main function of this office is to provide legal advice. This includes
advice not only regarding legislation, constitutional issues, reports, and
so forth, but also concerning rules of procedure. Legal advice for investi-
gating committees can be especially important.

The petitions office
This office serves as a kind of parliamentary ombudsman for the many
citizens who send requests or complaints to the parliament. The small staff
check whether the petitions are admissible, organize meetings of the petitions committee or, in Lower Saxony, the standing committees, and plan
visits by deputies to the locations of some complaints for a first-hand view
of the situation. Recommendations are made by the petitions committee or
other committees for relief or action by the bureaucracy or parliament.[99]

The plenary meeting and committee service
Here staff are responsible for preparing the regular committee meetings,
the plenary meetings, and the meetings of the praesidium (executive
committee) which sets the agenda and decides how much time should
be available for discussion of each item. The staff assemble and print all
relevant documents required for the plenary and committee meetings.

Stenographic services
Each parliament has several stenographers who have the task of recording
every word spoken in the plenary sessions, including questions raised that
interrupt the speeches and comments made by hecklers. They rotate
about every five minutes, and their reports are printed about fourteen
days after they were written. The record is not entirely verbatim, since
small and obvious corrections are made. For committee meetings notes
are kept rather than word-for-word accounts.

Public relations and media services
This is a more recent addition, and it has four areas of activity: the press,
publicity, political education, and visitor services. The staff keep the press
informed about parliamentary developments and the deputies informed

about press reports concerning them and parliament. Each party group also has a press office of its own.

The administration section[100]

Protocol
One civil servant has the responsibility to prepare for foreign visitors, official receptions, and other events. He or she also prepares visits of the parliamentary president and deputies to foreign countries, especially for the purpose of visiting regional legislative bodies such as selected American state legislatures.

The administration office
This office is responsible for administering the budget of the parliament, including payments of salaries to the deputies and staff, support payments to the party groups, printing costs and building maintenance. The deputies also have their own part-time secretaries paid from the budget. Payment of party group staff is the responsibility of the party groups themselves. There is also a small staff of technical personnel who maintain the building.

The information service
This service includes the library – which is some *Länder* is very good – archives, data collection, and so forth. The role of computers has become increasingly important in this area.

The parliamentary advisory service[101]

The purpose of this service is to advise and assist the party groups and the member deputies. The chair of the party group decides how to use the personnel assigned to the party group. They are selected by the parliamentary president in consultation with the party group, but they become public employees who must meet the civil service standards for the positions they occupy. Since they are civil servants, they cannot be released even if the party for whose parliamentary group they work no longer gains sufficient votes in parliamentary elections (i.e., 5 percent of the total) to be admitted to parliament. In this case they have to be assigned elsewhere. If the party groups hire persons not authorized in the budget, these persons do not become civil servants.

Conclusion

Land parliaments were established before the federal parliament in 1949, and Article 30 and Article 70 of the Basic Law seem to suggest that they have very important legislative functions. But the Basic Law also grants the federation broad legislative powers, concurrent powers, and the authority to pass framework legislation. These provisions, constitutional amendments, and Federal Constitutional Court decisions that have expanded the legislative powers of the federation, the growing role of the *Bundesrat* which increases the influence of *Land* governments rather than *Land* parliaments, the growing regulative activities of the EU, and *Politikverflechtung* in general, have had the overall effect of reducing the legislative powers of the *Land* parliaments.

On the other hand, *Land* deputies exercise many functions besides law making, including electoral and recruitment functions, control functions, debating functions, representative and articulation functions, service functions, and, to some extent, "laboratory" functions. Of these, the most time-consuming for most deputies is the service function performed especially for the home district. The deputies, who have few or no staff, serve as a link between citizens and the government, including administrative offices, and thereby help to bring government "closer to the people."

It could be argued that the decline of legislative powers of the *Land* parliaments is also to some extent a reflection of the operation of the parliamentary system. This system calls for the majority party or parties to support the government in order to give it the legitimacy it needs to govern and to provide political stability. A legislature that can and does defy the head of government or competes with him or her and the cabinet for control of the agenda and the power to pass legislation that may not be supported by the cabinet suggests a different political model, namely the presidential system, characterized by separation of powers and checks and balances. There is some evidence that many Germans seem to expect more of a separation of powers than the parliamentary system provides and do not understand or accept the conventional roles of government, majority, and opposition in this system; nor do they respect the politicians who operate within the system.[102] To the extent this thesis is correct, it is no wonder that there is widespread *Politikverdrossenheit* (alienation from or annoyance with politics) in Germany.

Notes

1 Hermann Eicher, *Der Machtverlust der Landesparlamente* (Berlin: Duncker & Humblot, 1988), pp. 23–27.

2 Ibid., pp. 31–38.

3 Ibid., pp. 38–40.

4 Ibid., pp. 77–78.

5 Martin Bullinger, "Die Zuständigkeit der Länder zur Gesetzgebung," *Die öffentliche Verwaltung* 23, no. 22 (November 1970), p. 765; Eicher, *Der Machtverlust*, p. 78.

6 Manfred Friedrich, *Landesparlamente in der Bundesrepublik* (Opladen: Westdeutscher Verlag, 1975), p. 55.

7 Otto Rundel, "Kontrolle der Fraktionsfinanzierung," in *Der Landtag – Standort und Entwicklungen*, edited by Erich Schneider (Baden-Baden: Nomos Verlagsgesellschaft, 1989), pp. 141–148.

8 For a list of rights and privileges associated with party group status, see Thomas Rösslein, "Die Fraktionen im Landtag," in Schneider, *Der Landtag*, p. 128.

9 Ibid., p. 126.

10 There is a vast literature in Germany on the tension between Article 21 of the Basic Law which is seen as promoting the "party state" and Article 38 of the Basic Law (and, of course, their counterparts in the *Land* constitutions) which prohibits deputies from acting on the basis of instructions against their own consciences. See, for example, Wilhelm Henke, *Das Recht der politischen Parteien* (2nd edn; Göttingen: Schwartz, 1972), p. 129 or Christoph Müller, *Das Imperative und Freie Mandat* (Leiden: Sijthoff, 1966), Ch. 5.

11 For a discussion of territorial and boundary reforms at the local level in Germany, see Arthur B. Gunlicks, "The Reorganization of Local Governments in the Federal Republic of Germany," in *Local Government Reform and Reorganization: An International Perspective*, edited by Arthur B. Gunlicks (Port Washington: Kennikat Press, 1981), pp. 169–181; and by the same author, *Local Government in the German Federal System* (Durham: Duke University Press, 1986), Ch. 4, and "Die parteipolitischen Präferenzen beim niedersächsischen Entscheidungsprozess für eine Gebietsreform im Spannungsfeld von Effizienz, Gleichheit und Freiheit," *Zeitschrift für Parlamentsfragen* 7, no. 4 (December 1976), pp. 472–488.

12 Herbert Schneider, *Länderparlamentarismus in der Bundesrepublik* (Opladen: Leske & Budrich, 1979), p. 83.

13 Rösslein, "Die Fraktionen im Landtag," pp. 129–134.

14 Ibid., pp. 134–135.

15 Schneider, *Länderparlamentarismus*, p. 82.

16 Walter Rudolf, "Die Bedeutung der Landesparlamente in Deutschland," in *Die Stellung der Landesparlamente aus deutscher, österreichischer, und spanischer Sicht*, edited by Detlef Merten (Berlin: Duncker & Humblot, 1997), p. 60;

Manfred Friedrich, *Der Landtag als Berufsparlament?* (Karl-Bräuer-Institut des Bundes der Steuerzahler, 1977), p. 29; Franz Gress, "Aktuelle Probleme und Perspektiven des Föderalismus in der Bundesrepublik Deutschland und den USA," in *Krise und Reform des Föderalismus,* edited by Reinhard C. Meier-Walser and Gerhard Hirscher (München : Olzog Verlag, 1999), pp. 123–124; Bullinger, "Die Zuständigkeit," p. 764.

17 Friedrich, *Der Landtag als Berufsparlament?*, p. 26.

18 I wish to thank Klaus-Eckart Gebauer, Director of the Cabinet Staff in Rhineland-Palatinate, for this reminder.

19 Gunlicks, "The Reorganization of Local Governments," pp. 169–181 and Gunlicks, *Local Government,* Ch. 4. For a comprehensive treatment, see Werner Thieme and Günther Prillwitz, *Durchführung und Ergebnisse der kommunalen Gebietsreform* (Baden-Baden: Nomos Verlagsgesellschaft, 1981).

20 See the resolution by the Conference of *Land* Parliament Presidents, who complained in 1983 of the loss of legislative powers to the federation and the European Community. Unterrichtung durch den Präsidenten des Landtags, "Standortbestimmung und Perspektiven der Landesparlamente," Landtag Rheinland-Pfalz, Drucksache 10/22 (1 June 1983).

21 This is the argument made by the president of the Bavarian *Land* parliament, Johann Böhm, in his "Grußwort," in *Die Abgeordneten: Stellung, Aufgaben und Selbstverständnis in der parlamentarischen Demokratie,* edited by Heinrich Oberreuter (Tutzing: Akademie für politische Bildung, 1995), pp. 9–10.

22 Albrecht Martin, "Möglichkeiten, dem Bedeutungsverlust der Landesparlamente entgegenzuwirken," *Zeitschrift für Parlamentsfragen* 15, no. 2 (1984), p. 279; Friedrich, *Der Landtag als Landesparlamente,* p. 55; Friedrich, *Berufsparlament?*, p. 26.

23 On the other hand, he has complained about the growing focus of attention in the parliaments on local matters and the decreasing attention paid to political leadership issues and principles. In this regard he has warned against the deputies' becoming mere spokespersons for public concerns. See Erik Spemann, "Schlanker Staat durch Schrumpfkur für das Parlament," *Das Parlament* (14 November 1997), p. 16.

24 Rudolf, "Die Bedeutung," p. 70.

25 Jens Kalke, "Bedeutungsverlust der Landtage? Ein empirischer Test anhand der Drogenpolitik," *Zeitschrift fürParlamentsfragen* 32 (May 2001), pp. 309–325.

26 Winfried Steffani, "Länderparlamentarismus im parlamentarischen Bundesstaat," in *Liberale Demokratie in Europa und den USA: Festschrift für Kurt L. Shell,* edited by Franz Gress and Hans Vorländer (Frankfurt: Campus Verlag, 1990), pp. 208–222.

27 Schneider, *Länderparlamentarismus,* p. 49.

28 Rudolf, "Die Bedeutung," p. 58. For a list of constitutional changes between 1963 and 1992 that granted more powers to the federation at the expense of

the *Länder*, see Albert Janssen, "Der Landtag im Leineschloß – Entwicklungslinien und Zukunftsperspektiven," in *Rückblicke – Ausblicke*, edited by Präsident des Niedersächsischen Landtages (Hannover: Hahn-Druckerei, 1992), pp. 38–40.

29   Rudolf, "Die Bedeutung," p. 52; Eicher, *Der Machtverlust*, p. 77.

30   Eicher, *Der Machtverlust*, pp. 103–104.

31   Ibid., p. 86.

32   Martin, "Möglichkeiten," pp. 279, 281.

33   Konrad Hesse, *Der unitarische Bundesstaat* (Karlsruhe: C. F. Müller, 1962).

34   Wilfried Erbguth, "Erosion der Länderstaatlichkeit," in *Verfassungsrecht im Wandel*, edited by Jörn Ipsen (Köln: Heymann, 1995), pp. 559–561.

35   Eicher, *Der Machtverlust*, p. 63.

36   Hartmut Klatt, "Beziehungen zwischen Bundestag and Landesparlamenten. (Selbst-) Entmachtung der Landesparlamente? Möglichkeiten und Gegenstrategien," in *Landesparlamente und Föderalismus: Hat das parlamentarische System in den Bundesländern eine Zukunft?*, edited by Franz Gress (Wiesbaden: Hessischer Landtag, 1990), p. 83.

37   The author most associated with this concept is Fritz Scharpf. For example, see Fritz Scharpf, Bernd Reissert, and Fritz Schnabel, *Politikverflechtung: Theorie und Empirie des kooperativen Föderalismus in der Bundesrepublik Deutschland* (Kronberg: Scriptor Verlag, 1976); Martin, "Möglichkeiten," pp. 280–281.

38   Rudolf, "Die Bedeutung," p. 64.

39   Friedrich, *Der Landtag als Berufsparlament?*, pp. 22–24.

40   Janssen, *Der Landtag*, p. 25.

41   Eicher, *Der Machtverlust*, p. 83.

42   Ibid., pp. 48–52.

43   Ibid., pp. 53–60.

44   Heiderose Kilper and Roland Lhotta, *Föderalismus in der Bundesrepublik Deutschland* (Opladen: Leske & Budrich, 1996), p. 199.

45   Ibid. See also Roland Johne, *Landesparlamentarismus im Zeichen der europäischen Integration* (Frankfurt/M.: Peter Lang, 1994), p. 36.

46   Eicher, *Der Machtverlust*, p. 30; Roland Hahn, *Macht und Ohnmacht des Landtages von Baden-Württemberg* (Kehl: N. P. Engel Verlag, 1987), p. 6; Franz Gress and Roland Huth, *Die Landesparlamente: Gesetzgeungsorgane in den deutschen Ländern* (Heidelberg Hüthig, 1998), Ch. 2.

47   Schneider, *Länderparlamentarismus*, p. 47.

48   Erich Schneider in the preface of *Der Landtag – Standort und Entwicklungen*, p. 8.

49   Schneider, *Länderparlamentarismus*, p. 51.

50   Roland Hahn, *Macht und Ohnmacht des Landtages von Baden-Württemberg* (Kehl: N. P. Engel Verlag, 1987), p. 7.

51   Schneider, *Länderparlamentarismus*, pp. 34–35.

52 Ibid., pp. 31–33.

53 Rudolf, "Die Bedeutung," p. 56.

54 Schneider, *Länderparlamentarismus*, p. 38; see also the allegations of Tammany Hall-like conditions in Cologne, in Erwin and Ute Scheuch, *Cliquen, Klüngel und Karrieren: Über den Verfall der politischen Pareien* (Reinbek bei Hamburg: Rowohlt, 1993).

55 Roland Hahn even notes that sometimes members of the *Bundestag* forward mail to their counterparts in the *Landtag*, because it concerns questions of administration that are the responsibility of the *Länder*. Hahn, *Macht und Ohnmacht*, p. 32.

56 Friedrich, *Landesparlamente*, p. 11; Hahn, *Macht und Ohnmacht*, p. 11; Rudolf, "Die Bedeutung," p. 70.

57 On the other hand, what appeared to be a rather routine change of leadership in mid-term for the SPD–FDP coalition in Lower Saxony in 1976 led to a change of government when the coalition majority failed in a secret ballot to provide the prime minister's replacement with an absolute majority vote. The end result was the election of the CDU's Ernst Albrecht as the new prime minister. Arthur B. Gunlicks, "Coalition Collapse in Lower Saxony: Political and Constitutional Implications," *Parliamentary Affairs* 29, no. 4 (Autumn 1976), pp. 437–449.

58 Joachim Linck, "Die parlamentarische Kontrolle der Landesparlamente," in *Die Kontrollfunktion der Landesparlamente*, edited by Heinz Schäffer (Wien: Manzsche Verlags- und Universitätsbuchhandlung, 1995), pp. 14–20.

59 Eicher, *Der Machtverlust*, pp. 96–98.

60 Frido Wagener, "Gemeinsame Rahmenplanung und Investitionsfinanzierung," *Die öffentliche Verwaltung* 30, no. 16 (August 1977), p. 588; "Milderungsmöglichkeiten nachteiliger Folgen vertikaler Politikverflechtung," in *Politikverflechtung im föderativen Staat*, edited by Joachim Jens Hesse (Baden-Baden: Nomos Verlagsgesellschaft, 1978), pp. 149–165.

61 Klaus-Eckart Gebauer, "Interessenregelung im föderalistischen System," in *Grundrechte, soziale Ordnung und Verfassungsgerichtsbarkeit*, edited by Eckart Klein (Heidelberg: C. F. Müller Juristischer Verlag, 1995), p. 89.

62 Schneider, *Länderparlamentarismus*, pp. 39–41; also Herbert Schneider, "Der Landtag," in *Baden-Württemberg: Eine politische Landeskunde*, edited by der Landeszentrale für politische Bildung (3rd edn; Stuttgart: Verlag W. Kohlhammer, 1985), pp. 97–99.

63 Gress and Huth, *Die Landesparlamente*, p. 47.

64 Gebauer, "Interessenregelung," p. 72.

65 Linck, "Die parlamentarische Kontrolle," p. 28.

66 Rüdiger Voigt, "Einfluß und Wirkungsmöglichkeiten der Landesparlamente," *Bayerische Verwaltungs-Blätter*, no. 4 (15 February 1977), p. 98.

67 Schneider, *Länderparlamentarismus*, p. 85

68 Friedrich, *Landesparlamente*, pp. 15–16, 20–21, 26–27.

69 Schneider, *Länderparlamentarismus*, pp. 85–86.

70 Ibid., pp. 42–43.

71 Walter Leisner, "Schwächung der Landesparlamente durch grundgesetzlichen Föderalismus," *Die öffentliche Verwaltung* 21, no. 11–12 (June 1968), pp. 389–396; Friedrich, *Landesparlamente*, p. 34.

72 Linck, "Die parlamentarische Kontrolle," p. 23.

73 Eicher, *Der Machtverlust*, pp. 66–69.

74 Hahn, *Macht und Ohnmacht*, p. 20.

75 Hans Meyer, "Was sollen und was können die Landesparlamente leisten?," in Gress, *Landesparlamente und Föderalismus*, p. 52; Schneider, *Länderparlamentarismus*, pp. 55–61.

76 Ibid., pp. 54–55.

77 Alan Rosenthal, *The Decline of Representative Democracy: Process, Participation, and Power in State Legislatures* (Washington, DC: CQ Press, 1998), pp. 27–31, 39–43; see also Werner Patzelt, *Abgeordnete und Repräsentation: Amtsvertändnis und Wahlkreisarbeit* (Passau: Wissenschaftsverlag Rothe, 1993), Ch 1. Chapter 1 draws heavily from Hanna F. Pitkin, *The Concept of Representation* (Berkeley: University of California Press, 1967).

78 Rosenthal, *The Decline*, pp. 31–39.

79 Eicher, *Der Machtverlust*, pp. 65–66.

80 Ibid., pp. 62–63.

81 Ibid., p. 63.

82 Rosenthal, *The Decline*, pp. 15–17.

83 Werner J. Patzelt, *Abgeordnete und ihr Beruf: Interviews – Umfragen – Analysen* (Berlin: Adademie Verlag, 1995), pp. 94–102.

84 Gress and Huth, *Die Landesparlamente*, pp. 54–57.

85 Thus it is the governments on which the press focuses its attention. Dietrich Herzog *et al.*, *Abgeordnete und Bürger: Ergebnisse einer Befragung der Mitglieder des 11. Deutschen Bundestages und der Bevölkerung* (Opladen: Westdeutscher Verlag, 1990), pp. 32–33.

86 Georg-Berndt Oschatz and Horst Risse, "Bemerkungen zum Gesetzesinitiativrecht des Bundesrates," *Zeitschrift für Gesetzgebung* 4, no. 4 (1989), pp. 316–331.

87 Eicher, *Der Machtverlust*, pp. 88–89; Friedrich, *Landesparlamente*, p. 71; Evelyn Haas, "Die Mitwirkung der Länder bei EG-Vorhaben," *Die öffentliche Verwaltung* 41, no. 15 (August 1988), pp. 621–622.

88 Eicher, *Der Machtverlust*, pp. 92–93.

89 Rudolf, "Die Bedeutung," p. 61.

90 Eicher, *Der Machtverlust*, p. 94.

91 Ibid., pp. 94–98; Martin, "Möglichkeiten," pp. 280–281.

92 Rosenthal, *The Decline*, pp. 327–328.

93 Paul Leo Giani, "Was könnte besser gemacht werden? Partei, Regierung, und Parlament. Die Praxis der Landespolitik," in Gress, *Landesparlamente und Föderalismus*, pp. 129–131, 133.

94 Hans Meyer, "Was sollen und was können die Landesparlamente leisten?," in Gress, *Landesparlamente und Föderalismis*, p. 36.
95 Werner Patzelt, "Ein latenter Verfassungskonflikt? Die Deutschen und ihr parlamentarisches Regierungssystem," *Politische Vierteljahresschrift* 39 (1998), pp. 725–757.
96 Rosenthal, *The Decline*, pp. 67–69, 340–343; Patzelt, *Abgeordnete und ihr Beruf*, pp. 193–197.
97 Wolfgang Krauter, "Die Verwaltungsinfrastruktur des Parlaments – ihre Entwicklung in den letzten 25 Jahren," in Schneider, *Der Landtag – Standort und Entwicklung*, pp. 155–156.
98 The information in this section is based on material describing the services provided in Baden-Württemberg as provided in ibid., pp. 159–164.
99 See also Schneider, *Länderparlamentarismus*, pp. 107–112.
100 Krauter, "Die Verwaltungsstruktur," pp. 166–168.
101 Ibid., pp. 172–175.
102 This is the theme of the article by Patzelt, "Ein latenter Verfassungskonflikt?," pp. 725–757.

7

The *Land* parliaments deputies in Germany

Introduction

When one reads of European parliaments and their members, one normally thinks of the national level. This is understandable with respect to the mostly unitary political systems, which have only national parliaments. But some of these states, such as Germany, Switzerland, Austria, and Belgium, are federal systems, and some others, such as Spain, have a semi-federal territorial organization. In these systems far more parliamentarians are members of regional parliaments than of the national parliament. Nevertheless, since the regional parliamentarians receive much less media coverage and relatively little public attention in general, less is known about them than about their counterparts in the national capital. In Germany there is some newspaper coverage of the *Land* parliaments and their members, but very little attention is paid them by television. On certain occasions there may be a development or incident in a parliament which receives considerable public attention, but in general politicians at the *Land* level are not in the public eye and are not all that well known. Nevertheless, one issue that has been discussed to some extent by the attentive public is legislative salary and various benefits along with the question of whether the *Land* politicians are overpaid and underworked.

The deputies: who they are

As of summer 2002 there were 1916 *Land* deputies in the thirteen territorial states and three city-states, ranging in number from fifty-one in the smallest territorial state, the Saarland, to 231 in the largest territorial state, North-Rhine Westphalia. The Christian Democrats (in Bavaria, the CSU) had the largest overall number, 815, while the SPD had 719. Among the small parties, the Greens had 107, the FDP ninety-three, the PDS 148, and others thirty-four. The Greens were represented in every West German *Land* parliament except for the Saarland, whereas in the new eastern *Länder* they had no seats except in Berlin. The FDP had representation in nine *Länder*, but in only one of the new *Länder*, and the PDS was confined to the five new *Länder* and Berlin. On the far right, the Republicans lost their last seats in Baden-Württemberg in 2001, but the German People's Union (DVU) had five seats in Brandenburg, and one in Bremen (Bremerhaven). The DVU lost all of its sixteen seats in Saxony-Anhalt in April 2002.

Each of the *Land* parliaments publishes a handbook with brief biographies and statistics about the deputies, including occupational and other data. Unfortunately, the organization of the data and categories are not standardized, and some of the handbooks provide more information than others. Indeed, some of the biographical information on occupational background is very limited. In 1994 Werner Patzelt sent a questionnaire to the 2,800 European, federal, and *Land* parliament deputies, about one-third of whom responded.[1] Of the respondents, 639 were *Land* deputies. The largest single group (21.6 percent) consisted of teachers, and all public employees together accounted for 45.3 percent of the deputies. The next largest group (15.4 percent) were employees in industry and trade. However, data collected by the author on deputies in the East show that a high proportion are or were employed in state-owned industry and trade firms and that many are or were engineers of various kinds. Different kinds of teachers also made up a significant proportion of the Eastern deputies, but otherwise public employees are a much smaller proportion of parliaments in the East than in the West (Table 7.1).

Patzelt found relatively few deputies who said they were still practicing their occupations on a full-time basis; indeed, on a five-point scale, about 70 percent selected points 4 or 5, i.e., they were engaged in their occupations very little or not at all. A sizable plurality of 44.5 percent considered themselves to be in the middle of a five-point scale on social class background. The average age was early fifties, and three-fourths of the deputies were male. A little more than 28 percent said they had served more than twelve years in office (20.4 percent said seven–twelve years).[2]

Based on the statistics collected by the author for half of the *Länder*, the proportion of women in the *Land* parliaments ranged from 21 percent in Bavaria to 39 percent in Bremen. The Greens consistently have the largest proportion of women (40–57 percent), the Christian Democrats the smallest (11–32 percent). The average age of the deputies is between

Table 7.1   **Parliamentary seats in the *Länder*, 1998–2001**

Land (Year of Last Election)	Total seats	SPD	CDU	FDP	Greens	PDS	Other
Baden-Württemberg (3/2001)	128	45	63	10	10	–	–
Bavaria (9/1998)	204	67	123[a]	–	14	–	–
Berlin (10/2001)	141	44	35	15	14	33	–
Brandenburg (9/1999)	89	37	25	–	–	22	5[b]
Bremen (6/1999)	100	47	42	–	10	–	1[b]
Hamburg (9/2001)	121	46	33	6	11	–	25[c]
Hesse (7/1999)	110	46	50	6	8	–	–
Lower Saxony (3/1998)	157	83	62	–	12	–	–
Mecklenburg-Vorpommern (9/1998)	71	27	24	–	–	20	–
North-Rhine Westphalia (5/2000)	231	102	88	24	17	–	–
Rhineland-Palatinate (3/2001)	101	49	38	8	6	–	–
Saarland (9/1999)	51	25	26	–	–	–	–
Saxony (9/1999)	120	14	76	–	–	30	–
Saxony-Anhalt (4/2002)	115	25	48	17	–	25	–
Schleswig-Holstein (2/2000)	89	41	33	7	5	–	3[d]
Thuringia (9/1999)	88	21	49	–	–	18	–
Total	1916	719	815	93	107	148	34

Notes: [a] Christlich Soziale Union (CSU); [b] Deutsche Volksunion (DVU); [c] Party for Rule of Law Offensive (PRO); [d] Südschleswigscher Wählerverband (SSW).
Sources: *Wahlergebnisse in Deutschland, 1946–1998* (Mannheim: Forschungsgruppe Wahlen, 1998); Karl-Rudolf Korte, *Wahlen in der Bundesrepublik Deutschland* (Bonn: Bundeszentrale für politische Bildung, 1998); www.wahlrecht.de/landtage with links.

forty-five and fifty. The Greens generally have the lowest average age, while the CDU and SPD are about the same.

Based again on data from about half of the *Länder*, a number of generalizations can clearly be made. In terms of occupation, a large majority of the delegations of the SPD and Greens are white-collar employees. Some of the SPD deputies are from the private sector, but relatively few Greens have worked for private employers. A large proportion of SPD and Green deputies, and a smaller but still sizable proportion of CDU deputies, have positions in the public service. Most of these are *Beamte*, i.e., persons holding positions in the public sector with some degree of responsibility at the *Land* and local levels. It is often asserted that most of the *Beamte* are school teachers and others involved in education, but the data suggest that this group is generally a sizable minority of the public employees who are deputies and from 5 to 30 percent of the total party delegation, depending both on the party and the *Land*. The SPD has from one to five union employees in its delegations, and both of the large parties and the

Greens often have employees of local public enterprises in their party groups. Frequently these three parties also have one or more political party employees in their delegations. The important point is that most deputies are economically dependent employees. This has consequences for compensation practices, which are said to reflect the lack of financial independence of the deputies. On the other hand, public employees are guaranteed the right to return to their positions, for example, as teachers, if and when they leave the parliament before retirement age.

A minority of deputies are self-employed. Lawyers are fairly well represented, though they constitute a small minority of the total and are a far less important occupational group than in many US legislative bodies. Housewives and an occasional househusband are represented in small numbers, and a few students are deputies, especially in some Green delegations. Retirees are small in number.

The deputies: what they do

In the early 1990s an intensive study was made of the deputies of the parliament of Lower Saxony. On the basis of personal observation of plenary meetings, committee meetings, party groups and their specialized subject working groups; lengthy interviews and discussions with deputies and staff; accompanying selected deputies during one week's activities; a questionnaire focusing on time spent on various activities during a particular month; and visits to constituencies with deputies, a comprehensive picture was developed of the activities of the then 155 deputies in Hanover.[3] One result of the study was that the average work week for deputies was 76.7 hours, which conforms with the results of studies done earlier in Baden-Württemberg and Schleswig-Holstein.[4] Excluding the hours worked in occupations in which some deputies were still engaged, the average number of hours in the workweek of a deputy was 62.1. The differences among party groups in hours worked in various occupations outside of parliament were significant: CDU deputies worked on average 15.9 hours; FDP 13.3 hours; and the SPD 10.4 hours. None of the Greens worked at another occupation while they were deputies. The range in the workweek as deputies was between 49.7 and 103 hours. There were minor differences between men and women, party leaders and backbenchers, newcomers and veterans, and those directly elected and those elected over the party lists. There were also few differences between deputies of the large parties, SPD and CDU, at 77.4 and 75.4 hours, respectively, while the much smaller FDP and Green delegations claimed to put in 81.2 and 83.9 hours, respectively. This was due in large part to the extra demands placed on their smaller numbers.[5]

Another important and even more thorough academic study, based on interviews in Bavaria in 1989 of representatives in the *Land*, federal, and European parliaments, was published in 1993. A second book by the same author, based on the same data but organized differently and designed more for the general reader, appeared in 1995.[6] The author, Werner Patzelt, concluded that *Land* deputies worked on average about 60 hours per week.[7] A third study, conducted by the same author in 1994 was based on the results of a mailed questionnaire of 2,800 deputies at the European, federal, and *Land* levels.[8] During the weeks when parliament met, which in most cases included committee meetings, the respondents from the federal and *Land* levels put in about 65 hours on average, excluding travel time, work in other occupations, etc. During weeks when the parliament did not meet and the focus was on the home district, the average was about 54 hours. According to the respondents, about one-half of their total working time was spent on parliamentary matters, about one-third on district activities and service.[9] Even if one is skeptical of the claims of some of the deputies, there can be little doubt that most of them have a very long work week.

What do they do that takes up so much time? There are three sets of activities in which all of the deputies engage: activities related directly to parliamentary work; activities in the election district, even if elected over the party list; and activities related to their political party. A fourth set of activities which takes up a good deal of time of most deputies is connected with an elected office at the municipal and/or county level.

Parliamentary work

With respect to parliamentary work, the deputies attend party group meetings and meetings of specialized party working groups in which party initiatives and positions related to their committee assignments are discussed and occasional trips are made to places within the *Land* to gather information and make contacts; these make up the core of parliamentary activity for the deputies, and it is in the working groups that they spend the most time, including reading and preparation. All deputies participate in committee meetings, which, depending on the committee, meet normally from once to seven or eight times a month. In contrast to other *Länder* that have special petition committees, the committees in Lower Saxony receive complaints, concerns, and inquiries from citizens that are related to the subject matter of the committees. These communications are checked first by parliamentary administrative staff who then direct them to the appropriate committees for action. Of course the activity most familiar to the general public is the plenary meeting of parliament; however, full meetings take place only for three successive days every month except in late summer for a total of about thirty days during the year. They can be time-consuming for party leaders and those who are making prepared speeches, but even these are seen as largely staking out party positions for public consumption, especially for the press, and for gaining some publicity back home. The plenary sessions are especially tedious for the Opposition deputies, who can achieve few concrete results against the majority party or coalition. The tendency to raise a large number of rather minor questions during question time is also time-consuming and tedious. Few deputies are willing to sit for any length of time through the speeches, questions and routine actions that do not interest or concern them directly, especially when they have many other things they would rather be doing. But from the gallery, of course, the public sees many empty seats, not the delegates who are actually meeting and talking with constituents, other deputies, interest groups, and others outside in the hallways or lobby.[10] The belief by the general public that the work of their deputies is or should be done in the legislative chambers is also a problem in the United States, where disappointed citizens often see from the visitors' gallery mostly empty seats and a few inattentive legislators.[11]

In contrast to the public view, legislators themselves see the plenary meetings as relatively unimportant. When asked to indicate the importance of various parliamentary activities, 95 percent of the respondents in Patzelt's 1994 study said committee meetings were important, 92 percent pointed to party group meetings, 91 percent listed specialized party working groups, and only 50 percent said plenary meetings were important. Seventy percent thought that informal contacts with members of their own party were important, 43 percent thought the same about contacts with members of coalition parties, and only 25 percent felt that contact with Opposition members were important; 57 percent thought contacts with journalists were important.[12]

District work

The second set of activities, which deputies see as crucial for reelection purposes, is their work in the district.[13] This consists of contacts with local citizens, local administrative offices, local businesses, groups of all kinds, and, of course, the local press. This work is not only a process of meeting people and remaining in contact; it also involves an ombudsman function,[14] including telephone calls at virtually all times of the day. These activities take up an average of one-third of the working time for the week. (In the study in Bavaria about 37 percent of the deputies suggested that more than 50 percent of the total time they spent on political work was connected with their districts.[15]) Not only do the deputies hear the wishes and concerns of their constituents; they also have an opportunity to express their views and the position of their party on relevant issues. Thus the deputy serves as the "transmission belt" between the district and the state capitol, possibly even assisting in gaining grants for local projects – although that is unlikely for an Opposition deputy. A common strategy is membership in or close contact with various local groups, for example, attendance at two or three functions or meetings every week and meeting with local politicians. One of the most damaging accusations against a deputy is that he or she is "distant" and "absent" or unconcerned about district voters and their views and wishes, and therefore deputies feel obligated to accept virtually every invitation to attend the various functions in their district. A study of deputies in the five new *Länder*, however, has shown that they were spending far more time on legislative than district activities in comparison to their counterparts in the West, at least in part due to the need to pass large amounts of legislation that had been passed in the western parliaments over several decades. On the other hand, the PDS, which, given its opposition status, carried much less parliamentary responsibility for this legislation, was focusing more attention on district work.[16]

Still, there are party differences among the deputies, e.g., the deputies from the small parties are generally unable to spend as much time in the district as their large party counterparts, and the Green deputies are less concerned with local "lobbying" activities for ideological reasons. The study in Lower Saxony also found differences between the governing party, SPD, and the Opposition CDU deputies, who were somewhat more likely to concentrate on district work than on parliamentary activities for the obvious reason that most of their parliamentary work was for naught. On the other hand, there were significant differences in approach to district work within both large parties.[17]

Deputies maintain contacts with the district population not only through attendance at various functions but also through personal communication. Telephone calls to the homes of deputies are common,

including on Sundays. Some deputies hold office hours in the district as a
service to their constituents. A majority of deputies in the Lower Saxon
study, however, did not, arguing in part that their experience showed that
many constituents felt uncomfortable about going to an office to discuss
their concerns and preferred individual contact, including home visits.
On average deputies made two or three such visits each week.[18]

Given the amount of time deputies at all levels devote to their districts,
it is not surprising that most of the responding deputies (53 percent) in
Patzelt's 1994 study believed their views reflect those of their constituents,
while only 6 percent were doubtful.[19] Unfortunately, polling data have
suggested that only 23 percent of the population believed *Land* deputies
are well informed about the views of their constituents, and 35 percent
assumed they are poorly informed. Only 13 percent said it is easy to meet
with a deputy, and 21 percent even thought it was nearly impossible.[20]
Needless to say, these are depressing figures for deputies who put so much
effort into making and maintaining contacts at home.

While 39 percent of the deputies thought citizens in their districts
would give them good grades for their work, 8 percent suspected they
would get bad grades; however, 70 percent thought they would be graded
favorably by the politically interested citizens. Most felt their constituents
had positive views about them individually, but they recognized that citizens generally had negative assessments of parliament as a body, which
76 percent said they found troubling (*belastend*).[21] The contrast in the
public views regarding their individual representative on the one hand
and the legislature as an institution on the other is also well known in the
United States, where polls commony indicate that citizens like their own
congressman but are contemptuous of Congress.

Political party work

A majority of *Land* deputies hold one or more offices in their political
parties at the local, regional and/or *Land* level. Party work is essential for
several reasons. There must be contact and cooperation between the
extra-parliamentary party and parliamentary party group. For example,
the deputy reports in local party meetings on developments in the parliament and receives feedback from the regular members. Holding party
office helps to integrate the deputy into the party organization and maintain contact with local party leaders. This is another means by which the
deputy serves as a "transmission belt" between local party members and
the parliamentary party group. Party office also increases the deputy's

influence over party policies and personnel matters. Finally, party office is an important means of retaining support for renomination as the party's candidate for the next election. Holding a party office and simultaneously serving in the *Land* parliament can lead to a variety of tensions, from complaints about party policy at the *Land* and federal levels for which the deputy is supposed to answer to envy from others in the party with whom the deputy has had a close relationship in the past.[22]

Local council offices

For the typical deputy, the list of activities does not end with parliamentary, district, and party work, but is complemented by office holding in local councils at the municipal or county level and, not infrequently, at both local levels. The practice of holding multiple offices is probably best known in France, where, in order to secure their local political base, deputies in the National Assembly and even ministers are often mayors or important officials in their communes. While members of the *Bundestag* rarely hold multiple offices, it is a common practice for *Land* deputies. This is because deputies usually serve at the local level before being nominated as a candidate for the *Land* level, and local office helps to provide the deputy with a political base in the home district; second, it is an important means of keeping the deputy in touch with the problems and concerns of local governments, which are an important responsibility of the *Land* parliaments. According to the personal bibliographies in the Handbook of the Lower Saxon parliament, 73 percent of the SPD and 60 percent of the CDU deputies served in a municipal council in the mid-1990s, while the percentage serving in county councils was 41 and 51 percent, respectively. Some had served in the past, but not while they were members of parliament. In some American state legislatures, a majority of the legislators may also have held a local government or party office, while in others the proportion with previous experience may be considerably less;[23] in any case they are not allowed to hold a local government office while they are members of the legislature.

In addition to the activities described above, most deputies are also members of various private and public boards, including charitable organizations; committees; and organizations, for example, local public savings and loan associations and public enterprises. Particularly from an American perspective, it is interesting that 4.5 percent of the CDU, 59 percent of the SPD, and 31 percent of the Green deputies in Lower Saxony were members of unions in the mid-1990s. Many of the SPD deputies were actively engaged in activities related to their union membership.

Taken together, the four general areas of activity of *Land* deputies require an inordinate amount of time, and it is not surprising that the deputies report an average workweek of over 60 hours excluding any time spent on activities not related to their work as office holders. But as with other professions, including academia, it is often difficult to explain the work load to outsiders who simply do not see the many obligations of deputies beyond their participation in plenary sessions, from which they absent themselves during much of the time when issues that do not interest or affect them are being discussed. This may be a problem that is common to legislators in all democratic societies. In Germany it is complicated by relatively high salaries and benefits, which can and do create considerable resentment and controversy.

The deputies: what they earn

The salaries and benefits of *Land* deputies are described in some detail in the "The Law Concerning Deputies" (*Abgeordnetengesetz*) contained in the respective *Land* parliamentary handbooks. The Law is divided into numerous sections, including "Compensation," "Reimbursement of Expenses," "Transition Payments," "Health Insurance," "Pensions," and so forth. Until the famous "compensation decision" (*Diätenurteil*) rendered by the Federal Constitutional Court in 1975,[24] most *Land* deputies were part-time with modest compensation packages. But the Court held that if deputies are full-time, they should be paid a full salary commensurate with the status and responsibilities of the office.[25] As a result the compensation for deputies in the *Länder* was increased dramatically.[26] Even though the Court revised the *Diätenurteil* in 1987,[27] the *Land* parliaments continued to increase compensation packages by significant amounts.

There are two parts to the compensation package received by the deputies. One part is literally "compensation" (*Entschädigung*), which includes base salary, transition pay, pension benefits, and assistance in meeting the costs of illness, births, and deaths. The other is the reimbursement of expenses (*Aufwandsentschädigung*), which is designed to cover office expenses, telephone and postage, travel and hotel expenses, public transportation, and office help. The legislative assembly of the city state of Hamburg used to be the exception to this two-part compensation package, since it perceived itself as a part-time body and provided only reimbursement of expense;[28] however, it now has a two-part package in spite of its continued self-perception as a part-time assembly.[29]

The base salaries of the deputies vary considerably from *Land* to *Land*. Salaries in the sixteen *Länder* in the mid-1990s ranged from DM 4,457 in Bremen (under certain circumstances supplemented by reimbursements for absences from regular work) to DM 1,1266 in Hesse (figured at $1.00/DM=1.60 – about the average exchange rate in the second half of the 1990s – this is $7041 per month!). The average in the old territorial states was DM 8,828 ($5330), in the new territorial states DM 6,633 ($4146). These are full-time salaries designed for full-time deputies, but some deputies, depending on the *Land*, do continue to work part-time as public employees or as self-employed persons in business or law.[30]

In addition to the base salary, *Entschädigung* includes transition money, i.e., full salary payments made to deputies who leave office for any reason, whether because of electoral defeat or voluntary departure for another job. Transition payments are made for one–three months to those who have served for as little as one year and for a maximum of twelve–thirty months for service of ten–twenty-two years. The total maximum payment could amount to DM 53,484 in Bremen to DM 214,500 ($134,063) in Schleswig-Holstein.[31] These payments have come under considerable attack, and they were reduced in recent years at the federal level.

A third major part of the *Entschädigung* consists of the retirement benefits. Lifetime retirement benefits amount to 25–35 percent of full salary for the minimum service of eight–ten years beginning at sixty years of age; these payments increase 3–5 percent each additional year of service to a maximum of 75 percent of salary beginning at age fifty-five in most *Länder* for long-time office holders (thirteen–twenty-three years). In four of the new *Länder* there are even provisions for modest pensions for deputies who served only one term in the first parliaments after unification. In addition to these very generous retirement benefits, deputies receive assistance for health care as well as birth and death payments.[32]

Ministers who still have their seats in the *Land* parliament receive a higher compensation; some even receive double payments, e.g., 50 percent of the deputy salary in addition to their ministers' salary in Bavaria, Berlin, North-Rhine Westphalia, and Saxony, and 70 percent in Baden-Württemberg. In the other territorial states the ministers receive 25–35 percent of the deputy salary. In Lower Saxony, however, there is no double payment, and in Bremen and Hamburg incompatibility rules prevent double office holding. Double payments also exist for pensions, e.g., full deputy pension plus one-half of a minister's pension. In Lower Saxony, again, only the higher of the two is paid.[33]

The second part of the total compensation package, as noted above, is reimbursement for expenses. This includes travel, hotel, and meals as well as free use of office space, government cars, telephones, and free public transportation. Two systems of payment are employed: lump sum and separate billing. The lump-sum payment is provided by Bavaria (DM 4711) and Berlin. Critics charge that some of this amounts to income, because payments are higher than actual expenses, especially for deputies who live near the capital, have no district offices, etc. The second system of payment is by separate billing for travel, hotel, and meals. The remaining range of partial lump sum payments for other expenses is from DM 769 in Bremen to DM 2,191 in North-Rhine Westphalia. According to two studies, these payments are also in excess of actual expenses.[34] Ministers and state secretaries also receive partial lump-sum payments that can range from DM 500 in Lower Saxony to DM 3,533 in Bavaria. In some *Länder* ministers even receive a lump-sum payment as deputies in spite of their chauffeured cars and other amenities.[35]

Given the high degree of regulation in German society and the "flood of legislation" that is the focus of many complaints among German legislators, it is surprising that some areas that are rather closely regulated in the United States have been ignored in Germany. A good example is the lack of regulation of private donations to legislators. In contrast to donations to political parties, there is no requirement of publicity for donations to individual politicians who may use the money received in any manner they wish, although they are most likely to pass it on to their party for campaign purposes. The only requirement at the federal level is that the deputy inform the President of the *Bundestag* of any donation of DM 1,000 or more. For donations of DM 20,000 or more to a *political party*, the donor must be named; that provision applies to individual legislators as well, according to the new party finance law of 1992. Only in Lower Saxony and Bremen is it illegal for a deputy to be paid a retainer by his firm or serve as a consultant while in office.[36]

It is clear from the above why the compensation packages received by office holders in the *Länder* – and at the federal and EU levels – have been so controversial in recent years.[37] And it certainly does not help when a report appears in the press about an SPD *Land* deputy from North-Rhine Westphalia who, in spite of a very generous salary and reimbursement package of about DM 12,000, was discovered to be receiving an additional DM 3,000 per month in unemployment compensation on the grounds that his regular job before he entered parliament had been eliminated![38]

By international comparison, even politicians at the *Land* level in Germany are well paid. They are also very well paid in comparison with "professional," full-time American state legislators, e.g., in New York or California.[39] But given the sixty-hour- plus weekly work loads of *Land* deputies, it can be argued they are not overpaid, especially when compared with high-salary employees in the private sector. This argument also applies to other Western democratic industrial societies, some of which, for example, Great Britain, pay their politicians far less than Germany. In fact, one reason why such a large proportion of the deputies are public and private employees, rather than more from the self-employed ranks as in the United States, is that the generous total compensation packages provide the office holders with higher incomes than they would receive in their regular positions, e.g., school teachers and other mid-level civil servants and private employees. This, together with the added prestige and social status – in spite of *Politikverdrossenheit* (alienation from or annoyance with politics) and the criticism directed toward the "political class" today in Germany – help explain why there is a tendency for office holders to cling to their positions. But this is a phenomenon observable among the more professionally oriented state legislators in the United States as well.[40] It is possible for legislators in Germany who entered parliament from the public service to return to their old pre-legislative positions, a prospect most seem to find uninviting; however, there is little tradition of moving to a well-paid, relatively high-status position in the private sector as is common in the United States. German "professional politicians" are more likely than many of the more financially independent American state legislators to live "off" politics, and, one might argue, as a result a larger proportion of Germans from the broad middle class rather than the middle to upper middle class are recruited into the legislature.

While it is clear that deputies in Germany are well paid, it should also be pointed out that they have high expenses. Like American politicians, they are not only invited to speak at and attend many functions and group meetings in their districts; they are also expected to contribute to the cause in many cases. Sizable contributions are especially expected – and required – by the political parties. Rarely, if ever, is anyone elected who is not a member of a party. This membership is not merely nominal, as is usually the case in the United States. Rather, "card-carrying" membership is the norm, which means monthly dues ranging from a dozen or so DM per month to hundreds of DM in the SPD, which has a dues structure graduated by income. In the past deputies were expected to contribute sizable funds to their party groups, while today this practice is supposed to have been banned with the party groups being funded generously by the public treasury. Nevertheless, some funding by deputies continues. Above all the deputies are expected to provide the parties with monthly donations amounting to DM 1,000 (about 500 Euro) or more, often referred to as a "party tax." The Greens pay an especially high party tax. This "tax" can be seen as a hidden form of party financing, especially given the provisions of the tax law that give private citizens a 50 percent tax credit and the party a 50 percent bonus designed to encourage private donations.[41] Deputies also give sizable amounts of money to their parties for election campaigns, since these are organized and fought by the parties, not by individual candidate organizations. One deputy told the author that he gives voluntarily about DM 20,000 to his party each year.

All in all, there is a considerable gulf between the often sharp criticisms of deputies and their salaries and benefits on the one hand and the views of the deputies themselves. Given the number of hours they devote to their work related directly and indirectly to parliamentary activities, to their districts and the services they perform, to the local government offices most of them occupy, and to their party activities, which are necessary both to maintain contact with supporters and retain the nomination for their seat in parliament, and the pressures these numerous and time-consuming obligations place on their family and private lives, most deputies believe they earn too little rather than too much.[42] Interviews which the author conducted with selected deputies in Lower Saxony also suggest they are resentful of charges that they are overpaid.

The deputies: part-time, full-time, or what?

In his influential essay, "Politics as a Profession," Max Weber distinguished among three kinds of elected office holders: the professional, the part-time, and the occasional politician.[43] Professionals can be distinguished further between those who live "off" of politics and those who live "for" politics. The former are dependent on the salaries they receive as office holders, the latter have independent sources of income.

In the United States, relatively high salaries, length of session, and staff support are the three variables that determine the degree of "professionalization." Most state delegates have traditionally been part-time politicians; however, in recent decades professional politicians have come to dominate the legislatures of at least nine states, with New York and California in the lead. Most of the legislators in these nine states with "professional legislatures" are full-time and live "off" politics, although some of the more affluent delegates live "for" politics. The salary range of these legislatures in 1997–98 was between $75,600 in California (raised to $99,000 in January 1999) and $35,000 in New Jersey, and the average annual duration of the legislative session in 1996–97 ranged from 365 calendar days in Wisconsin to 133 in Illinois. Legislative staff ranged from 3,899 in New York to 552 in Ohio. At the other end of the continuum, the legislatures in about sixteen American states can be categorized as "citizen" legislatures, with salaries ranging from $15,000 in West Virginia to $200 in New Hampshire, which also has the largest state legislative body with 400 delegates. Needless to say, few legislators in these states could live "off" politics, but not all of them are part-time. While the average annual duration of the session in 1996–97 was, as one would expect, shorter than for the professional legislatures, the range was from thirty-six days in Wyoming to 256 days in Rhode Island, which pays its legislators only $10,250. Staff support in these legislatures ranged from 742 in Georgia to fifty-eight in Vermont. The legislatures in about twenty-five states in between these two extremes are categorized as "hybrid," with salaries ranging from $32,000 in Hawaii to $1,040 in Alabama and an average annual duration of session ranging from 177 days in Delaware to fifty-two in Kentucky.[44] Staff support in the hybrid state legislatures ranged from 2,420 in Texas to 164 in Delaware. Most of the delegates in these hybrid states probably live "for" politics; nevertheless, many of them in both the citizen and hybrid legislatures, and particularly those with major responsibilities such as speakers, committee chairs, and party caucus leaders, are really full-time politicians.[45]

In Germany most *Land* deputies are full-time professionals who live "off" politics. The exception is perhaps the Hamburg assembly, which in law, if not in practice,[46] is part-time. The change from part-time to full-time professional took place after a Federal Constitutional Court decision in 1975 suggested – but did not require, as some *Land* deputies seemed to think[47] – that they should receive a full-time salary commensurate with their responsibilities. This has always been a controversial decision, because it served as the basis for very generous salary levels and benefits for *Land* deputies that approach or, in a few cases, are even roughly comparable to federal-level salaries. Some critics believe the compensation packages are not only unjustified; they are also the result of a sinister "self-service" in which deputies conspire to provide themselves economic benefits through legislation they pass without effective outside controls.[48]

There are, of course, various arguments pro and con regarding full-time professional status and part-time status for *Land* deputies. For the part-time option it can be argued that the work of the *Land* parliaments is fundamentally different from the federal parliament, that they do not have the powers and authority of the *Bundestag* and are not, therefore, the center of attention. *Land* deputies should be "closer to the people" and need to maintain close contact through an occupation. Being a professional politician at the *Land* level is too small a base for a deputy whose roots are only local, and clinging to office creates resentment in the electorate. Some critics readily admit that the deputies work long hours, but they counter that much of that work is "busy work" in parliament and, especially, in the districts designed to justify their salaries. The parliamentary example usually chosen is the large number of "*kleine Anfragen*," or written questions, that are said to have the effect mostly of tying up the ministerial bureaucracy with unnecessary and picky questions. There are, of course, many examples taken from district work, suggesting that the deputies could do a lot less. The critics are not impressed by the many hours put into party activities by deputies, nor do they consider local office holding an excuse for the burdens of *Land* office.[49]

While even some deputies agree to some extent with some of these criticisms,[50] they and others would also point to the importance of the parliament primarily as an instrument of control rather than of law making and the need to acquire expertise through legislative experience to exercise this control effectively. They would note the necessity of spending as much time in the district as possible in order to maintain close contacts with citizens, serve as ombudsmen, and retain or gain crucial popular support for the next election, and they would rebut strongly the argument that only part-time politicians with normal occupations are close to the people.[51] They would cite the importance of maintaining party support for renomination and for connecting the extra-parliamentary party and the party group in parliament. And they would certainly argue that local government office holding is an important source of political information and experience as well as an important political base. All of these functions also serve an important "transmission belt" function for the citizenry, and, in spite of *Politikverdrossenheit*, many citizens take it for granted that "their" deputy will hear their concerns and, to the extent possible, go to bat for them. In other words, there is an argument to be made for the quality of democracy in any discussion of these functions.[52] As we have seen above, it can also be argued that *Land* deputies, even if the sixty-hour week they claim to work *on average* is somewhat exaggerated, have too much to do to serve part-time. This is especially true in the larger *Länder*. The growth of the public sector and the need for deputies to serve as ombudsmen impose time demands on most deputies that exceed part-time capabilities.[53] It is precisely the alleged decline of the *Land* parliaments that requires professionals to prevent even further losses; according to this view, part-time status would reduce the parliamentary meeting time and therefore the control of the government. It would also mean less time spent on service functions for constituents. Some also insist that if deputies are not provided a decent salary, they will become more subject to the influence of lobbyists. One might add that without a decent salary, many potential candidates would also be discouraged from running for office, especially if legislative service takes too much time away from the occupation on which the person relies for an income. A further argument notes that the role of the bureaucracy is likely to increase under part-time deputies. There are also incompatibility rules for various public employees which would make it impossible for the many civil servants who are deputies – including many teachers and some university employees – to serve on a part-time basis.[54] Many Green deputies have no other employment,[55] and some deputies in the East are otherwise unemployed. Additional arguments, also common in the United States would include the need for legislative expertise in many fields that can be gained only through experience and the time spent in leadership positions, through service in committees, and participation in other meetings. American data also suggest that deputies in the more professional and full-time legislatures spend more time with their constituents.[56]

One observer has suggested that the belief that part-time deputies would be more broadly representative of the general population is based on a "thinking error" (*Denkfehler*). He points out that the *Land* parliament, like other democratic parliaments, is not designed to represent all social and economic groups. The office of a *Land* deputy has developed into a full-time position not unlike other positions, with various opportunities for advancement, recognition, etc. What the deputies did before in an earlier occupation is much less important than the political skills and effectiveness of the deputy in office.[57]

Conclusion

Like their counterparts in other countries, parliamentary deputies in Germany – whether at the federal or *Land* level – are not a representative sample of occupation, education, income, gender, and other character-stics; however, the proportions of women in German legislative bodies have increased significantly in all party groups in recent decades, especially with the advent of the Greens in 1979. In a politically more relevant sense, the deputies are representative of the broad currents of political views in the society, from the leftist PDS in the East and Greens in the West to the rightist *Republikaner* in the West and DVU in East and West. The vast majority of deputies, however, represent the center left SPD or the center right CDU (in Bavaria, the CSU). The proportional electoral system is a crucial factor, of course, in promoting this kind of political representation.

Even though it is often argued that the powers of the *Land* parliaments have declined over the decades, the *Land* legislatures do retain important, if limited, powers in certain areas such as education and culture, local government, law and order, and internal organization. And while their law making function may have declined, the deputies are still actively involved in committee meetings and party work groups associated with the parliament, in a variety of service and ombudsman functions in the home district, in political party activities, and, in most cases, in local government office holding. Studies suggest that the deputies work on average about sixty hours per week, excluding any hours they may have worked in their regular occupations as lawyers, businessmen, etc. American state legislators are also active in legislative and district work, but relatively few of them would have the added burden of political party work, and none of them would hold one or even two time-consuming local government offices.

Salaries and benefits for the *Land* deputies are relatively generous, especially if compared to the typical American state legislator. Only the legislators in the six or seven highest-paying American states are in a roughly equivalent situation. The benefits that German politicians take for granted that would undoubtedly raise the most questions in the United States are the transitional payments received when the deputy leaves office for almost any reason and the retirement benefits received after a relatively short period of time in office. Whether the deputies are overpaid, given the decline of legislative powers in recent decades, is a controversial question. On the one hand, it seems clear that they work long hours. The question some critics raise is whether all the work in which legislators engage is really productive or necessary. In response, deputies would point to their time-consuming work in various kinds of activities related to legislative and control functions, and to the importance of the linkage function between the population on the one hand and the *Land* government and administration on the other hand.

The discussion above also relates to the question of whether the deputies should or could be part-time. This debate has to do not only with assessments of the work load of the deputies and their salary and benefits, but also with attitudes concerning the political system in general and the "political class" in particular. As in the United States,[58] these attitudes are often quite negative.[59] For those who are contemptuous of politicians, it is doubtful that they could accept the very notion of full-time, reasonably well-paid "professional" politicians at the *Land* level.[60] Certainly it can be argued that the salary and benefits for some legislators are overly generous, but it is less clear that they are excessive for the majority of deputies.

Notes

1   Werner J. Patzelt, "Deutschlands Abgeordnete: Profil eines Berufstands, der weit besser ist als sein Ruf," *Zeitschrift für Parlamentsfragen* 27, no. 3 (1996), pp. 462–502.

2   Data provided to the author by Werner Patzelt.

3   Rolf Paprotny, *Der Alltag der niedersächsischen Landtagsabgeordneten* (Hannover: Niedersächsische Landeszentrale für politische Bildung, 1995), Ch. 2.

4   Ibid., p. 27.

5   Ibid., pp. 24–25.

6   Werner J. Patzelt, *Abgeordnete undRepräsentation: Amtsverständnis und Wahlkreisarbeit* (Passau: Wissenschaftsverlag, 1993) and *Abgeordnete und ihr Beruf: Interviews, Umfragen, Analysen* (Berlin: Akadamie Verlag, 1995).

7   Patzelt, *Abgeordnete und Repräsentation*, pp. 314–315, 451.

8   Patzelt, "Deutschlands Abgeordnete," pp. 462–502

9   Ibid., pp. 470–471, 480.

10 Paprotny, *Der Alltag*, pp. 46–61; Patzelt, *Abgeordnete und ihr Beruf*, pp. 56–59.

11 Alan Rosenthal, *The Decline of Representative Democracy: Process, Participation, and Power in State Legislatures* (Washington, DC: CQ Press, 1998), p. 69.

12 Patzelt, "Deutschlands Abgeordnete," p. 477.

13 Paprotny, *Der Alltag*, pp. 61–64; Patzelt, *Abgeordnete und Repräsentation,* part 3, and *Abgeordnete und ihr Beruf*, pp. 94–112. Of course not all *Land* deputies are elected in districts; up to one-half are elected over lists in the "mixed" district-list proportional representation system. But even most list candidates maintain close ties to their home towns, in order to secure renomination by the party and perhaps to gain the district-seat nomination in the future. Some deputies, however, make a clear distinction between deputies elected by district and list. One even told the author that "a respectable Emslander does not enter parliament over the list."

14 Many American state legislators, especially those with some staff support,

report that the most important part of their job is the service function they perform. Rosenthal, *The Decline*, p. 16.

15 Patzelt, *Abgeordnete und Repräsentation*, p. 136.

16 Werner Patzelt and Roland Schirmer, "Parlamentarismusgründung in den neuen Bundesländern," *Aus Politik und Zeitgeschichte* B27/96 (28 June 1996), pp. 23–24.

17 Paprotny, *Der Alltag*, p. 63.

18 Ibid., pp. 68–70.

19 Patzelt, "Deutschlands Abgeordnete," p. 469.

20 Werner Patzelt, "Was tun die Abgeordnete?," in *Die Abgeordneten: Stellung, Aufgaben und Selbstverständnis in der parlamentarischen Demokratie*, edited by Heinrich Oberreuter (Tutzing: Akademie für politische Bildung, 1996), pp. 25–26. The data are no better for federal parliament members. The same poll showed only 11 percent knew their federal deputy has office hours in the district, and only 6 percent knew that he/she talks to regular citizens (p. 25). Yet Dietrich Herzog *et al.* found that members of the federal parliament maintained close contacts to their districts, especially with individual citizens and via their district office hours! *Abgeordnete und Bürger: Ergebnisse einer Befragung der Mitglieder des 11. Deutschen Bundestages aund der Bevölkerung* (Opladen: Westdeutscher Verlag, 1990), pp. 20–21.

21 Patzelt, "Deutschlands Abgeordnete," pp. 497–498.

22 Paprotny, *Der Alltag*, pp. 73-74; for a more thorough discussion of the *Land* deputy and the role of the party, see Patzelt, *Abgeordnete und ihr Beruf*, pp. 140–156.

23 Rosenthal, *The Decline*, p. 61.

24 BVerfGE 40, 296.

25 Herbert Schneider, "Zum Abgeordnetenbild in den Landtagen," *Aus Politik und Zeitgeschichte*, B5/89 (27 January 1989), p. 6. But for an argument that the decision of the Court was misunderstood, see the comments of one of the judges, Willi Geiger, in *Zeitschrift für Parlamentsfragen* (1978), p. 528.

26 For critical comments, see Hans Herbert von Arnim, *Der Staat als Beute* (München: Knaur, 1993), pp. 21–23; a lengthy discussion of the Court's decision can be found in Hans H. Klein, "Diäten-Urteil und Diäten-Streit: Legendenbildung im Verfassungsrecht," in *Planung-Recht-Rechtschutz: Festschrift für Willi Blümel*, edited by Klaus Grupp (Berlin: Duncker & Humblot, 1999), pp. 225–257.

27 BVerfGE 76, 256.

28 Hans Herbert von Arnim, *Die Partei, der Abgeordnete und das Geld* (München: Knauer, 1996), pp. 202–203.

29 See www.hamburg.de/StadtPol/Brgschft.

30 For a table showing the base salaries of federal and *Land* deputies in the mid-1990s, von Arnim, *Die Partei*, p. 218.

31 Ibid., pp. 246–247.

32 Ibid., pp. 250–251.
33 Ibid., pp. 266–268.
34 Ibid., pp. 277–286.
35 Ibid., pp. 288–290.
36 Ibid., pp. 298–304.
37 Several books by Hans Herbert von Arnim have focused on a variety of abuses and even scandals in compensation packages in several *Länder* in the past decade. See, for example, *Der Staat als Beute, Staat ohne Diener,* or, for a book about federal office holders, *Der Staat sind wir!,* all published by Knaur, 1993 and 1995.
38 *Frankfurter Allgemeine Zeitung* (5 October 1996), p. 4.
39 Legislators in California receive $99,000 as of January 1999, whereas legislators in New York and Pennslyvania receive $57,000–58,000. California legislators probably receive more in salary than any of their German counterparts, but the latter also receive generous benefits such as retirement payments which a popular referendum has denied California legislators.
40 Rosenthal, *The Decline*, pp. 63–65.
41 Von Arnim, *Die Partei*, pp. 312–317.
42 Patzelt, "Deutschlands Abgeordnete," p. 476.
43 Not, as in the inaccurate translation by H. H. Gerth and C. Wright Mills, *From Max Weber: Essays in Sociology* (New York: Oxford University Press, 1946), only the two types of "vocational" and "occasional" politicians. See Arthur B. Gunlicks, "Max Weber's Typology of Politicians: A Reexamination," *The Journal of Politics* 40, no. 2 (May 1978), pp. 498–509.
44 Keith E. Hamm and Gary F. Moncrief, "Legislative Politics in the States," in *Politics in the American States*, edited by Virginia Gray, Russell L. Hanson, and Herbert Jacob (7th edn; Washington, DC: CQ Press, 1999), pp. 145–146.
45 Some legislators refuse to give their occupations as "legislator," even when it is obvious that they are. See Rosenthal, *The Decline*, p. 57.
46 Peter Raschke and Jens Kalke found that the deputies in Hamburg are generally as engaged in parliamentary activities as most other *Land* deputies in Germany and argue that they deserve professional status. See their article, "Quantative Analyse parlamentaischer Tätigkeiten der Landtage," *Zeitschrift für Parlamentsfragen* 25, no. 1 (January 1994), pp. 32–60.
47 Manfred Friedrich, *Der Landtag als Berufsparlament?* (Karl-Bräuer-Institut des Bundes der Steuerzahler, 1977), p. 54.
48 Hans Herbert von Arnim is the most severe and best-known critic who has revealed a number of scandals involving compensation schemes for *Land* parliamentary deputies. See, for example, *Der Staat als Beute* and *Staat ohne Diener.*
49 For a discussion of some of these arguments, see von Arnim, *Die Partei*, pp. 227–237.
50 Based on several interviews with deputies from Lower Saxony in autumn 1996.

51 Schneider, "Zum Abgeordnetenbild," p. 13; Patzelt, *Abgeordnete und Repräsentation*, Teil 3.

52 See also Schneider, "Zum Abgeordnetenbild," p. 13.

53 Herbert Schneider, *Länderparlamentarismus in der Bundesrepublik* (Opladen: Leske & Budrich, 1979), p. 119.

54 Friedrich, *Das Landtag als Berufsparlament?* pp. 13–15; Schneider, *Länderparlamentarismus*, pp. 116–117; Schneider, "Zum Abgeordnetenbild," pp. 3, 13.

55 Schneider, Zum Abgeordnetenbild," n. 59, p. 15.

56 In the declining number of American states with "citizen legislatures," some delegates report that they do not spend much time with constituents when parliament is not in session. Rosenthal, *The Decline*, p. 15.

57 Hans Meyer, "Was können und was sollen die Landesparlamente leisten?," in *Landesparlamente und Föderalismus: Hat das parlamentarische System in den Bundesländern eine Zukunft?*, edited by Franz Gress (Wiesbaden: Hessischer Landtag, 1990), pp. 56–57.

58 Rosenthal, *The Decline*, pp. 67–71.

59 Patzelt, *Abgeordnete und ihr Beruf*, pp. 198–206.

60 As indicated above for American legislators (n. 45), many German politicians are reluctant to admit they are professional politicians, even though 90 percent believe that serving in parliament is a career. See Patzelt, "Deutschlands Abgeordnete," p. 467.

8

Parties and politics
in the *Länder*

Introduction

In every federal system there is a national party system which, in spite of certain commonalities, is likely to be somewhat different from the regional and/or local party systems. In the United States there are two dominating, loosely organized, personality- and candidate-oriented, generally weakly disciplined parties with no single universally recognized national party leader except perhaps the president. They are financed by various private interest groups and individuals, including many supporters who are not members in any formal sense and pay no dues. In part because of these general characteristics, some differences can and do exist between the national and state parties and between various state parties and regions.[1] Thus the national party leadership may be more in conformity with the ideological or policy foci of the leading party personalities in one certain region or state than in another, for example, New England versus the South or Southwest.

The American party system stands in sharp contrast to the German parties, which, in spite of regional party organizations of varying strength, are hierarchically organized and member-based, programmatic, disciplined, and led by leaders, usually the Chancellor, certain prime ministers of the *Länder*, or other well-known office holders, who are elected by party organs for that purpose.[2] The parties are financed by a mixture of private and public funds, the latter of which are very generous by international standards.[3] Much of the private funding comes from the large dues-paying membership or supporters who, also in contrast to the United States, receive significant tax benefits for their contributions. While there is considerable evidence that German parties are changing, e.g., through declining membership and weakening ideology, and that there are some significant differences between parties in east and west Germany,[4] it is still the case that German and American parties represent rather starkly contrasting models.

Given the nature of the German party system, many questions arise about the relationship between federal and *Land* politics, including voting behavior in national and regional elections.[5]

Relationships between federal and *Land* politics

As in the United States, the subnational political systems in Germany are basically the same. All of the *Länder* have parliamentary systems with a government supported by a single party parliamentary majority (but in Saxony-Anhalt, the SPD governed alone as a minority party from April 1998 to April 2002) or, in a majority of cases, by a coalition of two and on rare occasions three parties, with one or more opposition parties. Each *Land* has one popularly elected chamber, called the *Landtag* in the thirteen territorial states, the *Bürgerschaft* in Bremen and Hamburg, and the *Abgeordnetenhaus* in Berlin. The legislative bodies vary in size from fifty-one in the Saarland to 231 in North-Rhine Westphalia. The party systems are also basically the same, although this is less true now than before unification, and the "establishment" *Land* parties are very similar to the national parties.[6] Of course each *Land* has a somewhat different history, tradition, culture, geography, and economy, but state politics are shaped to a large extent by the party political positions at the national level.[7]

The nature of the German party system, together with the penetration by the parties of much of the bureaucracy and public institutions and enterprises, explains in part the close relationship between the national and state parties. But constitutional provisions calling for the creation of uniform or equivalent living conditions; close interrelationships between the national, state, and local office holders and civil servants in the German federal system, often referred to as *Politikverflechtung*; the relatively small physical size of the country (about the size of Montana); the density of the population (over 80 million); the extensive German welfare state; and popular attitudes that favor equality over regional autonomy or diversity, have all contributed to strong centralizing tendencies, to what has been referred to as the "unitary federal state."[8] The question, then, is whether *Land* elections are just another form of federal elections, reflecting current public views of the government policy, personalities, or events at the national level.[9] This question is raised in different ways, e.g., whether *Land* elections are a kind of mid-term election, i.e., whether they are "barometer elections"; whether they are in effect *Bundesrat* elections, the results of which can and often do determine whether this *Länder* chamber will generally support or oppose the federal government and its majority in the popularly elected *Bundestag*; whether they serve as protest elections that have no direct effect on the national government but send a message; or whether they have much relevance to *Land* or regional politics at all. We will return to this subject in Chapter 9.

Parties and elections in the *Länder*

Parties in the Länder

The major German parties today are the Social Democratic Party of Germany (SPD); the Christian Democratic Union (CDU) and its Bavarian sister party, the Christian Social Union (CSU), together often referred to as the Christian Democrats or the Union parties; the Free Democratic Party (FDP); the Bündis 90 (Alliance 90)/Greens; and the Party of Democratic Socialism (PDS). Smaller parties that sometimes appear on the scene and even win a few seats, depending on the time and place, include the three radical right parties: the Republicans (Reps), the German People's Union (DVU), and the National Democratic Party of Germany (NPD). Numerous other smaller parties – sometimes more than twenty – take part in state elections, but they rarely receive more than 1 or 2 percent of the vote, if that much, and almost never win any seats. On the other hand, certain "flash parties" that form around personalities or movements expressing sentiments of protest have been quite successful in Bremen and Hamburg in recent years, the latest and best example being the law and order PRO party in Hamburg elections led by Judge Schill in the fall of 2001.

The Social Democratic Party of Germany is the oldest and traditionally largest social democratic party in Europe.[10] It was formed and developed in the latter half of the nineteenth century as an anti-capitalist, socialist, but non-revolutionary Marxist working- class party. It was outlawed by Bismarck in 1878 but allowed to re-emerge legally in 1890. Bismarck, in spite of his strong conservatism, introduced the first far-reaching social welfare reforms in the 1880s, such as health insurance and old-age pensions, at least in part as a means of securing the loyalty of the working class to the state and to weaken the appeal of the social democratic movement.

In spite of their leading opposition role after 1890 as a democratic but left-ist reform party that had numerous fundamental differences with the domestic and foreign policies of the Kaiserreich, the Social Democrats did vote for the credits to finance Germany's entrance in the First World War. Though in part a result of the desire of the leadership to demonstrate its loyalty to the German state, this support came back to haunt the party in many forms, one of which was its breakup into three parties after the First World War. The most important and permanent offshoot of the SPD was the Communist Party of Germany (KPD). In spite of a bitter and compet-itive relationship with the communists, the SPD remained the key party of the left in the Weimar Republic until it and other parties were outlawed by Hitler in 1933. After 1945 it was "relicensed" by the Allies as a democratic party, and it immediately became the leading left-wing party in West Germany. In its Godesberger Program of 1959, the party rejected Marxist dogma and became more of a center-left reformist party that was more interested in promoting a progressive capitalist welfare state on the Swedish model than in traditional socialist state ownership of the major means of production. In contrast to its successful transition in West Germany to one of the two leading parties that was capable of assuming government office at all levels,[11] it was soon undermined in East Germany after 1945 by the pro-Soviet communists and forced to merge with them to form the Socialist Unity Party (SED) in 1946.[12]

The Christian Democratic Union (CDU) was formed after 1945 as suc-cessor to and for a few years as competitor with the old, almost entirely Catholic, Center Party (Zentrum).[13] The Christian Democrats, while still supported mostly by Catholic voters, broadened the party's appeal to Protestants. While essentially a moderately conservative party that appealed not only to Catholics and practicing Protestants, the middle class, and voters in small towns and villages, it also had a special section that appealed to workers. Thus the CDU became the first catch-all, or "peoples' party" (*Volkspartei*) in Europe and soon forced the SPD also to broaden its appeal in its Godesberg Program of 1959.[14]

The FDP is the classical liberal party of Germany and the successor of two liberal parties in the Weimar Republic.[15] It combines two often com-peting traditions in classical liberalism, a focus on free enterprise and property rights and a focus on civil liberties, legal equality, and separa-tion of church and state. Known as a classical liberal democracy, the United States has two major parties, the Democrats and Republicans, which are derived from the same classical liberal traditions. One might argue, therefore, that basic elements of both major American parties can be found in the "economic liberal" right and the "social liberal" left wings of the FDP.

The FDP (it refers to itself as F.D.P.) is a "pivotal" party in the German party system that has served as a coalition partner of both the CDU and SPD over the past decades. It was the most likely coalition partner of the CDU at the national, *Land*, and local levels in the first decades after 1945, when the economic and national focus in the party was prevalent. In the late 1960s it joined a coalition with the SPD in North-Rhine Westphalia, and in 1969 it joined in a coalition with the SPD at the national level with the more international and civil liberties and equality wing of the party having gained the upper hand. In the fall of 1982 the economic wing of the party again become predominant, and the FDP left the national government under Chancellor Helmut Schmidt and joined the CDU/CSU in a new coalition government under Chancellor Helmut Kohl. When the SPD formed a coalition with the Bündnis 90/Greens after the federal elections of September 1998, it was the first time the FDP was not in a coalition at the federal level since 1969.[16] In the meantime the party remained in coalition with the SPD in Rhineland-Palatinate and with the CDU in Baden-Württemberg and joined the CDU in a coalition government in Hesse in 1999. It was not involved in more coalitions in the states because it had failed to win seats in all of the eastern and in several western *Land* parliaments until 2001 and 2002, when it gained entry into the parliament of Berlin and Saxony-Anhalt, respectively.

The problem for the FDP today is that its existence depends on coalitions.[17] Its focus is much less on ideology or program than on participating in government with leaders who are government office holders. Whether the party enters a coalition with the CDU or SPD at the *Land* level can be a signal of change at the federal level, and a change in partners at the federal level inevitably holds consequences for future partnerships at the *Land* level. The importance of coalitions makes changes of government and public statements during elections about coalition preferences of crucial importance for the party. By indicating preference for the CDU or SPD, the party tries to appeal to the voters of the favored party to help it with the second vote (explained below). It must exercise great caution in changing partners, because in 1969 as well as in 1982, when it did change national government partners, the FDP lost a significant proportion of its members and supporters who did not like the change in government. This means, of course, that it must pay attention to its voters, who are typically politically flexible higher-status white-collar, civil servants, urban, upper-income, well-educated, non-Catholic, and non-union. [18]

The Greens, who in 1993 combined with the East German Bündnis 90 (Alliance 90), are a classic postmaterialist "new politics" party which emerged in the late 1970s and early 1980s.[19] It stresses the environment, human rights, pacifism, social justice, and gender issues. It is to the left of the SPD on the political spectrum, although it is not as radical as it was in the 1980s, when it was deeply divided between "realists" (*Realos*) and "fundamentalists" (*Fundis*). The party saw itself at first as a "movement" or at most an anti-party party, and the fundamentalist wing was adamant in its insistence that there would be no collaboration with the establishment parties.[20] The party did join the SPD in a coalition in Hesse in 1985, but the coalition broke up in 1987 before the legislative term had ended. Later the party joined the SPD in other *Land* government coalitions, which were also controversial until most of the fundamentalist wing left the party. Today the party is divided between the "realists" who support coalitions with the SPD, and the left-wing elements who are less willing to compromise principles as a price for governing.[21] Since the Greens refuse to consider coalitions with the CDU, except at the local level, it is a much less flexible coalition party than the FDP. But, then, as a strongly programmatic party, governing is not its main goal.[22]

The Greens have always seen themselves as a grassroots (*basisdemokratisch*) party, and their most eager founders and adherents were idealistic, relatively affluent, well-educated young people with a mission to change the world. Needless to say, their strongholds have always been university towns. They have always taken seriously internal party democracy and are known for their meetings which often feature bitter open debate and discussion. As a result the *Land* parties are very jealous of their position in the party organizational hierarchy, and they enjoy a high degree of autonomy legally and in fact.[23]

The PDS (Party of Democratic Socialism) is the successor to the SED, the East German Socialist Unity Party that officially was united with the SPD in 1946 but which in fact was the Communist Party. With the collapse of the East German regime in November 1989, reform communists formed the PDS, hoping to save what they could of the old Marxist ideas and ideals.[24] The party has done well in the five new *Länder* and in the former East German part of united Berlin, receiving on average about 20 percent of the vote, but like the old West German Communist Party (DKP) formed in 1963, the PDS has not been able to gain more than 1–3 percent of the votes in western Germany. The party appeals mostly to former East German officials, many of whom lost power and prestige with unification, to farmers who fear they may lose land they gained from the

Soviet-imposed land reform of 1948, to people who have lost or fear loss of their jobs, and in general to the "losers" of unification. It has become the third party in the three-party system in eastern Germany in contrast to the four-party system in western Germany that excludes the PDS.

There are three radical right parties that sometimes compete against each other and sometimes cooperate by having one party withdraw from electoral competition to help the other. The first of these, the National Democratic Party of Germany (NPD), was formed in 1965 and flourished for a few years as a right-wing protest party during the grand coalition of CDU/CSU and SPD from 1966 to 1969.[25] Its counterpart on the left was the extraparliamentary opposition (APO), which did not form as a party but was a significant and powerful student-led movement. It helped bring about many reforms, but it also caused considerable disruption of university life as well as general political turmoil. Extremist elements in this movement became the core of the German terrorist movement. Of course the NPD profited from APO excesses, won seats in some of the *Land* parliaments and barely missed reaching the 5 percent barrier in the federal elections of 1969. Since then its successes have been very modest and limited.

Though first established in 1983, the Republicans (Reps) first received widespread attention with a sensational victory (in the sense of gaining more than 5 percent of the vote, i.e., 7.5 percent) in *Land* elections in West Berlin in 1989 and in elections for the European Parliament later in the same year (7.1 percent).[26] The party's founder and leader, Franz Schönhuber, had resigned from the Bavarian CSU out of opposition to the party's support for loans to East Germany. He had been a popular television talk show host and had volunteered to serve as an enlisted man in the SS during the Second World War. His book on his personal experiences during the War appealed to some veterans and nationalist anti-communist elements, and he appealed also to those who were concerned and upset about what they perceived to be a flood of unwanted refugees, asylum seekers, and illegal immigrants who had overwhelmed Germany's capacity to absorb them. The Reps suffered a series of setbacks after the collapse of the Wall and unification, including a palace revolt against Schönhuber, but the party continues on occasion to win seats in local and a few *Land* parliaments in the south of Germany, namely Baden-Württemberg.

The German Peoples' Union (DVU), is a party that is largely the creation of Gerhard Frey, a wealthy Hamburg publisher of right-wing newspapers and materials. The party has virtually no organization or members and exists only because of the financing and organizational input of its founder.[27] It is arguably the most right-wing of the radical right parties and, at the moment, the most successful. It won one seat in Bremen *Land* elections in June 1999, while it won sixteen seats in the 1998 elections in Saxony-Anhalt and five seats in the 1999 elections in Brandenburg. It appeals above all to disgruntled young males who are attracted by the party's strong opposition to the influx of foreigners in Germany. These are seen as a threat to German culture, jobs, and the welfare state which they are seen to be bankrupting.

The German party system changed at the national level from a multi-party system in the late 1940s and 1950s to a "2½"party system of CDU/CSU, SPD, and FDP by the end of the 1950s. In 1983 the Greens gained seats for the first time in the federal parliament, thus creating a four-party system. In 1990 the PDS joined the party system, benefiting from special provisions for that year's federal election that did not require 5 percent of the total German vote as a condition for entering the parliament. Since that time a five-party system has developed; however, not all five parties are capable of forming coalitions. The PDS is not acceptable to any of the other parties as a partner, and the differences between the Greens and the CDU are so deep that a coalition of these two parties is most unlikely. Given the potential effects of changes in the German economy and society, there are also some lingering questions about the long-term prospects of the FDP, Greens, and PDS.

The situation is quite different at the *Land* level. Here the FDP is represented in only eight of the *Land* parliaments, all in western Germany except Berlin since September 2001 and Saxony-Anhalt since April 2002. The Greens are generally comfortably above the 5 percent level and thus have seats in the western *Länder*, except in the Saarland, but they are not represented in any of the parliaments in the new *Länder*. In contrast, the PDS is the third party in the new *Länder* and even the second strongest party in Thuringia, Saxony, and Saxony-Anhalt, while it has no representation in any *Land* parliaments in western Germany. The radical right parties are represented in two *Land* parliaments, with five seats in Brandenburg and one in Bremen (Bremerhaven).

Thus there are two party systems at the *Land* level: a four-party system in the old *Länder*, consisting of the larger CDU (CSU in Bavaria) and SPD and the smaller Bündnis 90/Greens and FDP; and, at least until the recent successes by the FDP, a three-party system in the new *Länder*, consisting of the CDU, SPD, and PDS. Given the strength of the PDS (usually 20 percent or more) in *Land* elections, one can speak of three large parties in the new *Länder* and Berlin.[28] As at the national level, the CDU and Greens are unlikely coalition partners in the western *Länder*, and the PDS is not generally acceptable as a coalition partner for the CDU and SPD in the eastern *Länder*. This has changed recently, however, in that the SPD agreed in 1994 and 1998 to form a minority government in Saxony-Anhalt with the toleration of the PDS in parliament, and in the summer of 2001 the SPD formed a minority government in Berlin also with PDS toleration. In 1998 the SPD and PDS formed a regular government coalition in Mecklenburg-Vorpommern, and they formed a regular coalition in January 2002 after the new *Land* elections in October 2001. These concessions by the SPD have aroused considerable controversy,[29] not only between SPD and CDU/CSU, but also within the SPD. But these and other coalition arrangements do demonstrate the limited influence of the national parties on *Land* party coalition formation as well as the view that the *Land* parties should have more flexibility in forming coalitions than would be acceptable at the federal level.

At the end of the 1990s it was clear that the SPD had more opportunities than the CDU to form coalition governments in the *Länder*. It could form a grand coalition with the CDU in both the old and new *Länder*, a coalition with the Greens or the FDP in the former and a coalition with the PDS in the latter, at least in Mecklenburg-Vorpommern and Saxony-Anhalt. The CDU, in effect, was limited to forming a grand coalition or, in the West only, a small coalition with the FDP (however, in the fall of 2001 it formed a coalition with the FDP and the law and order "flash party," PRO).

The occasional success of a party outside the respective party systems, e.g., by one of the radical right parties, does not justify adding them to the two different party systems described above. Their success is too unpredictable even in those *Länder* in which they have shown the greatest strength. In any case the radical right parties are not acceptable coalition partners for any of the established parties, and as a result they have never held any government responsibility in any of the *Länder*. On the other hand, a middle class populist "flash party" in Hamburg (*STATT-Partei*) did join a coalition with the SPD from 1993 to 1997. A disgruntled working class voter group (AFB) was also able to gain temporary representation in Bremen from 1995 to 1999. And, as indicated above, the PRO party, led by Judge Schill, achieved success with almost 20 percent the of the vote in Hamburg in the fall of 2001. This was the largest vote ever received by a "flash party" in Germany.

Electoral systems in the Länder

German electoral systems are known for their complexity. Though less known, the electoral systems at the local level are especially complicated by American or British standards.[30] At the *Land* level, Bremen, Hamburg, and the Saarland have a simple proportional representation (PR) system, according to which voters cast one vote for a party list. Any party that receives at least 5 percent of the vote receives seats approximately in proportion to the proportion of votes it received, i.e., percent of votes = percent of seats, as determined by a particular mathematical scheme for calculation. Seven *Länder* use the d'Hondt method of calculation, nine use the Hare/Niemeyer method which is also used to calculate seats in the federal parliament.[31]

All other *Länder* have a personalized PR system (which British authors often call the "additional member system"). In North-Rhine Westphalia and Baden-Württemberg, voters have one vote that they cast for a direct candidate. The votes cast for all direct seat candidates are then totaled in order to determine the proportional distribution of total seats. In the other eleven *Länder*, voters have two votes, one for a direct candidate on the left side of the ballot, and one for a party list on the right side. The direct candidate represents a single-member district, and the candidate with the most votes (not necessarily an absolute majority) wins the seat, just as in the United States or Great Britain. But the system is basically a PR system, because the parties receive seats in proportion to the second votes cast. This means that small parties that receive 5 percent of the vote but not enough votes in any single district to win a direct seat still gain seats based on their proportion of the vote. On the other hand, the larger parties that did win direct seats have these deducted from the total they received based on their proportion of the vote. If they win more direct seats than they "deserve" based on their proportion of the vote, they get to keep these surplus seats (*Überhangsmandate*). This is why parliaments sometimes contain more members than the law would normally provide.

In order to qualify for the distribution of seats based on the proportion of votes received, a party must normally have a minimum of 5 percent of the vote (an exception is made in Schleswig-Holstein for the Danish minority party). At the federal level a second means of qualifying for this distribution is to win at least three direct seats. Thus the PDS won only 4.4 percent of the total German vote in 1994, but it won four direct seats and therefore entered the federal parliament with a total of 30 seats. If it had not won at least three direct seats, it would not have received any seats over its party list. If it had won only one or two direct seats, it would have entered parliament with that number. In Bremen, Hamburg, or the Saarland, the PDS would not have entered parliament, because there are no direct seats to contest in those *Länder*.

In Bavaria the voters select a direct candidate with the first vote, but with the second vote they may vote for the party list in their election district or select a particular candidate on the list ("personalized PR with open lists"). Both the first and the second votes count in determining the total distribution of seats for a party. Bavaria is divided into seven districts, which are the same as the government districts (*Regierungsbezirke*), with an equal or an almost equal number of direct and list seats per district, e.g., upper Bavaria has 33 district seats and 32 list seats, Lower Bavaria has ten of each.

In the federal parliament one-half of the deputies are elected directly and one-half enter based on the party lists. In the *Länder* the ratio of direct seats and party list seats varies. As a rule there are more direct seats, but they are equal in number in Brandenburg, Hesse, Saxony, and Thuringia.

Frequency of elections

As in the United States, some *Land* elections are held simultaneously with federal elections, while others are held sometime between federal elections, some soon afterwards, some soon before, but most at "mid-term." A major difference with the United States, however, lies in the fact that some of the *Länder* hold elections every four years, like the federal parliament, while others hold them every five years. An increasing number of cities are also holding council elections every five years, the basic idea being that parliaments and the governments they support must have sufficient time to develop and carry out their policies before they have to face re-election pressures. Table 8.1 shows the distribution of *Länder* according to their election calendar.

These are, of course, the official or normal cycles. If for some reason a government loses the support of a majority of the parliament, usually because of the collapse of a coalition, and it cannot or does not wish to form a minority government which exists only on the tolerance of one or more nongovernment parties in the parliament, then new elections will be called at a date different from the one scheduled. While this does not happen often, it has happened on numerous occasions over the past decades. Calling new elections in the *Länder* is made easier than at the

Table 8.1   **Election cycles in the *Länder***

Four-year election cycle	Five-year election cycle
Bremen	Baden-Württemberg (as of 1996)
Hamburg	Bavaria (as of 1998)
Hesse	Berlin (as of 1999)
Mecklenburg-Vorpommern	Brandenburg
Saxony-Anhalt	Lower Saxony (as of 1998)
	North-Rhine Westphalia
	Rhineland-Palatinate
	Saarland
	Saxony
	Schleswig-Holstein (as of 2000)
	Thuringia

federal level by provisions in all of the *Land* constitutions which allow *Land* parliaments to dissolve themselves under certain circumstances.

Voter turnout

Voter turnout in Germany has always been high in comparison with the United States, which is at the bottom or close to the bottom of any list which provides voting turnout figures in democratic countries. Registration is virtually automatic in Germany, which means that almost all eligible voters may vote. Germans do not have the problem found in the United States of having to decide whether to use all eligible voters or only those that have registered to vote as a statistical base. This can make a significant difference in the United States, because only about two-thirds of all eligible voters are registered. The most common practice in the United States is to use eligible voters as a base, which depresses the voting turnout statistics but which makes the figures more comparable to German and most European data.

As in the United States, voter turnout in federal elections is higher than in *Land* elections, the major difference being that the turnout at all levels in Germany is considerably higher than at comparable levels in the United States. The election in Germany most comparable to turnout figures for American presidential elections is the election for the European Parliament; however, in recent years turnout in some *Länder* has dropped to these levels as well. As in other democracies, the voting age in Germany at all levels is eighteen. This is also the minimum age for holding office, although some *Länder* have made twenty-one the minimum for office holding. In an effort to increase the interest of young people in politics (and to increase their percentage of the total vote), some SPD and Green politicians have pushed for a further reduction of the voting age to sixteen. In 1996 Lower Saxony reduced the voting age to sixteen for local elections, and Schleswig-Holstein has made it possible for sixteen-year-olds to participate in local planning projects.[32]

It is clear from Tables 8.2 and 8.3 that voter turnout in most elections has been generally declining over the years.[33] The decline has been dramatic at the European level and significant in most of the *Länder*, with the exception of Mecklenburg-Vorpommern which has seen a considerable increase in turnout since 1990 and Saxony-Anhalt, where turnout declined in 1994, surged in 1998, and declined again in 2000. The most common explanation for this decline is that there is a general alienation from politics (*Politikverdrossenheit*) at all levels. This is reflected not only in lower voting rates but also in declining membership in political parties, unions, and other organizations. If *Politikverdrossenheit* is a reason for the decline in voting participation, it certainly is not confined to Germany. Dissatisfaction with politics seems to be common to all developed democracies, so

Table 8.2 **Voter turnout in European Parliament and *Bundestag* elections, 1984–99**

Year	EU Parliament	*Bundestag*
1984	56.8	–
1985	–	–
1986	–	–
1987	–	84.3
1988	–	–
1989	62.3	–
1990	–	77.8
1991	–	–
1992	–	–
1993	–	–
1994	60	79
1995	–	–
1996	–	–
1997	–	–
1998	–	82.2
1999	45.2	–
2002	–	79.1
Average	56.1	80.5

Table 8.3 Voter turnout in Land elections, 1984–2002

Year	Baden-Württemberg	Bavaria	Berlin	Bremen	Hamburg	Hesse	Lower Saxony	NRW	Rhineland-Palatinate	Saarland	Schleswig-Holstein	Brandenburg	Mecklenb-Vorpom	Saxony	Saxony-Anhalt	Thuringia
1984	71.2	–	–	–	–	–	–	–	–	–	–	–	–	–	–	–
1985	–	–	–	–	–	–	–	75.2	–	85	–	–	–	–	–	–
1986	–	70.3	–	–	79.6	–	77.3	–	–	–	–	–	–	–	–	–
1987	–	–	–	75.5	–	80.3	–	–	77	–	76.6	–	–	–	–	–
1988	71.8	–	–	–	–	–	–	–	–	–	77.4	–	–	–	–	–
1989	–	–	79.6	–	–	–	–	–	–	–	–	–	–	–	–	–
1990	–	65.9	80.8	–	–	–	74.6	71.8	–	83.2	–	67.1	64.7	72.8	65.1	71.7
1991	–	–	–	72.2	66.1	70.8	–	–	73.9	–	–	–	–	–	–	–
1992	70.2	–	–	–	–	–	–	–	–	–	71.7	–	–	–	–	–
1993	–	–	–	–	69.6	–	–	–	–	–	–	–	–	–	–	–
1994	–	67.9	–	–	–	–	73.8	–	–	83.5	–	56.3	72.9	58.4	54.8	74.8
1995	–	–	68.6	68.6	–	66.3	–	64	–	–	–	–	–	–	–	–
1996	67.5	–	–	–	–	–	–	–	70.8	–	71.8	–	–	–	–	–
1997	–	–	–	–	69.5	–	–	–	–	–	–	–	–	–	–	–
1998	–	70	–	–	–	66.4	73.8	–	–	–	–	–	79.4	–	71.7	–
1999	–	–	65.9	60.1	–	–	–	–	–	68.7	–	60.1	–	61.1	–	59.9
2000	–	–	–	–	–	–	–	56.7	–	–	69.5	–	–	–	–	–
2001	62.6	–	68.1	–	71	–	–	–	62.1	–	–	–	–	–	–	–
2002	–	–	–	–	–	–	–	–	–	–	–	–	67.9	–	56.5	–
Average	68.7	68.5	72.6	69.1	71.16	70.95	74.9	66.925	71	80.1	73.4	61.2	71.2	64.1	63.9	68.8

Source: www.wahlrecht.de/landtage.

that the alleged specific German reasons are not very persuasive by themselves. Another problem is that disappointment and dissatisfaction are highest in the East, yet Mecklenburg-Vorpommern had the highest, Brandenburg the lowest, turnout in the most recent *Land* elections. It seems apparent, then, that factors other than dissatisfaction with parties and politics are also at work. One of these was probably the timing of the elections, i.e., Mecklenburg-Vorpommern and Saxony-Anhalt both had elections in 1998, and these were undoubtedly affected by the federal elections that year and the increased public focus on political issues.

Voting behavior[34]

In all advanced democracies the political parties depend on certain demographic, religious, occupational, regional, ethnic and other groups as foundations of electoral support, and the existence of such support provides stability to the party system and a certain predictability of election outcomes. A brief look at voting behavior in *Land* elections shows there are both similarities and differences between voting behavior in national and *Land* elections and between the old and the new *Länder*. The reader should be cautioned, however, that some generalizations are more persistent than others and that, for example, there is frequently a difference in voting patterns from one election to another in the same *Land* as well as changes over time.

Age has always been an important factor in voting behavior. The CDU tends to appeal more to older voters, while the SPD is generally given above-average support by younger voters. On the other hand, as suggested above, in some *Länder*, e.g., in the 1997 Hamburg elections, the SPD did best among voters over sixty. Also in some eastern states the CDU and SPD have done better with older groups and the FDP and PDS with middle-age groups. In some regions, though, support for the PDS increases with age. The SPD used to receive more votes from younger people than it does today, but since the 1980s many younger voters have given their votes to the Greens. Indeed, the Greens have relied heavily on younger voters; half of their voters have been under thirty-five and three-fourths under forty-five. However, in the most recent *Land* elections the Greens have lost support in the youngest group of eighteen–twenty-four. In the East the radical right has done especially well with the youngest voters.

Gender is not as important today as in the past, when the CDU tended to appeal more to women and the SPD more to men. In recent elections the CDU, CSU, Greens and PDS have received slightly more female than male votes, the FDP somewhat more male votes, and the SPD about the same number of female and male votes. Combining age and gender, the CDU receives a lower proportion of votes than the SPD from women in the youngest age groups but a higher proportion than the SPD in the 35 and older groups. In the East the CDU receives more votes from women than men, but it receives its lowest percentage of votes from younger women and its highest percentage from women over 60. A disproportionate number of younger women vote for the Greens, with that vote generally declining with age. The CDU does better than the SPD among younger men, while the Greens in the West and especially the radical right parties in East and West receive a large proportion of their votes from younger men.

In both the old and the new *Länder*, religion is a key determinant of voter behavior. In the West there is a strong relationship between Catholics and the CDU/CSU, although there are some exceptions such as the Saarland, which has a three-fourths Catholic population but has given the SPD strong support since 1980. Church-going Catholics are especially strong CDU/CSU voters, but the proportion of those attending church regularly is declining. Protestants in the West are more likely to vote for the SPD or FDP. In the East both the Catholic and Protestant population strongly favor the CDU, although Protestants are more likely to vote SPD in Brandenburg. The Greens and the PDS are strongly favored by unaffiliated voters; indeed, the PDS has its weakest support among church-affiliated voters who are almost immune from voting PDS.[35] However, a serious problem for the CDU in the new *Länder* is that the unaffiliated make up about two-thirds of the population, which tends to favor the SPD, PDS, and the radical right.

Occupational differences are also important factors in explaining voting behavior. Workers have always tended to support the SPD, and unionized workers have been the party's staunchest supporters. Exceptions occur primarily when heavy cross-pressures exist, e.g., among strongly Catholic workers. In the new *Länder* a majority of workers voted for the CDU in the 1990 *Land* elections, and the CDU still receives above-average support from workers in Saxony and Thuringia, and, in 1999, in Berlin. The SPD has made strong gains among workers since 1990 in the other new *Länder*. In the old *Länder* the CDU has generally received above-average support among civil servants, but the SPD has done better among white-collar workers. The PDS has received below-average support from workers but above-average support from civil servants and white collar workers. The CDU and FDP receive significant support from

the self-employed, and especially in the West the CDU is generally supported by farmers. Unionized workers in the new *Länder* have given
strong support to the SPD and PDS, while non-unionized workers have
given above-average support to the DVU. The DVU has also received
strong support from manual apprentices. Both the DVU and PDS have
done well among the unemployed in the new *Länder*. Generally the less
educated give above-average support to the SPD, the better educated to
the CDU, FDP, and PDS. The Greens receive a large proportion of their
support from the better-educated young people.

A good deal of attention has been paid in Germany to those voters who
support the far right and far left parties, i.e., the NPD, Reps, and DVU or
PDS. It was noted above that younger voters, especially younger males, are
more likely to vote for the far right parties. *Politikverdrossenheit* is obviously one reason for the dissatisfaction of young male voters, but ideology
is also important.[36] Religious affiliation has been noted above as a key
factor in support for the PDS, but ideological conflict in the East is also a
factor. It is most clearly reflected between voters of the PDS and the CDU.
CDU voters in the East reject the PDS, but they also reject the attempt on
the part of the CDU in the West to isolate the PDS, as in the "red socks"
campaign in the federal elections of 1994. Even more PDS voters reject
the CDU. This places the SPD in the middle in the East, whereas the basic
conflict in the West is between the SPD and the CDU/CSU.[37]

Direct democracy

As noted in Chapter 4, the Basic Law of the Federal Republic, like the
United States Constitution, does not provide for direct democracy. The
one exception is Article 29, which deals with the rearrangement of *Länder*
boundaries. In contrast, all *Land* constitutions today provide for direct
democracy. The older constitutions generally had a two-step process
which involved a petition for a referendum (*Volksbegehren*) and the referendum (*Volksentscheid*). The Constitution of Schleswig-Holstein in 1990
provides for three steps: an initiative, i.e., a petition to place an item on
the *Land* parliament's agenda; if that fails to produce action, a petition
(*Volksbegehren*) for a popular referendum on a specific item; and, if the
parliament does not act within a set period of time, a referendum. Four
of the new *Länder* followed the example of Schleswig-Holstein, but signature requirements for the first two petitions and percentage thresholds
required for approval of the referendum vary from *Land* to *Land* in both
eastern and western Germany.

The changes in the Constitution of Schleswig-Holstein not only encouraged the new *Länder* to follow; it also raised the interest of many political activists in the West to reconsider their constitutional arrangements and to think also about the adoption of some other aspects of direct democracy, including the direct election of mayors. In general the 1990s were a period when there was a sharp increase in the discussion of various features of "plebiscitary" democracy, including the direct election of the prime ministers of the *Länder*.

Initiatives, petitions for referenda, and referenda are hardly everyday occurrences in the *Länder*. Between 1946 and 1992 there were only twenty-three referenda, including referenda on seven *Land* constitutions in the American and French occupation zones in 1946–47 and in North-Rhine Westphalia in 1950. There were also three special referenda in these early years: one in Hesse on socialization of industry; one in Rhineland-Palatinate on schools; and one in Bremen regarding co-determination. There were three referenda in Bavaria dealing with voting age in 1970; with the electoral law in 1973; and with the addition of environmental protection to the *Land* constitution in 1984. There were four referenda in Hesse: on the election law in 1950; on the voting age in 1970; on the direct election of mayors and country managers in 1991; and on the protection of the environment as a state goal in 1991.[38]

There have been several legislative initiatives. In Bavaria there was a petition and a referendum on schools, in 1973 a constitutional change regarding television and radio, and in 1991 a petition and referendum on waste collection. In each case the *Land* parliament passed a competing proposal for the final referendum which was close to the original initiative and which then succeeded. In North-Rhine Westphalia in 1978 the CDU, the Catholic Church, and parents' groups stopped a school reform proposed by the SPD. The SPD government dropped the legislative bill after 30 percent of the electorate signed a petition for a referendum.[39]

A parliamentary dissolution was attempted in Baden-Württemberg in 1971 by those opposed to the local government territorial reforms, but it failed because the 50 percent threshold of eligible voters required for passage was not reached. In 1981 unofficial petitions for the dissolution of the West Berlin city parliament were signed by more than 18 percent of the voters (20 percent were required for an official, formal petition), and in response the parliament dissolved itself.[40]

In the 1990s there were referenda in three of the new *Länder* (1992 and 1994) and in Berlin (1995) on their constitutions. Bremen held a referendum on a partial reform of its Constitution in 1994, Hesse on lowering the age for voting in 1995, and Bavaria on introducing referenda at the local level in 1995. There were also examples of the *Land* parliaments taking action under the threat of popular action. In North-Rhine Westphalia the SPD-controlled *Land* parliament agreed to a law providing for the direct election of mayors after the CDU had collected 50,000 signatures for a petition in favor of the change. In Lower Saxony the *Land* parliament added a statement referring to God in the preamble of its 1993 constitution after a citizens' initiative collected 120,000 signatures for a petition calling for this change. In the Rhineland-Palatinate the SPD/FDP government revoked its legislation on human organ transplantations after the CDU Opposition took steps to initiate a petition against the law. In Baden-Württemberg the grand coalition government dropped its intention in 1995 to eliminate Whit Monday as a holiday to help finance the new nursing home insurance program, after 30,000 signatures were collected for an initiative petition.[41]

In the meantime a referendum was held in Berlin and Brandenburg in 1996 in which the merger of the two territorial units was rejected, and referenda were held in Bavaria in February 1998 on eliminating the second chamber, the Senate, and in March 2000 on schools. In 1998 Schleswig-Holstein held a referendum on the very controversial spelling reforms (*Rechtsschreibreform*) introduced by all of the *Land* governments, Austria, and Switzerland. To the consternation of the government, the reforms were rejected, and for a while it looked as though Schleswig-Holstein would be the only German-speaking region that would not introduce the reforms in its schools as the new standard German spelling. But in 1999 the parliament reversed the referendum decision, a highly controversial act that the Federal Constitutional Court refused to hear.

Conclusion

In spite of basic similarities among the American states in their political systems, there are differences among them in terms of the powers exercised by the governors, the number of state-wide officers elected directly by the voters, the party constellations in the two legislative chambers (except for the unicameral Nebraska Senate), the degree of competition for state-wide officials as opposed to state legislators, and so forth. In Germany there is also a basic similarity in the political systems of the *Länder*, but there are also some differences in the powers of the prime ministers of the territorial *Länder* and lord mayors of the city-states, in the degree of competition among the parties, in the strength of certain parties (Greens and FDP in the West, PDS in the East), in the frequency of elections, and so forth. Germany's federal system is politically more complicated in the sense that there is a multi-party system in all of the *Länder* (generally consisting of four parties in the West and three parties in the East), supported and encouraged by an electoral system of PR (often combined with a number of directly elected candidates), which leads to the necessity of forming coalition governments which vary in membership from *Land* to *Land*.

This means that the *Länder* can and do often have very interesting governments that are quite different from the federal model. For example, though the CDU and SPD are usually strongly divided on most important issues at the federal level, they may be partners in a coalition government in a *Land*, as they were at the turn of the twentieth century in Brandenburg, Bremen, and Berlin (until June 2001). Such coalitions can and do have considerable influence on the *Bundesrat*, the policy positions of which can be crucial to important legislation passed by the government-dominated *Bundestag*, because it is likely that these coalition governments will abstain in cases involving controversial legislation. *Land* governments may also be especially interesting because of coalitions that would not be acceptable at the national level, e.g., the SPD–PDS coalition in Mecklenburg-Vorpommern and Berlin or even the toleration of the SPD–Green government by the PDS in Saxony-Anhalt. Furthermore, *Land* elections can serve as indications of dissatisfaction regarding certain policies or conditions owing to the success of certain protest parties, especially the parties of the far right in both West and East Germany and the PDS in East Germany.

Generalizations are often made about voting behavior in *Land* elections. Age is one obvious factor, with the CDU/CSU and FDP generally appealing to older voters and the SPD and, especially Greens, appealing to younger voters. The CDU used to appeal more to females, and it still does so among older women voters; however, the CDU today appeals more to older women and the Greens to younger women. The CDU tends to do better with younger male voters, but young males are especially important to the Greens in the West and to the far right parties in the East. Strong religious affiliation makes voters virtually immune from voting PDS in the East, whereas in the West the Catholic voters tend to support the Christian Democrats and the Protestants the SPD and FDP. Unionized workers are strong supporters of the SPD, while the CDU and FDP have usually received the votes of most of the self-employed. The CDU also does well with civil servants and farmers, while the SPD has picked up support from white-collar workers. The PDS does better with white-collar workers and civil servants than with workers. But caution must be exercised in drawing generalizations from one *Land*, one region, one election, or only a few election cycles, because voting behavior has not been entirely consistent over the years.

Direct democracy was rejected by the German founding fathers for the national level exept for changing *Land* boundaries, but advocates have turned it into an increasingly important topic in recent years. During the 1990s there were numerous changes at the *Land* and local levels expanding the opportunities for initiatives and referenda, and many examples can be cited when some form of direct democracy was put into play in a variety of *Länder*.

Notes

1 James Gimpel, *National Elections and the Autonomy of American State Party Systems* (Pittsburgh: University of Pittsburgh Press, 1996).

2 For a general overview of the German party system, see, for example, Gerard Braunthal, *Parties and Politics in Modern Germany* (Boulder: Westview Press, 1996) and Christopher S. Allen (ed.), *The Transformation of the German Political Party System* (New York: Berghahn, 1999). See also Thomas Poguntke, "Das Parteiensystem der Bundesrepublik Deutschland: Von Krise zu Krise?," in *50 Jahre Bundesrepublik Deutschland*, edited by Thomas Ellwein and Everhard Holtmann (Opladen: Westdeutscher Verlag, 1999), pp. 429–439.

3 For a description and analysis of party financing in Germany, see Arthur B. Gunlicks, "The New German Party Finance Law," *German Politics* 4, no. 1 (April 1995), pp. 101–121.

4 See, for example, Ursula Birsl and Peter Lösche, "Parteien in West- und Ostdeutschland: Der gar nicht so feine Unterschied," *Zeitschrift für Parlamentsfragen* 29, no. 1 (February 1998), pp. 7–24.

5 In Germany today internal differences between parties exist less between federal and *Land* levels than between west and east Germany. See Ann L. Phillips, "Agents of Democratization and Unification: Political Parties in the New German States," in Allen, *The Transformation of the German Party System*, pp. 179–206.

6 But Phillips, cited above, notes that given the particular experiences of East Germans, the weakness of party organizations, the resentment of western influence and dominance, and other factors, there is a considerable disconnect between the national, western-dominated party organizations and the state and local parties in eastern Germany.

7   Uwe Jun, *Koalitionsbildung in den deutschen Bundesländern* (Opladen: Leske & Budrich, 1994), p. 88.

8   Konrad Hesse, *Der unitarische Bundesstaat* (Karlsruhe: C. F. Müller, 1962).

9   Georg Fabritius, *Wechselwirkungen zwischen Landtagswahlen und Bundespolitik* (Meisenheim am Glan: Verlag Anton Hain, 1978), pp. 1–2.

10   For a general overview of the SPD from the origin of the party from 1863 to the early 1960s, see Ludwig Bergsträsser, *Geschichte der politischen Parteien in Deutschland* (München: Günter Olzog Verlag, 1965), pp. 107–118, 248–252; Heino Kaack, *Geschichte und Struktur des deutschen Parteiensystems* (Opladen: Westdeutscher Verlag, 1971); see also Braunthal, *Parties and Politics*, Ch. 5, pp. 22–25.

11   For an overview, see Andrew B. Denison, "The SPD: Between Political Drift and Direction," in *Between Bonn and Berlin: German Politics Adrift?*, edited by Mary N. Hampton and Christian Soe (New York: Rowman & Littlefield, 1999), pp. 73–101.

12   Geoffrey K. Roberts, *Party Politics in the New Germany* (London: Pinter, 1997), p. 26.

13   Bergsträsser, *Geschichte*, pp. 238–244; Kaack, *Geschichte*, pp. 170–178; Braunthal, *Parties and Politics*, Ch. 4.

14   For a review of Christian Democratic fortunes to the end of the Kohl era, see Clay Clemens, "The CDU/CSU: Undercurrents in an Ebb Tide," in Hampton and Soe, *Between Bonn and Berlin*, pp. 51–71 and, by the same author, "Kohl's Legacy: The CDU/CSU in a New Era," in *The Federal Republic of Germany at Fifty*, edited by Peter H. Merkl (London: Macmillan Press, 1999), pp. 100–111.

15   Bergsträsser, *Geschichte*, pp. 244–248; Braunthal, *Parties and Politics*, Ch 6.

16   Christoph Hanterman and Christian Soe, "The FDP: Do the Liberals Still Matter?," in Hampton and Soe, *Between Bonn and Berlin*, pp. 119–136.

17   Gudrun Heinrich, "Der kleine Koalitionspartner in den Ländern: Koalitionsstrategien von F.D.P. und Bündnis 90/Die Grünen im Vergleich," in *Hinter den Kulissen von Regierungsbündnissen: Koalitionspolitik in Bund, Ländern und Gemeinden*, edited by Roland Sturm und Sabine Kropp (Baden-Baden: Nomos Verlagsgesellschaft, 1999), p. 123.

18   Ibid.

19   Braunthal, *Parties and Politics*, Ch 7; Andrei S. Markovits and Philip S. Gorski, *The German Left: Red, Green and Beyond* (New York: Oxford University Press, 1993), Ch. 8; E. Gene Frankland and Donald Schoonmaker, *Between Protest and Power* (Boulder: Westview Press, 1992).

20   Heinrich, "Der kleine Koalitionspartner," p. 129.

21   Ibid., p. 130.

22   The Greens were, however, far more pragmatic at the end of the 1990s than before. E. Gene Frankland, "Alliance 90/The Greens: Party of Ecological and Social Reform," in Hampton and Soe, *Between Bonn and Berlin*, pp. 103–117;

also, by the same author, "The Green Party's Transformation: The 'New Politics' Party Grows Up," in Merkl, *The Federal Republic of Germany at Fifty*, pp. 147–159.

23 Ibid., p. 134.

24 For an overview of the PDS between 1990 and 1994, see Gerald R. Kleinfeld, "The Return of the PDS," in *Germany's New Politics*, edited by David P. Conradt *et al.* (Tempe: German Studies Review, 1995), pp. 193–220; also, by the same author, "The PDS: Between Socialism and Regionalism," in Hampton and Soe, *Between Bonn and Berlin*, pp. 137–154.

25 Fred H. Richards, *Die NPD: Alternative oder Wiederkehr?* (München: Günter Olzog Verlag, 1967).

26 Hans-Joachim Veen *et al.*, *The Republikaner Party in Germany: Right-Wing Menace or Protest Catchall?* (Westport: Praeger, 1993).

27 Dietrich Thränhardt, "Die DVU: eine virtuelle Partei, durch manipulierbares Wahlrecht begünstigt – ein Plädoyer zur Wahlrechtsreform," *Zeitschrift für Parlamentsfragen* 3, no. 3 (September 1998), pp. 441–448.

28 Eckhard Jesse, "Koalitionen in den neuen Bundesländern," in Sturm and Kropp, *Hinter den Kulissen*, p. 163.

29 See, for example, ibid., pp. 156–159. Also Wolfgang Renzsch and Stefan Schieren, "Grosse Koalition ohne Alternative?" and Winfried Steffani, "Wer trägt die Verantwortung? Wider die wissenschaftliche und politische Verharmlosung des 'Magdeburger Modells,'" *Zeitschrift für Parlamentsfragen* 29, no. 1 (February 1998), pp. 187–190.

30 Arthur B. Gunlicks, *Local Government in the German Federal System* (Durham: Duke University Press, 1986), pp. 174–177.

31 For a description and demonstration of both methods of calculation, see ibid., pp. 176–177.

32 Christoph Knödler, "Wahlrecht für Minderjährige – eine gute Wahl?," *Zeitschrift für Parlamentsfragen* 27, no. 4 (November 1996), pp. 553–555; Ursula Hoffmann-Lange and Johann de Rijke, "16jährige Wähler – erwachsen genug?," *Zeitschrift für Parlamentsfragen* 27, no. 4 (November 1996), pp. 572–585.

33 For an analysis of nonvoting in Germany, see Ursula Feist, "Nichtwähler 1994: Eine Analyse der Bundestagswahl 1994," *Aus Politik und Zeitgeschichte* 51–52 (23 December 1994), pp. 35–46.

34 The discussion below is based on Wolfgang G. Gibowski, "Germany's General Election in 1994: Who Voted for Whom?," in *Germany's New Politics*, edited by David P. Conradt *et al.* (Tempe: German Studies Review, 1995), pp. 102–110; Reinhold Roth, "Die Bremer Bürgerschaftswahl," *Zeitschrift für Parlamentsfragen* 26, no. 2 (May 1995), p. 24; Wolfram Brunner and Dieter Walz, "Die Hamburger Bürgerschaftswahl," *Zeitschrift für Parlamentsfragen* 29, no. 2 (May 1998), p. 283; Oskar Niedermayer and Richard Stöss, "Die Wahl zum Berliner Abgeordnetenhaus," *Zeitschrift für Parlamentsfragen* 31, no. 1 (arch

2000), p. 98; Thomas Renz and Günter Rieger, "Die bayerische Landtagswahl," *Zeitschrift für Parlamentsfragen* 30, no. 1 (February 1999), pp. 84–85; Rita Miller-Hilmer, "Die niedersächsische Landtagswahl," *Zeitschrift für Parlamentsfragen* 30, no. 1 (February 1999), pp. 49–51; Kai Arzheim and Cornelia Weinss, "Zerfallen die sozialstrukturellen Bindungen an die Union . . . ?," *Zeitschrift für Parlamentsfragen* 28, no. 2 (May 1997), pp. 208–212; Karl Schmitt, "Die Landtagswahlen in Brandenburg und Thüringen," *Zeitschrift für Parlamentsfragen* 31, no. 1 (March 2000), pp. 59–61; Nikolaus Werz and Jochen Schmidt, "Die mecklenburg-vorpommersche Landtagswahl," *Zeitschrift für Parlamentsfragen* 30, no. 1 (February 1999), p. 109–111; Eckhard Jesse, "Die Landtagswahl in Sachsen," *Zeitschrift für Parlamentsfragen* 31, no. 1 (March 2000), p. 79; Stefan Schieren, "Die Landtagswahl in Sachsen-Anhalt," *Zeitschrift für Parlamentsfragen* 30, no. 1 (February 1999), p. 67.

35   Rudolf Günter Deinert, "Die PDS, die rechten Parteien und das Alibi der 'Politikverdrossenheit'," *Zeitschrift für Parlamentsfragen* 29, no. 3 (September 1998), pp. 438–439.

36   Ibid.

37   Henry Krikenbom, "Nachwirkungen der SED-Ära: Die PDS als Katalysator der Partei- und Wahlpräferenzen in den neuen Bundesländern," *Zeitschrift für Parlamentsfragen* 29, no. 1 (February 1998), pp. 25–31.

38   Otmar Jung, "Daten zu Volksentscheiden in Deutschland auf Landesebene (1946–1992)," *Zeitschrift für Parlamentsfragen* 24, no. 1 (February 993), pp. 5–9.

39   Ibid., pp. 9–11.

40   Ibid., p. 11.

41   Otmar Jung, "Direkte Demokratie: Forschungsstand und Forschungsaufgaben 1995," *Zeitschrift für Parlamentsfragen* 26, no. 4 (November 1995), pp. 660–661.

9

Elections
in the *Länder*

Introduction

Five phases can be distinguished in the development of political parties in the *Länder*. The first phase, from 1945 to 1953, was the period during which older parties were reestablished, e.g., SPD, and new parties were founded, e.g., the refugee party (BHE), CDU, and FDP (although the CDU has its roots in the old Center Party [Zentrum] and the FDP could be traced back to liberal parties of the Empire and Weimar Republic). The second phase, from 1953 to 1969, saw the developing concentration of parties culminating in the three- (or "2½")-party system of CDU/CSU, SPD, and FDP. The third phase, from 1969 to 1983, was the period of three-party dominance, while in the fourth phase, from 1983 to 1990, the Greens emerged as a fourth party. Finally, following a reorientation after unification in 1990, a five-party system has developed at the national level with the rise of the PDS which, however, has a special regional character, and in *Land* elections has been confined to the new *Länder* and Berlin in the East just as the Greens and FDP have been successful only or mostly in the West.[1]

In order to provide the reader with some of the flavor and spice of *Landtag* elections, and to assess better some of the hypotheses about *Land* elections and parties that were mentioned in the previous chapter (pp. 267–273), a very brief overview of political developments in the *Länder* since 1945 is presented below. This overview also contains a summary of the major issues, personalities, and events associated with the most recent *Land* elections.

The old *Länder*

Baden-Württemberg

Baden-Württemberg is an industrialized region with important sectors in engineering, automobiles (Daimler-Benz and Porsche), and many industrial suppliers. It also boasts many renowned educational and scientific institutions.[2] The last *Land* to be formed from previous *Länder* in 1952 – this time by the Germans themselves rather than by the Allies – Baden-Württemberg held its first parliamentary (*Landtag*) election in 1952. Since then the CDU has been the leading party. Nevertheless, the first government was made up of a coalition of SPD, FDP/DVP, and GB/BHE (a refugee party that played an important role in the politics of several *Länder* after 1945 until the early 1960s), and the first prime minister (*Ministerpräsident*) was from the FDP. By 1953 the CDU had joined the coalition to form an all-party government. From that time until 1972, the CDU provided the prime minister in a variety of coalition governments with changing partners from the parties above. After 1972 the CDU controlled the government alone. During this time the SPD ranged from 29 to 37 percent of the vote, while the liberals (FDP/DVP) sank from 18 towards 5 percent. But this picture of stability was shaken by the success of the radical right parties, the NPD in 1968 and the Republicans in 1992, and the Greens in the 1980s and 1990s. In 1992 the CDU suffered a major loss to 39.6 percent and formed a grand coalition with the SPD, which had sunk below 30 percent. The "Reps" and the Greens had received 10.9 percent and 12.1 percent, respectively, which then complicated coalition formation,[3] because the Reps were not considered by the other parties to be acceptable coalition partners and the CDU and Greens did not consider seriously sharing governmental power.

In 1996 the most important questions were whether the CDU and SPD would be forced to continue their grand coalition and whether the FDP would receive the required 5 percent of the vote to gain seats in the *Landtag*. As it turned out, the FDP got a surprising 9.6 percent, which made it possible for it to form a coalition with the CDU. The Greens also increased their vote, and the Reps were pleased with the surprising 9.1 percent they received. The SPD was the big loser, receiving only 25.1 percent of the vote and only one of the 70 direct seats. Since the CDU won only 41.3 percent of the vote but 69 direct seats, it ended up with a surplus of 18 seats (*Überhangsmandate*). As a balance, the other parties were given 17 additional seats, so that the parliament after 1996 had 155 instead of the official 120 seats.[4]

In spite of the positive trends in the polls for Chancellor Schröder and his government, the decline in popularity for the Christian Democrats since the party financial scandal centering around former Chancellor Kohl became an issue at the end of 1999, and increasingly favorable polling results for the SPD and its leading candidate, Ute Vogt, the *Land* election in 2001 went well for the CDU. It received 44.8 percent of the vote, 3.5 percent more than in 1996. This was due apparently to the popularity of the prime minister, Erwin Teufel, and his government during the five years since the last election. Nevertheless, the SPD made unusually large gains and received 33.3 percent or 8.2 percent more than in 1996. In spite of its partnership with the CDU in a successful coalition government, the FDP went from 9.6 percent to 8.1 percent. The Greens had trouble mobilizing their voters, many of whom went over to the SPD, and received 7.7 percent in comparison to 12.1 percent in 1996. The Republicans, who received 9.1 percent of the protest vote in 1996, declined to 4.4 percent in 2001 and were no longer in the parliament. In contrast to many other *Länder*, the CDU received substantially more support than the SPD among workers and voters with modest educations. The SPD led the CDU in support among civil servants and educated women (especially the younger categories), and picked up support among younger women in general at the cost of the Greens (figure 9.1).[5]

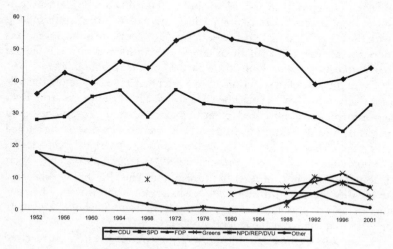

Figure 9.1   **Election results in Baden-Württemberg, 1952–2001**
Source: www.wahlrecht.de/landtage

Bavaria

Politics in Bavaria are different from the other *Länder* in some important ways. First, Bavaria is more rural, much more Catholic, and less unionized than elsewhere. All of these factors favor a Christian–conservative party. Second, there is a widespread political–cultural consciousness favoring political independence and cultural uniqueness. Third, economic modernization came late and without the baggage of old conflicts associated with industrialization. Fourth, these background elements brought about an asymmetric party system established in the 1960s, with the Christian Social Union (CSU, the sister party of the CDU) as the hegemonial party vs an opposition with no real chance of dislodging the CSU from government. The CSU won an absolute majority of seats in the *Landtag* in 1962, and it has won an absolute majority of votes since 1970. The SPD was a government party only between 1954 and 1957 in a four-party coalition. The FDP has failed to pass the 5 percent barrier on several occasions: 1966, 1982, 1986, 1994, and 1998.[6] Characteristic of the CSU's hegemony is its single-party rule since 1966, its presence in all aspects of society, and its penetration of the state apparatus and mass media, all of which lead to a tendency to identify the party with the *Land*.[7]

The CSU has responded to this identity with Bavaria with a nebulous ideology, because its policy positions are a mix of free-market economics, social democracy, catholic–clerical traditionalism in cultural and family policy, and a conservative domestic policy. The SPD has been unsuccessful in its attempts to offer an appealing alternative, and it suffers along with the Greens and FDP from a variety of problems, including organizational weakness, recruitment of elites, little influence with the federal party, and competition with "flash parties" on the right and left.[8]

Given the date of the election on 13 September 1998 just before the federal election two weeks later, the CSU stressed its distance from the Kohl government and emphasized its various successes under the leadership of its prime minister, Edmund Stoiber. These were contrasted to the alleged failed policies of the SPD's Chancellor candidate, Gerhard Schröder, as prime minister in Lower Saxony and the SPD's federal party chair, Oskar Lafontaine, as prime minister in the Saarland. The SPD and Greens tried to identify the CSU with the CDU's Chancellor Kohl, who had become increasingly unpopular, and to focus on the nation-wide political climate that favored change at the federal level.[9]

The results of the election were very positive for the CSU. It received an absolute majority again (52.9 percent), which was about what it received in 1994, while the SPD and Greens suffered slight losses and declined to 28.7 and 5.7 percent, respectively. Only these three of nineteen parties received more than the required 5 percent of the vote to enter parliament.[10]

The CSU received above average support (58 percent) from Catholics, below- average support among Protestants (47 percent), and only 28 percent of the non-affiliated vote. It received 77 percent of the frequent church-goers among Catholics, 60 percent among Protestants. Since two-thirds of the voters are Catholic, the CSU has a strong electoral advantage in this population. But the traditionally high percentage of church- goers is declining, and in 1998 only 19 percent of the voters said they attended church every Sunday. The CSU is also the strongest party in all occupational groups and, of course, in rural areas.[11]

The CSU's very slight gain in 1998 over 1994 was the first since its high-point in 1974, when it received 62.1 percent of the vote. This success was attributed to the appeal of the prime minister, Edmund Stoiber, who was able to attract uncommitted voters and younger voters. In spite of high unemployment, concerns about the influx of foreigners and asylum seekers, concerns about the environment, and a general disillusionment with politics (*Politikverdrossenheit*), Stoiber was able to point to numerous positive developments in the *Land*. As a result, polls suggested that the CSU more than the SPD enjoyed the confidence of voters in the ability to deal with key issues such as the economy and crime.[12] This election seemed to rebut the thesis that *Land* elections are basically partial federal elections,[13] as has been suggested by Georg Fabritius (see p. 327).

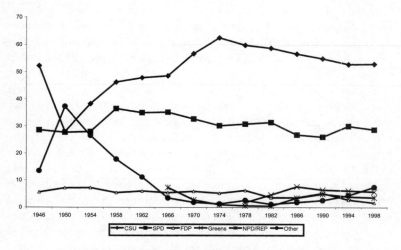

Figure 9.2   **Election results in Bavaria, 1946–98**
Source: www.wahlrecht.de/landtage

Hesse

For the first twenty-five years after the war, Hesse had the reputation of being "red," i.e., SPD. In the 1974, 1978, and 1982 elections the CDU received relative majorities, but the SPD formed a coalition government with the FDP in the 1970s and tried to muddle through as a minority government after 1982. However, failure to pass its budget led to early elections in 1983. The SPD gained votes in these elections, the CDU lost more than six points, the Greens entered the parliament for the second time, and the FDP returned again, having failed to clear the 5 percent barrier in 1982. At first the SPD formed a minority government that was "tolerated" by the Greens in parliament; then, in 1985, the first Red–Green coalition government at the state level was formed. However, tensions between the SPD and Greens within the government led to the calling of elections six months early in April 1987. The result was that for the first time the CDU and FDP were able to gain a majority of seats and remove the SPD from forty years of uninterrupted rule.[14]

In the election of 1991, held only seven weeks after the federal election which the SPD and Greens lost badly, the SPD and Greens both gained votes and were able to replace the CDU and FDP coalition government with a coalition of their own.[15] In 1995, even though the CDU received a narrow relative majority, its 39.2 percent of the vote was not enough to form a coalition with the FDP. The FDP was nevertheless very relieved with its success at gaining 7.4 percent, since it had failed to gain the required 5 percent of the vote for representation in parliament in the last nine *Land* elections and the European elections. With a two-seat majority in parliament, the SPD, with 38 percent, and Greens, with 11.2 percent, were able to continue their governing coalition under the leadership of Hans Eichel.[16]

The election in Hesse in February 1999 was not only of great interest due to its timing as the first *Land* election following the SPD–Green victory in the September 1998 federal elections; it turned out also to be the first in a series of state elections that shocked and seriously damaged the new national government. The press had judged harshly the first 100 days of the Red–Green government in Bonn, and the same coalition of parties in Hesse had been only moderately successful. Hesse had the highest *per capita* income, and it was the largest net payer in the system of fiscal equalization among the states. But it was unable to balance its budget, and many of the government's goals remained unmet. Also the SPD prime minister, Hans Eichel, did not enjoy the same degree of personal support often accorded the *Landesvater*, although he had more personal appeal than his lesser-known CDU challenger.[17]

The CDU started with the issues of education and crime, but during the campaign it picked up another theme as a main focus: the federal government's plans to reform the citizenship laws for foreigners. The CDU and CSU started a national campaign to gather signatures for petitions against the dual-citizenship proposals, and the CDU in Hesse initiated its own successful campaign in Hesse three weeks before the election. The SPD, but especially the Greens, objected to the CDU signature campaign, while the FDP sought a compromise formula. Though most voters were also critical of the CDU campaign, even more were critical of the national government's proposals.[18]

The CDU emerged with an unexpected victory, receiving 43.4 percent of the vote to 39.4 percent for the SPD. The Greens lost 4 points and ended up with 7.2 percent. The FDP also lost votes, but it still remained barely above the 5 percent clause. As a result the CDU and FDP were able to form a coalition for the second time since 1987 with a bare majority of 56 to 54 seats in parliament. In spite of the agreement by the far-right German Peoples' Union (DVU) to withdraw from the race in favor of the Republicans (Reps), the far right received only 2.7 percent of the vote.[19]

The loss of the election by the SPD–Green coalition in Hesse was not only the first of several embarrassing losses in 1999; it also meant the

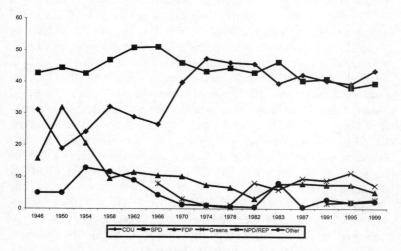

Figure 9.3   **Election results in Hesse, 1946–99**
Source: www.wahlrecht.de/landtage

loss of the federal government's majority in the *Bundesrat*. This did not mean that the Opposition had gained the majority, however, because several states had grand coalitions or SPD–FDP coalitions which were generally neutral on controversial issues in the *Bundesrat*. A second direct consequence of the election for the national government was that it revised its plans for changing the citizenship law and adopted in principle the FDP compromise proposal according to which a foreigner born in Germany would become a citizen at birth but would have to choose between German and foreign citizenship at age twenty-three (figure 9.3).[20]

Lower Saxony

After a seventeen-year period of rule, the SPD proposed a candidate in 1976 to replace the governing SPD prime minister in the middle of the 1974–78 legislative term. To the surprise and consternation of the SPD, their candidate failed to gain the requisite absolute majority of secret votes in the parliament, in spite of a one-vote SPD–FDP coalition majority in the parliament. The CDU, under the leadership of Ernst Albrecht, first formed a government alone and later a coalition government with the FDP.[21] For fourteen years Albrecht remained a highly influential prime minister until his defeat by Gerhard Schröder in 1990.

Schröder and the SPD won re-election in 1994 with virtually the same percentage of the vote as the party received in 1990; however, their Green coalition partner received almost 2 percent more than in 1990. In spite of having received an absolute majority of the vote together, the Red–Green coalition was not renewed; instead, the SPD, with its one-vote majority in parliament, formed a government alone.[22]

The election of March 1998 was special, because it was the first test election before the national election of September, and because it featured Gerhard Schröder again not only as the SPD's candidate for prime minister of Lower Saxony but now also as a leading candidate for the federal chancellorship. Schröder said before the election that he would not be a candidate for chancellor if the SPD lost more than 2 percent of the vote received in 1994. This was a risky condition, because the party had lost between 2.8 and 6.8 percent in all of the state elections since 1994. The SPD also had to answer for bad economic data in Lower Saxony, including higher-than-average unemployment and a large budget deficit. But as state issues receded into the background and federal themes became more prominent during the campaign, polling data for the SPD improved. Most voters saw the federal government as being more responsible for

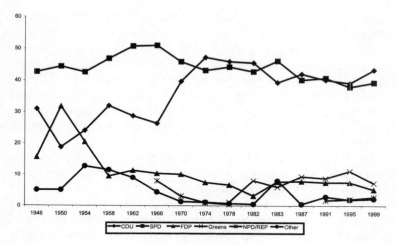

Figure 9.4   **Election results in Lower Saxony, 1947–99**
Source: www.wahlrecht.de/landtage

unemployment than the state government, and Schröder's name recognition and personal appeal made him more popular than his party. Voters also realized the importance of the election to Schröder's candidacy for the chancellorship, and this consideration also affected their vote. Indeed, the election was perceived by many as a kind of primary.[23]

The results of the election were very satisfactory from the perspective of Schröder and the SPD, which received its highest share ever (47.9 percent) in Lower Saxony. The CDU lost less than 1 percent, but that left it with the lowest percentage it had received since 1959. The Greens lost slightly (7.4 to 7 percent), while the FDP gained votes but at 4.9 percent barely missed clearing the 5 percent hurdle.[24] Another important result for Schröder in particular was that he was now the unchallenged chancellorship candidate for the SPD, in spite of previous strong support among party office holders around the country for the prime minister of the Saarland, Oskar Lafontaine (figure 9.4).

North-Rhine Westphalia

For the first two decades after the war, the CDU was the strongest party in North-Rhine Westphalia, but the 1960s and 1970s were periods of strong competition between the CDU and SPD. The SPD has been the governing party since 1966, and it governed alone from 1980 to 1995 with an absolute majority of seats in the parliament. Starting with the 1980 election, it looked as though the economically distressed areas of the Rhine and Ruhr had become as strongly SPD as the economically prosperous areas of Baden-Württemberg and Bavaria were entrenched strongholds of the CDU and CSU. In 1995, however, the SPD lost its absolute majority and formed a shaky coalition with the Greens. This coalition was destined for trouble, especially because of a fundamental disagreement from the beginning over the issues of surface coal mining, highway construction, and airport noise.[25]

Like Schleswig-Holstein, North-Rhine Westphalia was expected to turn toward the CDU in the elections of 2000. The SPD's long-serving popular prime minister, Johannes Rau, had become Federal President in the summer of 1999, and the new prime minister, Wolfgang Clement, did not yet have the kind of broad-based personal appeal enjoyed so many years by Rau. The conflicts between the Red–Green coalition parties during the 1995–2000 legislative period had not left a positive impression of government competence, unemployment remained high, and the Schröder government's policies were not popular. To complicate matters for the SPD, it was revealed that government ministers had received free air flights and other benefits in past years from a publicly owned bank.

Having won a series of *Land* elections and the European elections in 1999, and having emerged as the winner of local elections in September, the CDU was in a strong position to make substantial gains or perhaps even challenge the SPD for leadership in the election of 14 May 2000. But the party finance scandal that erupted at the end of 1999 concerning in particular former Chancellor Helmut Kohl and the CDU leadership in Hesse changed the political atmosphere dramatically, and the CDU candidate for prime minister, Jürgen Rüttgers, did not help his image with his campaign against the federal government's plan to issue "green cards" for foreign computer experts. The Greens had not gained public confidence as a result of their participation in the government in coalition with the SPD, and they no longer appealed in particular to young voters. The FDP, under the leadership of Jürgen Möllemann, profited from the weaknesses of the other parties and their leaders and was the only party to gain voters from every category of age and vocation.[26]

The SPD emerged with its smallest proportion of votes since 1958, declining by 3.2 points to 42.8 percent, while its coalition partner, the Greens, lost 2.9 points and ended up with 7.1 percent. The results of the election were unusual in that the opposition CDU failed – because of the party finance scandal involving former Chancellor Kohl – to gain against

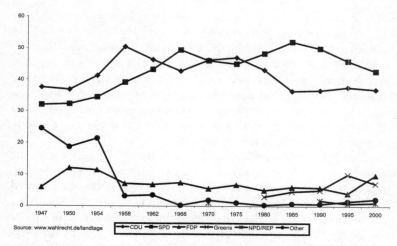

Figure 9.5   **Election results in North-Rhine Westphalia, 1947–2000**
Source: www.wahlrecht.de/landtage

the government parties in spite of the widespread dissatisfaction with these parties at the national level, receiving 37 percent, or 0.7 percent less than 1995. The only winner was the FDP, which received a sensational 9.8 percent, up from a mere 4 percent from 1995 when the party failed to enter parliament. Voter turnout, at 56.7 percent, was among the lowest ever in a state election since the war.[27]

In theory the SPD had three coalition alternatives: CDU, Greens, and FDP. Even though there was considerable speculation about an SPD–FDP coalition that Prime Minister Clement reportedly favored, the SPD agreed in June to stay with its partner of the previous five years, the Greens, under the continued leadership Wolfgang Clement (figure 9.5).[28]

Rhineland-Palatinate

The CDU dominated the electoral scene in Rhineland-Palatinate for forty-four years beginning with the first election in 1947, and it received absolute majorities in 1975, 1979, and 1983. It was able to govern alone from 1971 to 1987. But the CDU suffered serious losses in 1987 and was forced to form a coalition with the FDP. This led to a considerable loss of authority for the long-serving CDU prime minister, Bernhard Vogel (now prime minister of Thuringia), who then became the object of internal party conflict. In November 1988 Vogel lost his party chairmanship and resigned as prime minister a short time later. Unfortunately for the CDU, this did not end internal divisions, and the party entered the 1991 elections with weak leadership and a frustrated membership. The SPD became the strongest party in local elections in 1989, and in the 1991 *Land* election it gained an additional 6 points to reach 44.8 percent of the votes.[29] The CDU lost more than 6 points and dropped to its lowest percentage ever, 38.7 percent. The result was a coalition between SPD and FDP led by the SPD's Rudolf Scharping[30] and the loss of the Kohl government's majority in the *Bundesrat*.

In 1994 prime minister Scharping became the SPD's candidate for the chancellorship in the federal elections, after which he moved to the *Bundestag* as party group leader. His successor was Kurt Beck, who assumed office in October 1994 and continued the coalition with the FDP. In the 1996 election, which marked the end of the first five-year term for the state, the SPD lost 5 points and dropped to 39.8 percent, but the CDU was unable to benefit from this loss and remained at 38.7 percent. The FDP, which was concerned not only about remaining in the government in coalition with the SPD but even about passing the 5 percent barrier, actually gained 2 percent and had its best result since 1963 with 8.9 percent. The Greens gained slightly, but the SPD and FDP remained in coalition under the leadership of Prime Minister Beck.[31]

In contrast to the political climate in 1999, when elections first in Hesse and then several other *Länder* led to gains for the CDU, the 2001 elections in Rhineland-Palatinate were held under conditions that favored the SPD. The CDU was still reeling from the party finance scandal surrounding former Chancellor Kohl, Chancellor Schröder had reshuffled his cabinet and gained considerable popularity through his policies and personality, and Prime Minister Beck had proven to be a capable and popular leader. The SPD gained an impressive 4.9 percent over 1994 to reach 44.7 percent, while its coalition partner, the FDP, lost 1.1 percent but still remained well above the 5 percent clause at 7.8 percent. The CDU lost another 3.4 percent from 1994 and received its lowest percentage ever in the *Land* elections, 35.3 percent. With 5.2 percent, barely above the 5 percent minimum, the Greens also lost votes compared to their 6.9 percent in 1994. In spite of the lowest voter turnout ever (62.1 percent), the SPD picked up voters from both the CDU and the Greens and enjoyed especially strong support among workers and voters with modest educational backgrounds. It also increased its support among the better educated and the youngest and oldest voters (especially women) (figure 9.6).[32]

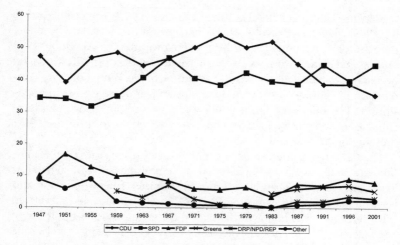

Figure 9.6   **Election results in Rhineland-Palatinate, 1947–2001**
Source: www.wahlrecht.de/landtage

Saarland

In 1945 the Saarland was not only occupied by the French; it was incorporated economically into France which had the intention of annexing it later as it had done three centuries before with Alsace-Lorraine. However, as after the First World War, the voters in the Saarland chose in a referendum in 1955 to remain with Germany, and the Saarland was reincorporated into Germany as a separate state in 1957.

In the first state election in 1955, the CDU received a relative majority of the votes with 25.4 percent, and the party's share increased rapidly thereafter to place the CDU in a dominant position until 1980, when it was eclipsed slightly by the SPD. The SPD gained votes every election from 1955 until 1994, when it still emerged as the strongest party with 49.4 percent. Its high mark of 54.4 percent was reached in 1990. Given the fact that three-fourths of the population of the state is Catholic and except for Saarbrücken and Neunkirchen basically rural and small-town – factors that generally favor the CDU – the CDU should be the dominant party. But severe economic problems, especially the decline of the coal and steel industry, have made the economy the main issue for decades and given the advantage to the SPD. Much of the SPD's success was due also to the popularity of the prime minister, Oskar Lafontaine, the former mayor of Saarbrücken and a more traditional socialist with populist tendencies. Lafontaine became the SPD national party leader in November 1995, when he defeated Rudolf Scharping for that post, and he joined the Schröder government as Minister of Finance after the September 1998 federal election. Lafontaine was succeeded by Rudolf Klimmt, who became a popular figure soon after assuming office. But Lafontaine's resignation in February 1999 from his ministerial and party posts in opposition to Schröder's economic policy direction and the changed political climate in the country in 1999 had a very negative effect on the SPD's standing in the Saarland.[33]

The CDU had gained votes in the 1994 elections over its 1990 results, but with 38.6 percent it still remained far behind the SPD, which had lost 5 percent. The CDU's candidate for prime minister, Peter Müller, was also less popular than prime minister Rudolf Klimmt. The Greens had cleared the 5 percent barrier in the Saarland for the first time in 1994, but the FDP had failed in 1994 to enter the parliament. The FDP had failed to clear the 5 percent hurdle in seven of the last eight state elections, it had lost almost half of its members, it had no strong personalities to offer, and it had few loyal supporters.[34]

With a voter turnout of 68.7 percent, a decline of 15 percent from 1994 and the lowest turnout in the state since 1955, the results were dramatic. The CDU became the strongest party with 45.5 percent, barely defeating the SPD which received 44.4 percent. The CDU increased its percentage by a stunning 6.9 percent over 1994 (an increase of 12.1 percent since 1990), while the SPD lost 5 percent (10 percent since 1990). The Greens failed to return to parliament, and the FDP, though gaining 0.5 percent, received only 2.6 percent of the vote. With an absolute majority in parliament of 26 seats to 25 seats for the SPD, the CDU formed a new government, and Peter Müller replaced the very short-term Rudolf Klimmt as prime minister. In spite of his criticism of the federal government during the campaign, the former SPD prime minister entered the federal cabinet as the Minister of Transportation[35] but was later forced to resign due to a financial scandal involving his government while he was prime minister (figure 9.7).

Schleswig-Holstein

In the first elections after the war, the SPD received the most votes in this northernmost German state known for shipbuilding, fishing, and agriculture. However, the party's total vote was reduced sharply in the 1950s. This was due largely to the influx of refugees and expellees from the East

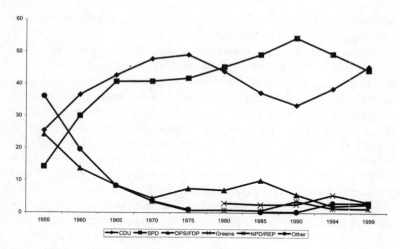

Figure 9.7   **Election results in the Saarland, 1955–99**
Source: www.wahlrecht.de/landtage

who became a significant proportion of the population and formed their own refugee party, the BHE. As the refugees slowly became assimilated, they tended to turn to the CDU, which was the governing party from 1950 to 1988, in coalition with other parties until 1971, alone from 1971 to 1987. In the meantime the SPD steadily increased its percentage of the vote, due in part to the crisis in the shipbuilding industry and in agriculture, bypassing the CDU in 1987 for the first time.

Just as the 1987 election campaign was beginning, the CDU Prime Minister, Uwe Barschel, was involved in an airplane accident in which he was the only survivor. Seriously injured, Barschel did not become active in the campaign until four weeks before the election date. Then one week before the 1987 elections, it was revealed that the SPD's candidate for prime minister, Björn Engholm, was being followed by two private detectives and that an anonymous charge had been made that Engholm had cheated on his taxes. The CDU government, under Prime Minister Barschel, denied all charges implicating it, but hours before the election it was revealed that a close associate of Barschel had signed a statement according to which Barschel had been advised of the plan to accuse Engholm with tax fraud, to have Engholm followed, and to engage in other practices that would embarrass the Opposition. Barschel rejected these revelations as lies, and the suspicion arose that because of its timing and reputation, *Der Spiegel*, the news magazine that printed the exposé, had itself engaged in highly questionable behavior.[36]

The results of the election were a tie in seats for the CDU and FDP vs the SPD and *Südschleswigscher Wählerverband* (*SSW*), the Danish minority party that does not have to receive 5 percent of the vote to enter parliament. Only two weeks after the election, during negotiations with the FDP and SSW to form a new government, Prime Minister Barschel resigned from office. The tumult surrounding him refused to subside, and he left for a vacation in Switzerland. On 12 October he was found dead in his hotel in Geneva.[37] Whether it was murder or suicide has never been determined with certainty. Given the circumstances, the CDU, FDP and SPD agreed to hold new elections in May 1988.

Not surprisingly, the "Barschel affair" completely dominated the spring campaign, and the vote received by the CDU declined from 42.6 percent in 1987 to 33.3 percent in 1988. The SPD, on the other hand, increased its vote from 45.2 percent to its first absolute majority of 54.8 percent. The FDP, which had hoped to gain votes in comparison with 1987, failed to pass the 5 percent barrier, as did the Greens. Björn Engholm became the first SPD prime minister in thirty-eight years.[38]

By the time the election of 1992 was held, the SPD could no longer expect to benefit from the "scandal bonus," and it received 46.2 percent. This figure was still historically very high and enough to give the party an absolute majority of the *Landtag* largely because the Greens, with 4.97 percent, barely missed passing the 5 percent barrier. In spite of the SPD's losses, the CDU did no better than in 1988 with 33.8 percent. Engholm, who had assumed a national leadership role in the SPD, became prime minister again, but a year later he and one of his ministers were forced to resign owing to additional revelations concerning the "Barschel affair." The Minister of Finance, Heidi Simonis, replaced Engholm as prime minister, and by the time the 1996 elections were held she had made quite an impression as a successful and ambitious "Powerfrau."[39] While far more popular than her challenger from the CDU, she could not prevent her party from receiving only 39.8 percent of the vote while the CDU gained 3.4 percent to reach 37.2 percent. The Greens increased their proportion of the vote to 8.1 percent, and the FDP entered the *Landtag* again with 5.7 percent. These results meant that a coalition government would be necessary, and only the SPD had a realistic chance of forming a government. With some reservations owing to a number of differences in policy positions, especially regarding highway construction, the SPD joined with the Greens.[40]

Toward the end of 1999, it looked as though the CDU would have a very good chance of becoming the strongest party again after twelve years in opposition and recapturing the prime ministership with its leading candidate, former defense minister Volker Rühe. The SPD and Greens had lost a significant percentage of votes in a series of *Land* elections following the federal election of September 1998, and there was no reason to believe the losses sustained elsewhere would not occur in Schleswig-Holstein as well. But the party finance scandal involving former Chancellor Helmut Kohl broke in December 1999, and the favorable prospects of the CDU suddenly turned bleak. The elections in Schleswig-Holstein were the first *Land* elections to take place after the scandal broke, so a great deal of attention – even from American newspapers – was devoted to the elections.[41]

The CDU lost votes, but not as many as expected, receiving 35.2 percent as opposed to 37.2 percent in 1996. The SPD received 43.1 percent, 3.3 percent more than its proportion of the 1996 vote (39.8 percent). The FDP improved its position also by almost 2 percentage points, receiving 7.6 percent in contrast to 5.7 percent in 1996. The Greens dropped from 8.1 percent in 1996 to 6.2 percent in 2000, which was the same percentage loss as the FDP's gain. The Danish minority party, SSW, improved its position rather dramatically, receiving 4.1 percent as opposed to 2.5 percent in 1996 which was also more than it normally receives. Neither the PDS on the far left nor the NPD on the far right received significant

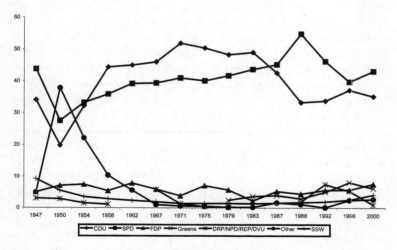

Figure 9.8   **Election results in Schleswig-Holstein, 1947–2000**
Source: www.wahlrecht.de/landtage

support (1.4 and 1.0 percent, respectively), and three other small splinter parties received a total of 1.5 percent. Thirty days after the election, the SPD and the Greens formed a new coalition government headed again by Heide Simonis, still the only female prime minister in the sixteen German *Länder* (figure 9.8).[42]

The city-states

Bremen

Bremen (which includes Bremerhaven), an old Hanseatic League city-state like Hamburg, is the smallest in population of the sixteen German *Länder*. It is also one of the three former West German *Länder* (together with Hamburg and Bavaria) that existed long before 1933, when the then existing German states were dissolved by Hitler. For more than four decades after the war, the SPD was the hegemonic party. Not until the 1990s did it become merely the strongest party, in part because of the emergence of the Greens. In 1991, when it lost 12 percentage points, it was forced to form a coalition government. It did so with both the Greens and the FDP, which had received 11.4 and 9.5 percent, respectively.[43]

Owing to strong conflicts within the cabinet, particularly between FDP and Greens,[44] new elections were called for under the newly revised constitution. The results of the May 1995 elections were that the SPD received slightly more, the CDU slightly less, than one-third of the vote, the Greens gained almost 2 points to reach 13.1 percent, and the FDP failed to clear the 5 percent barrier. On the other hand, a new party, "Jobs for Bremen and Bremerhaven" (AFB), formed only a few months before the election by leaders who were interested in promoting a nonpartisan coalition to deal more effectively with the serious economic and fiscal problems confronting the city, received a remarkable 10.7 percent.

The Lord Mayor, Klaus Wedemeier, resigned the day after the election and was succeeded as the result of an unprecedented selection by vote of party members by former Minister (*Senator*) of Education and Justice, Henning Scherf. Negotiation between SPD and CDU then led to the formation of a grand coalition between the two parties. Each party received four ministers in the cabinet, and both parties agreed to the necessity of reducing the extemely high public debt and bringing some order to the city state's finances.[45]

In spite of the closing of a major shipbuilder in 1996, Bremen achieved above- average economic growth after 1995, success in reducing the debt,

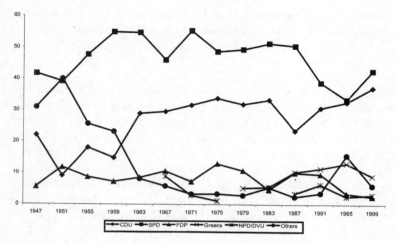

Figure 9.9   **Election results in Bremen, 1947–99**
Source: www.wahlrecht.de/landtage

and success in attracting new business to the city; however, high unemployment remained a serious issue. Still, the population had become more optimistic, and the prospects of the AFB had declined dramatically by the time the September 1999 elections were held. Though his party preferred an SPD–Green coalition, Scherf made clear he wanted a renewal of the grand coalition with the CDU. The CDU had demonstrated government competence in the ministries it controlled, and polls showed the voters liked Scherf and the SPD but thought the CDU was more competent in dealing with some of the major issues, especially the economy. The CDU campaigned for a renewal of the grand coalition, while the SPD hoped for an absolute majority.[46]

In spite of the lowest voter turnout (60.1 percent) since the Second World War, the results of the election were an increase of over 9 percent for the SPD to 42.6 percent and of 4.5 percent for the CDU to a high of 37.1 percent.[47] The Greens campaigned against a grand coalition and for an SPD–Green coalition and lost clearly, receiving 8.9 percent. The FDP warned precisely against such an alliance in its campaign and still received only 2.5 percent, about the same as the AFB.[48]

Although a Red–Green coalition would have been possible, Scherf announced on the evening of the election that the grand coalition would be continued with the goal of "saving" Bremen from those who would like to see it consolidated into Lower Saxony. The SPD and CDU agreed to reduce the size of parliament from 100 to 80 over the next four years and to continue to focus on the economy and city finances (figure 9.9).[49]

Hamburg

As in Bremen, the SPD has been the dominant party in Hamburg since the end of the war; however, the CDU has been able on three occasions (including 1953, when it was part of a larger alliance) to gain more votes than the SPD, though, unlike the SPD, never an absolute majority. In June 1982 and June 1986 the CDU received 0.5 percent and 0.2 percent more than the SPD but was unable to form a coalition; the SPD was also unable to form a coalition with either the CDU or the Greens.[50] In each case new elections had to be called in which the CDU lost votes and the SPD regained a relative majority. In 1991 the CDU declined further to 35.1 percent, and the SPD gained more votes to reach 48 percent. After the 1991 election, a CDU member, Markus Wegner, complained before the courts that the CDU had been nominating its candidates in an undemocratic and therefore illegal manner, and in 1993 the Hamburg Constitutional Court agreed. The parliament was forced to dissolve itself, and new elections were called for September 1993.[51]

Following his success in court, Wegner announced that he would form a new voter group that would be against the party-dominated politics of the past. Common sense and citizen expertise rather than party dogma and discipline would be stressed. Thus he named his new group the *STATT-Partei*, literally the "instead-of-party." Its slogan was "Citizen responsibility *instead of* party power." There was no need to take stands on controversial issues, such as the city debt, housing, crime, or unemployment; solutions to such problems would be found by engaging normal citizens in the political process, including measures of direct elections and direct democracy.[52]

The CDU, of course, was on the defensive as the party whose practices had led to the early election which a majority of people opposed. As expected, its fortunes declined sharply, and it lost 10 points, reaching an all-time low of 25 percent. The SPD also lost 7.6 percent, down to 40.4 percent. The Greens, led by a candidate who had defeated her more left-wing female opponent, increased their vote by 6.3 points to 13.9 percent. The FDP failed to clear the 5 percent barrier, but the new *STATT* Party entered the parliament with 5.6 percent of the vote.[53]

While a variety of coalition options for the SPD were available, the Lord Mayor, Henning Voscherau, made it clear he preferred a coalition with the *STATT* Party. His party, however, favored a coalition with the Greens, and Voscherau was forced to enter negotiations with them. Unable to reach agreement with the Greens on fundamental issues, negotiations with the *STATT* Party were begun and a cooperation agreement reached according to which the *STATT* Party would not join a coalition but would receive two cabinet positions for independents with expertise. It also received promises by the SPD to introduce a number of direct democratic practices, cuts in expenditures, and a reduction in the number of cabinet positions.[54]

After the new government was formed in 1993, there were, as expected,numerous conflicts between the SPD and the *STATT* Party. In 1996 the parliament gave up its formal part-time status and, like all of the other *Land* parliaments, became a full-time professional parliament. One result, of course, was considerably more compensation for the deputies. By 1997 the economy was somewhat better than average in Hamburg, but unemployment and crime were persistent problems. Only about one-third of the electorate expressed satisfaction with government performance, and the SPD–*STATT* Party cooperation agreement was not viewed with favor. Indeed, voters preferred either a Red–Green or a grand coalition, not another agreement with the *STATT* Party.[55]

Some saw the September 1997 election in Hamburg as a test election for the national level a year later, and both the CDU and SPD had high hopes that they could give their parties a boost. Mayor Voscherau retained majority support in the polls, but only about one-third of the voters were satisfied with government performance. The results of the election were not particularly favorable for either party. The SPD lost a little more than four points to 36.2 percent, the CDU gained 5.7 points to 30.7 percent, still far below their results in 1991 or the 1980s. The Greens continued to improve their standing, but only slightly, to 13.9 percent, the highest percentage the Greens had received in any state or national election to that time. The *STATT* Party failed to pass the 5 percent barrier, as did the FDP and the numerous small parties that participated in the election. With 4.9 percent the right-wing DVU barely missed clearing the 5 percent hurdle; however, together with the Reps and NPD the far-right parties received a total of 6.8 percent of the vote, even though they failed to gain any seats. Accepting responsibility for the SPD losses, Henning Voscherau resigned as lord mayor. Ortwin Runde succeeded him and formed a coalition with the Greens.[56]

Those who thought the failure of the *STATT* Party to win any seats in 1997 meant the return to political party "normalcy" were shocked on 23

September 23 2001, when a brand new party, the "party for a rule of law offensive" (PRO, i.e., *Partei Rechtsstaatliche Offensive*), emerged suddenly in the city election to win almost 20 percent of the vote, the most ever received by a "flash party" in Germany. This party, founded by a local judge, Ronald Schill, promoted itself as the "law and order" alternative to the political establishment which had allegedly failed to protect the citizens of Hamburg from growing crime, drugs, and violence and a feeling of general insecurity, especially after the 11 September terrorist attacks in the United States. The SPD received 36.5 percent, about the same percentage as in 1997, but this was not enough to form a majority coalition government with its former partner, the Greens, who saw their vote reduced from 13.9 to 8.5 percent. On the other hand, the CDU, in spite of dropping from 30.7 percent in 1997 to 26.2 percent, was nevertheless able to think about forming a coalition with the FDP, which had re-entered the city parliament with 5.1 percent, and the upstart "Schill Party." The CDU rejected the idea of a grand coalition with the SPD.[57]

So, in spite of its rather poor showing, the CDU, under the leadership of Ole von Beust, was able to form a government with the FDP and Ronald Schill without the SPD, which had been the leading party in all coalitions in Hamburg for forty-four years.[58] Whether the "Schill Party" is a strictly temporary Hamburg phenomenon or whether it will be able to spread to other areas of Germany as it hopes to do remains to be seen (figure 9.10).

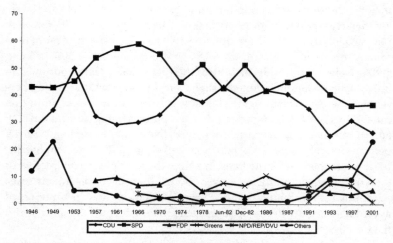

Figure 9.10   **Election results in Hamburg, 1946–2001**
Source: www.wahlrecht.de/landtage

Berlin

Berlin differs from most other *Länder* not only because it is one of three city-states but also because it combines the former West Berlin and East Berlin, which were very separate and divided cities during most of the period from 1948 to 1990. West Berlin was especially isolated and cut off from its surrounding territory by the infamous Berlin Wall which was constructed in 1961 to prevent the flow of people from East Germany to the West via Berlin. In 1990 not only were East and West Germany united, but also East and West Berlin. The result was that politics in Berlin changed dramatically, and it was no longer possible to generalize from previous experience. In some respects, Berlin has become a microcosm of the two-party systems described above, i.e., one party system in the former West Berlin, another in the former East Berlin.

From 1946 to the 1970s, the SPD was the dominant party in West Berlin. Starting in 1975, the CDU gained at first a small lead over the SPD, and then an ever-larger lead until 1989, when the two parties received virtually the same percentage of the vote. The decline in support for the SPD was due in large part to the rise of the Greens, whereas the CDU suffered a sharp decline in 1989 owing to the sudden success of the far-right Republikaner, who received 7.5 percent of the vote but never gained more than 3.1 percent after that year. From 1990 to 1999 the CDU and SPD formed a grand coalition, with the CDU as senior partner.

The election in 1999 was supposed to bring about a change in Berlin just as the federal election in 1998 had brought change at the national level. It had been difficult for the SPD to join a coalition with the CDU in 1995, at which time the SPD received its lowest percentage of votes ever in the postwar era. But with the CDU and Greens too far apart and the PDS not acceptable as a coalition partner, there was no alternative to a grand coalition. The conflicts in the coalition between the parties and the numerous problems confronting the city led to considerable public dissatisfaction with the performance of the government in spite of its successes, for example, in putting its finances in order and introducing territorial and administrative reforms along with implementing a reduction in the size of parliament. But several major projects were not realized, e.g., the construction of a new airport and consolidation with the surrounding state of Brandenburg; unemployment remained high, and economic growth was the lowest in all of Germany.[59]

The continuing deindustrialization of Berlin has resulted in a decline in the traditional base for the SPD. The SPD also suffered from its reputation as a party of patronage and personal favoritism. Nevertheless, the SPD had reason to hope for more support after its success in the national elections in 1998. But the change in the political climate in Germany by the beginning of 1999 and mistakes during the campaign led to the party's lowest percentage of the vote (22.4 percent) in a *Land* election since 1950 and failure to win a single direct seat.[60]

The CDU not only benefited from the change in the national political climate but also from the popularity of the Lord Mayor, Eberhard Diepgen. Diepgen enjoyed the support of a unified party, while the SPD was divided by personality, by the participation of the party in a grand coalition with the CDU which made it difficult for it to be too critical of the cuts its own finance minister had made to consolidate the city's finances, and by attacks from unions and the leftist PDS. The CDU received 49.3 percent in West Berlin but only 26.9 percent in the East for a total of 40.8 percent of second votes.[61]

The Greens also suffered from the changed political climate. There was considerable dissension in the party over German involvement in Kosovo, but the party focused its campaign on its leading female candidate and ended up receiving 9.9 percent of the vote, or 3.3 percent less than in 1995. The FDP's efforts to get CDU voters to give it their second vote were largely ignored, and the Reps did not play a major role in the campaign in spite of the withdrawal of the DVU in its favor. Neither party received the requisite 5 percent. The PDS, next to the CDU the major victor in the 1999 elections, gained 17.7 percent of the vote, up 3.1 percent from 1995.[62]

In West Berlin after unification in 1990 the CDU enjoyed generally stable support of around 50 percent , while the Greens and the PDS improved their standings by a few percentage points. The SPD and FDP lost about 4 or 5 percent each. In East Berlin the CDU gained about 5 percentage points, while the SPD dropped from about one-third to less than one-fifth of the vote. The FDP and Greens also suffered sharp declines. The PDS increased its vote from about one-fourth to almost 40 percent, becoming the largest party in the East. By the election of 1999 the results for Berlin as a whole were that the FDP was no longer in the parliament, while the PDS, with increasing numbers of seats, was not a viable coalition partner for either the SPD or CDU, and the Greens could hardly coalesce with the CDU. This left a grand coalition between the CDU and a reluctant SPD as the only alternative for a functioning government.[63] However, in June 2001 the SPD withdrew from the grand coalition owing to a financial scandal involving a publicly owned bank in Berlin that was managed by a member of the CDU. After joining with the Greens and

PDS against the CDU in a vote of no-confidence, the SPD, under the leadership of Klaus Wowereit, formed a minority government with the Greens with the toleration of the PDS. Soon thereafter the parliament agreed to call for new elections on 21 October 2001.[64]

The results of the election for the CDU were disastrous. It received 23.8 percent, or a loss of 17.1 percent from its best result ever in 1999, the largest loss it had ever suffered in a *Land* election since 1945 and the largest any party has suffered since 1950. It lost its only 2 direct seats in East Berlin and most of its direct seats in West Berlin, where it had dominated during the 1990s. Its leading candidate, Frank Steffel, had ranked a distant third, behind the SPD's Klaus Wowereit and the PDS's Gregor Gysi, when the public was polled about their choice for mayor. Though in a coalition government with the SPD until June of 2001, the CDU was blamed far more than the SPD for the severe financial problems of the city, which at the end of 2001 had a debt of DM 80 billion (about 40 billion Euros).[65]

The SPD gained 7.3 percent and ended up with 29.7 percent. The PDS also gained 4.9 percent, which, at 22.6 percent, was only about 1 percent less than the CDU's total. In East Berlin the PDS came close to an absolute majority, and it enjoyed widespread support among young people and the better educated. With 9.9 percent, the FDP was also a big winner, returning to the parliament which it had failed to enter for the past six years. The Greens received 9.1 percent which, while only a slight reduction from 1999, was the seventeenth electoral loss in a row for them in *Land* elections.[66]

The question after the election was what kind of coalition government should be formed. An SPD–CDU coalition would have a majority in the parliament, but the SPD and its mayoral candidate, Klaus Wowereit, were no longer willing to share power with the CDU. That left two alternatives: a so-called "traffic light coalition" (*Ampelkoalition*) made up of the SPD (Red), FDP (Yellow), and Greens, or a Red–Red coalition of SPD and PDS. The charismatic leader of the PDS, Gregor Gysi, argued that only with its participation could the deep division of the city be overcome. In the meantime the national leadership of the SPD, including Chancellor Schröder, made known their preference for a Red–Yellow–Green coalition.[67]

By the beginning of December 2001, it was clear that a traffic light coalition would not be formed, because the FDP rejected tax increases favored by the SPD and Greens. Especially the Greens and the FDP disagreed sharply on other issues as well. As a result the SPD began negotiations with the PDS, and the SPD national leadership signaled its approval in spite of its doubts about the PDS position on various issues, including its

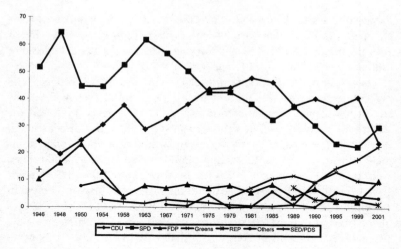

Figure 9.11   **Election results in Berlin, 1946–2001**
Source: www.wahlrecht.de/landtage

opposition to German participation in the international military actions against terrorism. Though eager to join the SPD in governing the city, the PDS was faced with the problem of having to share responsibility for cutting the budget deficit of around DM 10 billion and reducing the city's debt of DM 80 billion (figure 9.11).[68]

The five new *Länder*

Brandenburg

Before the Wall fell in November 1989, conventional wisdom held that the SPD would be the strongest party in any free election in the former East Germany. This assertion was based on voting history before 1933, especially in the industrialized areas of the East around Berlin and Saxony, and on the presumably leftist political culture inculcated by the East German regime for forty years. As it turned out, the CDU emerged as the strongest party in the first and only elections for the East German parliament (*Volkskammer*) in March 1990 – except in East Berlin – and as the strongest party in the *Land* and federal elections in the Fall of 1990 following unification. The one exception was the *Land* election in Brandenburg in 1990, when the SPD won by about 9 points.

Manfred Stolpe, a former high official of the Lutheran Church in East Germany, became the prime minister in 1990. In spite of charges raised by the CDU opposition and others – but never proved – that he had collaborated with the Communist regime, Stolpe became immensely popular in Brandenburg. This was due in part without doubt to his identification with the East, in contrast to his counterparts in the other new *Länder*, and his reputation as a fighter for Eastern interests even, if necessary, against his own national party.[69] In 1994 the SPD under Stolpe's leadership increased its lead by more than 15 points to over 54 percent, while the CDU and PDS tied at 18.7 percent.

Nevertheless, the popular assessment of the Stolpe government before the elections in 1999 was mixed. In spite of government efforts to improve economic conditions, unemployment remained high (17.4 percent in summer 1999). The poor economy had undoubtedly contributed to anti-foreigner incidents. Popular programs such as the 1000 DM "welcome money" for each newborn child had to be cancelled, but the bloated bureaucracy was not cut. Consolidation with Berlin had been rejected in a referendum in 1996 in spite of Stolpe's support,[70] and no progress was made on major infrastructure projects, such as the new airport for Berlin and Brandenburg. There had been considerable turnover in the cabinet, and controversy surrounded Welfare Minister Regine Hildebrandt's management of money. The Education Minister pushed through a "life-formation, ethics and religious studies" course that replaced the conventional religious instruction classes in the public schools in spite of the vehement opposition of the Catholic and Protestant Churches and the CDU.[71] The Minister was forced to back down in the summer before the September 1999 elections, and she resigned. But Stolpe enjoyed the benefit of an ineffective opposition by the CDU and PDS, and the CDU had received the lowest percentage of the party's vote in any *Land* in the 1998 national election.[72]

In spite of the past support for Stolpe, most voters indicated before the election that they favored change, including if necessary a grand coalition of SPD and CDU. The SPD had received only 2.5 percent more votes than the CDU in the June 1999 European Parliament elections (with only 30.1 percent voter turnout, the lowest of all the *Länder*!). The change in the political climate since the national elections in 1998 also made the SPD defensive a year later, having to fight a two-front battle against the CDU on the right and the PDS on the left. In the latter case the SPD had also to decide during the campaign whether to exclude the PDS from a possible coalition, which was an internally divisive issue. Stolpe refused to commit

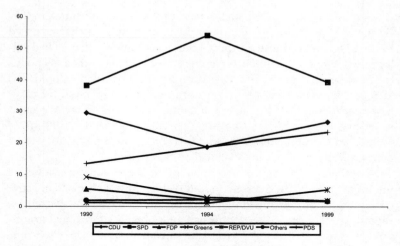

Figure 9.12   **Election results in Brandenburg, 1990–99**
Source: www.wahlrecht.de/landtage

himself one way or the other, but Welfare Minister Hildebrandt said a coalition with the CDU would be unthinkable for her.[73]

The result of the election of September 1999 was a continuation of the trend toward a concentration of the many parties that had run. A three-party system was evident, with the PDS receiving more than 20 percent for the first time. The SPD lost almost 15 percent but still emerged as the strongest party with 39.3 percent, and the CDU increased its vote by almost 8 points to 26.5 percent. The DVU, which as a "phantom party" had campaigned with slogans but hardly with candidates or an organization, received somewhat more than the required 5 percent for gaining seats in the parliament. Both the FDP and Greens received less than 2 percent.[74]

Following the election, Stolpe held negotiations with both the CDU and PDS, but he rejected the PDS offer because he said the goals of the PDS could not be financed. After strenuous negotiations with the CDU, a grand coalition was formed; however, Regine Hildebrandt refused to accept any position in the cabinet and even gave up her seat in parliament in opposition to the CDU's participation in government.[75] Manfred Stolpe, of course, remained prime minister until he stepped down in a surprise move in June 2002. He was replaced by the mayor of Potsdam and former Brandenburg cabinet minister, Matthias Platzeck (figure 9.12).[76]

Mecklenburg-Vorpommern

The elections in Mecklenburg-Vorpommern were held on the same day as the federal elections in both 1994 and 1998, so there can be little doubt about the influence of federal politics and themes in these elections. In 1990 the CDU won a plurality of the votes with 38.3 percent, followed by the SPD with a mere 27 percent. While the FDP gained entry into the parliament with 5.5 percent, the Greens did not. The PDS was the third most popular party with 15.7 percent. The combined seats of the CDU and FDP were matched by those of the SPD and PDS, so neither a coalition of CDU and FDP nor SPD and FDP would have had a majority. Then an unhappy SPD deputy joined the CDU party group, so a shaky CDU–FDP coalition was formed. However, a series of personnel problems soon plagued the CDU and the government: several CDU deputies lost their seats owing to their activities on behalf of the communist regime before unification; more than half of the cabinet ministers were relieved of their posts; the prime minister, Alfred Gomolka, was replaced in midstream by Berndt Seite; and the CDU state party chair, Günther Krause, was replaced by Angela Merkel, who was finally able to discourage the internal conflicts within the party. In the meantime the SPD, under its leader, Harald Ringstorff, presented a picture of relative unity and seriousness.[77]

In 1994 the CDU lost slightly but still retained a plurality with 37.7 percent. The SPD gained 2.5 percent, and the PDS gained 7 points. The FDP and the Greens failed to pass the 5 percent barrier. The leader of the SPD, Ringstorff, had indicated before the elections that he might be interested in the "Magdeburger Modell," i.e., the example set in Saxony-Anhalt where an SPD minority government was being "tolerated" by the PDS in parliament. He even held exploratory talks with the PDS after the election simultaneously with the CDU. But in the end, in spite of considerable tension between the two parties and, especially, between Seite and Ringstorff, the CDU and the SPD formed a grand coalition for the period 1994–98 with Seite as prime minister.[78] Relations between the parties were not good, and Ringstorff renewed discussions with the PDS, only to have the national party leaders intervene against any kind of coalition with the former communists. The result was that the CDU–SPD coalition limped along under a climate of "mutual contempt."[79]

By the summer of 1998 the national SPD leadership had decided to give Ringstorff a free hand, and the PDS made it clear that it was willing to cooperate with Ringstorff. The CDU was in a difficult situation, since on the one hand Prime Minister Seite tried to point to coalition successes,

while the CDU party group leader focused on the differences with the
SPD and its power-hungry leader. The CDU was also hurt by the general
climate in the country at the time that favored the SPD and change. The
state was known as the "poor house of the republic" and had an unemployment rate of 20 percent and in some regions over 30 percent. In addition, the CDU had to ward off charges that it wanted to repeal the land
reforms that had taken place under Russian occupation between 1946 and
1948 and return land to the former large land owners. Warning against
the "SPDS" did not have much effect. Ringstorff and the SPD could
emphasize the need for change and the need to create jobs, while the PDS
could appeal to the need for "full employment before profit."[80]

It was no surprise that the results of the election favored the SPD,
though less than one might have expected. The SPD received 34.3 percent,
the CDU 30.2 percent, and the PDS 24.4 percent. No other parties cleared
the 5 percent hurdle. After the election the SPD took up negotiations with
the CDU and PDS, but it was soon clear that it favored a coalition with the
PDS. The PDS made certain concessions, such as agreeing to a signed
statement that political forces that do not recognize the Basic Law should
have no influence on state policy making and admitting that the SED
(the Communist Party of the former East Germany) was responsible for
political injustice in the old German Democratic Republic (GDR). The
SPD, in return, agreed to stop checking backgrounds of public servants for
connections with the old regime (figure 9.13).[81]

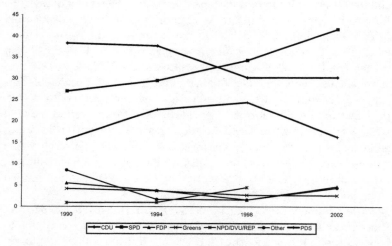

Figure 9.13   **Election results in Mecklenburg-Vorpommern, 1990–98**
Source: www.wahlrecht.de/landtage

Saxony

In spite of its reputation gained during the Weimar Republic of being a socialist stronghold, Saxony was the only state in the East to give the CDU an absolute majority in the 1990 elections. Kurt Biedenkopf, a longtime member of the *Bundestag* and state legislature in North-Rhine West-phalia, General Secretary of the CDU in the mid-1970s, and state party chair, had gone to the University of Leipzig as a guest professor in March 1990 and become the CDU candidate for prime minister in the October 1990 state elections. His leadership proved decisive then and later.[82]

Being matched in popularity only by Prime Minister Manfred Stolpe in Brandenburg, Biedenkopf and the CDU could face the elections in 1994 with confidence. Indeed, the CDU's 58.1 percent was the highest percentage of the vote ever received by the CDU in a state election and was exceeded only by the CSU in Bavaria in the mid-to-late 1970s and early 1980s. The SPD lost 2.5 points and dropped down to 16.6 percent, while the PDS gained 6.3 points to tie the SPD. Neither the FDP nor the Greens received the required 5 percent to return to the parliament.[83] As in 1990, the CDU formed a government alone with Biedenkopf as prime minister.

The CDU did not do so well in Saxony in the federal election of September 1998, but it rebounded in the European elections in June 1999. At the time of the state elections in September 1999, the CDU was at a high point and the SPD at a low point because of the national political climate. The state CDU, the "Saxon Union," could point to several successes as well: Saxony was in fourth place nation-wide in the number of jobs per 1,000 inhabitants; no other state had so many self-employed or so few public employees; and it had the fewest people receiving public assistance. The only question was whether the SPD or the PDS would come in second. The CDU victory, with 56.9 percent of the vote, was expected; however, the success of the PDS in gaining another 5.6 points to reach 22.2 percent and the decline in support for the SPD from 16.6 to 10.7 percent were not expected. This was the lowest percentage of votes for the SPD in any state election since 1949. In spite of the influence of federal politics on the outcome, it was clear that Prime Minister Biedenkopf had been a key factor in the "Saxon Union's" victory.[84]

But Biedenkopf turned 70 in 2000, and he appeared to resist the idea of a "crown prince." Indeed, internal conflict between Biedenkopf and others plagued the CDU in 2000 and 2001. Nevertheless, Biedenkopf was succeeded in May 2002 by Georg Milbradt, a long-serving CDU minister of finance in Biedenkopf's cabinet (figure 9.14).[85]

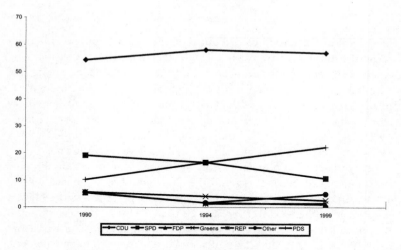

Figure 9.14   **Election results in Saxony, 1990–99**
Source: www.wahlrecht.de/landtage

Saxony-Anhalt

Politics in Saxony-Anhalt have been more tumultuous since 1990 than in any of the other new or old states. In the first election in 1990, the CDU received a plurality with 39 percent of the vote and formed a coalition with the FDP, which had received 13.5 percent.[86] The SPD had received 26 percent, the Greens 5.3 percent, and the PDS 12 percent. Less than a year after the coalition government was formed under Prime Minister Gerd Gies, who had emerged from the pre-unification East CDU, Gies was replaced by Werner Münch, who had been serving as finance minister and was from the West. Two years later Münch and his cabinet resigned over charges that he and several cabinet ministers had arranged excessive compensation packages for themselves. In November 1993 Münch was replaced by the CDU party group leader, Christoph Bergner, while the SPD and Greens demanded new elections. The FDP was divided over new elections, but soon after Bergner was elected prime minister in December with FDP support, elections were called for June 1994 before, rather than after, the summer vacation time.[87]

With a decline of 10.3 percent to 54.8 percent, the lowest voter turnout figure in any state election in Germany since the war, the CDU still received a plurality with 34.4 percent, followed closely by the SPD with 34 percent. The Greens squeaked through with 5.1 percent, whereas the FDP lost almost 10 points and fell to 3.6 percent. The PDS was able to gain almost 8 points to reach 19.9 percent. On the morning after the election, both Bergner and the SPD's leading candidate, Reinhard Höppner, laid claim to the right to form a cabinet. A minority government seemed inevitable, since the SPD ruled out a grand coalition with the CDU and the CDU had no other potential coalition partners. The SPD, like the CDU, also rejected the idea of a coalition with the PDS. That left the possibility of a minority SPD government with the Greens tolerated by the PDS, which had indicated its willingness to play such a role. A coalition government with Höppner as prime minister was formed, and the CDU became the opposition party with Christoph Bergner as party group leader.[88]

The state election in April 1998 took place under unusual circumstances in that for the first time since the war a government was up for reelection that had not had a majority throughout the legislative term but had depended, instead, on the toleration of the PDS. This had become known as the "Magdeburg Model," named after the state's capital city. This had inspired the CDU to initiate a campaign in 1994 against the SPD–PDS "red socks," but the campaign was not very effective. The SPD–Green government had been unable to do much to reduce unemployment, which was the highest in the country, and it had accumulated a huge debt, the largest on a *per capita* basis in Germany. The Greens were frustrated over their limited influence in the government and divided over the proper course to follow. The CDU had been obstructionist during the first two years of the legislative term, but then it realized its strategy merely encouraged more cooperation between the government and PDS. After discussions with the government, the CDU took a somewhat more cooperative stance after 1996 and actually supported the government on some occasions. A CDU-sponsored vote of no confidence was rejected by all three of the other parties. The PDS had demonstrated its dependability by tolerating the government in parliament, but it also ignored any sense of fiscal responsibility by demanding increased funds for teachers and local government social services.[89]

Since the election was only five months before the national elections in September, many prominent federal politicians appeared during the campaign, the main theme of which was unemployment. The CDU tried to tie unemployment to the "Magdeburg Model," but the polls showed that most dissatisfaction about the economy was directed at the federal government under Helmut Kohl. The CDU rejected a new "red socks" campaign, but it did focus on cooperation between the SPD and PDS. Prime Minister Höppner rejected the idea of a grand coalition after the election as well as a coalition with the PDS. But he also rejected demands by the Greens and PDS that he drop his economics minister who had good relations with the CDU. The PDS could not really campaign as a normal opposition party, because it had tolerated the government thoughout the legislative term. This had apparently led to some confusion in the party.[90]

The results of the election were dramatic. Not because the CDU lost more than 12 points and received only 22 percent of the vote, not because the Greens failed to return to parliament and the FDP again failed to pass the 5 percent barrier, not because the SPD gained a little less than 2 points at 35.9 percent, and not because the PDS remained stagnant with 19.6 percent. The sensational and unexpected development was the explosion of votes for the far-right DVU, which jumped from 1.3 percent in 1994 to 13.6 percent in 1998. The party's massive campaign spending in the last few days before the election had obviously paid off. With slogans such as "German Workplaces for German Workers," "Expel Criminal Foreigners Immediately," and "Save the D-Mark!" (a reference to the Euro), the DVU appealed as a protest party to a young, especially male, xenophobic proletariat in spite of a mere 1.8 percent foreign population in the state.[91] This success was less attributable to CDU voters switching to the DVU than to a significant increase in voter turnout (54.8 to 71.7 percent), which stands in sharp contrast to Brandenburg, Saxony, and Thuringia. Indeed, 28 percent of all new voters gave their votes to the DVU.[92]

It was again apparent that a single party could not form a majority government, and it was apparent that the new party in parliament, the DVU, was even less acceptable as a coalition partner for the SPD – or CDU – than the PDS. After unsuccessful talks with the CDU, Prime Minister Höppner again rejected both a grand coalition[93] and a coalition with the PDS, which left as the only option a return to the simple toleration of an SPD government by the PDS. Attacked by the CDU for being soft on the PDS, Gerhard Schröder, the Chancellor candidate for the SPD in the upcoming federal elections, tried to get Höppner to form a grand coalition, but Höppner refused, thus increasing his popularity in the state. The SPD was in a stronger position than before, because as long as the PDS abstained, it could outvote the CDU and DVU together. This was seen as an inducement for the CDU to be more cooperative, since it did not want to be associated in fundamental opposition with the DVU.[94]

In 2002 elections were again held in Saxony-Anhalt five months before the federal elections, and with devastating results for the SPD. Voter turnout was 56.5 percent, down more than 15 points from 1998, and neither the previously successful DVU, the Greens, nor the "Schill Party" received the 5 percent required for admission to the parliament. But the FDP did gain seats, with a sensational 13.3 percent, and the CDU saw its support rise from 22 to 37.3 percent. The SPD, on the other hand, dropped from 35.9 to 20 percent, mirroring the CDU's loss in the previous *Land* election in Berlin. The PDS experienced a slight gain of 0.8 percent to 20.4 percent, which put it in second place, as in Saxony. The SPD blamed its loss on its leader, Reinhard Höppner, high unemployment, and the "Magdeburg model," while the CDU saw its success tied to the dissatisfaction with the policies of Chancellor Gerhard Schröder, high unemployment, and the SPD's party finance scandal in Cologne which pushed the older scandal involving former Chancellor Kohl into the background. In any case the results were a very bad omen for the SPD in the upcoming federal elections, and, more to the point, the SPD lost its working majority in the *Bundesrat* with the gain of four votes for the CDU–FDP coalition government led by Wolfgang Böhmer (figure 9.15).[95]

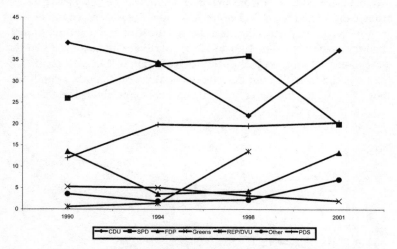

Figure 9.15   **Election results in Saxony-Anhalt, 1990–2001**
Source: www.wahlrecht.de/landtage

Thuringia

Like the other new *Länder*, excluding Brandenburg, the CDU received the most votes in the first state election in 1990; however, only in Thuringia and Saxony did the CDU remain the leading party in 1994 and 1999.

Following the 1990 elections, the native East German, Josef Duchac, formed a coalition government with the FDP. Duchac was prime minister for only fourteen months, however, owing to revelations of his past involvement with the Communist regime. In 1992 he was replaced by Bernhard Vogel, who was the former CDU prime minister of Rhineland-Palatinate and the only state prime minister since 1945 to hold that office in two different states. In 1994 the FDP and Greens both failed to receive the required 5 percent of the vote, and, as in the other eastern *Länder*, a three-party system emerged with the CDU, SPD, and PDS gaining seats in the parliament. Though by far the largest of the three, the CDU needed a coalition partner, and it formed a government with the SPD from 1994 to 1999.[96]

In contrast to Mecklenburg-Vorpommern, the grand coalition in Thuringia was not controversial. The SPD leadership never considered either a toleration model or a coalition with the PDS, relations between the two coalition partners remained relatively good, and the PDS faced a united cabinet and a relatively quiet legislative session. Favored by geography over some of its counterparts, Thuringia enjoyed the strongest economic growth of all the new states from 1991 to 1998. Together with Saxony, it had the most industrial jobs, and its unemployment rate of 15.1 percent in July 1999 was the lowest in the East. Its public debt, on the other hand, was above average for the states. Nevertheless, concerns about the economy,

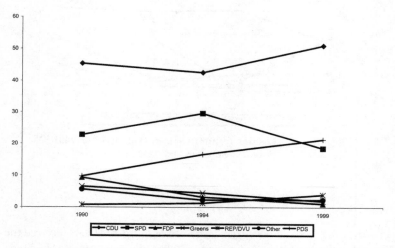

Figure 9.16   **Election results in Thuringia, 1990–99**
Source: www.wahlrecht.de/landtage

jobs, social justice, education, crime, and traffic were major issues. According to the polls, Vogel and the CDU enjoyed more public confidence in their competence to deal with these issues than did the SPD or PDS.[97]

As in Brandenburg, the SPD suffered in the 1999 *Land* elections from the declining popularity of the SPD–Green government in Bonn, it could not criticize effectively the government of which it had been a partner, and its leading candidate could hardly challenge seriously the popular CDU prime minister. The result was an absolute majority of votes for the CDU, which won all 44 direct seats. The SPD lost 11 points, fell below its 1990 vote, and, for the first time in one of the new *Länder*, received fewer votes than the PDS. The PDS, with 21.3 percent, gained almost 5 percent over 1994. No other party cleared the 5 percent barrier (figure 9.16).[98]

Summary

Since elections in one or more of the *Länder* take place every year, only a kind of temporary snapshot of the array of leading parties and governments can be made at any particular time. Table 9.1 presents the governing parties and prime ministers of the *Länder* as of summer 2002. The Christian Democrats governed alone in four *Länder*, together with the FDP in three *Länder*, and with the FDP and PRO in one *Land*. The SPD governed alone in only one *Land* and together with the CDU in two *Länder*, with the Greens in two *Länder*, with the FDP in one *Land*, and with the PDS in two *Länder*.

These variations show clearly both the volatility of *Land* elections and the "promiscuity" of the two major parties in forming governments.[99]

Are *Land* elections "partial" federal elections?

As in other federal systems, a recurring question in Germany is the extent to which the elections in the *Länder* reflect more the popular assessment of political developments and policies of the individual *Länder* governments or of the federal government. In the United States one general school of thought centers around the idea that state gubernatorial elections are basically national referenda which express approval or disapproval of the sitting president and his policies, especially in terms of the economy. Another school suggests that voters focus on the performance of the incumbent governor and the state of the regional economy. In any

Table 9.1   **Governments in the *Länder* (as of November 2002)**

Länder governed by the CDU or CSU alone:	Bavaria since 1996	Prime Minister Edmund Stoiber
	Saxony since 1990	Prime Minister Kurt Biedenkopf (since 5/2002, Georg Milbradt)
	Saarland since 1999	Prime Minister Peter Müller
	Thuringia since 1990	Prime Minister Bernhard Vogel
Länder with CDU/FDP coalition governments:	Baden-Württemberg since 1996	Prime Minister Erwin Teufel
	Hesse since 1999	Prime Minister Roland Koch
	Saxony-Anhalt since 2002	Prime Minister Wolfgang Böhmer
	Lower Saxony since 2003	Prime Minister Christian Wulff
Länder with CDU/FDP/ PRO coalition government:	Hamburg since 2001	Lord Mayor Ole von Beust
Länder with SPD/CDU coalition governments:	Bremen since 1995	Lord Mayor Henning Scherf
	Brandenburg since 1999	Prime Minister Manfred Stolpe (since 6/2002, Matthias Platzeck)
Länder with SPD/Green coalition governments:	North-Rhine Westphalia since 1995	Prime Minister Wolfgang Clement (since 11/2002, Peer Steinbrück)
	Schleswig-Holstein since 1996	Prime Minister Heide Simonis
Länder with SPD/FDP coalition governments:	Rhineland-Palatinate since 1991	Prime Minister Kurt Beck
Länder with SPD/PDS coalition governments:	Mecklenburg-Vorpommern since 1998	Prime Minister Harald Ringstorff
	Berlin since 2002	Lord Mayor Klaus Wowereit

case state contests are affected by news media which focus on national and international events, and the national political parties exercise some influence in the states through their funding and assistance in state campaigns. It also seems clear that evaluations of the president and the national and international environment can lead to a form of referendum voting in the states. On the other hand, incumbent governors, like incumbent politicians in Congress, are not easily defeated.[100]

Rainer Dinkel, who has studied the relationship between *Land* elections and federal influences, found that in sixty-five of sixty-seven *Land* elections the federal government coalition received less support than expected based on federal election results. He also cited polls showing that public support for the federal government tended to be higher shortly after and shortly before federal elections, i.e., the federal coalition parties were likely to lose votes in the *Länder* especially at mid-term. The reduced support was due especially to floating voters who expressed their judgment of federal policies by voting against the federal coalition in *Land* elections. Lack of support of the federal coalition might also be seen in the lower voter turnout in *Land* elections. He did not find, in contrast to some other scholars,[101] that *Land* elections could be seen as a barometer that measured the strength of the federal government and opposition parties. It is clear, however, that *Land* elections, like European Parliament elections, are barometer elections in so far as they can and do send signals to the federal government.[102] Dinkel's general conclusion was that both federal and *Land* politics were factors in *Land* elections.[103]

The German scholar who is probably most identified with the question of the relationships between federal and *Land* politics, Georg Fabritius,[104] has offered a useful set of hypotheses about federal politics and elections in the *Länder*. First, he suggests that *Land* elections have not been purely *Land*-based since the founding of the Federal Republic. Like a number of other observers, he notes the federal themes taken up by the political parties in *Land* elections, the appearance of national political leaders in the *Land* during campaigns, the joint membership of *Land* political leaders in *Land* and national party committees, and the difficulty voters have in distinguishing between federal and *Land* politics.[105] For example, the economic conditions in a *Land*, as is generally the case for an American state, have more to do with federal than *Land* policies, yet the state of the economy can have a powerful influence on a *Land* (or, in the United States, state) election.

The second thesis is that in spite of the influence of federal politics, the themes of *Land* politics are also important. The popularity of the prime minister is a key variable, and *Land* politics, for example, policies regarding schools, teachers, and curricula have become major issues over the years. But the popularity of the prime minister sinks when his party at the federal level is held in lower esteem. Fabritius argues, furthermore, that the "normal vote" is more likely to be seen in *Land* elections, because federal elections exaggerate support or opposition. This "normality" exists especially when there is no protest against federal policies. Like Dinkel, he

also suggests that *Land* election results hardly carry over to the next federal election or vice versa, when the elections do not take place too closely
to each other.[106] While there may be some evidence for the hypothesis that
the popularity of the prime minister suffers when his party at the federal
level is held in low esteem, a counterexample would be the Bavarian election of 1998 which was held only a few months before the federal election.
In this election the prime minister remained very popular, and the CSU
actually picked up additional votes in spite of the national party's weakness. It also seems clear that the personal appeal of the prime ministers in
the Eastern *Länder* is a crucial factor in explaining election results in
Brandenburg, Thuringia, and Saxony.[107]

Thirdly, Fabritius argues that the degree of federal influence on the
results of elections in the *Länder* varies and is greatest in crisis periods.
Then *Land* elections most clearly have the character of protest elections,
where there is a kind of referendum for or against federal policies. He
notes that the chief beneficiary of the protest is not necessarily the major
opposition party; instead, it is frequently a protest party or group that
may have just formed or been relatively dormant.[108] Examples in the mid-
to-late 1960s would be the rightist NPD and the *Ausserparlamentarische
Opposition* (*APO*) or extra-parliamentary opposition which consisted
especially of radical left students, the Greens from the late 1970s throughout the 1980s, the right-wing Reps and DVU in the 1980s and 1990s, and
the PDS in the East in the 1990s and after 2000.

Land elections are also more likely to take on the characteristics of
protest elections when they occur at mid-term, i.e., not too soon before
or after a federal election. Here they may be seen as a kind of plebiscite –
though an unclear one – for or against the federal government, or, in any
case, as a kind of barometer or measurement of the current political
climate. Voters can abstain or vote for a different party and still return to
their normal party in the federal election, which also applies to elections
for the European Parliament. Thus there appears to be more solidarity
with one's normal party in federal elections.[109] If this is true, though, it
seems inconsistent with Fabritius' previous assertion that *Land* elections
are the more "normal" elections. Indeed, a recent empirical study, which
otherwise generally confirms Dinkel's and Fabritius' hypotheses above,
lends strong support to the argument that federal elections reflect more
the "normal" vote.[110]

The fourth hypothesis is that the "coordination" between *Land* elections
and federal politics which exists to some extent is the result of the interlocking relations (*Politikverflechtung*) between and among the *Länder* and

the federation and the German party state. Thus the division of power between the federation and the *Länder* does not mean a separation in terms of policies or parties. The thesis of the "unitary federal state" is confirmed in *Land* elections. Party images are set by the federal parties, but there is a strong mutual dependence between the federal and *Land* parties. Most obviously the *Länder* are closely associated with federal politics via the *Bundesrat*.[111] This is reflected in a clever CDU campaign advertisement in the 1958 *Land* elections in Hesse:

Deine Wahl in Hessenstaat
zählt im Bonner Bundesrat.
Regierung Zinn stützt Ollenauer,
wählt CDU für Adenauer.

A somewhat related theme to Fabritius' last hypothesis has been developed by Gerhard Lehmbruch, who suggests that there is an incongruence between the German party system and the federal system. The British parties form a strong party system which leads to majority rule, i.e., the "Westminster parliamentary system" of strong, disciplined party government under the leadership of the prime minister with little necessity of bargaining between Government and Opposition. The strong German parties, in contrast, are forced to bargain because of cooperative federalism or the *Politikverflechtung* which exists between the federation and the *Länder* and the role of the *Länder* in the *Bundesrat*. The German party system, therefore, is unable to provide the kind of party government found in Great Britain, but must, instead, engage in a highly complex system of bargaining and consensus politics. This can and does lead to blockage, which can frustrate decision makers who are held accountable by the public for their political promises. As a result, the federal cabinet ministers try to work with *Land* politicians to support their policies, while the Opposition leaders do the opposite.[112]

In a recent empirical study of the relationship between federal and *Land* elections, Charlie Jeffery and Daniel Hough note that evidence of a cyclical pattern of support for the main political parties and the national level is now commonplace. Examples are mid-term congressional elections in the United States and other "second-order" elections such as the European Parliament elections in the EU member states.[113] Following a review of the literature and data, and focusing especially on the findings of Rainer Dinkel, cited above, the authors conclude that the data for 1949–90 generally support Dinkel's picture of

Land elections as 'subordinate', or second-order elections subject to an electoral cycle whose turning points were set by the rhythm of the federal rather
than the Länder electoral arenas. Incumbency in federal government was
punished, especially at mid-term. The main federal opposition party held
up its vote share better, on occasion doing significantly better than expected,
while the gamut of smaller parties, apparently benefiting from voter experimentation when less was at stake, generally did well.[114]

They also note the importance of voter turnout as a factor in explaining
Land election results. Turnout is generally considerably lower in *Land* elections, as it is in European Parliament elections, which punishes government
parties that fail to mobilize "their broadly contented supporters when less
is at stake," hurts opposition parties less "as their voters are typically willing
to get out and make a point," and reduces barriers to smaller parties, "especially those capable of mobilizing a concerted protest vote."[115]

When they looked at the data for the period from 1990 to 1998, however, Jeffery and Hough reached somewhat different conclusions. The
trend since 1990 of increasingly lower turnout in *Land* elections appears
to be associated with reduced support for both the government and
opposition parties, so that "the success of small parties suggests less of
an anti-government effect post-unity than a more indiscriminate effect
penalising the wider federal party 'establishment.'"[116] Jeffery and Hough
reserve judgment on the question of whether this means that *Land* elections might have become uncoupled from federal politics and are no
longer "second-order" elections. They note the relevance of a number of
factors, such as holding *Land* elections on the same day as the federal
election and the important role of the personal appeal of the incumbent
prime minister. But a brief look at the results of the *Land* elections since
1998 suggests that the relevance of federal politics is still strong, e.g., the
CDU opposition made strong gains in all of the *Land* elections in 1998
and 1999, when the SPD–Green federal government seemed to be
floundering, but it lost significantly after December 1999 when the
party finance scandal involving former Chancellor Helmut Kohl was
revealed. On the other hand, the most recent elections in Hamburg and
Berlin suggested that local issues dominated the campaigns. Thus the
question seems still to be unresolved. There can be no doubt that federal politics can have a decisive influence on *Land* elections, but it is also
clear that local conditions and personalities can be important and even
decisive as well.[117]

Conclusion

The brief overview of elections in the *Länder* provided above suggests some major differences between regional parties and elections in Germany and the United States. Some of these differences, of course, are due in part to the presidential system (directly elected governor and separation of powers) in the American states and the parliamentary system in the German *Länder*. Germany also has a multiple-party system ("limited pluralism"[118]) in contrast to the American two-party system; indeed, there may be as many as twenty or more parties participating in German *Land* elections. Even though most of these parties fail to win seats in the parliament, usually three or four parties cross the 5 percent hurdle which is the minimum needed to benefit from the proportional representation features of the electoral laws. But the party systems vary, as they do in the United States, between dominant SPD and CDU parties in some *Länder* and more competitive systems in others; between *Länder* that have gone through party realignments and those that have not; and, most importantly today, between the old *Länder* and the new, where the PDS has replaced the Greens and FDP as the "third force." The result today is the three-party system of SPD, CDU, and PDS in the East and the four-party system of SPD, CDU, FDP, and Greens in the West. This difference complements the north–south division between SPD and CDU/CSU that increasingly characterized the Federal Republic before unification.

Another difference is that most governments that are formed in the *Länder* – as well as at the federal level – are two-party coalitions. Most of these are between the SPD or CDU and a smaller party, such as the SPD and Greens or the CDU and FDP; however, by early 2002 there were also two SPD–CDU grand coalitions, one SPD–FDP coalition, one CDU–FDP–PRO coalition, and even two SPD–PDS coalition governments, with the PDS "tolerating" an SPD minority government in Saxony-Anhalt until 2002. Coalition governments are, of course, common in parliamentary systems, while they are virtually unknown in the United States. But the direct election of the governor, lieutenant governor, attorney general, and frequently other state-level officials often results in the representation of both parties in state executive positions. These are not, however, coalition governments in the parliamentary sense of two or more parties sharing responsibility for policy making initiatives. Nor does a governor of one party who faces one or both legislative houses with an opposing majority enter into a coalition, even if and when some cooperation may be required to get legislation or appointments approved.

The timing of elections and voter turnout are related in both countries. Voter turnout rises when the regional elections are held close to or simultaneously with federal elections, and it also rises under the impact of federal politics. For this reason about three-fourths of the American states hold their state elections between federal elections. In Germany most *Land* elections are held between federal elections, and even when held in the same year they are usually scheduled for different months. But the federal influence on German *Land* elections is clearly stronger than the federal impact on American gubernatorial elections – there is little federal influence on American state legislative races – as is demonstrated by the fact that during the Reagan and Bush I presidencies the Republicans never had a majority of state governorships. Even for mid-term congressional races, incumbency is more important than federal politics. Yet state politics in the United States are not entirely immune from federal influence as can be seen in the role of the national media and decline of regional differences in helping to bring about a narrowing of the margins in the state voting for president.[119]

Still another difference is the rise – usually temporary – of anti-establishment protest parties in some of the *Länder* at certain times. An important example in the 1960s was the radical right NPD. In the late 1970s and early 1980s the leftist Greens made their first appearance. In the late 1980s and 1990s it was the radical right Republikaner and somewhat later the DVU which largely, but not entirely, replaced the NPD. In the mid-1990s it was the middle-class *STATT Partei* in Hamburg and the working-class AFB in Bremen; in 2001 it was the PRO in Hamburg. And in all of the new *Länder*, the PDS offered an alternative to voters who were disappointed and even disgusted with the CDU and SPD. The closest parallels in the United States would be the extreme right-wing David Duke in Louisiana, who tried to run as a Republican, and the Reform Party, which enjoyed its greatest success with the election of Jesse Ventura in Minnesota in 1998.

In sum, the overview of elections in the German *Länder* shows a rich variety of political patterns and developments in the different regions of the country. As in the United States, no two *Länder* are the same, and some have a politics and party system that differ dramatically from other regions, e.g., Bavaria vs North-Rhine Westphalia, Mecklenburg-Vorpommern vs Saxony. The overview suggests that the north–south cleavage of the old Federal Republic has been complemented since unification by an east–west cleavage; however, it also shows that the north–south gap may now include the new *Länder* (i.e., Saxony and Thuringia in the south), so that in the future a north–south gap may be more prominent and enduring than an east–west divide.

Notes

1 Andreas Galonska, *Landesparteiensysteme im Föderalismus: Rheinland-Pfalz und Hessen, 1945–1996* (Wiesbaden: Deutscher Universitätsverlag, 1999), p. 42.

2 David Broughton and Neil Bentley, "The 1996 Länder Elections in Baden-Württemberg, Rheinland-Pfalz and Schleswig-Holstein: The Ebbing of the Tides of March?," *German Politics* 5, no. 3 (ecember 1996), pp. 505–506.

3 Ibid., pp. 506–507 and Galonska, *Landesparteiensysteme*, pp. 48–49.

4 Broughton and Bentley, "The 1996 Länder Elections," pp. 508–509.

5 *Das Parlament*, no. 15 (6 April 2001), p. 4 and Oscar W. Gabriel, "Die baden-württembergische Landtagswahl vom 25. März 2001," *Zeitschrift für Parlamentsfragen* 33, no. 1 (March 2002), pp. 10–26.

6 Galonska, *Landerparteiensysteme*, pp. 49–50.

7 Thomas Renz and Günter Rieger, "Die bayerische Landtagswahl vom 13. September 1998," *Zeitschrift für Parlamentsfragen* 30, no. 1 (February 1999), p. 78.

8 Ibid., pp. 79–80.

9 Ibid., pp. 81–82.

10 Ibid., p. 84.

11 Ibid., pp. 84–85.

12 Ibid., pp. 85–93.

13 Ibid., pp. 89–91.

14 Rüdiger Schmitt, "Die hessische Landtagswahl vom 5 April 1987," *Zeitschrift für Parlamentsfragen* 18, no. 3 (September 1987), pp. 343–345.

15 Rüdiger Schmitt-Beck, "Die hessische Landtagswahl vom 20. Januar 1991," *Zeitschrift für Parlamentsfragen* 22, no. 2 (June 1991), pp. 226–228.

16 Rüdiger Schmitt-Beck, "Die hessische Landtagswahl vom 19. Februar 1995," *Zeitschrift für Parlamentsfragen* 27, no. 2 (May 1996), pp. 243–245.

17 Rüdiger Schmitt-Beck, "Die hessische Landtagswahl vom 7. Februar 1999," *Zeitschrift für Parlamentsfragen* 31, no. 1 (March 2000), pp. 3–5, 9.

18 Ibid., pp. 8–9.

19 Ibid., pp. 12–13.

20 Ibid., p. 15.

21 Arthur B. Gunlicks, "Coalition Collapse in Lower Saxony: Political and Constitutional Implications," *Parliamentary Affairs* 24, No. 4 (Autumn 1976), pp. 437–449.

22 Reinhold Roth, "Die niedersächsische Landtagswahl vom 13. März 1994," *Zeitschrift für Parlamentsfragen* 26, no. 2 (May 1996), pp. 204, 212.

23 Rita Müller-Hilmer, "Die niedersächsiche Landtagswahl vom 1. März 1998," *Zeitschrift für Parlamentsfragen* 30, no. 2 (February 1999), pp. 41–46.

24 Ibid., pp. 47–48.

25 Stefan Bajohr, "Fünf Jahre und zwei Koalitionsveträge: Die Wandlung der Grünen in Nordrhein-Westfalen," *Zeitschrift für Parlamentsfragen* 32, no. 1 (March 2001), p. 148.

26 Ursula Feist and Hans-Jürgen Hoffmann, "Die nordrhein-westfälische Landtagswahl vom 14. Mai 2000: Gelbe Karte für Rot-Grün," *Zeitschrift für Parlamentsfragen* 32, no. 1 (March 2001), pp. 124–145.

27 Ibid., pp. 134–136.

28 Ibid., pp. 142–144.

29 Broughton and Bentley, "The 1996 Länder Elections," p. 511.

30 Werner Billing, "Die rheinland-pfälzische Landtagswahl vom 21. April 1991," *Zeitschrift für Parlamentsfragen* 22, no. 4 (December 1991), pp. 584–586.

31 Angelika Scheuer, "Die rheinland-pfälzische Landtagswahl vom 24. März 1996," *Zeitschrift für Parlamentsfragen* 27, no. 4 (November 1996), pp. 617–622; Broughton and Bentley, "The 1996 Länder Elections," p. 513.

32 *Das Parlament*, no. 15 (6. April 2001), p. 4; "Die rheinland-pfälzische Landtagswahl vom 25. März 2001," *Zeitschrift für Parlamentsfragen* 33, no. 1 (March 2002), pp. 26–43.

33 Jürgen R. Winkler, "Die saarländische Landtagswahl vom 5. September 1999," *Zeitschrift für Parlamentsfragen* 31, no. 1 (March 2000), pp. 28–30.

34 Ibid., p. 29.

35 Ibid., pp. 33–34.

36 Wilhelm Bürklin, "Die schleswig-holsteinische Landtagswahl vom 13. September 1987," *Zeitschrift für Parlamentsfragen* 19, no. 1 (March 1988), pp. 49–51.

37 Ibid., pp. 56–58.

38 Wilhelm Bürklin, "Die schleswig-holsteinische Wahl vom 8. Mai 1988," *Zeitschrift für Parlamentsfragen* 19, no. 4 (December 1988), pp. 482–495.

39 Peter Mnich, "Die schleswig-holsteinische Landtagswahl vom 24. März 1966: Grüne am Ziel, SPD wider Willen im rot-grünen Regierungsbündnis," *Zeitschrift für Parlamentsfragen* 27, no. 4 (November 1996), pp. 628–630.

40 Ibid., pp. 638–640.

41 Peter Mnich, Die schleswig-holsteinische Landtagswahl vom 27. Februar 2000: Das erste Wählervotum nach der CDU-Finanzaffäre," *Zeitschrift für Parlamentsfragen* 32, no. 1 (March 2001), p. 173.

42 Ibid., pp. 173–176.

43 Reinhold Roth, "Die Bremer Bürgerschaftswahl vom 29. September 1991," *Zeitschrift für Parlamentsfragen* 23, no. 2 (June 1992), pp. 281–290.

44 The conflict reached its peak with the unauthorized placement under an EU nature program by the Green environmental minister of open land that had been set aside for development. This led to the first removal of office in Bremen since 1945 of a minister (*Senator*) by a parliamentary vote of no-confidence. See Reinhold Roth, "Die Bremer Bürgerschaftswahl vom 14. Mai 1995," *Zeitschrift für Parlamentsfragen* 27, no. 2 (May 1996), pp. 272–273.

45 Ibid., pp. 272–283.

46 Reinhold Roth, "Die Bremer Bürgerschaftswahl vom 6. Juni 1999," *Zeitschrift für Parlamentsfragen* 31, no. 1 (March 2000), pp. 18–27.

47 David Broughton, "The First Six Länder Elections of 1999: Initial Electoral Consequences and Political Fallout of the *Neue Mitte* in Action," *German Politics* 9, no. 2 (August 2000), p. 57.

48 Roth, "Die Bremer Bürgerschaftswahl," p. 23.

49 Ibid., p. 25.

50 Early elections in 1982 and 1987 were made necessary by the inability of the SPD or CDU to form a coalition with each other or the Greens. See Ferdinand Müller-Rommel, "Die Wahl zur Hamburger Bürgerschaft vom 19. Dezember 1982," *Zeitschrift für Parlamentsfragen* 14, no. 1 (February 1983), p. 96 and Thomas Saretzki, "Die Wahl zur Hamburger Bürgerschaft vom 17. Mai 1987," *Zeitschrift für Parlamentsfragen* 19, no. 1 (March 1988), pp. 26–27.

51 Ursula Feist and Hans-Jürgen Hoffmann, "Die Hamburger Bürgerschaftswahl vom 19. September 1993," *Zeitschrift für Parlamentsfragen* 25, no. 2 (May 1994), pp. 217–218. This was the third time that early elections were called in Hamburg. See n. 50 above.

52 Ibid., p. 221.

53 Ibid., pp. 219–220, 222.

54 Ibid., p. 232.

55 Wolfram Brunner and Dieter Walz, "Die Hamburger Bürgerschaftswahl vom 21. September 1997," *Zeitschrift für Parlamentsfragen* 25, no. 2 (May 1998), pp. 275–289.

56 Ibid., pp. 282, 287.

57 Florian Kain, "Der Machtwechsel ist ziemlich sicher," and Christa Hategan, "Lehren aus dem Wahlkampf an der Elbe," *Das Parlament* 40 (28 September 2001), p. 3 and Patrick Horst, "Die Hamburger Bürgerschaftswahl vom 23. September 2001," *Zeitschrift für Parlamentsfragen* 33, no. 1 (March 2002), pp. 43–63.

58 Florian Kain, "Historischer Regierungswechsel in Hamburg," *Das Parlament* 47 (19. November 2001), p. 3.

59 Oskar Niedermayer and Richard Stöss, "Die Wahl zum Berliner Abgeordnetenhaus vom 10. Oktober 1999," *Zeitschrift für Parlamentsfragen* 31, no. 1 (March 2000), p. 86.

60 Ibid., pp. 88 and 93.

61 Ibid., pp. 89–90, 93.

62 Ibid., pp. 92–93.

63 Ibid., pp. 95 and 99.

64 K. Rüdiger Durth, "Erste Bilanz des Übergangssenat," *Das Parlament* 40 (28 September 2001), p. 3 and Oskar Niedermayer and Richard Stöss, "Die Wahl zum Berliner Abgeordnetenhaus vom 21. Oktober 2001," *Zeitschrift für Parlamentsfragen* 33, no. 2 (June 2002), pp. 244–246.

65 Ibid., pp. 250–251.

66 Ibid.

67 K. Rüdiger Durth, "SPD, FDP und PDS sind die Gewinner der Berlin-Wahl,"

Das Parlament 44 (26 October 2001), p. 3.
68 K. Rüdiger Durth, "Nun kommt die PDS doch noch zum Zuge," *Das Parlament* 50 (7 December 2001), p. 3 and Niedermayer and Stöss, "Die Wahl . . . ," pp. 257–258.
69 In 1992 Stolpe refused to follow the SPD line in the *Bundesrat* opposing a tax change proposed by the Kohl government, on the grounds that the tax would benefit the East which desperately needed the additional funds.
70 For an analysis of the referendum, see Joanna McKay, "Berlin-Brandenburg? Nein danke! The Referendum on the Proposed *Länderfusion*," *German Politics* 5, no. 3 (December 1996), pp. 485–502; also Otmar Jung, "Die Volksabstimmungen über die Länderfusion Berlin-Brandenburg: Was hast sich bewährt – wer ist gescheitert?," *Zeitschrift für Parlamentsfragen* 28, no. 1 (February 1997), pp. 13–20.
71 See Arthur B. Gunlicks, "Fifty Years of German Federalism: An Overview and Some Current Developments," in *The Federal Republic of Germany at Fifty*, edited by Peter H. Merkl (London: Macmillan Press, 1999), p. 193.
72 Karl Schmitt, "Die Landtagswahlen in Brandenburg und Thüringen vom 5. und 12. September 1999," *Zeitschrift für Parlamentsfragen* 31, no. 1 (March 2000), pp. 45–46.
73 Ibid., pp. 52–53.
74 Ibid., pp. 54–55.
75 Ibid., pp. 63–64.
76 K. Rüdiger Durth, "Grosse Aufgaben warten auf den 'Deichgrafen'", *Das Parlament* 26 (1 July 2002), p. 10.
77 Karl Schmitt, "Die Landtagswahlen 1994 im Osten Deutschlands," *Zeitschrift für Parlamentsfragen* 26, no. 2 (May 1995), p. 266.
78 Ibid., pp. 291–292.
79 Nikolaus Werz and Jochen Schmidt, "Die mecklenburg-vorpommersche Landtagswahl vom 27. September 1998," *Zeitschrift für Parlamentsfragen* 30, no. 1 (February 1999), pp. 97–98.
80 Ibid., pp. 99–104.
81 Ibid., pp. 112–115.
82 Schmitt, "Die Landtagswahlen 1994 im Osten," pp. 266–267.
83 Ibid., pp. 276–277.
84 Eckhard Jesse, "Die Landtagswahl in Sachsen vom 19. September 1999," *Zeitschrift für Parlamentsfragen* 31, no. 1 (March 2000), pp. 69–73, 80–81.
85 Astrid Pawassar, "Das Land soll Spitze bleiben," *Das Parlament* 21 (24 May 2002), p. 3.
86 The FDP's initial electoral success in the federal and state elections in Saxony-Anhalt was due in large part to the "Genscher Effect," i.e, Hans-Dietrich Genscher, the West German foreign minister at the time of unification, who had been born and raised in Halle, one of the larger cities in the state.
87 Jürgen Plöhn, "Die Landtagswahl in Sachsen-Anhalt vom 26. Juni 1994," *Zeitschrift für Parlamentsfragen* 26, no. 2 (May 1995), pp. 215–217.

88 Ibid., pp. 221–222 and 227–230.
89 Stefan Schieren, "Die Landtagswahl in Sachsen-Anhalt vom 26. April 1998," *Zeitschrift für Parlamentsfragen* 30, no. 1 (February 1999), pp. 56–59.
90 Ibid., pp. 59–61.
91 Ibid., p. 62.
92 Ibid., p. 63.
93 This was due in part because with a grand coalition both opposition parties would be of questionable loyalty to the democratic system and thus the alternative to the government would be anti-system parties. The counterargument, of course, was that the SPD was breaking a general consensus that democratic parties would not cooperate with anti-system parties. See *Zeitschrift für Parlamentsfragen* 30, no. 1 (February 1999), pp. 71–72.
94 Ibid., pp. 70–75.
95 K. Rüdiger Durth, "Die Union hat jetzt im Bundesrat wieder die Mehrheit," *Das Parlament* 17 (26 April 2002), p. 1 and *Das Parlament* 21 (24 May 2002), p. 3.
96 Ursula Feist and Hans-Jürgen Hoffmann, "Landtagswahlen in der ehemaligen DDR am 14. Oktober 1990," *Zeitschrift für Parlamentsfragen* 22, no. 1 (March 1991), pp. 5–34; Karl Schmidt, "Die Landtagswahlen 1994 im Osten Deutschlands," *Zeitschrift für Parlamentsfragen* 26, no. 2 (May 1995), pp. 261–295.
97 Schmitt, "Die Landtagswahlen in Brandenburg und Thüringen," pp. 47–50.
98 Ibid., p. 56.
99 Charlie Jeffery and Daniel Hough, "The Electoral Cycle and Multi-Level Voting in Germany," *German Politics* 10 (August 2001), p. 93.
100 Malcolm E. Jewell and Sarah M. Morehouse, *Political Parties and Elections in American States* (4th edn; Washington, DC: CQ Press, 2001), Ch. 6.
101 For example, Hein Kaack, "Landtagswahlen und Bundespolitik 1970–1972," *Aus Politik und Zeitgeschichte* 13/74 (30 March 1974), pp. 4–5.
102 Christopher J. Anderson and Daniel S. Ward, "Barometer Elections in Comparative Perspective," *Electoral Studies* 14, no. 1 (1995), pp. 1–14; Uwe Jun, *Koalitionsbildung in den deutschen Bundesländern* (Opladen: Leske & Budrich, 1994), p. 93.
103 Rainer Dinkel, "Der Zusammenhang zwischen Bundes- und Landtagswahlergebnissen," *Politische Vierteljahresschrift* 18 (1977), pp. 348–359.
104 Georg Fabritius, *Wechselwirkungen zwischen Landtagswahlen und Bundespolitik* (Meisenheim am Glan: Verlag Anton Hain, 1978) and "Sind Landtagswahlen Bundesteilwahlen?," *Aus Politik und Zeitgeschichte* 21/79 (26 May 1979), pp. 23–38.
105 Georg Fabritius, "Landtagswahlen und Bundespolitik," in *Westeuropas Parteiensysteme im Wandel*, edited by Hans-Georg Wehling (Stuttgart: Kohlhammer Verlag, 1983), pp. 113–116.
106 Ibid., pp. 118–119.
107 Tilo Görl, "Regionalisierung der politischen Landschaft in den neuen Bundesländern am Beispiel der Landtagswahlen 1999 in Brandenburg,

Thüringen und Sachsen," *Zeitschrift für Parlamentsfragen* 32, no. 1 (March 2001), pp. 94–95, 123.

108 Ibid., pp. 121–122.

109 Ibid., p. 123.

110 Frank Decker and Julia von Blumenthal, "Die bundepolitische Durchdringung der Landtagswahlen. Eine empirische Analyse von 1970 bis 2001," *Das Parlament* 33, no. 1 (March 2002), pp. 144–165.

111 Görl, "Regionalisierung," pp. 113–114, 124–125.

112 Gerhard Lehmbruch, *Parteienwettbewerb im Bundesstaat* (2nd expanded edn; Opladen: Westdeutscher Verlag, 1998).

113 Jeffery and Hough, "The Electoral Cycle," pp. 76–77.

114 Ibid., p. 84.

115 Ibid., p. 85.

116 Ibid., p. 89.

117 Decker and von Blumenthal, "Die bundespolitische Durchdringung," p. 164.

118 Giovanni Sartori, *Parties and Party Systems: A Framework for Analysis* (Cambridge: Cambridge University Press, 1976), p. 125.

119 Paul Allen Beck, "Party Realignment in America: The View from the States," in *Party Realignment and State Politics*, edited by Maureen Moakley (Columbus: Ohio State University Press, 1992), pp. 261–265.

10

The *Länder*, the *Bundesrat*, and the legislative process in Germany and Europe

The Federal Council, or *Bundesrat*

All federal states have some kind of second chamber that participates in the legislative process and represents the constituent parts of the whole, but Germany's second chamber is unique in the world's federal systems.[1] It is unique in that it is a *federal*, not a *Land*, organ, in which the member states are represented by their *governments* (i.e., cabinets). This means it is an executive as well as a legislative body, and it means also that it is *not* a part of parliament, which is the *Bundestag* alone. Rather, it is a constitutional organ along with the *Bundestag*, the federal government, the Federal President, and the Federal Constitutional Court that makes it possible for the *Länder,* via their governments, to participate in the legislative process. Of course this means that the *Bundesrat* is also a product of the historical development of federalism in Germany and of the German second chamber.[2]

History

The North German Federation and the Kaiserreich

Germany did not become a nation-state until 1871, following the Franco-Prussian War. From that time to the present, there have been five clearly delineated time periods and six – or possibly seven – political systems on German territory. These are the Kaiserreich, also known as Hohenzollern Reich or Bismarck Reich, of 187–1918; the Weimar Republic of 1918–33; Hitler's "Third Reich" of 1933–45; Allied occupation from 1945 to 1949; the German Democratic Republic (GDR) in the East from 1949 to 1989;

and the Federal Republic of Germany (FRG) in the West from 1949 to the present. Some might argue that the unification of the latter two states in October 1990 by which the West German Federal Republic absorbed the former East Germany created yet another political system, but that is a questionable thesis that cannot be developed here. These different regimes range from monarchy to democracy to fascist dictatorship to military rule to communist dictatorship to Western democratic welfare state capitalism. No other Western country has gone through so many political changes in modern times.

In 1867 the North German Federation was formed under the guidance of the Prussian Prime Minister, Otto von Bismarck. It consisted of twenty-two states, all of which were monarchies, and three city-states, Hamburg, Bremen and Lübeck; not included were Austria or the south German states of Bavaria, Württemberg, and Baden. It represented a compromise between German tradition and the institutions of confederation on the one hand and the demands for some form of national union with a central government and the constitutionally guaranteed participation of the population on the other hand. It was, therefore, a compromise among monarchical, democratic, federal, and unitary principles within a constitutional framework that provided for a complicated division of powers and the *de facto* dominance of Prussia. Prussian dominance continued even after the founding of the Kaiserreich in 1871 that adopted with some revisions the North German Constitution as its own.

The Kaiserreich included the three south German states for a total of twenty-five states, ranging in size from Prussia, with three-fifths of the population and two-thirds of the area of the Reich, to tiny Schaumburg-Lippe with 32,000 inhabitants. Again, three of the states were "free" city-states and all of the twenty-two territorial states were monarchies.[3] There were two chambers in the Reich, the popularly elected *Reichstag* and the *Bundesrat* which represented the states. Like the old *Bundestag* of the German Confederation, the *Bundesrat* was comprised of members who were rather like ambassadors sent by the state governments and instructed by them on how to vote. Therefore, in contrast to the *Staatenhaus* proposed by the Frankfurt Assembly of 1848–49, which was to be a part of parliament with members at least legally free to vote their consciences, the *Bundesrat* of the Kaiserreich was not a parliamentary body but rather a chamber representing the monarchical governments in the states.[4] Indeed, sovereignty in the Reich resided in the *Bundesrat*.[5]

The distribution of seats in the *Bundesrat* was similar to that of the old imperial *Bundestag*. Prussia had 17 of 58 votes, more than the 14 needed to block constitutional amendments, and the members were instructed delegates sent by the state government to vote en bloc. But there was a crucial difference: the North German Federation of 1867 and the Kaiserreich of 1871 were federations with a central state, while the German Confederation of 1815 was a loose association of sovereign princes.[6]

Bismarck had thought originally of the *Bundesrat* as a potential government, or cabinet, which would counter the democratic pressures in the country as well as the fear that the Prussians would dominate the government. In fact the *Bundesrat* did not become either the basis of a cabinet or as strong a legislative body as the *Reichstag,* because the idea of the nation-state, which favored the Kaiser and the popularly elected *Reichstag,* was more powerful than the old-fashioned notion of a confederation of princes.[7]

The Constitution of the Kaiserreich thus held two principles of legitimacy in balance: the rising principle of democracy and the traditional principle of monarchy. On the other hand, the principle of government responsibility to parliament, as in Great Britain, was not yet established at the national or state level. The *Bundesrat* stood for the principle of federalism, but also for monarchy. Even though it was overshadowed by the *Reichstag* in the legislative process, it exercised veto power over the *Reichstag* and over constitutional change. It was, then, more than merely a chamber representing the states.[8]

The Weimar Republic

With the collapse of the Kaiserreich in 1918, a new Constitution, often seen as a model of democracy, was drafted and approved in a constitutional assembly in the quiet town of Weimar, southwest of and away from the then turbulent Berlin. The Weimar Constitution also provided for a federal system with eighteen, then seventeen, member states and a second chamber, now called the *Reichsrat.* Several different ideas concerning this body were discussed, but in the end it remained a chamber consisting of delegates selected by the governments of the states,[9] now called *Länder.* Prussian dominance was broken by having the different provincial governments, rather than the central Prussian government, select delegates. A major difference to the past, of course, was that now the governments were democratically elected. The monarchies had been swept away in the wake of the lost war.

But the powers of the *Reichsrat,* in comparison with its predecessor, the *Bundesrat,* were reduced. It had no absolute veto, only a suspensive veto, the effect of which depended on the actions of the *Reich* President. It could not even stop constitutional changes. Like federalism in general, the *Reichsrat* proved to be a weak institution in a state that, confronted by a series of foreign and domestic crises, became more centralized and unitary than originally conceived. But the trend toward centralization was nothing in comparison to the Nazi dictatorship that overthrew the Weimar Republic in January 1933 and eliminated the *Länder* and dissolved the *Reichsrat* in 1934.[10]

The new Länder *after 1945 and the founding of the Federal Republic*

Between 1945 and 1949, when the Basic Law came into effect, eleven *Länder* emerged in the Western Allied zones of occupation, only four of which, Baden, Bavaria, and the city-states of Hamburg and Bremen, had existed before 1934. Prussia, half of which was annexed by Russia and Poland in 1945 and seen by the Allies as having been too large and its influence too militaristic (although this was not the case in the Weimar Republic), was dissolved altogether in 1946. The Americans re-established Bavaria and Bremen and created the *Länder* Hesse and Württemberg-Baden. The French created the Rhineland-Palatinate and Württemberg-Hohenzollern and considered annexing the Saarland until agreeing in the 1950s to return it to Germany. The British re-established Hamburg and created North-Rhine Westphalia, Lower Saxony, and Schleswig-Holstein as *Länder*. West Berlin remained an occupied city. Baden, Württemberg-Baden, and Württemberg-Hohenzollern were combined by the *Germans* – unlike the other new states – to form Baden-Württemberg in 1952. By this time, then, there were two large *Länder* in the North – North-Rhine Westphalia and Lower Saxony – and two large *Länder* in the South – Bavaria and Baden-Württemberg. Never before in German history had there been this kind of rough regional balance. In the East, the GDR had also created or revived five *Länder* after 1945, but they were virtually abolished in 1952 and replaced by fourteen districts in a highly centralized communist state.

In 1948 the Western Allies directed the *Land* governments to prepare a draft Constitution that, among other things, would have to provide for a federal system.[11] Some Germans have argued or at least suspected that federalism after 1945 was imposed on them,[12] but it is clear that the German constitutional founders also wanted a federal state.[13] Federalism as such did not become a major issue in the Herrenchiemsee Conference that drafted the constitution; rather, it was the nature of the second chamber that created controversy.[14] The SPD generally favored a more powerful elected parliament and a second chamber with reduced powers, while the CDU and CSU were more supportive of a second chamber equal in power to the parliament. The SPD and the CDU in the British Zone also favored a chamber comprised of uninstructed members selected by the *Land* parliaments, rather like the United States Senate before 1913, while the CSU and southwest German CDU preferred the German tradition of instructed members representing their governments, i.e., the old *Bundesrat* model. The FDP position was not clear.[15]

When the Herrenchiemsee Conference, a preparatory committee of experts, turned over its draft document in September 1948 to the Parliamentary Council – the official constitution-making body established by the *Länder* – it offered both the Senate and the *Bundesrat* solutions, the latter of which could be subdivided into "classic" and "weakened" alternatives.[16] The Parliamentary Council finally reached a compromise favoring the "weakened" *Bundesrat* model. The *Bundesrat* was not given powers equal to those of the parliament, or *Bundestag,* as in the "classic" model, but the Constitution did grant membership on the basis of instructed delegates appointed by the *Land* governments. German federalists, after all, believed that the *Länder* should participate in law making *and* in the administration of federal laws, both of which were very much in the German tradition.[17] This favored the representation of the *Land governments* in a second chamber of the *Länder* that would mediate between the federal and *Land* governments. This is the solution that is most *federal,* in the sense that it provides for a *federal* division of powers in which both levels are represented by governments. A Senate solution would have duplicated in the *Bundesrat* the *party* representation in the *Bundestag,* whereas representation in the *Bundesrat* was to be based on the different principles of continuity, stability (i.e., long-standing interests of the *Länder)* and administrative expertise.[18] Thus the *Bundesrat* of the Federal Republic represents a special form of German federalism but not the old federalism of the German princes.[19]

The *Bundesrat* today

Functions, composition, organization, and general procedures

Even though Chapter IV (Articles 50–53) of the Basic Law is devoted to the *Bundesrat,* it focuses only on the basic function of the chamber, i.e., participation in the legislative process and administration of the federation and in matters affecting the EU; membership, representative principles and voting; rules of order, certain procedures and committees; and provisions concerning participation of federal cabinet members in *Bundesrat* proceedings. Many other key provisions concerning this body are found in other parts of the Basic Law. For example, details about the legislative process involving the federal government, *Bundesrat*, and *Bundestag* are contained in Articles 76 and 77; constitutional amendments, which require a two-thirds vote in each chamber, are discussed in Article 79; the *Bundesrat's* role in finance legislation is found in Articles 104a, 105–109, 134, and 135; its role in approving federal regulations regarding the administration of federal laws by the *Länder* is outlined in Articles 84 and 85; its role in joint tasks is contained in Article 91a; the election by the *Bundesrat* of one-half of the judges of the Federal Constitutional Court is provided in Article 94; and other, generally less important, matters are found in a variety of other Articles.[20]

Together with the *Bundestag*, Federal Government, Federal President, and Federal Constitutional Court, the *Bundesrat* is a constitutional organ of the *federation*, but with a focus on federalism. It is a second chamber but not an "upper house" of parliament; nor is it a *Länderkammer*, or chamber of the *Länder*, in which the *Länder* deal with matters that affect them internally as regional units. Rather, *Länderkammer*, if that term is to be used, should be understood as a *federal* organ which allows the constituent parts of the union to participate in the governmental process of the whole state.[21] This has led some observers to use the term "participatory federalism" in describing the German federal system.

Unlike the *Bundestag* which begins a new session after each federal election, the *Bundesrat* is a continuous body. *Land* governments decide if and when the members change, usually as the result of a change in the cabinet due to *Land* elections. The *Bundesrat* is not a body that represents the people directly, but rather one that represents elected *Land* governments. It is, therefore, in part an executive and in part a legislative body.[22] The goal is not so much a democratic one as one that focuses on a German version of separation of powers and checks and balances.[23] This, in turn, promotes use of the term, "administrative federalism" in Germany.

The *Bundesrat* is composed of members of and is appointed by the *Land* governments (cabinets). Only these cabinet members may vote in the plenary sessions; civil servants may participate in the regular committee meetings. The number of delegates each *Land* sends to the *Bundesrat* varies roughly according to population. Each *Land* has at least three votes. *Länder* with more than 2 million inhabitants have 4 votes; with more than 6 million, 5 votes; and with more than 7 million, 6 votes (see table 10.1). Before unification the maximum number of votes for a *Land* was 5. In contrast to Prussia in the Kaiserreich, no one *Land* dominates the voting or has a veto over constitutional amendments. But while population is considered, the differences in size of population and territory between North-Rhine Westphalia or Bavaria on the one hand and Bremen or the Saarland on the other hand are dramatic. When the five new *Länder* were created in the former GDR, concern was expressed in the West that this would give the East, with a total of 16.4 million inhabitants, 15 votes and leave North-Rhine Westphalia, with 17 million inhabitants, 5 votes. To ensure that they would at least be able to block constitutional amendments that they might see as damaging their interests, in particular fiscal equalization among the *Länder*, the four large *Länder* in the West were given 6 votes each in the Unification Treaty of 1990 and in the amendment to the Basic Law of September 1990. In the *Bundesrat* tradition, the votes are cast as a block and on

Table 10.1   **The German *Länder*: their populations, representation in the *Bundesrat*, and their capitals**

State (*Land*)	Population	Seats in *Bundesrat*	Capital city
Baden-Württemberg	10,300,000	6	Stuttgart
Bavaria	11,900,000	6	Munich
Berlin[a]	3,400,000	4	
Brandenburg	2,600,000	4	Potsdam
Bremen[a]	700,000	3	
Hamburg[a]	1,700,000	3	
Hesse	6,000,000	5	Wiesbaden
Lower Saxony	7,700,000	6	Hanover
Mecklenburg-West Pomerania	1,800,000	3	Schwerin
North-Rhine Westphalia	17,800,000	6	Düsseldorf
Rhineland-Palatinate	3,900,000	4	Mainz
Saarland	1,100,000	3	Saarbrücken
Saxony	4,600,000	4	Dresden
Saxony-Anhalt	2,800,000	4	Magdeburg
Schleswig-Holstein	2,700,000	4	Kiel
Thuringia	2,500,000	4	Erfurt
Federal Republic of Germany	81,400,000	69	Berlin[b]

Notes: [a] City-states; [b] Berlin is now the official capital, but some ministries will remain in Bonn even after 2000.

instruction of the *Land* governments. In case the *Land* has a coalition government and the parties in the government do not agree on how to vote, the *Bundesrat* members from that *Land* will most likely abstain; this has the effect of a negative vote, since only positive votes are counted. All coalition governments sign detailed agreements before they form a government, and these include provisions concerning voting procedures in the *Bundesrat*.[24] An obvious breakdown occurred in March 2002 when the delegation from Brandenburg was divided between the senior coalition partner, the SPD, and the junior partner, the CDU, over the vote for or against the SPD–Green government's immigration reform bill. In spite of a vote against cast by a CDU minister, the SPD prime minister, Manfred Stolpe, cast a vote in favor which provided the needed majority of 35 to 34. Stolpe's vote was accepted as official by the then president of the *Bundesrat*, the SPD lord mayor of Berlin, Klaus Wowereit.[25] Though this vote was considered to be unconstitutional by many experts, the president of the Federal Republic, Johannes Rau, reluctantly signed the bill which officially had passed the *Bundestag* and *Bundesrat*. That decision was then appealed to the Federal Constitutional Court, which ruled in autumn 2002 that the vote in the *Bundesrat* was, indeed, unconstitutional.

The *Bundesrat* elects a President each year on a rotating basis, beginning with the largest *Land*, North-Rhine Westphalia. The President is always a current *Land* prime minister or lord mayor of a city-state, and he is second only to the Federal President in terms of protocol. He calls and presides at the meetings of the *Bundesrat*, usually every third Friday, for a total of about twelve meetings per year. The meetings are public, but the public may be excluded under certain circumstances. Members of the federal government have the right to attend and speak at the plenary meetings as well as to participate in meetings of committees in which federal civil servants also may participate.

There is much less hierarchy in the *Bundesrat* than in the *Bundestag*. The prime ministers and ministers in the *Bundesrat* are formally equal, and the presidency changes every year. There is a certain hierarchy in the so-called "political committees" – foreign affairs and defense, in which the members are usually the *Land* prime ministers. The plenary meetings, which are prepared in advance and therefore generally dispose of the long agenda quickly and efficiently, are far more relaxed and business-like than in the *Bundestag*, and expressions of approval or disapproval from the listening members are very rare.[26]

The Bundesrat *and the legislative process*

The *Bundesrat* has the right to initiate legislation, but most bills come from the federal government (cabinet) or, to a lesser extent, from the *Bundestag*.[27] In the most common case, the government sends its bill to the *Bundesrat*, which then has six weeks to respond. (If the bill is initiated by the *Bundestag*, that chamber deals with it first; if the bill emerges from the *Bundesrat*, it goes first to the federal cabinet and then to the *Bundestag*.) The President of the *Bundesrat* sends the bill directly to the relevant committees.

Most of the real work of the *Bundesrat* takes place in the committees, in which each *Land* is represented officially by the relevant *Land* cabinet minister. In the committee on foreign relations, the *Länder* are normally represented by the prime minister. Each *Land* has 1 seat and 1 vote in the committee, and majority votes there generally suggest how the *Bundesrat* will vote. However, since each *Land*, depending on its population, has from 3 to 6 votes in the plenary meetings, the majorities in the committee and later in the plenary meeting can be different. It is common for civil servants rather than for ministers to represent their *Land* in the committee, which, together with the pressures of time, explains why the bureaucratic influence in the *Bundesrat* is high. But having access to the expertise of *Land* bureaucrats in the legislative process that affects the *Länder* was one of the reasons for adopting the *Bundesrat* over the Senate alternative in the negotiations that led to the final version of the Basic Law.[28]

The committee must normally complete its work by Thursday, eight days before the next Friday plenary meeting of the *Bundesrat* before the end of the six weeks. The *Land* missions then begin a tightly organized process by informing their prime minister's staff (*Staatskanzlei*) of the committee's recommendation. The staff spends much of the week, and especially the weekend, discussing and coordinating views in the *Land* government. On Monday the chief of staff contacts his counterparts in other *Länder* with the same party majority to arrive at a common position. This means that the *Land* cabinets, which meet on Tuesdays, have only a few but well-prepared days to consider the legislation and to decide how to vote on Friday, when the *Bundesrat* meets. Thus the decisive stage for *Bundesrat* decisions is the cabinet meetings of the *Land* governments, but for ministerial coordination it is usually the committee stage.[29]

In effect the votes in the plenary meetings generally register the decisions taken in committees and, in case of disagreement there, in a special standing committee, the Permanent Advisory Committee, composed of the *Land* plenipotentiaries of the sixteen *Länder*, the Director of the *Bundesrat*, and a representative of the Federal Chancery. When the *Bundesrat* was still in Bonn, these meetings were held in "Room 13" of the *Bundesrat* building, and this tradition has been continued in Berlin. The Committee receives reports from the Federal Chancellor's Office regarding the meeting of the Federal Cabinet earlier in the afternoon. The members comment to the Federal "Reporter" from the perspective of their respective *Länder*, which provides a useful confidential communication link between the two levels. The meetings of the Committee are chaired by the oldest serving member, who also formulates statements if and when such are forthcoming.

For our purposes the more important functions of the Committee are the assistance it gives the President and Praesidium of the *Bundesrat* in preparing the plenary meetings and its advice regarding administrative tasks. Shortly before the plenary meeting of the *Bundesrat* the Committee meets again and, if it discovers that there are different views regarding the course or procedures of the upcoming meeting, the Committee, led by the *Bundesrat* President, attempts to reach a quick compromise regarding procedures or other disagreements.[30]

No later than the last Friday of the six weeks allowed the *Bundesrat* for action, that chamber votes on the bill. The votes for each *Land* are cast as a block, i.e., one member of the *Land* delegation casts from three to six votes. Normally no more than two members are present from any one *Land*, and sometimes only one member is present, since one member casts the votes for the *Land*. The results are then sent to the federal government which sends the bill to the *Bundestag* with its statement on any issues in dispute. After considering the bill in committee and possibly making certain changes with the approval of the government, the *Bundestag* either passes or rejects the bill. If the bill passes, it is sent to the *Bundesrat* a second time. The *Bundesrat* then has three weeks to react. The consequences of its actions depend on the kind of legislation being proposed (figure 10.1).

If it is a "simple bill" or "objection bill" (*Einspruchsgesetz*), i.e., one which does not involve the *Länder* in the bill's administration or finances, and the *Bundesrat* approves, it goes back to the government which gives it to the Federal President for his signature. If the *Bundesrat* does not approve, it can call for a meeting of the Mediation Committee,[31] composed of one member from each *Land* and an equal number of *Bundestag* members, for a total of thirty-two. The number of members each party sends from the *Bundestag* is based on proportional representation. If the Mediation Committee reaches a compromise and first the *Bundestag* and then the *Bundesrat* accept, the bill goes to the government and the Federal President for his signature. If the *Bundesrat* does not accept the compromise, it has the right of a suspensive veto. If the veto represents a majority of the *Bundesrat,* i.e., at least 35 of 69 votes, it can be overridden by an absolute majority vote of the *Bundestag.* But if the suspensive veto represents a two-thirds majority of the *Bundesrat,* i.e., 46 votes, the *Bundestag* can override only by a two-thirds vote, which would be virtually impossible in all but the rarest of cases. Since the Opposition would rarely have a two-thirds majority in the *Bundesrat,* the government and its majority in the *Bundestag* can normally count on passage of their "objection bills."

If it is a "consent bill" (*Zustimmungsgesetz*) which is the case for about 55–60 percent of all bills (but about 90 percent of the more important bills[32]), the *Bundesrat* has potentially an absolute veto and is equal to the *Bundestag* in legislative power. This occurs when any part of the bill contains a provision concerning administrative procedures or certain issues of public finances, which are the province of the *Länder.* If the *Bundesrat* approves the bill, which it does in most cases, it goes back to the government which gives it to the Federal President for signing. If the *Bundesrat* does not approve, which is more likely to occur when the Opposition in the *Bundestag* has a majority in the *Bundesrat,* i.e., when there is "divided government," the *Bundesrat,* the federal government, or the *Bundestag* can each call one time for a meeting of the Mediation Committee. If the Mediation Committee is unable to reach any compromise agreement, the bill is dead. If it does reach a compromise, the bill goes back to the *Bundestag,* which must vote the compromise up or down without amendment. If accepted, the bill goes back to the *Bundesrat* for its consent. Whether an objection bill or a consent bill is involved, the *Bundesrat* has three weeks to respond to the *Bundestag* in its "second reading." In the case of a constitutional amendment, the *Bundesrat* also has an absolute veto in that both the *Bundestag* and the *Bundesrat* must approve the amendment by a two-thirds vote.[33]

If one looks at the statistics from 1949 to 1994, one sees that the federal government, which initiates about 60 percent of all legislation, has a success rate of final passage of about 86 percent. The *Bundestag,* with about 33 percent of the initiatives, has a success rate of about 33 percent, and the *Bundesrat,* with less than 10 percent of the initiatives, also has a success rate of about 33 percent. Surprisingly, the *Bundesrat* has approved 98 percent of the bills sent to it after approval by the *Bundestag.*[34] Thus, it tends either to approve legislation sent to it or to accept compromises in the Mediation Committee when it disagrees.

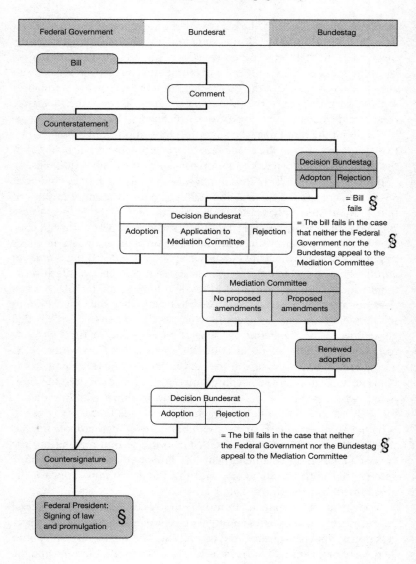

Figure 10.1   The legislative process and the *Bundesrat*
Source: Deutscher Bundesrat.

"Simple" or "objection" bill (Einspruchsgesetz)

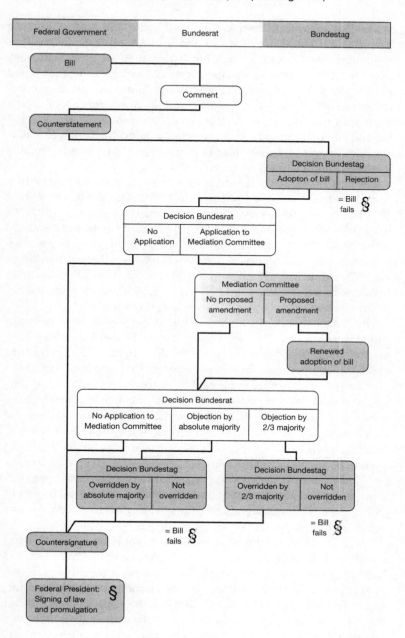

This does not mean, however, that the *Bundesrat* in practice has little power. In the first place, it is involved in the legislative process from beginning to end, except for bills initiated by the *Bundestag*, with many opportunities to exercise varying degrees of influence. In the second place, most deliberations in the Mediation Committee end in compromise acceptable to both the *Bundestag* and the *Bundesrat* and, of course, the federal government. In the third place, when the *Bundesrat* rejects a bill and any attempts to reach a compromise in the Mediation Committee, it is virtually by definition an important piece of legislation, whether it is an objection bill or a consent bill.

The range in the percentage of consent bills vetoed in four-year periods from 1949 to 1998 was 0–5.7. The most contentious periods were from 1972 to 1983 and from 1990 to 1998, when the Opposition (in the 1970s the CDU/CSU, in the 1990s the SPD) had a majority in the *Bundesrat* and was accused of a politics of "blockade" *vis-à-vis* the government. Even though a number of important government bills were, indeed, blocked by the SPD and their Green allies in the divided government of the 1990s (twenty-one each in the period 1990–94 and 1994–98), the percentage of all consent bills vetoed was only 2.6 and 2.3, respectively.[35]

The *Bundesrat* can call for a meeting of the Mediation Committee within three weeks of the receipt of a bill passed by the *Bundestag*. (Or, in the case of a consent bill, it can reject the bill outright, p. 350.) In contrast to the plenary meetings, the sixteen members from the *Bundesrat* in the Mediation Committee are not bound by instructions from their governments, and members from the *Bundestag* are also free to vote with their consciences under Article 38 of the Basic Law. Needless to say, given the strong party discipline in Germany, one can be skeptical about just how "free" members from either organ really are, and some see the *Bundesrat* as a crucial location for party politics.[36] Nevertheless, on certain occasions the *Länder* do break party ranks because of competing *Land* interests.[37] Some observers even suggest that party politics has had a real impact in only a minority of cases overall, even though party interests become more important in conditions of divided government.[38]

Members of the Mediation Committee may not bring any civil servant experts with them; only "genuine" members, i.e., *Land* ministers and *Bundestag* members may participate. The Committee is seen as an instrument of political compromise and consensus, and its meetings are confidential and not open to the public. Minutes are published only after an intervening session of the *Bundestag*, i.e., at the earliest about five years after the meeting took place. Members are not legally required to report back to their respective bodies, and the compromise proposals that emerge from the Mediation Committee must normally be accepted or rejected by the *Bundestag* and *Bundesrat* without change.[39]

As indicated in the analysis above, the Mediation Committee is a powerful and, therefore, somewhat controversial body. It combines the principles of territorial and political representation and serves as a balance between democratic and federal elements. But the fact that its meetings are closed to the public, that reporting back to the two chambers is not required, and that the Committee's compromise proposals are not normally subject to amendments are viewed by some critics as having the combined effect of reducing the legislative powers of the democratically legitimated *Bundestag*. On the other hand, these procedures are also seen as the conditions for promoting compromise.[40] The Mediation Committee becomes especially controversial when, as in the 1970s up to 1982 and during the 1990s, the Opposition in the *Bundestag* has a majority in the *Bundesrat* and the Mediation Committee is used sometimes as an instrument of opposition.[41] In such cases it is especially clear that the *Bundesrat* is not just a constitutional organ; it is also a political instrument.[42]

This development is a result in part of the proportion of bills that are consent bills, i.e., bills over which the *Bundesrat* has an absolute veto. As indicated above, the proportion of consent bills has been about 55–60 percent for several decades. In the very first session of the *Bundestag* from 1949 to 1953, the proportion of 43 percent was higher than expected. While this could be seen as a positive development for German federalism, it can also be interpreted negatively. Constitutional experts have noted that consent by the *Bundesrat* is now required for many bills because their legislative content was given to the federal government by constitutional changes that, in fact, were made at the expense of the *Land* parliaments. This is especially the case in concurrent legislation. Thus, there has been an increase in federal laws that are administered with considerable uniformity by the *Länder* and therefore require *Bundesrat* consent. On the other hand, the increase in consent laws has given the *Bundesrat* more influence over the contents of federal legislation, not just their administrative features, which then can lead to controversy over whether the *Bundesrat* can reject a government bill on the grounds of its contents rather than because of administrative procedures, as was the intent of the constitutional founders. The *Bundesrat* is not obliged to give reasons for its rejection of a bill. This has led to the federal government's attempts on occasion to divide bills into multiple parts in order to avoid as much as possible rejection of the whole package in the *Bundesrat*.[43]

It is often argued that while the federal government has gained legislative powers since 1949, especially in the area of concurrent legislation, the *Länder* have been compensated by their rights of administration and the increase in the proportion of consent laws. As we have seen above, however, it is the *Land governments*, not the *Land* parliaments, that have been compensated. It is generally agreed that the *Land* parliaments have been the net losers in the federal legislative process and in the transfer of general *Land* legislative powers to the federal government. This is a major reason why some observers refer to German federalism as "executive federalism."[44]

Territorial vs partisan politics in the Bundesrat

As noted above, there were two periods in the 1970s and 1990s in particular, when strong criticism of the *Bundesrat* arose because of the "gridlock" between the government and its majority in the *Bundestag* and the majority of *Länder* votes in the *Bundesrat*. This criticism is based not only on the traditional view that the *Bundesrat* has the function of territorial representation, while the *Bundestag* has the function of partisan political representation, but also on the more modern argument that a politics of "blockage" in the *Bundesrat* undermines the political responsibility or accountability of the popularly elected *Bundestag*. This is the main thesis of Gerhard Lehmbruch, cited in Chapter 9, who pointed to the bargaining and cooperation required by *Politikverflechtung* in general and in the *Bundesrat* in particular and the kind of hidden grand coalition or all-party politics that resulted. But the partisan disagreements that were perceived in the 1990s appeared to go beyond a kind of all-party government to "gridlock" between the two legislative bodies and the parties that controlled them. There was strong public criticism of the *Bundesrat*, especially in the electoral period between 1994 and 1998, because it appeared that some of the Kohl government's badly needed economic reforms were being blocked as a result of opposition by the Social Democrats and Greens who together had won enough elections in the *Länder* to gain a majority of votes in the *Bundesrat*. But while the general public and many scholars complained about "gridlock" or at least noted the questionable role of partisan politics in the *Bundesrat*, some scholars argued that the failures to agree were exaggerated and, in the case of the important tax reform proposal, not so much the fault of the Opposition as that of the smaller coalition parties, FDP and CSU[45] (a view strongly contested by others).[46] Two non-German scholars even suggested that in fact territorial politics were increasingly replacing the more partisan relationships in the *Bundesrat*[47] or that disagreements between the *Bundestag* and *Bundesrat* are a natural result of different electoral outcomes at the federal and *Land* levels and should therefore be considered part of the normal political process.[48]

The Land *missions in Berlin*[49]

All of the *Länder* have missions in Berlin headed by an official *Land* representative who serves as a kind of *Land* ambassador, lobbyist, liaison officer, and spokesperson for the *Land* government. The *Land* representative normally divides his or her time between Berlin and the home capital. A number of high-level civil servants are also assigned to the mission. They normally staff the *Bundesrat* committees for their *Land* and assist in liaison functions between *Land* and federal ministers and among civil servants of other missions, especially with regard to *Bundesrat* matters. The missions also are informed by the federal government of issues affecting the *Länder.*

In order to be able to report back to their governments, the civil servants in the missions have the right to attend all *Bundestag* plenary meetings and committee meetings, with the right to be heard in the latter. In plenary sessions this right is reserved in practice for *Land* prime ministers or subject ministers (department heads). Attendance of *Bundestag* committee meetings by *Land* civil servants is important so that they can report back immediately to their governments; this is essential in order that the *Länder* can react to *Bundestag* actions within the generally limited time they have at their disposal.

In addition to the above functions, the *Land* missions serve as a place where the *Land* delegation in the *Bundestag* can meet, regardless of party affiliation. The missions also perform public relations tasks, such as providing information and organizing cultural events, lectures, and various social gatherings. They serve as places for interest groups from the *Land* to meet with members of the *Land* delegation in the *Bundestag* or federal ministers. From this brief description, it is understandable that the *Land* missions have been called the "spiders in the web"[50] of relationships between the *Länder* and the federal government.

Conclusion

For several centuries the states were represented, first, in the Holy Roman Empire, by a *Reichstag;* then in the German Confederation by a *Bundestag;*

and in the North German Federation and the Bismarck Reich by a *Bundesrat*. During the Weimar Republic of 1919–33, the states were represented by a *Reichsrat*, and since the emergence of the Federal Republic in 1949 the *Bundesrat* has made its reappearance. It is clear, then, that in spite of the numerous changes of regime, composition, and functions, the current *Bundesrat* has deep roots in German history.

Its historical function was to create some degree of union from many separate states and in the process secure the autonomy of the individual parts from the central authority. But this is no longer true in the Federal Republic. The legitimacy of the federal state in Germany today is based on constitutional postulates: democracy, rule of law, the welfare state, and federalism. Federalism today serves as an additional means of dividing power and thus of encouraging liberty.[51]

The *Bundesrat* today is very different in some key respects from its predecessors. It shares the function of representing the constituent parts of Germany before the central authority and of participating in the decision making process of that central authority. Its decision making powers are especially important in legislation that deals with the administrative responsibilities of the *Länder*. But with the exception of the short-lived Weimar Republic, it differs sharply from the past in that it consists of representatives of democratically elected *Land* governments. It is not dominated by any single state or a combination of a few large states, and it serves both as an important check on the federal government and *Bundestag* as well as a joint decision maker on a majority of laws. For all of these reasons German federalism is sometimes referred to as "participatory," "administrative," or "executive federalism." In any case, the *Bundesrat*, next to the United States Senate, is arguably the most important second chamber in any other democracy, let alone any other federation.

Notes

1 Hans-Georg Wehling, "The Bundesrat," *Publius: The Journal of Federalism* 19, no. 4 (Autumn 1989), p. 53.

2 Peter Graf Kielmansegg, "Vom Bundestag zum Bundesrat: Die Länderkammer in der jüngsten deutschen Verfassungsgeschichte," in *Vierzig Jahre Bundesrat*, edited by the Bundesrat (Baden-Baden: Nomos Verlagsgesellschaft, 1989), p. 43.

3 Wehling, "The Bundesrat," p. 56.

4 Kielmansegg, "Vom Bundestag zum Bundesrat," pp. 44–45.

5 Uwe Thaysen, "The *Bundesrat*, the *Länder* and German Federalism," *German*

Issues 13 (Washington, DC: American Institute for Contemporary German Studies, 1993), p. 5.

6   Kielmansegg, "Vom Bundestag zum Bundesrat," pp. 46–47.

7   Ibid., pp. 48–49; Thaysen, "The *Bundesrat,*" pp. 5–6.

8   Ibid., p. 50.

9   Ibid., pp. 52–53.

10 Thaysen, "The *Bundesrat,*" pp. 6–7.

11 For an excellent study of the developments leading to the Allied decisions regarding the drafting of a German Constitution, see John Ford Golay, *The Founding of the Federal Republic of Germany* (Chicago: University of Chicago Press, 1958), Ch. 1.

12 Kai-Uwe von Hassel, "Der Bundesrat zwischen Länderinteressen, gesamt-staatlicher Verantwortung und Parteipolitik," in Bundesrat, *Vierzig Jahre Bundesrat,* p. 72.

13 Thaysen, "The *Bundesrat,*" p. 12.

14 Heiderose Kilper and Roland Lhotta, *Föderalismus in der Bundesrepublik Deutschland: Eine Einführung* (Opladen: Leske & Budrich, 1996), pp. 93–95.

15 Kielmansegg, "Vom Bundestag zum Bundesrat," pp. 53–54.

16 Thaysen, "The *Bundesrat,*" pp. 12–13; Golay, *The Founding,* p. 41.

17 Wehling, "The Bundesrat," p. 55.

18 Kilper and Lhotta, *Föderalismus,* p. 94.

19 Kielmansegg, "Vom Bundestag zum Bundesrat," pp. 55–60.

20 For a table containing the locations of provisions throughout the Basic Law that relate to the *Bundesrat,* see Kilper and Lhotta, *Föderalismus,* p. 113.

21 Ibid., pp. 114–115. See also Heinz Laufer and Ursula Münch, *Das föderative System der Bundesrepublik Deutschland* (Bonn: Bundeszentrale für politische Bildung, 1997), pp. 111–112.

22 Peter Lerche, "Principles of German Federalism," in *Germany and Its Basic Law,* edited by Paul Kirchhof and Donald P. Kommers (Baden-Baden: Nomos Verlagsgesellschaft, 1993), pp. 71–90. A German language edition of this book is also available under the title, *Deutschland und sein Grundgesetz.*

23 Karlheinz Neunreither, "Politics and Bureaucracy in the West German Bun-desrat," *American Political Science Review* 53, no. 3 (September 1959), pp. 713 and 723; Kilper and Lhotta, *Föderalismus,* p. 115.

24 Thaysen, "The *Bundesrat,*" p. 28.

25 See several articles in *Das Parlament* 13–14 (2–5 April 2002), p. 3.

26 Helmut Herles, "Der Stil von Bundesrat und Bundestag: Kammerton und Schaubühne," in Bundesrat, *Vierzig Jahre Bundesrat,* pp. 231–250.

27 For a discussion by the previous director of the Bundesrat's legislative initia-tives, see Georg-Berndt Oschatz and Horst Risse, "Bemerkungen zum Geset-zesinitiativrecht des Bundesrates," *Zeitschrift für Gesetzgebung* 4, no. 4 (1989), pp. 316–331.

28 Kilper and Lhotta, *Föderalismus,* pp. 120–121.

29 Interview with a former *Bundesrat* member.
30 Peter M. Schmidhuber, "Zimmer 13," *Miterlebt – Mitgestaltet: Der Bundesrat im Rückblick*, edited by Rudolf Hrbek (Stuttgart: Bonn Aktuell, 1989), pp. 266–270; Laufer and Münch, *Das föderative System*, pp. 118–119.
31 For a detailed discussion of the Mediation Committee, see Diether Posser, "Der Vermittlungsausschuß," in Bundesrat, *Vierzig Jahre Bundesrat*, pp. 203–211.
32 Kilper and Lhotta, *Föderalismus*, p. 175.
33 For a detailed description of the legislatve process and the *Bundesrat*, see Kilper and Lhotta, *Föderalismus*, pp. 122–126.
34 Ibid., pp. 125–126.
35 Roland Sturm, *Föderalismus in Deutschland* (Berlin: Landeszentrale für politische Bildungsarbeit, 2001), pp. 62–63.
36 Uwe Leonardy, "Parteien im Föderalismus der Bundesrepublik Deutschland: Scharniere zwischen Staat und Politik," *Zeitschrift für Parlamentsfragen* 33, no. 1 (March 2002), pp. 183–185; Thaysen, "The *Bundesrat*," pp. 25–27.
37 Posser, "Der Vermittlungsausschuß," p. 208. There are some dramatic examples of the national parties being ignored by the *Land* parties. One was in 1992 when the refusal of the SPD *Land* government of Brandenburg to back the national SPD led to the passage of the CDU/CSU–FDP government bill to raise the VAT from 14 to 15 percent and thus increase funds going to the *Länder*. The most recent example concerns tax reform legislation of the SPD–Green government which passed the *Bundesrat* in July 2000 because the CDU, which was a grand coalition partner in three *Länder*, and the FDP, which was a minority coalition partner in one *Land*, agreed to support a compromise solution which was, at least in the case of the CDU, against the wishes of the national party leaders.
38 Wehling, "The Bundesrat," p. 59.
39 Kilper and Lhotta, *Föderalismus*, pp. 127–128.
40 Posser, "Der Vermittlungsausschuß," p. 206; Thaysen, "The *Bundesrat*," p. 21.
41 Kilper and Lhotta, *Föderalismus*, pp. 126, 128–129.
42 Friedrich Vogel, "Der Vermittlungsausschuß," in Bundesrat, *Vierzig Jahre Bundesrat*, pp. 213–214.
43 Peter Lerche, "Zustimmungsgesetze," in Bundesrat, *Vierzig Jahre Bundesrat*, pp. 185–189, 196.
44 See, for example, Wilhelm Hennis, "Am Föderalismus liegt es nicht: Aber der Bundesrat hat sich als kapitale Fehlkonstruktion erwiesen," *Frankfurter Allgemeine Zeitung* (14 August 1997), p. 31. "Executive federalism" is not a new term; nor is it the only term that focuses on the role of the executive in German federalism. See, for example, Peter Merkl, "Executive–Legislative Federalism in West Germany," *American Political Science Review* 53, no. 3 (September 1959), pp. 732–741, in which Merkl contrasts German executive-legislative federalism to the US model of "mutual-independence" or dual federalism.

45 Wolfgand Renzsch, "Die grosse Steuerreform 1998/99: Kein Strukturbruch, sondern Koalitionspartner as Vetospieler und Parteien als Mehrebenensysteme," *Zeitschrift für Parlamentsfragen* 31, no. 1 (March 2000), pp. 187–191.

46 Raimut Zohlnhöfer, "Der Parteienwettbewerb, die kleinen Koaltionspartner und das Scheitern der Steuerreform. Eine Erwiderung auf Wolfgang Renzsch," *Zeitschrift für Parlamentsfragen* 31, no. 3 (September 2000), pp. 719–724.

47 Charlie Jeffery, "Party Politics and Territorial Representation in the Federal Republic of Germany," *West European Politics* 22, no. 2 (April 1999), pp. 159–161; for a somewhat similar view, see Roland Sturm, "Party Competition and the Federal System: The Lehmbruch Hypothesis Revisited," in *Recasting German Federalism*, edited by Charlie Jeffery (London and New York: Pinter, 1999), pp. 197–216.

48 Stephen J. Silvia, "Reform Gridlock and the Role of the Bundesrat in German Politics," *West European Politics* 22 (April 1999), pp. 167–181.

49 This section is based on Uwe Leonardy, "The Working Relationships between *Bund* and *Länder* in the Federal Republic of Germany," in *German Federalism Today*, edited by Charlie Jeffery and Peter Savigeau (London: Leicester University Press, 1991), pp. 48–50.

50 Ibid.

51 Alfred Kubel, "Bewährungen und Versäumnisse im Bundesstaat," in Hrbek, *Miterlebt–Mitgestaltet*, pp. 50–51.

11

European and foreign policy
of the *Länder*

Introduction

At first it would appear that this chapter is misnamed. Surely "European and Foreign Policy" are themes that belong to the federal government. They do, of course, but the *Länder* are not irrelevant in these areas. Indeed, European policy is now to a considerable extent domestic policy, and many responsibilities that have traditionally belonged to the *Länder* have been and are today the subjects of European Community – now EU – regulations and legislation. The efforts by the *Länder* to protect their sphere of responsibility from EU incursions or, at the very least, to participate in the decision making that affects them directly, have been of varying success over the years. However, it seems as if they are now in a stronger position than ever before to influence decisions in Brussels. They also continue to have a modest impact on foreign policy, particularly in the area of foreign aid, where they have been quite successful in very specific areas of activity.

The *Länder* and European integration

European integration as a challenge to the Länder

European integration, which dates back at least to the creation of the European Coal and Steel Community (ECSC) in 1951, has from the start been supported strongly not only by all federal governments, regardless of party or coalition, but also by the *Länder*. Nevertheless, the *Länder* have often been frustrated by the loss of powers and influence they have suffered in the process of European integration in addition to the continuing erosion of legislative powers to the federation. Some transfer of sovereignty must take place by definition in forming a more integrated Europe. But whereas the federal government has been a participant in negotiating such transfers, and therefore has agreed voluntarily to them, the *Länder* have generally had little to say. Where federal powers have been transferred, legislation thereafter is drafted in the European Commission and, possibly after some input from the European Parliament, adopted by the European Council of Ministers. Of course the federal government is an important participant in the Council. But the effect for the *Länder* has been that they no longer have a voice in these matters in the domestic legislative process via the *Bundesrat*.

To add insult to injury, Article 24 of the Basic Law has been used as the authorization for the federal government to transfer not only federal but also *Land* powers to the EC/EU without *Land* participation.[1] Indeed, after the transfer of a *Land* power, the federal government gains the right to participate in legislation in the Council of Ministers on the matter over which it had no voice before. One should also note that the EC/EU has preempted certain *Land* powers by invoking Article 235 (now Article 308) of the European Economic Union (EEC) Treaty which serves as a kind of enabling or implied powers clause or by referring to other articles, e.g., Article 100, which also provide the European Community (EC) with a basis for action.[2] Thus, European integration has meant an erosion of *Land* powers from the beginning.[3]

While the complaint is often made that *Land* powers have been transferred to or preempted by the EC over the years, it is useful to ask just which functions these were. First, we have already noted the indirect transfer of *Land* powers that occurs when the federal government transfers federal powers to the EC/EU over which the *Länder* then have no voice via the *Bundesrat*. But this also applies to the *Bundestag*. That is, both legislative chambers in Germany lose to the Council of Ministers when federal powers are transferred. Second, there is the direct loss of *Land* powers owing to EC/EU preemptions. Thus, in the area of education and training and more recently in research, technology and environment, it is often claimed that EC policies have preempted certain *Land* powers. The European Court of Justice (ECJ) has said the EC/EU has no powers in the field of education, but it has used its jurisdiction over economic policy to promote worker mobility. "Mobility" includes mutual recognition of standards and certification in vocational and professional training. Thus, the ERASMUS and LINGUA programs that provide scholarships for students in EC/EU member states to study in other member states require mutual

recognition of academic standards.[4] In the area of TV and radio, there has
been a dispute over whether the mass media fall under Article 92 (now
Article 87) of the EEC Treaty that permits regulation of regional economic
policy or under "culture," which is a responsibility belonging to the *Länder*.[5] In 1989 the federal government approved EC guidelines to which the
Länder objected, and Bavaria took the issue to the Federal Constitutional
Court. The Court sided with the federal government, but this incident
made the *Länder* all the more determined to gain access to EC decision
making by the federal government regarding EC policy.[6] Construction,
water, and general environmental protection have come under EC law in
varying degrees, as have subsidies involved in regional economic policies.[7]
Since the member states implement most EC/EU legislation, this means
administration by the *Länder* for Germany. Some laws allow more leeway
than others, but the *Länder* are restricted especially in regional economic
policy, e.g., subsidies, and they must pay the costs of administration.[8]

It is common and understandable for the *Länder* to be critical of these
developments, but it is doubtful that such problems can be avoided in a
common market.[9] In 1990 a commission established by the parliament of
North-Rhine Westphalia looked at the question of task transfers and
reported that it is not at all clear what exactly has been lost. This may be
due in part to the fact that transfers have also been made to the federation
via constitutional amendment, federal preemptions have occurred
through concurrent legislation and provisions in the Basic Law regarding
"uniform living conditions," and Federal Constitutional Court decisions
have generally favored broader powers for the federation.[10] Self-coordination among the *Länder* at the *domestic* "third level," where *Land* officials meet in extra-legal forms to promote cooperation and coordination,
has also been a factor in the decline of *Land* legislative powers.[11] Thus, the
intergovernmental relations or joint decision making (*Politikverflechtung*) between the federation and the *Länder* and among the latter also
make any assessment difficult, since powers and responsibilities are
mixed. It might be more accurate to speak of a redistribution of powers
among the three levels of EC/EU, federation and *Länder*, and the difficulty of compensating the *Länder* in this process.[12]

In any case conventional wisdom states that there has been a steady erosion of *Land powers*, which could be seen as contradicting the "eternal
federalism" clause of Article 79, para. 3, of the Basic Law.[13] This real or
perceived erosion became a major reason for the search by the *Länder* for
procedures by which the federal government could continue to participate constructively in the process of European integration and at the same

time provide adequate opportunities for *Land* participation that would protect their interests.[14]

Early efforts to protect Länder rights in European integration

During the ratification process of the ECSC in 1951, concern was expressed that the process of European integration could eventually turn the *Länder* into mere administrative units.[15] As a result the *Bundesrat* insisted in its official reaction to the ratification law sent to it by the federal government that the participation of the *Länder* be secured in the German decision making process regarding the ECSC. This demand was not met, and in the end the *Bundesrat* was assured only that a subcommittee of its foreign affairs committee would be kept informed by the federal government.

In the ratification process regarding the Treaties of Rome in 1957, the *Länder* were a little more successful. The federal government agreed to keep both the *Bundestag* and the *Bundesrat* informed of developments in the EEC and European Atomic Energy Community (Euratom) and to make this information available before any decisions were reached in the Council of Ministers which would have a direct effect on Germany or would require implementing legislation. In fact, however, this did not go much beyond the requirements of Article 53, para. 3, of the Basic Law which states that the federal government is to keep the *Bundesrat* informed. Real participation by the *Länder* in Community matters did not occur.[16]

It took another twenty years before the *Länder* tried again to improve their position in the European Community – or, technically, *Communities* (after 1967, ECSC, EEC and Euratom combined). This time the *Länder* as such, rather than the *Bundesrat*, started negotiations with the federal government over procedures to involve the *Länder* in cases in which their exclusive powers or essential interests would be affected. After more than two years of talks, an exchange of letters took place in 1979 between Chancellor Helmut Schmidt and the prime minister of North-Rhine Westphalia, Johannes Rau, who was then chair of the Conference of Prime Ministers. In the letter it was agreed that the federal government would inform the *Länder* in a complete and timely manner about EC proposals, and, insofar as these affected the exclusive powers of the *Länder*, would give them the opportunity to present their positions completely and in depth. Only for compelling reasons of foreign and integration policy could the federal government exclude the *Länder*.

The idea behind this letter was to involve the *Länder* directly rather than via the *Bundesrat*. This idea was not applied consistently, however, since it was soon agreed that overlap with the *Bundesrat* should be avoided when it became involved in the process.[17] There were also structural problems, such as the lack of *Land* instruments to coordinate the flood of information and direct it to the appropriate subject ministries and the difficulty of coordinating *Land* responses and arriving at some consensus among the *Länder*. Thus, while it seemed as though the *Länder* had now been able to secure their position in matters involving European integration, practice proved otherwise.[18]

The Bundesrat *and the ratification of the Single European Act*

Various proposals and efforts in the early 1980s to reform the EC became an increasing focus of attention, with the Single European Act (SEA) emerging in 1986 as the most important development since the Treaties of Rome in 1957 which the SEA amended. The *Länder* saw another opportunity to replace the old procedures and devise new ones to protect their interests, and when the federal government submitted the draft ratification law for the SEA in February 1986, the *Bundesrat* was determined to improve its position. It passed a resolution insisting that the position of the *Bundesrat* be strengthened and suggested that Article 24 of the Basic Law be amended to provide for the approval of the *Länder* in transfering any of their autonomous powers to the EC. This led to charges that the *Länder* were trying to interfere in the realm of foreign policy that belonged to the federal government; but for the *Länder* European policy had become domestic policy, and they were reacting accordingly.

In any case the resolution had the effect of persuading the federal government to make the ratification law a consent law, thus conceding to the *Bundesrat* the right of veto. But the ratification bill still did not grant the *Bundesrat* the right of participation in the federal government's decision making process concerning EC legislation affecting the *Länder*. This led to the *Bundesrat's* insistence that the ratification bill be changed to provide for its participation and that the Basic Law be amended so that the transfer of autonomous rights under Article 24 could be made subject to *Bundesrat* approval. The result was that the federal government was forced to accept a change in the ratification bill which provided that the federal government had to obtain the position of the *Bundesrat* before it could approve any decisions of the EC Council of Ministers that wholly or partially affected the exclusive legislative powers of the *Länder* or their essential interests. Furthermore, the federal government could deviate from this position only for compelling reasons. In this case the federal government was to provide the reasons and, upon the demand of the *Bundesrat*, engage as far as possible representatives of the *Länder* in the negotiations with the consultative organs of the Commission and Council of Ministers.[19]

In the meantime the *Länder* continued to push for more rights regarding the EC, and at the *Länder* Prime Ministers' Conference in Munich in October 1987 ten theses were presented which outlined the demands of the *Länder* concerning the nature of the EC and their rights. This was followed in December by the "Federation–*Länder* Agreement" which again outlined various information and participation rights of the *Länder*, including *Bundesrat* representatives in the German delegation in Brussels when negotiations were taking place on matters that affected the *Länder* directly. In such cases, however, the leadership of the delegation which still had only one vote in the Council of Ministers was to remain with the federal government.

The success of the *Bundesrat* in improving its ability to protect its interests in matters concerning the EC has, of course, been criticized as an example of cooperative federalism carried too far; indeed, the provisions described above have been characterized as interfering in the responsibilities of the federal government for foreign policy and even as unconstitutional to some extent. At the very least a confusing picture is presented: the *Land* representatives in the German delegation in Brussels receive a double status; to the outsider they are representatives of the federal government, but internally they are representatives of the *Länder*.[20]

The negotiation and ratification of the Maastricht Treaty (TEU)

The Maastricht Treaty on the EC and EU, which we will refer to as the Treaty on European Union (TEU), represents a new stage in the process of European integration.[21] It was designed not only to adapt the EC to a new Europe following the events of 1989 but also to integrate further and bind the larger, united Germany to Europe ("a European Germany, not a German Europe"). Given the various rights of information and participation which the *Länder* had gained since the SEA, they were well prepared for the challenge of Maastricht.

Even before the first summit meeting in Dublin in June 1990 concerning the EC and EU, the prime ministers of the *Länder* had placed Europe on their permanent agenda, including the idea of a "Europe of the

Regions."[22] In the late summer of 1990, the federal government declared its willingness to let the *Länder* participate in the internal preparations as well as in intergovernmental conferences (IGCs) on the Maastricht treaties. Delegates from Baden-Württemberg and North-Rhine Westphalia represented the *Länder* in IGC meetings on the EU, and representatives from Bavaria and Hamburg participated in similar meetings on a European Economic and Currency Union. Next to Germany, only Belgium had subnational units involved in both intergovernmental conferences. Parallel to these conferences, the *Bundesrat* created a Europe-Commission in which all sixteen *Länder* and the federal government participated.[23]

In August 1990 the *Bundesrat* passed a resolution outlining its expectations for the Maastricht Treaty. These included anchoring the principle of subsidiarity in the treaties with a specific reference to a *European* "third level"[24] of *Länder* and regions (if taken seriously, this would mean an expectation that all member states become federal systems); opening the meetings of the Council of Ministers to representatives of the *Länder* and the regions; creating a special council for the regions; and providing for the right of *Länder* and regions to bring cases before the ECJ to protect the right of subsidiarity. These expectations were then confirmed by the *Länder* Prime Ministers' Conference in Munich in December 1990.[25]

In the negotiations on the treaties during 1991, the German delegation presented a position that was a compromise between the views of the federal government and the *Länder*. The delegation accepted the demand for a regional council, but only as a consultative body, and the *Länder* agreed to attach it to the Economic and Social Committee that advises the EU Commission and Council of Ministers. The demand for anchoring the principle of subsidiarity in the Treaty was accepted, but the demand for regional participation in the Council of Ministers was not. The demand to have the right to bring cases to the ECJ was revised.[26]

From the above one can already see the German influence on the final results of the IGC meetings. The principle of subsidiarity was included in the Treaty, which was seen as a significant accomplishment. However, in the Munich Declaration of the *Land* prime ministers in December 1990, the expectation was for three levels throughout the EU and a clear separation of tasks between each of these. This was designed to counter the "creeping accession of powers" by the EC and to oppose the provisions of Article 235 (now Article 308) of the EEC Treaty of Rome that serve as a kind of general or implied powers. Unfortunately, there are problems with the expectations associated with the principle of subsidiarity: first, its meaning is not clear, especially to non-Germans; second, as written in the TEU it applies to the member states, and subnational levels are not mentioned; and, third, not even in German federalism is there a clear division of tasks between the federal and *Land* levels. Rather, widespread joint decision making and cooperation (*Politikverflechtung*) and a trend toward a "unitary federal state" make it difficult to take seriously a demand by the prime ministers of the *Länder* that there should be clear divisions of powers in the EU.[27]

Another major achievement from the perspective of the *Länder* and some other regions was the establishment of a Committee of the Regions (CoR), even if it has only advisory functions *vis-à-vis* the Commission and Council of Ministers. With the three new member states that joined the EU in 1995, the CoR has 222 regional and local representatives; Germany has twenty-four members. It is not nearly as important a body as the prime ministers of the *Länder* hoped it would be. It is neither an independent nor a homogeneous regional organ, and its influence seems quite limited. Nevertheless, it appears to have more than a mere symbolic purpose;[28] though weak, analyses of its actions in the short time it has existed suggest that it has had some impact on the Commission and Council and in representing the regions before the "Reflection Group" that reported to the IGC in 1996.[29] On the other hand, the representation in the CoR of mostly large cities, rather than regions in the German sense, has altered considerably the original idea behind the concept of the CoR and perhaps even weakened the status of the German, Belgian, and Austrian regions while providing no incentive to nonfederal member states to create regions.[30]

A third victory for the *Länder* and regions in Europe was the introduction of Article 146 in the EC Treaty that provides for subnational ministers to represent member states in the Council of Ministers when their autonomous rights are affected. The *Länder* had insisted on this right all along, but they were forced to drop the issue in the IGC. It was then revived by the Belgian regions and later accepted as part of the Treaty.[31]

It should be noted that the German local governments, which play a very significant role in German politics and administration, were not absent from the developments outlined above. The principle of "subsidiarity" that was pushed so hard by the *Länder* received the "fervent" support of German municipalities, which were also concerned about the transfer of their powers to the EU.[32] There was disagreement between them and the *Länder* governments, however, over their respective representation in the new CoR. A compromise was reached according to which three of the twenty-four

German seats would be municipal representatives, one each nominated by the three local government associations representing the larger German cities (*Deutscher Städtetag*), the smaller cities and towns (*Deutscher Städte- und Gemeindetag*), and the counties (*Deutscher Kreistag*). German municipalities are not represented as strongly as those of other EU states, of course, because the German *Länder* consider themselves to be the appropriate "regions." Nevertheless, the three local government associations, like the *Länder*, have established a small combined office in Brussels which serves as an "antenna" for gathering relevant information.[33]

EU policy making affects local governments in two general ways: through regulations on a variety of topics and through grants. Regulations affect the procurement of goods, services, and construction work by municipal and county governments which are responsible for two-thirds of all public spending on capital investments in Germany; second, as noted above in the example from Saxony, the EU controls public subsidies to the private sector; third, EU environmental regulations have become more intrusive over the years; fourth, personnel polices are regulated by the anti-discrimination provisions of the TEU; and lastly, drinking water and sewage treatment are covered by EU regulations.[34]

The EU presence in Germany was small before unification with regard to grants. But the Ruhr area has qualified for some aid owing to its troubled smokestack industries, and all of former East Germany now qualifies. As a result of EU funding and regulations, some municipalities have created an office that deals with EU matters; however, these require only part-time attention in most cases. EU activities still have a low profile in most local governments.[35]

As noted above, the *Länder* had rather high expectations of the TEU concerning the European "third level" of regions below the national governments. In the meantime it has become clear that these expectations could not be realized. As Jeffery has noted, the *Länder* have "run up against the buffers not so much of the limitations of their achievements in the Maastricht Treaty, but rather a more insuperable problem: the sheer heterogeneity of forms of sub-national governmental organization in the EU."[36]

The appropriate regional level simply does not exist in most EU member states, as is reflected clearly in the CoR in which local governments, rather than regions, are strongly represented.[37] One result of the region–local division in the EU is the encouragement this gives to different and even conflicting interpretations of the concept of subsidiarity, which is so important to the Germans.[38]

The Länder, *the EU, and constitutional changes*

After the Maastricht Meeting of December 1991, a Joint Constitutional Commission consisting of members of the *Bundestag* and *Bundesrat* was formed in January 1992 to consider amendments to the Basic Law that were deemed necessary after unification and continuing developments in European integration. In June the Commission agreed to recommend a new "Europe" article and to change Article 24.[39]

Thus, the old Article 23, which had been used by the five new *Länder* in the former East Germany to accede to the Federal Republic and was now obsolete, was replaced by a new Article 23 focusing on Europe. Article 23 and some other changes concerning Europe, including a new paragraph for Article 24, were approved by the *Bundestag* and *Bundesrat* at the same time they ratified the TEU in December 1992 (however, owing to a challenge made before the Federal Constitutional Court, ratification did not go into effect until 1 November 1993, after the Court approved the German ratification of the TEU).

The new Article 23 and the laws that have been passed pursuant to it replace the various agreements that were made between the *Länder* and the federal government in the past concerning *Länder* rights in the integration process.[40] Article 23, para. 1 suggests that the EU will preserve the principles of federalism and subsidiarity, and it binds future transfers of sovereignty to the consent of the *Bundesrat*. It provides for a comprehensive exchange of information concerning the EU between the federal government and the *Bundestag* and *Bundesrat*, and it gives the *Bundesrat* the opportunity to state its opinion before the federal government participates in the EU legislative process. The *Bundesrat* is to have the right to participate in the decision making process of the federal government. Where the federal government has exclusive power but the interests of the *Länder* are affected, the federal government is to take into account the opinion of the *Bundesrat*. Where the autonomous rights of the *Länder* are affected, the opinion of the *Bundesrat* shall prevail while keeping in mind the overall responsibility of the federal government. And where the exclusive legislative authority of the *Länder* is involved, the Federal Republic shall be represented in EU councils by a representative of the *Länder* sent by the *Bundesrat*. In this case the representation shall take place with the participation and agreement of the federal government in order to preserve the interests of the federation. This last provision can be seen as an exception to the rule that the federal government represents the country as a whole in foreign affairs; on the other hand, the *Bundesrat* representative must cooperate with the federal government. By 1995 representatives of the *Länder* nominated by the *Bundesrat* were participating in about 400 EU committees and other bodies.[41]

It is worth noting that the "Law Regarding the Cooperation of the Federation and *Länder* in Matters Concerning the EU of March 1993" provides that a two-thirds majority in the *Bundesrat* can force the federal government to accept its position in case of conflict on a matter covered by Article 23, para. 5, of the Basic Law. This, of course, underlines the view that European policy is no longer foreign policy but a form of domestic politics.[42]

A serious problem for the *Bundesrat* and *Länder* in actually being able to take advantage of their new rights concerning the EU is the flood of information that comes from Brussels. The problem is not new, and the *Bundesrat* has had an "EC Committee" since the Treaties of Rome to consider proposals for regulations from the EC Commission and proposals to the Council of Ministers sent to the *Bundesrat* by the federal government. This EC Committee has been very busy, which can be seen by the fact that the *Bundesrat* considered 6,355 proposals from the EC between 1957 and 1994. The EC Committee has recommended a *Bundesrat* position for most of these proposals. The numbers exceed the number of domestic bills sent to the *Bundesrat* by the federal government over the same period of time. The "flood of paper" has increased since 1989, when it began to reach 70–80 documents each day. These are placed in a computer and sent to all or some of the *Länder* on demand. Relevant documents are also sent to *Bundesrat* committees. For proposals in the Council of Ministers that affect the autonomous powers of the *Länder*, the federal government informs the *Länder* of the time frame for decision making in the Council, and the *Bundesrat* secretariat ensures that the appropriate committees hold meetings on the proposals in time to meet the deadlines. All of this requires close cooperation between the federal government and the *Bundesrat* and the *Bundesrat* and the *Länder* and demonstrates the demands and complexity involved in *Bundesrat* participation in matters involving the EU.[43] Having "chosen a consensual approach in dealings with the Federal Government" throughout the first half of the 1990s, "there have been no great trials of strength pitting *Bundesrat* against Federal Government in the exercise of Article 23 powers."[44]

A relatively new instrument in the *Bundesrat* is the EC Chamber, authorized in 1988, and called the "Europe Chamber" since 1992 with the amendment of Article 52, para. 3a, of the Basic Law. This Chamber is to decide for the *Bundesrat* when there are serious time pressures or when confidential material is involved. Each *Land* has one member or a representative with the same voting rights as in the plenary sessions. So far, this chamber has met only three times. The last meeting was in December 1999, when the Chamber majority voted to ask the federal government to oppose an EU environmental proposal that was to be considered in a few days. The federal government voted for the measure anyway "for reasons of state." If, however, the *Länder* had opposed the measure by a two-thirds majority, the federal government would probably have been bound to accept the Chamber's decision.[45]

Other reactions by the Länder to the EU

Observer of the Länder at the EU

Since the establishment of the EEC in 1958, the *Länder* have had an official observer who keeps them informed directly or via the *Bundesrat* of events in Bonn and Brussels. The scope of his activity was expanded to include the ECSC and Euratom in 1965. He is appointed by the Conference of *Land* EU Ministers. He serves in the German delegation, if only as an observer; but he is also a direct contact person for European institutions. From his offices in Bonn and Brussels, he was originally expected to keep the *Länder* informed of activities that were to be dealt with by the *Bundesrat* and to provide them with information over developments in Brussels that affected *Land* responsibilities. This information was in addition to materials supplied by the federal government, which were not always timely or sufficiently complete. These and many other duties were focused on the *Länder*, but the difficulties they experienced in handling the information and in arriving at a timely consensus, along with other problems, encouraged more focus on the *Bundesrat*. This came especially with the rights of information and participation gained during the ratification process of the SEA in 1986. As a result the *Länder* Observer no longer transfers to the *Länder* routine drafts and documents from the Commission and the Council of Ministers, since the *Bundesrat* now receives these. The federal government also sends its materials directly to the *Bundesrat* which transfers them to the *Land* Missions that are now in Berlin. Where necessary or useful, the Observer now sends materials to the *Bundesrat*. Since the SEA, the Observer has focused more on Brussels, and his offices in Bonn were closed in 1999. He continues to gather relevant information, assist the *Länder* with the organization and explanation of materials sent to the *Bundesrat*, report on the activities of other EU organs, and attend *Bundesrat* EU Committee and Europe Chamber meetings. New duties include above all assisting the Representives of the *Länder* in Brussels.[46]

Land *liaison offices in Brussels*

The German *Länder* were the first "regions" in Europe to establish liaison offices in Brussels in 1985 – an office for a local government, Birmingham, was opened in 1984[47] – and today all of the *Länder* are represented. Each *Land* has its own office except for Schleswig-Holstein and Hamburg, which share a "Hanse" office. The purpose of these offices is to provide information and documents relevant to their respective *Land* through their contacts with EU organs, the German Permanent Representative's Office, other member states, and various interest groups in Brussels; to explain their *Land's* views on various issues; to help economic enterprises in their *Land* with matters involving the EU; to try to obtain grants from the EU structural funds for the weak *Länder*, especially in former East Germany; to organize visits by politicians and others from the *Land*; and to lobby in favor of their *Land* through exhibits and various personal contacts; to promote efforts to educate the public concerning the EU, etc.[48] These offices have often been models for more than 140 offices established by the end of 1995 by other European regions and cities since 1984.[49] German cities, towns, and counties are represented collectively by a European Office in Brussels. In addition, some individual *Länder* have established an office to represent their own local governments.[50]

Questions have been raised about the extent to which the *Land* liaison offices might interfere with the federal government's responsibilities for foreign policy, but the conventional view seems to be that the *Länder* are not prohibited from trying to influence EU organs which pursue policies that affect the *Länder*. Of course the *Länder* may not try to transform their offices into diplomatic institutions.[51]

The main differences between the *Länder* Observer and the *Land* Representatives in the liaison offices is that the former is concerned with continuing, broad issues that affect various subject ministries but not particular *Länder*. He enjoys a privileged position in his information-gathering functions, and it is more efficient for him to send materials to the *Bundesrat* than for the individual representatives in the *Land* liaison offices to gather information on their own. The *Land* Representatives are more concerned with lobbying and public relations and look for contacts and influence for their *Land*. These activities can, of course, bring the *Länder* into competition for EU projects. While the functions of the *Länder* Observer and the *Land* Representatives of the *Land* liaison offices are separate, they complement each other in the general effort to improve the "*Europafähigkeit*" of the *Länder*, i.e., the capacity of the *Länder* to handle their EU responsibilities.[52]

"*Europe ministers*" in the Länder

In recent years the *Länder* have appointed "Europe ministers" to take responsibility for the various relationships among the EU organs, federal government, *Bundesrat* and *Länder*. In most cases these are ministers who share this responsibility with other fields, e.g., justice or economics, or who are simultaneously the *Land* "ambassadors" in the *Land* missions in Berlin. In 1992 the Conference of "Europe Ministers" of the *Länder* (EMK) was formed to watch over the EU's consideration of the principle of subsidiarity. The Conference replaced the "Europe Commission" of the *Land* Prime Ministers' Conference. In their first meeting they agreed to coordinate the interests of the *Länder* in matters concerning Europe. This included their interests *vis-à-vis* the federal government and the organs of the EU as well as their own activities, such as the dissemination of information about Europe. The operating assumption of the new Europe Ministers' Conference seems to be that European politics are now domestic politics, and the *Länder* must act accordingly.[53]

Länder involvement in other foreign relations

Cross-border regions

Since the establishment of the EEC in 1958, forty transnational or cross-border economic regions have been created in Europe. With nine states on neighboring borders, it is no surprise that Germany is a member of fifteen of these.[54] Examples include the "Euregio Maas–Rhine" consisting of a Dutch province, two Belgian provinces and the Aachen (Aix-la-Chapelle) region of North-Rhine Westphalia; the "Saar–Lor–Lux" region comprising the Saarland, Lorraine, and Luxembourg; the "Arge Alp" consisting of German, Swiss, Austrian and Italian Alpine regions; the "Four Motors for Europe," which includes Baden-Württemberg, Lombardy, Catalonia, and the Rhône-Alpes regions; the "Euroregion Neisse" which joins border areas of Germany, Poland and the Czech Republic; and the "Euroregion Elbe/Labe," which joins German counties around Dresden with counties in Northern Bohemia in the Czech Republic.[55] These regions have their own administrative structures that promote cooperation and coordination of

policies in areas such as regional economic development, traffic, environmental protection, health services, and culture, education and sport.[56] The
involvement of the *Länder* in such cross-border arrangements, with agreement of the federal government, are now constitutionally authorized in the
new para. 1a of Article 24. The view that the Europe of the future will be a
"Europe of the Regions" that will eventually replace the current national
states is based in large part on examples such as the above.[57]

Other "foreign relations" of the Länder

German states that comprised the Holy Roman Empire and the German
Confederation – if they were large enough – had their own foreign offices
and diplomatic relations. Even in the North German Federation and the
Kaiserreich, the powers associated with foreign relations were shared to a
limited extent by the central government and the states. Thus Bavaria,
Württemberg, Baden and Saxony had some form of diplomatic relations
to certain states until the early twentieth century. The *Länder* in the
Weimar Republic between 1919 and 1933 had some limited treaty power,
but foreign affairs was now a matter for the central government.[58]

Article 32, para. 1, of the Basic Law gives the federal government
jurisdiction over the conduct of foreign affairs. However, para. 2 calls
upon the federal government to "hear" a *Land* before the conclusion of a
treaty if special circumstances affect the *Land*. Such "circumstances"
might involve shipping in the Baltic or North Sea or Rhine River traffic.
Being heard does not necessarily mean the *Land* must approve; but it
probably does.

Article 32, para. 3 gives the *Länder* the right to make treaties with foreign countries with the federal government's approval, if the contents of
the treaty fall within the legislative competence of the *Länder*. This paragraph has led to some controversy between the *Länder* and the federal
government, because two different interpretations are possible. The federal government has argued that it has a concurrent power which allows
it to make treaties even when they affect the exclusive legislative powers of
the *Länder* (compare the American constitutional case of *Missouri* v. *Holland*, which confirmed that treaties are the "supreme law of the land!"[59]).
The *Länder* insist that they alone have the power to make treaties when
these affect their autonomous authority.[60] They also point out that only
they are in a position to implement the treaty's provisions, since they are
responsible for administration; that is, there are no "transformation
rights" that accrue to the federal government by treaty as occurred in the

United States after *Missouri* v. *Holland.* Federal comity makes it highly unlikely that the federal government would try to commit the *Länder* to administering a treaty they did not approve.[61]

The two sides have found a compromise in the "Lindau Agreement" of November 1957. This agreement stipulates that the two sides disagree on treaty powers, but that the federal government has the responsibility for consular treaties, commercial treaties, and treaties with international organizations. Where the *Länder* believe their exclusive rights of legislation are concerned, especially regarding culture, the *Länder* must consent to federal treaties and must be given time to react. Finally, it was agreed that in the case of treaties where the essential interests of the *Länder* are affected, whether exclusive powers of the *Länder* are involved or not, they are to be consulted in time.[62]

As a result of the Lindau Agreement, a Permanent Treaty Commission of the *Länder* was also formed. This Commission meets monthy and consists of civil servants from the *Land* missions in Berlin. They consider draft treaties sent to them by the Foreign Office or by another ministry interested in negotiating a treaty. The examination of the draft treaty begins with a focus on which part of the Lindau Agreement it falls under and normally ends with the consent of all of the *Länder* before the federal government submits the treaty to the *Bundesrat* for ratification.[63]

Beyond certain treaty rights, the *Länder* have no power to conduct foreign affairs, and it cannot be said they conduct foreign policy on the side (*Nebenaußenpolitik*).[64] Visits abroad by *Land* ministers are for information purposes only, in agreement with the federal government. The *Land* offices in Brussels do not violate the foreign policy powers of the federal government so long as they confine themselves to information-gathering, forming contacts, and trying to exercise influence on EU organs. They are separate from the German Permanent Representative's Office in Brussels, which does fall under federal foreign relations powers.[65]

Foreign aid and the Länder

As we have seen above, according to Article 32, para. 1, of the Basic Law, foreign relations are the concern of the federal government. On the other hand, the federal government must consult a *Land* before it concludes a treaty with another country if the *Land* is affected in some special way. And in those areas that fall under the legislative powers of the *Länder*, especially culture – which includes education – the *Länder* may conclude treaties with other countries.

The *Länder* have always considered themselves free to conclude agreements with subnational regions of other countries. Informal relations with foreign states are also maintained, and, as long as federal comity is not disregarded, this does not normally present the federal government with any difficulties.[66]

Examples of *Länder* activities abroad are public and private foreign aid projects, the latter of which is provided by nongovernmental organizations (NGOs) such as the Red Cross, church organizations, foundations, schools, etc. The *Länder* become involved in foreign aid activities in three ways: first, they sometimes participate in aid projects of the federal government in which, for example, they provide education, training or research facilities or make available experts employed by the *Länder*; second, they promote educational activities in their schools and elsewhere to increase awareness of the developing world; third, they finance their own development projects in Germany and abroad. In the domestic arena, for example, they finance university and specialist college students (*Fachhochschüler*) and certain foundations. In the target developing countries, they manage and finance their own projects or operate through an NGO. These are usually modest programs ranging from emergency humanitarian aid to the construction of village wells and rural hospitals to the training of midwives and classes to teach women how to use hand-operated sewing machines. They do not become involved in large and expensive projects. In 1993 they spent a total of DM 172 million (depending on the exchange rate, about $105–115 million) on foreign aid, not including student stipends in Germany; from 1962 to 1993 they provided almost DM 2.2 billion in aid.[67]

The *Länder* are in a particularly good position to offer aid in the form of training in crafts and trades, given their highly respected "dual system" of concurrent vocational education and practical apprenticeship training. They also take great pride in providing relatively inexpensive but effective practical aid that involves a good deal of personal contact with native populations.[68] Of course the impact of such programs is generally limited, unless a multiplier effect can take place.[69]

Since the *Länder* do not provide enough aid to justify a *Land* ministry for such purposes, there can be problems of coordination among the various ministers and their modest programs. Coordination does exist, especially via the prime ministers' staffs (*Staatskanzleien*), but problems do arise, given the German tradition of ministerial responsibility, especially in the case of coalition governments. Formal treaties or contracts are not the rule, so that a successor minister may not follow closely the plans of his or her predecessor. *Land* budget planning helps with coordination, but it does not solve all potential problems by any means. Given the lack of public enthusiasm for foreign aid in Germany as in other donor countries, it is also tempting to cut back projects that may be in fact quite promising over time.

Problems between the *Länder* and the federal government can arise for a variety of reasons. The *Länder* may make promises, real or perceived, that they do not keep because of the nature of the agreement with the target country. Of course, if there is a legal commitment under international law, the federal government feels bound to abide by the agreement. This raises the question of the extent to which the federal government should coordinate *Land* aid projects. The *Länder* and the federal government do cooperate in many ways, and the Federal Ministry of Economic Cooperation and Development meets two or three times a year with a "Federal–Land Committee on Development Aid." In addition there is some contact between the Federal Ministry and the Foreign Office with individual *Länder*. But the federal ministries have no authority to instruct or direct the *Länder* in this area of activity. Thus a *Land* or an NGO supported by a *Land* may build a hospital or school in Cuba or Nicaragua, which for foreign policy reasons the federal government could or would not do, whether it secretly approves or not.[70]

The responsibility of the federal government is limited by the fact that the agreements between the *Länder* and the target countries do not normally fall under international law and therefore do not involve the federal government. Otherwise, the *Länder* have to receive the consent of the federal government. But with few exceptions the federal government has come to accept a kind of customary legal basis for *Land* practices. In return, however, a strong sense of federal comity has prevented the *Länder* from abusing this customary right.[71]

Foreign trade policy and the Länder

In 1995 a major national newspaper in Germany reported that in April of that year the prime minister of Bavaria was leading a delegation of businessmen from his *Land* to Beijing, only to be met there by delegations from North-Rhine Westphalia, Baden-Württemberg, and Stuttgart, as well as executive board members from three large German enterprises. All were trying to arrange meetings with the same responsible Chinese economic policy makers. This coincidental meeting was not only an example of the lack of coordination among public officials but also generally symbolic of overlapping activities and competition in the efforts by *Land* and even city officials to secure economic advantages for their constituents. The result is that "Germany" may not be represented by any one office with separate divisions but by multiple offices representing various *Länder*, cities, foundations, and agencies.[72]

It may be that other countries also face problems of coordination, but these are probably more severe in federal systems where the constituent units compete not only with other countries but also among themselves. In meeting the competition for export promotion, they have four instruments at their disposal: they provide grants for export consulting services, especially to their medium-sized enterprises; they provide businesses in their territories with subsidies to help them participate in foreign trade fairs or organize their own trade fairs, e.g., Hanover and Leipzig; they reduce the risks of exporting by giving certain guarantees against non-payment for goods and services received; and they establish a temporary or even permanent presence in selected foreign countries. In some cases, as the report above demonstrates, *Land* ministers and prime ministers, accompanied by business representatives, travel abroad on trade missions. In some cases, especially in China, trade partnerships are made with certain regions. *Land* activites in Western countries, such as the United States, are usually focused more on attracting investment in Germany. As already noted above, the *Land* offices in Brussels are more interested in lobbying for various EU funds for regional development plans.[73]

Of course such activities can affect foreign policy and, under certain circumstances, involve the federal government. Thus if a prime minister or minister makes a controversial public political statement in the country he or she is visiting, e.g., concerning human rights, it makes a difference whether he or she is doing so as a party leader or as the representative of the *Land* government. In the first case he is not speaking for any government; in the latter case his statement might be seen as interference in the internal affairs of the country and cause an international incident directly affecting the federal government's responsibility for foreign policy making. Needless to say, the fine line might not always be understood in all cases.[74]

As we saw on p. 374, foreign policy is an activity that belongs to the federal government in principle; however, whether in the area of foreign aid or in foreign trade relationships, the *Länder* can act on their own within certain limitations.[75] They can conclude treaties with foreign states only with the consent of the federal government; they may not interfere with federal government responsibilities; *Land* spokespersons must abide by standards of international behavior, e.g., regarding interference in the internal affairs of other states; and they must act in concert with the German conventions of federal comity. On the other hand *Land* government officials are generally free to comment in debates on foreign affairs in Germany and to react critically to federal government policies.[76]

Conclusion

The *Länder* have not only experienced an erosion of their powers owing to federal government actions and constitutional amendments, they have also seen the EC (now EU) Commission and other EU organs make policy decisions that affect their powers. In some cases the federal government, which has no authority in areas of exclusive *Land* powers, has agreed in the Council of Ministers to legislation affecting the *Länder*, thus undermining the constitutional protection the *Länder* thought they enjoyed. As a result of these developments, the *Länder* have tried since the beginning of European integration in the 1950s to gain meaningful rights of participation in federal government decision making in Brussels. While they had some limited success in the 1970s and early 1980s, they were basically unable to gain the kind of influence that would provide them with real protection against further incursions on their powers.

With the negotiations between the federal government and the *Bundesrat* over ratification of the 1986 SEA, however, the *Länder* were successful in forcing the federal government to take the position of the *Bundesrat* into account when voting on issues in EC councils that affected *Land* interests and even to allow the *Länder* to participate in negotiations in Brussels when exclusive *Land* interests were involved. These rights were then confirmed after German unification by the addition of the new Article 23 to the Basic Law. The result is that today the *Bundesrat* has constitutional rights of participation that place the *Länder* in a stronger position than ever before in the area of European integration.

The *Länder* have had liaison offices in Brussels for several decades, but these have been strengthened over the years to provide them with a variety of services and contacts. More recently, the *Länder* have been appointing "Europe ministers" to help meet the many demands made upon them by the increasing number of EU regulations and actions.

The *Länder* like to argue – and for good reasons – that European policy is now domestic policy. That may be overstated in some areas, just as it would not be correct to suggest – as some have – that the *Länder* have their own foreign policies in general. On the other hand, they do participate in limited foreign aid projects, especially with subnational regions in third world countries, and they appear to have had considerable success with the education and training they have provided and the relatively small amounts of money they have spent on their activities. Like American states, they engage also in trade policies designed to increase exports of home industries throughout the world. The *Länder* are, then, active if limited participants in the general arena of foreign affairs.

Notes

1 Charlie Jeffery, "Farewell to the Third Level? The German Länder and the European Policy Process," in *The Regional Dimension of the European Union*, edited by Charlie Jeffery (London: Frank Cass, 1997), p. 57.

2 Rudolf Hrbek, "Doppelte Politikverflechtung: Deutscher Föderalismus und Europäische Integration," in *Die Deutschen Länder und die Europäische Gemeinschaften*, edited by Rudolf Hrbek and Uwe Thaysen (Baden-Baden: Nomos Verlagsgesellschaften, 1986), p. 19.

3 Georg-Berndt Oschatz and Horst Risse, "Europäische Integration und deutscher Föderalismus," *Europa-Archiv* 43, no. 1 (10 January 1988), p. 9; Wolfgang Renzsch, "Deutsche Länder und europäische Integration," *Aus Politik und Zeitgeschichte* B28/90 (6 July 1990), pp. 29–31.

4 Thoma Remmers, *Europäische Gemeinschaften und Kompetenzverluste der deutschen Länder* (Frankfurt/M.: Peter Lang, 1992), pp. 84–86.

5 Ibid., p. 87 and Jochen Abr. Frowein, "Bundesrat, Länder und europäische Einigung," in *Vierzig Jahre Bundesrat* (Baden-Baden: Nomos Verlagsgesellschaft, 1989), p. 290.

6 Matthias Knothe and Endress Wanckel, "Europäische Rundfunkpolitik als Aufgabe der Länder," *Zeitschrift für Urheber- und Medienrecht* 39, no. 1 (1995), pp. 20–28.

7 In the summer of 1996, Kurt Biedenkopf, the prime minister of Saxony in eastern Germany, defied the European Commission by granting VW a higher subsidy for investing in his *Land* than the Commission had authorized. After a year of serious conflict between Saxony and the Commission, with the German federal government caught more or less in the middle, a compromise was reached according to which VW had to repay most of the subsidy. See *Frankfurter Allgemeine Zeitung*, 7 August 1997.

8 Remmers, *Europäische Gemeinschaften*, pp. 88–91.

9 Christian Tomuschat, "Bundesstaats- und Integrationsprinzip in der Verfassungsordnung des Grundgesetzes," in *Bundesländer und Europäische Gemeinschaft*, edited by Siegfried Magiera and Detlef Merten (Berlin: Duncker & Humblot, 1988), pp. 28–32.

10 See also Jeffery, "Farewell to the Third Level?," p. 58.
11 Georg-Berndt Oschatz, "Normsetzung der Länder in einem Europa der Regionen: Gesetzgebung oder Satzungserlaß?," *Zeitschrift für Gesetzgebung* 5, no. 1 (1990), pp. 16–18.
12 Heiderose Kilper and Roland Lhotta, *Föderalismus in der Bundesrepublik Deutschland: Eine Einführung* (Opladen: Leske & Budrich, 1996), pp. 214–215.
13 Remmers, *Europäische Gemeinschaften*, pp. 159–176.
14 Ibid., pp. 211–212.
15 Oschatz and Risse, "Europäische Integration," p. 10.
16 Ibi., pp. 10–11; Kilper and Lhotta, *Föderalismus*, p. 216.
17 Ibid., p. 11.
18 Ibid., pp. 11–12.
19 Ibid., pp. 12–13, 217–218; JoEllyn Murillo Fountain, "The 'Constituent' Diplomacy of the German Länder in Europe: Federalism in the 1990s," paper delivered at the annual meeting of the American Political Science Association, 29 August–1 September 1996, pp. 15–16.
20 Kilper and Lhotta, *Föderalismus*, p. 219.
21 For a general discussion in English of the TEU from a German perspective, see Uwe Leonardy, "Regionalism within Federalism: The German Constitution Prepared for European Union," in *Evaluating Federal Systems*, edited by Bertus de Villiers (Boston: Martinus Nijhoff Publishers, 1994), pp. 299–315.
22 See also Jeffery, "Farewell to the Third Level?," p. 64.
23 Kilper and Lhotta, *Föderalismus*, pp. 223–224.
24 Jeffery, "Farewell to the Third Level?," pp. 63–65.
25 Kilper and Lhotta, *Föderalismus*, pp. 224–225.
26 Ibid., p. 225.
27 Ibid., pp. 226–228.
28 Ibid., p. 229.
29 JoEllyn Murillo Fountain, "German Cooperative Federalism in Europe: *Länder* as Architects of Integration," paper delivered at the Annual Meeting of the American Political Science Association, 29 August–1 September 1996, pp. 13–14.
30 Uwe Leonardy, "Deutscher Föderalismus jenseits 2000: Reformiert oder deformiert," *Zeitschrift für Parlamentsfragen* 30, no. 1 (February 1999), pp. 158–159.
31 Fountain, "German Cooperative Federalism," pp. 1012 and Jeffery, "Farewell to the Third Level?," p. 67.
32 Helmut Wollmann and Silke Lund, "European Integration and the Local Authorities in Germany: Impacts and Perceptions," *European Integration and Local Governments*, edited by M. J. F. Goldsmith and K. K. Klausen (Brookfield, VT: Edward Elgar, 1997), p. 62.
33 Ibid., pp. 62–63.
34 Ibid., p. 64.

35 Ibid., pp. 66–68.
36 Jeffery, "Farewell to the Third Level?," p. 69.
37 Jeffery, "Regional Information Offices in Brussels and Multi-Level Governance in the EU: A UK–German Comparison," in *The Regional Dimension of the European Union*, edited by Charlie Jeffery (London: Frank Cass, 1997), p. 187.
38 Jeffery, "Farewell to the Third Level?," pp. 69–71.
39 For a general discussion in English, see Leonardy, "Regionalism within Federalism," pp. 303–308.
40 Jeffery, "Farewell to the Third Level?," pp. 61–62.
41 Walter Rudolf, "Die Bedeutung der Landesparlamente in Deutschland," in *Die Stellung der Landesparlamente aus deutscher Sicht*," edited by Detlef Merten (Berlin: Duncker & Humblot, 1997), p. 68.
42 Kilper and Lhotta, *Föderalismus*, pp. 229–231 and Jeffery, "Farewell to the Third Level?," pp. 56–57, 59.
43 Ibid., pp. 219–221; for a detailed discussion of the activities of the EC Committee, see Georg-Berndt Oschatz and Horst Risse, "Bundesrat und Europäische Gemeinschaften," *Die öffentliche Verwaltung* 42, no. 12 (June 1989), pp. 510–512.
44 Jeffery, "Farewell to the Third Level?," p. 72.
45 Wolfgang Fischer and Claus Dieter Koggel, "Die Europakammer des Bundesrates," *Deutsches Verwaltungsblatt* (1 December 2000), pp. 1742–1751.
46 Fritz Stöger, "Aufgaben und Tätigkeit des Beobachters der Länder bei den Europäischen Gemeinschaften," in *Bundesländer und Europäische Gemeinschaften*, edited by Siegfried Magiera and Detlef Merten (Berlin: Duncker & Humblot, 1988), pp. 101–112; Elisabeth Dette-Koch, "Die Rolle des 'Länderbeobachters' im Rahmen der Mitwirkung der Länder an der europäischen Integration," *Thüringer Verwaltungsblätter*, no. 8 (3 August 1997), S. 169–171.
47 Jeffery, "Regional Information Offices in Brussels," p. 183.
48 Ibid., pp. 192–196; Konrad Zumschlinge, "Das Verhältnis der Bundesländer zu den Europäischen Gemeinschaften," *Die Verwaltung* 22, no. 2 (1989), pp. 229–230.
49 Jeffery, "Regional Information Offices in Brussels," p. 183; Fountain, "German Cooperative Federalism," p. 9, speaks of over ninety regional offices.
50 Not surprisingly, Bavaria has done so. *Europa Regions Magazine*, no. 2 (April–May–June 1996), pp. 27–28, 30.
51 Jeffery, "Regional Information Offices in Brussels," p. 199, notes, however, that the German Permanent Representative in Brussels has been perturbed by some of the larger *Länder* calling their offices "missions." See also Ulrich Fastenrath, "Länderbüros in Brussel: Zur Kompetenzverteilung für informales Handeln im auswärtigen Bereich," *Die öffentliche Verwaltung* 43, no. 4 (February 1990), pp. 125–136.
52 Stöger, "Aufgaben," pp. 113–114.
53 Hartmut Klatt, "Die Identität der Regionen soll gesichert werden," *Das*

Parlament (16 October 1992), p. 20. See also Jeffery, "Farewell to the Third Level?," pp. 62–63.

54 For a review of the cross-border relations and many other foreign activities of Rhineland-Palatinate, see Jacqueline Kraege, "Die Rolle der deutschen Länder in den internationalen Beziehungen am Beispiel von Rheinland-Pfalz," in *Die Rolle der deutschen Länder und der US-Bundesstaaten in den internationalen Beziehungen*, edited by Johannes Ch. Traut (Kaiserslauten: Atlantische Akademie Rheinland-Pfalz, 1996), pp. 38–51.

55 Kilper and Lhotta, *Föderalismus*, p. 237; Fountain, "German Cooperative Federalism," p. 15.

56 See, for example,the information handout for "Euroregion Elbe/Labe," issued by the Kommunalgemeinschaft Euroregion EEL, Pirna, Germany.

57 Oschatz, "Normsetzung," p. 21.

58 Uwe Leonardy, "Federation and Länder in German Foreign Relations: Power-Sharing in Treaty-Making and European Affairs," *German Politics* 1, no. 3 (December 1992), p. 120.

59 252 U.S. 416 (1920).

60 Rudolf, "Die Bedeutung," p. 65.

61 Bruno Schmidt-Bleibtreu and Franz Klein, *Kommentar zum Grundgesetz* (8th edn; Neuwied: Luchterhand Verlag, 1995), Article 32, p. 646.

62 The Lindau Agreement is reprinted in most constitutional commentaries on Article 32. See, for example, ibid., pp. 644–645.

63 Leonardy, "Federation and Länder," pp. 124–126.

64 Siegfried Magiera, "Verfassungsrechtliche Aspekte der Rolle der Länder in den internationalen Beziehungen – Aus der Sicht der Länder," in Traut, *Die Rolle der deutschen Länder*, p. 111.

65 Schmidt-Bleibtreu and Klein, *Kommentar*, p. 642.

66 Leonardy, "Federation and Länder," p. 123.

67 Klaus Otto Naß, "Recht und Praxis der Entwicklungspolitik der deutschen Länder," *Die öffentliche Verwaltung*, no. 7 (April 1996), pp. 274–275. For a breakdown of aid by *Land*, see n. 8, p. 275. Total federal foreign aid in 1994 was almost DM 8.3 billion, almost 6 billion of which was for bilateral aid and 2 billion for multilateral aid (n. 10, p. 276).

68 Interview with a former *Land* prime minister, September 1996.

69 Naß, "Recht und Praxis," p. 276.

70 Ibid., pp. 278–279; for a discussion in English, see Klaus Otto Naß, "The Foreign and Economic Power of the German *Länder*," *Publius: The Journal of Federalism* 19, no. 4 (Autumn 1989), pp. 169–171.

71 Ibid., pp. 279–281.

72 *Frankfurter Allgemeine Zeitung*, 13 July 1995, p. 11.

73 Klaus Otto Naß, "'Nebenaußenpolitik' der Bundesländer," *Europa Archiv* 41, no. 21 (10 November 1986), pp. 620–621; Naß, "Foreign and Economic Power," pp. 168–169.

74 Ibid., p. 625; ibid., pp. 172–173.
75 And apparently in some other areas as well, as indicated by the prime minister of an East German *Land* who suggested in a meeting with visiting American scholars that he maintains official contacts with bordering Central European states without seeking approval of the Federal Ministry for Foreign Affairs. Wayne Thompson, "Germany and Central Europe: A Fulbright Journey," unpublished manuscript, 1998.
76 Naß, "'Nebenaußenpolitik' der Bundesländer," pp. 627–628; Naß, "Foreign and Economic Power," pp. 183–184.

12

Conclusion:
the German model
of federalism

The German model

The most commonly cited characteristic of American federalism is "dual federalism." This refers to constitutionally delegated powers for the federal government and reserve powers for the states, with each level of government responsible for making, financing, implementing, and administering its own policies. In case of conflict, federal law is supreme so long as the federal government is authorized to act by the constitution. German federalism is also sometimes described by German scholars as "dual federalism," but sometimes this means the same as above (*Trennsystem*) and at other times something quite different. That is, it often means "dualism" in the sense that the federal level is responsible for passing most legislation and the *Länder* for implementing this legislation on their own responsibility, usually with only legal supervision by the federation. Some Germans also refer to their system as "functional federalism," by which they mean that the legislative function is largely a national responsibility, the administrative function largely a matter for the *Länder*.

These terms are confusing in fact, not only because of the different interpretations of "dual federalism," but also because American dual federalism was abandoned to a considerable, though not complete, extent with the emergence of President Franklin Roosevelt's New Deal in the 1930s and policies of following Administrations that were faced with the challenges of the growing welfare state. These changes brought about what became known as "cooperative federalism," which was characterized above all by the sharing of fiscal and administrative responsibility for a wide variety of activities. Indeed, by the 1970s there were few government programs that did not involve the federal government in some combination with the states and/or local governments. The federal government claimed the authority to pass legislation in almost any area it chose by use of the implied powers and interstate commerce clauses of the constitution, and, after the 1930s and 1940s, the Supreme Court generally accepted this interpretation of broad federal powers. Cooperative federalism was championed most enthusiastically during Lyndon Johnson's Great Society programs in the 1960s, and it continued to grow even under the more cautious Richard Nixon, whose "new federalism" tried to remove to some extent the federal bureaucracy from its heavy involvement in state and local governments through such innovations as revenue sharing. A reaction set in with Ronald Reagan, whose "new federalism" was more like the old dual federalism in that he sought to "sort out" the responsibilities of the different levels and, in the process, return a number of important functions to the states. Since this was to include the financing of these activities, the support of many governors and interest groups was not very strong, and in the end little actual "sorting out" occurred. But the enthusiasm for federal involvement in so many activities was dampened during the Reagan era, and with the appointment of a majority of conservative Supreme Court judges during the Reagan and Bush Administrations from 1980 to 1992, the Supreme Court has become much less supportive of and even hostile in some cases to federal actions that can be seen as interfering with state autonomy.

The German era of cooperative federalism also weakened, but certainly did not eliminate, the German dualism of federal legislation and *Land* administration. Cooperative federalism is usually identified with the finance reforms of 1969 which were passed by the grand coalition of CDU/CSU and SPD. These reforms provided for the sharing of the most important taxes for federal and *Land* levels, authorized federal grants for certain purposes, and even initiated a traditionally rejected "mixed administration" in several "joint tasks" in which the *Länder* were deemed to need financial assistance to meet the constitutional requirement of "uniform living conditions." In the meantime the joint decision making and mixed administration called for by these reforms and other features of German cooperative federalism came under increasing attack for their inefficiency and lack of transparency.[1]

"Functional federalism" is also problematic, because Germans use "functional" in contradictory ways. As already indicated, to some Germans "functional" refers to federal legislation and *Land* administration. But Frido Wagener, a leading legal scholar of public administration, distinguished between administration by function, as in the case of special districts that are especially characteristic of American public administration, and the "territorial administration" typical of Germany, France, and many other European states in which there is a high degree of unity of command. The classical examples would be the fragmented administration of American local governments that have numerous special districts responsible for schools, public housing, airports, parks, sewerage, public transport, etc., and the French prefectures or German cities and counties in which virtually all public activities are the administrative responsibility of the local general purpose executives.

"Participatory federalism" is another term frequently applied to Germany. This refers to the participation by the *Länder* in federal legislation, that is, national policy making. This occurs informally through a variety of committees and conferences, such as the conference of *Land* prime ministers associated with the chancellor's party, and more formally through the *Länder* chamber, the *Bundesrat*. Federal legislation that affects the *Länder*, which is about 60 percent of all federal legislation, is subject to the absolute veto of the majority in the *Bundesrat*, while other matters are subject to a suspensive veto. This regional level participation in national policy making has no counterpart in American federalism, where the governors may have some informal influence with the Administration and/or Congress but no formal access to decision making. Indeed, governors can be ignored in the policy making process, especially if they are not of the same party as that of the President. The federation in Germany has gained a variety of powers or competences since 1949 largely at the expense of the *Länder* through concurrent and framework legislation, but almost always with the approval of a majority of the *Länder* in the *Bundesrat*. In other words, the *Länder* relinquished certain powers over the years, mostly for financial reasons and because federal responsibility was deemed more rational or appropriate, or because federal action was seen as more likely to produce more uniformity (since 1994 "equivalency") of living conditions. These voluntary acts of relinquishing powers were, however, always done in return for *Länder* participation in the federal policy making process. The powers relinquished usually belonged to the *Land* parliaments, while the increased rights of participation went to the *Land* governments, so that the exchange was at the expense of the *Land* parliaments.

"Executive federalism" is therefore a term which is related to "participatory federalism," but it refers more to the increased role of *Land* executives in federal policy making in the *Bundesrat* and to the role of prime ministers, subject ministers, and civil servants in discussing, coordinating, and even drafting common policies and procedures in various committees and groups (sometimes referred to as the "third level"). The Conference of Minister-Presidents (prime ministers), the conference of education ministers (*Kultusministerkonferenz* (*KMK*)), and the science council which deals with higher education are well-known examples, but there are also informal conferences of the chancellor and prime ministers of his party that are very influential in policy making.

The term "administrative federalism" is used to describe the administration of most federal laws by the *Länder*. The general rule is still that the *Länder* administer these laws on their own responsibility without interference or supervision by the federation except with regard to the legality of *Land* practices. This stands in sharp contrast to the mixed responsibilities found in the administration of many American grant programs, which is a part of the American concept of cooperative federalism or intergovernmental relations.

A term often heard in Germany that seems contradictory to American ears is "unitary federalism." It seems contradictory, of course, because "unitary" suggests a unitary as opposed to a federal system, or at the very least a highly centralized federal system. There is more centralization of legislation and other matters in Germany than in the United States, but "unitary" refers more to various policies, ideas, formal and informal coordination, and constitutional provisions that lead to more uniformity of public policy making and implementation with or without action by the federal government and *Bundesrat*. The requirement of uniform or equivalent living conditions is not only a constitutional requirement, it is also a reflection of the value Germans hold for equality. It does not mean that everyone should have the same standard of living – which some foreign observers and even some Germans seem to believe. Rather, it refers to "living conditions" such as school facilities and salaries of teachers, public transportation, roads, athletic facilities (including outdoor and indoor swimming pools), public assistance, and general welfare. The conferences of ministers and other committees and groups are also concerned among other things with coordination and standardized practices throughout the country. The most obvious result of the constitutional requirement and ideology of equivalent living conditions is found in the fiscal equalization procedures which, in the final analysis, bring the poor *Länder* to 99.5 percent of the average total revenues of all of the *Länder* but at considerable cost to the richer *Länder*.

A relatively new concept in Germany is "competitive federalism." Over the past several years, an increasing number of voices have been heard that argue that the practices of German federalism have discouraged experimentation and autonomous actions of all kinds in the *Länder*. Bavaria, joined by Baden-Württemberg and Hesse, has complained that fiscal equalization in Germany rewards *Länder* that are perhaps less concerned with cost-saving practices or more autonomy, because they receive the average revenues of all the *Länder* regardless of their own policies. On the other hand, the richer *Länder* have little incentive to be more cost-effective, because as much as 80 percent of their above average revenues are taken from them for transfer to the poorer *Länder*. The focus on federal policy making regarding most issues with only *Land* executive participation in the *Bundesrat* also discourages the *Länder* from engaging in autonomous experimentation. They have also addressed the more fundamental issue of *Land* autonomy and have insisted on the return of significant powers to the *Land* parliaments. The question, of course, is whether the value of equality and the consitutional provision regarding equivalent living conditions do not preclude serious efforts at autonomous decision making in the *Länder* beyond relatively minor actions.

In summary, the German federal model is characterized by parliamentary institutions, a strong party system, and a national government which is responsible for policy making at the federal level in most areas outside of education, culture, local government, and police, and autonomous administration of these policies by the *Land* governments. However, the *Länder* governments (which also means opposition parties) participate in this policy making and can even exercise an absolute veto over most important bills in the *Bundesrat*, so that it is not accurate to think of federal law making as being highly centralized. Administration is generally carried out according to the principle of unity of command by the local governments to which most federal laws are transferred by the *Länder* for implementation. The most important tax revenues are shared by the federal, *Land*, and to some extent local governments, which reduces pressures for widespread resort to American-style federal grants. However, some federal grants are provided under certain conditions, and there is some joint financing of certain "joint tasks." A key characteristic is also the requirement to promote equivalent living conditions in the country as a whole. The accretion of powers over the years by the federation; the perfectionist and highly complex fiscal equalization procedures; the numerous conferences of prime ministers, subject ministers, and civil servants regarding specific policy arenas; and the requirement of equivalent living standards which is a reflection of the value Germans place on equality together form complex pressures for policy conformity which is captured in the term, "unitary federalism."

The characteristics of German federalism described above have major consequences for the general political system. Peter Katzenstein pointed to the inability of the Kohl government after 1982 to match the kinds of significant changes brought about by the Thatcher and Mitterrand governments or the Reagan Administration, in spite of the talk of a major shift in direction (*Wende*) when the Kohl government assumed office. Indeed, one could also argue that the SPD–Green coalition government of Gerhard Schröder that came into office in 1998, after sixteen years of Kohl and his CDU/CSU–FDP coalition government, has also proceeded cautiously and incrementally. This is because the Federal Republic, in spite of being in many ways a centralized society, is also a decentralized, "semisovereign state" with "coalition governments, cooperative federalism, a wide range of parapublic institutions, and . . . the state bureaucracy itself" which together create "domestic shackles that have tamed the power of the West German state."[2]

Challenges confronting the German model

Many Germans express considerable pride in and satisfaction with their system of federalism, and some are eager to point to the advantages and accomplishments they believe have resulted from the federal system since 1949. A long list would include opportunities for greater grassroots participation; the political experience gained by numerous political leaders at the regional level and in the interlocking arrangements between the regions and the center; the opportunities available to regional politicians to be recruited into national politics; the identity which many Germans have with their regions; the fact that the *Länder*, while not as autonomous as American states, do provide for generally effective and honest administration; the division of powers which finds expression especially in the *Bundesrat* (also seen by some as a disadvantage); and, in spite of unification in 1990, the high degree of uniform living conditions throughout the country.

On the other hand, one German scholar has written that "it is apparent that German federalism is seen as permanently in need of reform."[3] The evidence for this statement is strong. Of the fifty amendments to the Constitution since 1949, most have some connection with federalism. There have been several reforms of financial relationships between the federation and the *Länder* and among the latter, the last of which was in the summer of 2001. From the beginning the German *Länder* enjoyed little autonomy.[4] By the 1960s Germany was being described as a "unitary federal state," which suggested not just a tendency toward centralization but also various practices and policies that brought about a high degree of coordination and participation in federal policy making. The finance reform of 1969 ushered in the era of cooperative federalism which soon became identified with *Politikverflechtung*, or a kind of intergovernmental, interlocking decision making process in the *Bundesrat*, in joint tasks, in conferences and expert committees, etc., all subject to the "joint-decision trap" according to which the requirement of unanimity or near-unanimity leads to inefficient, ineffective, and fiscally wasteful decision making based on the lowest common denominator.[5] A study commissions on *Land* boundary reform was formed in the early 1970s, and it recommended a consolidation of the then ten West German *Länder* to five or six *Länder* of roughly equal size. In spite of considerable discussion, no action was taken beyond some changes made in the Basic Law in 1976 concerning procedures for territorial revisions. Another study commission recommended in the mid-1970s some changes in the Basic Law regarding federalism, but again no action was taken. The SPD–FDP coalition government tried to expand federal authority even more in the 1970s, but it was thwarted to a large extent by the opposition in the *Bundesrat* and by growing economic problems.[6] By the early 1990s, one scholar in an admittedly somewhat polemical book called Germany a "disguised unitary state" and argued that history, political structures, procedures, actions of political parties, public attitudes and other factors did not favor genuine federalism.[7] Following unification in 1990, some changes were made in fiscal legislation, especially in order to accommodate the five new *Länder*, but no significant permanent changes in the existing system were made. There were also some relatively minor changes in the Basic Law in 1994 concerning federalism and other matters, but those who wanted a thorough revision were certainly disappointed. As noted above, considerable dissatisfaction arose during the 1990s over fiscal relations, and, following a decision of the Federal Constitutional Court in November 1999 requiring some rather major changes, the prime ministers and Chancellor Gerhard Schröder hammered out an agreement that will go into effect on January 2005 and last until the end of 2019.

Voices calling for some major changes in German federalism were hardly quieted by the financial agreement of 2001, because it did relatively little to satisfy those who now argue that Germany needs a system of "competitive federalism."[8] As indicated on pp. 192–194, the general theme is the need for more fiscal and policy making autonomy for the *Länder*. This has been a long-standing demand of many *Land* politicians, but it seems not to have been taken very seriously in the past. In more recent years, especially since unification and the huge transfers of funds to the East, it has become a serious demand. This can be demonstrated by two examples. First, Bavaria, Baden-Württemberg, and Hesse went before the Federal Constitutional Court in 1998 and argued that the existing system of fiscal equalization was unconstitutional. In November 1999 the Court agreed in part and ruled that the *Bundestag* would have to revise the law by the end of 2002 so that a new system of financing the *Länder* could go into effect by 2005. As noted on p. 199, Chancellor Schröder and the prime ministers of the *Länder* met in June 2001, after the recommendations of a special expert commission had been rejected, and hammered out an agreement for the period 2005–19. This agreement was reached at the expense of the Federation, which agreed to increase its contributions so that the richer *Länder* could retain a larger portion of their above- average revenues. Another part of the agreement provides for a continued transfer of large amounts of money to the five new *Länder* in the East.

A second example is the announcement in August 2001 by Prime Minister Roland Koch of Hesse that he would seek authorization from the *Bundesrat* to engage in an experiment regarding the administration of public assistance (*Sozialhilfe*) based on the "Wisconsin model" introduced by Governor Tommy Thompson in the 1990s. This model, which focuses on consultation, child care for single parents, basic job training, and assistance in getting a job offer which must be accepted to avoid a reduction in monetary aid, immediately became a focus of discussion in the German media. Not surprisingly, many supported the idea, while others rejected it. It is interesting to note that some opponents said it would not work in Germany, while others claimed that the model was already being applied to a considerable extent. In any case it is doubtful that Hesse will receive permission by the *Bundesrat* majority to begin a process that could be seen as undermining the strong belief in Germany that welfare is a national responsibility and that all citizens must be treated equally.

The probable failure of Prime Minister Koch's initiative is an example of why it will be difficult to give the *Länder* more autonomy. More *Land* autonomy means less attention paid to the constitutional requirement of equivalent living conditions. This can be seen clearly in the United States, where there are rather significant differences in social policy among the more autonomous states. These differences will probably grow in time under the Welfare Reform Act of 1996 which eliminated the old federal program of Aid to Families with Dependent Children (AFDC) and turned the new program, Temporary Aid to Needy Families (TANF), over to the states with federal guidelines. Given the value that Germans place on equality, which, after all, is reflected in the provision for uniformity or equivalence of living conditions, it is difficult to see how the *Länder* can be granted more autonomy without a negative public reaction which would surely be even stronger in the five new *Länder* than in the West. The poorer *Länder* would find it difficult to maintain the generous welfare programs to which many Germans have become accustomed and which many would argue are necessary to keep current recipients from threatening political stability through protests or even violence.

It should be noted in this context that conventional wisdom in Germany holds that the *Länder* have little opportunity to be innovative, whether because of the dominant policy role of the Federation, the interlocking relationships between the federation and the *Länder* and among themselves, the lack of own source revenues, political culture and public expectations, or for other reasons. Yet one might hypothesize that this conventional wisdom is based in part the lack of studies on comparative public policy in the *Länder*. It is at least possible that there are greater differences than is generally recognized, and that the *Länder* do indeed engage in some innovations within the constraints in which they operate. This is one of the conclusions of Schmid and Blancke, whose careful and sophisticated comparative study of employment policy demonstrated that some differences exist in the initiatives taken by the *Länder*. These are based to some extent on party differences, but, as in the United States, more on social–economic pressures confronting the *Land* governments.[9]

Whether or not employment policies or welfare policies are exceptions to the ability of the *Länder* to act with some autonomy, one might argue that they could regain some greater initiative if they could achieve a lessening of the joint decision making processes which seem to hinder effective policy making and reform efforts.[10] But this would probably require some sorting out of responsibilities, and as Americans learned under President Reagan's "new federalism," a sorting out of responsibilities in the modern state is not a simple matter. In determining what is a matter of federal concern as opposed to what is a matter for the *Länder*, it may well be decided that the responsibility should be shared. This means cooperative federalism, which is what those demanding more autonomy appear to reject.

A successful sorting out of responsibilities would also mean that more pressure would be placed on the smaller and poorer *Länder* to consolidate with their neighbors in order to reduce political costs, for example, for separate cabinet ministers, parliamentary deputies, *Land* political parties, etc.; reduce potentially costly competition for economic investments; and to realize savings in scale. But besides the problem of the low likelihood and feasibility of territorial reform, it is not clear how the joining of two or perhaps even three small and poor *Länder* would improve significantly their fiscal potential.

Another interesting question raised by the demand for more autonomy is the extent to which the *Land* governments are willing to give up their participatory rights in the *Bundesrat* and elsewhere in making federal policy.[11] Indeed, there is reason to believe that some *Land* politicians would not be willing to trade their rights to participate in "high politics" in return for more *Länder* autonomy. Another question is the extent to which the strong party system in Germany can be brought into conformity with more autonomous *Länder*, since they have also been agents of a more "unitary" federalism. (On the other hand, some scholars have suggested that the parties are acting more autonomously today than in the past.)[12] And it must be asked, of course, to what degree the autonomy of the *Länder* has already been or will be in the future affected by the responsibilities assumed by the EU. The *Länder* have some influence via the *Bundesrat* on EU policy making that affects them directly, and they are represented in the EU's CoR, but so far they do not seem to have been able to gain the voice in EU policy making in the Committee that they had hoped for when the TEU was negotiated in Maastricht in 1991.

Today German federalism is under discussion more perhaps than ever before,[13] and some of the criticism, which has always existed, has become so extreme as to suggest that German federalism is a farce and should be abandoned.[14] The addition of five poor new *Länder* as a result of unification has made the achievement of equivalent living conditions even more difficult than it was before, in spite of the massive transfers to the five new *Länder*. Old questions about the extent to which the *Länder* have lost most of their important legislative functions in return for the right of participation in federal policy making by *Land* executives are being raised again with a new vehemence, and a serious discussion of more autonomy for the *Länder* can be found today in the major newspapers, academic journals, and in numerous books. Apparently in part as a response to the EU's 2002 Convention on the Future of Europe, the presidents of the German *Land* parliaments began their own "Convention of *Land* Parliaments" in the summer of 2002 in the Wartburg on devising means of gaining more autonomy and drawing a clearer separation of federal and

Land responsibilities. Their report is due by 2004, before the EU Convention has submitted its findings. How this body deals with the issue of equivalent living conditions will be a major question. There seems to be little doubt that the pressures for changes will have some impact on German federalism in the near future, and that these changes will not be limited to the rather modest revisions made in the Basic Law in 1994 or in the financing of the *Länder* in June 2001. Those interested in federalism, in Germany and elsewhere, will be eager to learn about the changes which finally emerge.

Notes

1 Fritz W. Scharpf, "The Joint-Decision Trap: Lessons from German Federalism and European integration," *Public Administration* 66 (Autumn 1988), pp. 255–267.

2 Peter J. Katzenstein, *Policy and Politics in West Germany: The Growth of a Semisovereign State* (Philadelphia: Temple University Press, 1987), pp. 15 ff., 350.

3 Heidrun Abromeit, *Der verkappte Einheitsstaat* (Opladen: Leske & Budrich, 1992), p. 71.

4 Ursula Münch, "Die Diskussion um eine Reform des bundesdeutschen Föderalismus vor dem Hintergrund der Entwicklungslinien des deutschen Bundestaates vor und nach der Vereinigung," in *Krise und Reform des Föderalismus*, edited by Reinhard C. Meier-Walser and Gerhard Hirscher (München: Olzog Verlag), pp. 89–90, 97; Abromeit, *Der verkappte Einheitsstaat*, p. 9.

5 Scharpf, "The Joint-Decision Trap," pp. 254–271.

6 Münch, "Die Diskussion," p. 100.

7 Abromeit, *Der verkappte Einheitsstaat*, pp. 7–12.

8 There is a rapidly growing literature on the subject of competitive federalism. One recent example is Heribert Schatz *et al.*, *Wettbewerbsföderalismus: Aufstieg und Fall eines politischen Streitbegriffs* (Baden-Baden: Nomos Verlagsgesellschaft, 2000). Several chapters in Meier-Walser and Hirscher, *Krise und Reform des Föderalismus*, also deal with competitive federalism.

9 Josef Schmid and Susanne Blancke, *Arbeitsmarktpolitik der Bundesländer* (Berlin: Sigma, 2001).

10 Münch, "Die Diskussion," p. 109.

11 Ibid., pp. 109–110.

12 Charlie Jeffery, "Party Politics and Territorial Representation in the Federal Republic of Germany," *West European Politics* 22, no. 2 (April 1999), pp. 159–161 and Roland Sturm, "Party Competition and the Federal System: The

Lehmbruch Hypothesis Revisited," in *Recasting German Federalism*, edited by Charlie Jeffery (London and New York: Pinter, 1999), pp. 197–216.

13 Münch, "Die Diskussion," p. 108.

14 See the harsh assessment of German federalism made by Hans Herbert von Arnim, *Vom schönen Schein der Demokratie* (München: Droemer Verlag, 2000), pp. 49–165.

Index

initiatives 150, 281–2
petitions (*Volksbegehren*) 150, 281
referenda (*Volksentscheid*) 103–4,
143–7, 149–51, 156, 281–3
direct election of mayors 282–3
division of power 4, 5
dual federalism 5, 60–1, 202, 385
as concept in Germany xi, 60
as concept in U.S. xi, 61
Duchac, Prime Minister Josef 324
Duke, David 332

education reforms 217, 227
Eichel, Prime Minister Hans 294
Elazar, Daniel xi, 54, 69
election results in the *Länder*
Baden-Württemberg 291
Bavaria 293
Berlin 314
Brandenburg 316
Bremen 307
Hamburg 310
Hesse 295
Lower Saxony 297
Mecklenburg-Vorpommern 318
North-Rhine Westphalia 299
Rhineland-Palatinate 301
Saarland 303
Saxony 320
Saxony-Anhalt 323
Schleswig-Holstein 305
Thuringia 324
elections in the *Länder* as "partial"
federal elections 325–9
electoral systems 274–5, 279
election cycles 275–6
frequency 275–6
proportional representation 147,
215, 274, 331
single-member districts, direct seats
215, 274
Engholm, Prime Minister Björn
303–4

equivalent living conditions
definition of, 148, 182
see also uniform living conditions
Erhard, Chancellor Ludwig 170–1
Erzberger, Matthias 165
Europe Ministers of the *Länder*,
Conference of (EMK) 373
"Europe of the Regions" 200
European integration 172, 360–73
European Union (EU) 3, 56, 64–5, 70,
87, 149, 197, 254
Bundesrat and *Länder* 221
Commission 200, 361
Committee of the Regions (CoR)
367–8, 397
Convention on the Future of
Europe 394–5
Council of Ministers 200, 220, 361,
363–4
decline of *Land* parliament powers
220, 222, 232
European Parliament 271, 361, 315,
327–30
federal government
(*Bundesregierung*) and *Länder*
363–4
Land liaison offices 372–3
Land parliaments 236, 363–4
local governments 367–8
exclusive legislation, federal 56–7, 213
executive dominance, comparative
and general 218, 220
"executive federalism" 220, 230, 354,
356, 387–8

Fabritius, Georg 293, 327–8
federal administration 62–3, 83–84
direct and indirect 83–4
supreme and high authorities 83
federal comity 64, 178
Federal Constitutional Court 1, 54–5,
59, 63, 65, 70–2, 83, 110, 112,
146–7, 153, 169, 173, 178, 191,